AT THE PARIS
PEACE CONFERENCE

THE MACMILLAN COMPANY
NEW YORK · BOSTON · CHICAGO · DALLAS
ATLANTA · SAN FRANCISCO

MACMILLAN & CO., Limited
LONDON · BOMBAY · CALCUTTA
MELBOURNE

THE MACMILLAN COMPANY
OF CANADA, Limited
TORONTO

THE HÔTEL DE CRILLON DURING THE PEACE CONFERENCE

AT THE PARIS PEACE CONFERENCE

By JAMES T. SHOTWELL

Professor of History, Columbia University;
Director, Division of Economics and History,
Carnegie Endowment for International Peace

NEW YORK
THE MACMILLAN COMPANY
1937

SET UP BY BROWN BROTHERS LINOTYPERS
PRINTED IN THE UNITED STATES OF AMERICA
BY THE FERRIS PRINTING COMPANY

19248

PREFACE

THE Paris Peace Conference is now a thing of history. The action of the League of Nations at the Assembly of 1937, in taking up the thorny question of the separation of its Covenant from the peace settlement, marks a turning point away from "Versailles" to new realities and forces. The crises through which the League itself has been passing are steadily carrying it over into a new era. But, although the Peace Conference is receding into the background of politics, it is still a living influence in world affairs.

The way in which the peace settlement became a symbol and a register of conflict lies outside the field of this narrative; but the student of history may find in it an explanation of how that process began. When diplomacy succeeded to war, the unreconciled nations drew from the treaties their slogans of discord, and the settlements made by the Peace Conference imposed themselves upon the imagination of a whole generation as the cause of most of the evils from which the post-war world was suffering. That this was an oversimplification even for Germany was clear to all judicious students of contemporary Europe. The war was chiefly responsible for much that was attributed to the treaties, and pre-war Europe was responsible for the issues of the war. But the war was over and the treaties were still operative. Moreover, the war was too vast, too long and varied, for anyone anywhere to appreciate to the full its impact upon the normal or established routine of Europe and the world generally. The treaties, on the other hand, lengthy and involved as they were, expressed in words and figures the cost of defeat—and of victory. Therefore it was but natural that the treaties should be charged with much for which they were not to blame. The post-war years witnessed the creation of a myth in which the Peace Conference figured as a sinister thing, sowing dragons' teeth, vindictively, subtly, while high-minded idealists looked on confused and frustrated. Myths like this do not die readily, especially while the attitude of mind which produced them still persist. In time, however, they cease to dominate the springs of action, as new situations crowd to the forefront of

v

the international arena. Then they can be examined with something more nearly approaching fair-mindedness. The signs are multiplying that this is now the case with the history of the Peace Conference.

The narrative which follows deals only incidentally with these fundamental problems. It is a day-to-day record of what one of the many present at the Paris Peace Conference saw of the making of the treaties. Much of that record was of interest only to family and friends, but with the passing of the years it is often the casual incident that throws into relief the really significant events and prevents their outlines from being blurred. The academic flavor of some of the comments on men and things is not wholly academic if it registers the opinions of the actors at the time. Even the omissions from the story reveal the limitations of contact and information in a conference with so vast a program and so many participants. But, as is pointed out in both the Retrospect and in the explanatory material, inserted later as parentheses with many of the entries, the text, such as it is, throws new light on some of the central problems of the peace settlement and especially upon the work of the American Delegation.

As for the text itself, the contemporary record is taken from three sources. By far the largest of these was a diary, dictated about midnight regularly from early in January until the final negotiations with the Germans, except when interrupted by absence from Paris or by extreme pressure of work. These missing sections were filled up as soon as possible, sometimes a day or two late, from notes taken at the time. Dr. Preston Slosson labored with me on this record, which we kept in diary form even when he had to go back to cover two or three days of belated description. Its original purpose was to serve as a substitute for letters home and to my parents. Therefore it had many blind references and omissions when dealing with matters under negotiation. But alongside the diary went letters bearing the same date in which not infrequently were descriptive items. At first it was planned to include passages from these letters only as notes to the diary, but it was finally decided to make no difference between them, because they were all written for the same readers at the same time by the same person. There was this difference, however, that the letters were more personal, and those to my parents contained descriptions necessary for those who had never traveled abroad, while the recipients of the other letters knew Paris and Europe intimately. Some flavor of these varied influences will be detected in the entries, but they supplement each other here as they were intended to do at the time.

The question which the historian has a right to ask is what if any changes were made in the original texts. After much study of the problem I decided not to regard the dictated diary as sacrosanct in such matters as arrangement of incident when the diary itself recorded its own shortcomings at the time. Thus a reference to something that happened in the morning was sometimes recalled after the notes on the afternoon had been dictated. There was no way to change it then, because the text was dictated directly to the typewriting machine. Neither of us had shorthand at our disposal, so there was no other way to correct the text than by inserting the correction later. The intention then was to put the insertions where they belonged, and this has now been done. When the text plainly indicated its own inadequacy, I have taken the liberty with it which I would have taken at the time but for the rigidity of the typewritten page and the lack of opportunity. There are also deletions, more especially in the case of names of casual acquaintances and of some characterizations. Not all of a personal record is of interest to others.

The volume as it stands will remind the readers of Mr. Harold Nicolson's *Peacemaking,* both by reason of the Retrospect and its handling of the text. It should be said, however, that the pages which follow were substantially ready for the printer some years before *Peacemaking* was published. The Retrospect, with the exception of part of the last two chapters, and most of the notes were written some six years ago. The chief reason for delay was a reluctance to publish so personal a document. But it is also a document of history, and as such it is now offered for the scrutiny of those interested in the study of a great event and of the motives and actions of those who, at that vital moment, governed the affairs of men.

J. T. S.

November 1, 1937.

CONTENTS

ix

APPENDICES

ILLUSTRATIONS AND MAPS

PART ONE

RETROSPECT

CHAPTER I

THE INQUIRY

ONE day in September, 1917, there was a telephone message from Mr. Herbert Croly, Editor of the *New Republic*, that Colonel House wanted to see me. I had spent the late spring and most of the summer in Washington, from the first weeks of America's entry into the World War, as chairman of the National Board for Historical Service, the war-time organization of the historians of the country, and then had fallen ill, a victim to heat and germs, and spent most of August and September in the country. I had, therefore, no knowledge of any antecedent action which led to the telephone call, but gathered from Mr. Croly's few cautious words that "the Colonel" wanted to see me in connection with preparations for the Peace Conference which would sooner or later have to be called at the end of the World War.

Mr. Croly had no further information or directions for me, except one personal caution, that I must be at my appointment next morning with Colonel House at the exact time set for it, for not only does he insist on punctuality, but this was to be too important an appointment to be a moment late.

I met Colonel House for the first time in his own apartment, where he introduced me to his brother-in-law, Dr. Sidney E. Mezes, President of the College of the City of New York. I learned that Dr. Mezes was to have charge of the organization of a group of students of international affairs drawn chiefly from the faculties of the universities, whose duty it would be to study the political, economic, legal, and historical elements of the problems which would have to be faced in the treaty of peace. Technically it was connected with the State Department [1] but really it was to be the President's personal staff under Colonel House's direction. The interview with Colonel House was not of long duration, but it was extremely businesslike and straight to the point. After the Colonel had outlined

[1] Cf. Robert Lansing, *The Peace Negotiations: A Personal Narrative* (Houghton Mifflin, 1921), pp. 17 and 18.

the problem in a few sentences, Dr. Mezes informed me that the organization had not yet begun, and that apart from Mr. Walter Lippmann and myself, our only other colleague as yet was Mr. David Hunter Miller, whom I then came to know as a lawyer in whose judgment Colonel House had learned to place great confidence. It was not long before the basis of that confidence became evident. Mr. Miller's great services at the Peace Conference are known to the few who have studied the documents of its history which he had printed for researchers, but from the first days of the preparation for it his sound judgment and unerring scholarly instinct held that work to practical ends without yielding at any point President Wilson's program of constructive statesmanship, which it was our duty to translate into terms definite enough for a treaty. Tireless in physical as well as mental energy and quick to discern the bearing of a complicated question upon the essential lines of American policy, Mr. Miller became at Paris one of the President's most trusted advisers. At the opposite pole from this quiet but sure jurist was the sensitive and imaginative genius of his associate, Mr. Lippmann, who during the early months of the work of the organization (he left it to become a captain in Military Intelligence in the following summer) acted as secretary under Dr. Mezes, and so became the chief liaison between it and Colonel House, as well as being directly in touch with the President. This was but setting the seal of formal approval upon a relationship already begun. Mr. Lippmann's unique gift for clarifying the issues of politics, so widely known in the post-war period, explains the importance of the rôle he played in interpreting and phrasing policy. Professor Seymour's summary of the trend of Mr. Lippmann's contribution is correct when he says, "It is my impression that Lippmann furnished the abstract ideas which found their way into a good many of the memoranda of the American Delegation and ultimately into some of President Wilson's public speeches," [1] if "abstract ideas" is another term for general principles. They were ideas, moreover, which Mr. Lippmann sought to make concrete by testing them in the laboratory of research. My own tendency was to work the other way on, from the historical background out into the problems of the day. But this method of work at once called for an extended organization with technical experts competent to deal with each phase of

---

[1] *The Intimate Papers of Colonel House* (Houghton Mifflin, 1928), III, 171.

the vast field that would have to be covered by the Peace Conference. My first task, therefore, was to help secure the acceptance of a group of associates in the fields of history, geography and economics who would be able to concentrate upon specific questions and have the results of their research ready when these issues came up for decision at the Peace Conference.

Dr. Mezes himself had had long experience as an educator. President of the University of Texas before he came to New York, he was acquainted with the political currents of American life in the Southwest as well as with the problems of university administration. It was but natural, therefore, that Colonel House, when entrusted by the President with a task that called for the co-operation of university men, should turn to one who had shared so much of his own early environment. In Dr. Mezes' discretion and capacity for silence he could repose absolute confidence—qualities essential in the director of an enterprise of this kind which, while the war was still on, was to analyze and apply in definite terms the conditions of a peace yet to be won. Those who joined the group in the autumn of 1917 found in its director a quiet-mannered gentleman of the old school, devoted to his task with patriotic ardor and modestly aware of the fact that not only was the task an unfamiliar one—for never before had universities been mobilized for such a service—but that it called for specialists whose interests lay in a different academic world from that of undergraduate instruction, in which he had been chiefly engaged. The distinction between research and education consists almost as much in an attitude of mind as in a difference of occupation. The problems of education call for different administrative methods from those of research. Researchers in proportion to their competence must be granted freedom in methods and conclusions. The researchers in this instance were to be drawn from the highest academic capacity in the country and it was not long before they began to form a democracy of their own. Dr. Mezes clearly felt that he was not one of them, but now and again made the mistake of attempting to control when he could not direct. This happened both before the Peace Conference and at it; and, as will be evident from the narrative which follows, it led to other misunderstandings of much greater importance. At the beginning we had little idea of either the difficulties or the possibilities ahead. We only knew that the task was too vast for any small group to deal with it effectively, and Dr. Mezes assured me of Colonel House's agreement with my suggestion that we at once enlarge the organization by adding colleagues in the various political and social sciences.

One of the first to join us was Professor Archibald Coolidge, of Harvard, recognized as the outstanding authority in the American academic world on the history of Eastern Europe and a master of the literature of European diplomatic history. Coolidge and I were in agreement that in preparation for the coming Peace Conference, geography would play a large part, and this led to the suggestion that we should at once secure the co-operation of Dr. Isaiah Bowman,[1] Director of the American Geographical Society, the one scientific body for geographical research in America. So secret was the organization as yet, however, that Dr. Bowman could not lay the matter before the whole body of his trustees, and it was only towards the close of the year that a conservative statement was made to the Council of the American Geographical Society. Nevertheless, not only Dr. Bowman's services, but ultimately those of almost the entire staff, were placed freely at the disposal of the Government. It is impossible to estimate Dr. Bowman's services both before the Peace Conference and during it, for there was more than one critical period in the history of the research organization in which his steadfastness and directness of purpose, as well as the confidence of his colleagues in his high scientific competence, saved the organization not only from disintegration but almost from complete collapse. Under the circumstances it was but natural that while the organization remained under the titular chairmanship of Dr. Mezes, as time went on the burden of the day fell more and more upon Dr. Bowman, who was both Chief Territorial Expert and Executive Officer. When the records are all laid bare, the full extent of Dr. Bowman's contribution to the Peace Conference will be made known. His unyielding spirit in the face of obstacles was as necessary for the structure of the whole American Delegation as it was for that of the technical experts. In his genius for organization, based upon a deep sense of the necessity for co-operative work in so vast an undertaking, Dr. Bowman was almost the exact opposite of Mr. Lippmann, whose natural trend was more toward the use of individual than of corporate methods.

Very different from his associates, both in temperament and in

[1] Now President of Johns Hopkins University.

method of work, was George Louis Beer, to whom was assigned the important section of Anglo-American relations and questions of colonial policy as well as certain economic problems. Mr. Beer was looked upon by many as having a pro-British bias, but his ancestry was Continental and German, and the judgments which he had reached concerning British colonial policy had been based solely upon historical investigation. There were few in the United States or elsewhere who could rival him in solidity of learning and grasp of detail. Carefully discriminating between prejudice and fact, he had written in outspoken protest against false conceptions of British history which had so largely colored popular American opinion. Most of these distortions in perspective have now disappeared or are ridiculous in the eyes of the average reader; but in this work of historical reform, Beer was a pioneer. A gentleman of leisure, who had for years devoted himself to scholarship, he was to justify his appointment by earning the confidence of every person at the Peace Conference. During this preparatory period, however, he worked alone in his own library, having an incurable dislike to public appearances of any kind, and, while generous with advice and help for all serious matters, was quick to react against the restraints of organization which seemed to him to block research or lead to one-sided judgments. His death a year after the Peace Conference was over was a greater loss to his country and the organization of world affairs than can ever be measured.[1]

Our first quarters were in the New York Public Library, where Mr. Lippmann was already beginning work in a small private room next to that of the Librarian. For the short time that our office was in that building I shared the room with him. Our work was to be carried on in absolute secrecy. The Librarian, Dr. Anderson, and the Reference Librarian, Dr. Lydenberg, were in the secret; but there were to be no names or labels attached to any of our material which would give an outsider the least idea of what we were doing. Mr. Miller, working at his own law offices, had the assistance of Mr. Frank Warrin, whose accuracy in the control of document material was matched by his scholarly detachment.

Dr. Bowman's membership opened up the chance for obtaining more suitable quarters than could be secured for us in the crowded

[1] I have written an account of Mr. Beer's services at the Peace Conference in a memorial volume, *George Louis Beer*, published after his death by The Macmillan Company (New York, 1924).

conditions of the Public Library. The building of the American Geographical Society, at the corner of Broadway and 156th Street, had perfect equipment for the preparation of maps, which would form so large a part of our documentation. It was also fireproof, with plenty of space for expansion, and it could be well protected at its one and only entrance door which opened into the courtyard, the street door being kept locked. Moreover, it was in a quiet part of New York where one would hardly expect to find the staff of the personal adviser of the President preparing materials for world policy.[1]

It was necessary now, however, to find some name for the organization which would be perfectly blind to the general public, but which, nevertheless, would serve to identify it among the initiated. To meet this peculiar situation, I suggested "The Inquiry," and although none of us was quite satisfied that this was a good name for it, it was adopted at first only provisionally, but later retained by the paradox that its very inadequacy was its best recommendation. We soon established ourselves in the new quarters in a row of offices on the second floor looking out onto the quadrangle, with the map rooms on the floor above. When Colonel House was in the country we had access to him if there was anything to be taken up by any of us, but the only members of the group who saw him with any regularity in the early months were Dr. Mezes and Mr. Lippmann.

Meanwhile our staff was rapidly increasing. Professor Allyn A. Young of Cornell came from Washington to take the headship of the Division of Economics. Professor Charles H. Haskins, Dean of the Harvard Graduate School, and the best known to Europe of American historical scholars, was assigned the problems of the eastern frontier of France; while his colleague, Professor R. H. Lord, as the only specialist in American universities in Polish history, was given the problems of Poland. Yale University contributed two of the most important chiefs of divisions in Professor Charles Seymour,[2] the historian, who took charge of the problems of Austria-Hungary, and Professor Clive Day, equally well known as historian and economist, who was assigned those of the Balkans. The prob-

---

[1] The fact that Colonel House had begun to create a commission to study the facts likely to come up in the Peace Conference at the end of the War could not be kept secret, however. On September 29 the *New York Times* carried the full story on its front page.

[2] Now President of Yale University.

lems connected with Turkey and the Near East were turned over
first to a medievalist, Professor Dana Munro of Princeton, and then
to a professor of ancient history, W. L. Westermann of Cornell.
Professor W. E. Lunt of Haverford College came in to study the
historical background of Italian boundary claims, while Professor
Douglas Johnson of Columbia University made the area of the
Adriatic—especially on the eastern side—the chief center of his
geographical researches. Professor Stanley K. Hornbeck of the University of Wisconsin—later of Harvard and now Chief of the Division of Far Eastern Affairs of the State Department—took charge
of a field involving the relations of China and Japan which was destined to prove one of the most thorny at the Peace Conference.
Others joined the organization as months went on. Professor Frank
Anderson of Dartmouth was associated with me in work on diplomatic history, Dr. Parker T. Moon of Columbia worked with Mr.
Lippmann and Dr. Bowman, and Dr. Preston W. Slosson of Columbia, now Professor of History in the University of Michigan,[1] served
as my secretary both during the preliminary work of the Inquiry
and in Paris.

The preparation of geographical apparatus, under Dr. Bowman's
direction, with Professor Mark Jefferson, of the Michigan State
Normal College, as chief cartographer, proceeded apace; and, with
each of the separate divisions rounding out its own special subject,
my work slipped back into that of history, diplomatic and social,
dealing with problems that on the one side were germane to those of
international law—as for instance in the study of the question of
the Straits and Constantinople—and on the other hand on the fringe
of the Economics Division under Professor Young, especially the
study of labor programs, both political and economic. At this juncture, I transferred my office to the Library of Columbia University,
partly because the Geographical Building became rather crowded
and partly because Columbia had a more nearly complete collection
of source material in my field.[2] Mr. Miller similarly moved most of
his work to Washington where his colleague of the International
Law Division, Dr. James Brown Scott, had his office. It is surely

[1] My long and intimate relationship with Dr. Slosson will always remain one of
the pleasantest memories of those years. As tireless in research as he was alert to
reality in the deceptive material with which we dealt, he played a larger part in the
events chronicled in this book than, I fear, is indicated in the text.
[2] I had been on leave of absence from Columbia University from the time the
United States entered the war.

unnecessary to comment on the added strength which came to the Inquiry from Dr. Scott's membership, the breadth of his scholarship and the wealth of his experience, an experience of international conferences unique in the United States with the exception of that of Dr. Scott's own chief in the Carnegie Endowment, Mr. Elihu Root. Dr. Scott not only threw himself into the work with his usual energy and decision of action, but brought along a competent staff as well.

Properly enough, as time went on, the Inquiry developed most in the field of geography in the broadest sense of that term; that is to say, it developed a splendid equipment, both technical and scholarly, with reference to all territorial problems. Its Division of Economics was also well manned and well supported. Professor Young, its head, was competent to the point of genius, bringing as his contribution the rare combination of a philosopher, statistician, and economist, one whose well-poised judgment was never captured by war-time psychology. He was even then stating the case for reparations in almost exactly the terms which came later to be recognized as the only practical basis of international action, until the long-drawn-out effects of extravagant folly ruined even that possibility.[1] My own division contributed miscellaneous studies on all kinds of subjects—ready reference guides to European diplomatic history, studies on German, British and French foreign policy, the alignment of European political parties on questions like those which might come up at the Peace Conference, analysis of public opinion in Trade Unions, Chambers of Commerce, speeches and periodicals. While some of this work was academic and unusable in the rapid hours of the Peace Conference, the proportion of such waste effort was surprisingly small in view of the unprecedented situation which the Peace Conference was bound to present; and some of the most obscure studies proved to be of real importance, as for instance in the field of labor legislation. Moreover the purely documentary contribution of my division was supplemented by a series of meetings with the representatives of European governments or factions, held for the most part in the evenings and in a private dining room at the Columbia University Club. Not the least interesting of these occasions were those when Professor Masaryk ex-

---

[1] The relation between the Division of Economics, under Professor Young, and the War Trade Board, under Mr. Baruch and his associates, and the War Finance Corporation and other economic organizations at Washington was never fully worked out, even at the Peace Conference itself, except on a personal basis.

pounded the philosophy of self-determination for Eastern Europe, with the map which he had prepared hanging on the wall and the members of the Inquiry gathered like a class in a seminar to listen to his exposition of how liberty would develop responsible government among the nations that would be set free by the war. It should be added, however, that not all members of the seminar were convinced.[1]

This is not the place for a history of the Inquiry, beyond what is necessary for the understanding of the rôle which it and its members played in the shaping up of the Treaties of Peace at Paris. Even that is too large a theme for this narrative. Some day the Inquiry will find its historian, and this strange experiment in the mobilization of the political and social sciences to help in shaping the outlines of the new world structure which had to be built out of the ruins of the war will offer a subject with unique possibilities. My own connection with the Inquiry varied from time to time for both technical and personal reasons. In the summer of 1918, when the organization was losing coherence and effectiveness, Colonel House intervened and asked Dr. Bowman to assume administrative control. This position he accepted on condition that he be permitted to restore the democratic character of the association which it had largely lost in the preceding months. Dr. Mezes still continued to hold the nominal position of Director.

If there were problems in the administration as well as the program of the Inquiry, there were others more obvious to the outside

---

[1] As a memorial of these occasions, the Czechoslovak Government presented me, in 1937, with a full-length portrait of President Masaryk which hangs on the wall of the room in the Columbia University Club in which these meetings were held.

As soon as the existence of the Inquiry became known to the representatives of European governments and to the propagandists of the "new nations," we were all flooded with the literature of their claims and, in some instances, pursued even to our homes by their protagonists. There were also transient visitors such as Premier Hughes of Australia, who gave us a foretaste of his diplomatic technique at the Peace Conference by laying his electric ear-trumpet on the table when he didn't want to hear any objections to his point of view. More picturesque still were the personalities from Eastern Europe, from Macedonian bandits to the Lithuanians whose claim rested partly on linguistic affiliations with Sanscrit! This is perhaps the place for a comment that upon the whole it was easy to distinguish propaganda from information and that the former had little or no effect upon the Inquiry reports except to put the researcher on his guard against being duped by it.

The co-operation with the British and French Governments was, of course, on a different level, and we had cordial and intimate relations with some of their diplomatic and technical staffs in Washington and in New York. On the French side there was the Commission under M. Tardieu, of which M. Aubert was a member. Lord Eustace Percy, an intimate friend of some of the Inquiry members, was especially helpful in securing documents and information from the British side, a service which we were later to return in kind.

world in the relations between Colonel House's staff and the State Department. Even before the Armistice there had been some indications, although none of these serious, that there were those in the State Department who were by no means happy at the way in which the preparations for the Peace Conference were being made. This was not only natural under the circumstances but, from the standpoint of public law, had apparent justification. If the State Department did not have full control of the preparation for negotiations, how could it play any effective part in their actual conduct? Men whose lives had been spent in diplomatic service could hardly be expected to regard favorably the creation of a temporary body of so-called experts as the President's advisers in so many important aspects of the negotiation of peace, nor to look forward with equanimity to the prospect of having this improvised organization take any formal part in the work of the Peace Conference. Although the Inquiry might be regarded as simply an *ad hoc* commission to deal with a single problem, the State Department properly felt that the problem in this particular case covered practically the whole field of our foreign relations at the most critical, and even revolutionary, turning point in the history of American diplomacy. In their eyes it was one thing for the President to have a personal adviser in Colonel House, but quite a different thing for the Colonel's staff to develop to the point of displacing the established governmental organ for foreign affairs.

The staff of the State Department therefore had strong reasons, apart from their personal feelings, for objecting to the development of anything resembling a rival staff made up of amateurs in diplomacy, who would escape from any continuing responsibility for their acts after the Conference was over by their immediate return to private life. But a subsequent study of war-time organizations has convinced me that the method of preparation for the Peace Conference and of organization at it, which at the time seemed rather haphazard and improvised, was nevertheless based upon the soundest principles. It was in harmony with the method pursued in practically every instance of successful war-time administration. Neither in England nor in the United States had the peace-time organization of government proved adequate to the handling of the new tasks imposed upon the government by the war. The result in this country was the creation of such bodies as the War Industries

Board, the War Trade Board, the United States Shipping Board, etc., forming a war-time government by itself, separate from the permanent government departments. The creation of these separate bodies left the regular organs of government free to continue their normal course, and permitted the emergency organizations to devote their entire energies to the one task in hand, undisturbed by the continuance of any routine questions. Although the United States Government had not wittingly copied European war-time governments in this new framework which it had erected in Washington, but had simply met a practical situation in a practical way, it is of interest to the historian to see that the actual method developed in Washington followed the lines of those which were most successful in the war-time governments of Europe, as well as in the field of inter-Allied co-operation. In short, crisis organizations seem to follow a definite law, which is quite distinct from the ordinary principles of government. The crisis must be met by organs either specially created or specially adapted for that purpose. In proportion as the crisis becomes real, these specialized organs must free themselves from any other controls or bureaucratic impediments and act directly with or under the chief executive. So far as I know, there has never been a study of "crisis government." [1] It would be one of the most enlightening essays in the art and practice of politics, and would throw a new light upon some of the great turning points in history. For example, the most perfect model of the kind of government which all nations finally accepted in the World War was the Committee of Public Safety in the French Reign of Terror, an instrument of government, the precision and efficiency of which have been completely obscured in the popular mind because of that one activity—the Terror—with which its name is always associated.

There was, therefore, a theoretical as well as a practical justification for the method of preparation for the Peace Conference, especially in view of the fact that President Wilson laid down in his Fourteen Points a basis of peace which had to be worked out with little regard to those diplomatic secrets which constitute so much of the political asset of foreign offices. The Peace Treaty was not to be a return to the old diplomacy, but the establishment of a new world order. For this task specialists in history, economics, and public

---

[1] This was written before the publication of *Crisis Government* by Professor Lindsay Rogers of Columbia University (New York, 1934).

or international law were perhaps as well qualified as those who knew what the foreign minister of one country had written to another in a state system that had now broken down both by revolution and by the emergence of new nations on the soil of Europe.

The case for the Inquiry, however, passes beyond argument when we find that the same kind of organization was established by the governments of Great Britain and France and that when Germany began seriously to face a peace that would not be dictated by it, in October, 1918, it similarly drew upon the work of specialists, at first in various departments of the Government and then from outside. The British body was set up in the spring of 1917, under the direction of Dr. (later Sir) George W. Prothero, distinguished historian and publicist. Its program was very similar to that of the Inquiry, extending into the fields of geography, history, and economics, as well as those of politics and diplomacy. The monographs which it produced were freely turned over to us in so far as they had to do with the general problems common to both governments.[1] The French preparations began with the erection of a Comité d'Etudes for territorial questions, under the dean of French historians, Ernest Lavisse, and a committee on economics under Senator Jean Morel. We were kept directly in touch with its activities through the French Mission at Washington. As for the preparations which were being made at the same time in Berlin, we naturally knew nothing, although the archives of the Inquiry reveal that we took for granted that the Germans would be making at least as careful preparations as their enemies and we tried to guess what lay behind the veil of secrecy.

So long as the Inquiry was simply preparing memoranda for future use, it did not create for the State Department the problem of a rival organization. Throughout the war the whole world had become accustomed to regard President Wilson as his own foreign minister. The State Department, however, knew only too well that this had been the case from the first days of his presidency. Owing to Colonel House's personal relations with the President, the Inquiry was, in a sense, the President's personal staff. Through its Division of International Law it also had a liaison with the State Department,

---

[1] They were published in 1920 by the British Stationery Office under the title "Peace Handbooks."

especially as Dr. James Brown Scott had his office in Washington, and not in New York.

But before the Armistice came Colonel House was in Europe, and the President formally commissioned Secretary Lansing to organize the "American Delegation to Negotiate Peace." The question then arose as to whether the Inquiry had not completed its task by the preparation of the preliminary material already in its files. Dr. Mezes wished to make changes in the personnel, and after negotiations with Secretary Lansing it was decided that Dr. Bowman should go as head of a small group of territorial experts, taking with him Dr. Young to strengthen the State Department's economic staff and in this way prepare to deal with those problems which the War Industries Board and War Trade Board had so largely made their own in the course of the war. There was naturally no place in this revamping of the Inquiry for any Division of History, but Dr. Bowman camouflaged my position by asking that I be given charge of the reference material and the library; and until the Inquiry was reorganized at the end of the first week of our residence in Paris my position was technically that of Librarian and nothing else.

This position was not a sinecure, however, for our staff was one that had definitely refused to make bricks without straw, and the straw in this case consisted of a collection of material in the form of books, reports and documents which had drawn upon both government material and the great reference libraries of the country. The Library of Congress was especially liberal and helpful in co-operation, sending not only books and documents but a highly qualified specialist to assist in the cataloguing and packing. Dr. Putnam assured me, both in New York and in Paris, that the Library of Congress would meet any possible demands upon our part. It is, perhaps, even more interesting now to note that the actual shipping of the books in their heavy oak cases, ready to open on the walls of their Paris office, was in the hands of James Truslow Adams, who was later commissioned a captain and sent to the Peace Conference. He had not at that time written his major histories.[1] There was not a little humorous comment in the press at the time on the "shipload of Peace Conference munitions," and some of the experienced diplo-

---

[1] At the Peace Conference Captain Adams was archivist for Dr. Bowman's office. At the close of the Peace Conference the library contained 4,612 books, of which 2,735 were loaned by the Library of Congress, the great universities and the American Geographical Society.

mats of the old school were frankly critical of the air of academic amateurishness which in their eyes this apparatus seemed to imply. Nevertheless the event completely justified the precaution.

As will be apparent from the narrative of the voyage over, the question of an adjustment between the State Department and its staff and the members of the Inquiry was one of the first problems confronting the American Delegation to Negotiate Peace. On board the "George Washington" it was left in abeyance, except for the clear intimation on the part of President Wilson that he would continue to look to the Inquiry for technical help.

On arriving at Paris [1] it was evident that there must be some unified control of these two bodies. It would not do for Mr. Lansing to have one staff advising him and Colonel House another, acting separately and independently, especially as General Bliss would have the Intelligence Divisions of Army and Navy reporting independently to him. This would have meant that three of the Commissioners would each be having recommendations drawn up without regard to the information or instructions of the others. Mr. White had only a small staff of his own, but his affiliations would naturally have thrown him more closely with the State Department. An effort had been made to deal with this situation prior to our arrival by the appointment of Mr. Joseph Grew as Secretary General of the American Commission to Negotiate Peace; and Mr. Grew had drafted a general chart of organization which was the blueprint upon which the first form of the American Commission was built up. As he was an old and tried official of the State Department with diplomatic experience, it was natural that the Inquiry should find itself definitely subordinated alongside Military and Naval Intelligence. All communications were to pass through Mr. Grew's office, the chief personnel of which was drawn from the diplomatic and State Department staff. This state of affairs lasted, however, only three days after our arrival in Paris, as is noted in my diary under December 17. Dr. Bowman, who had been Executive Officer of the Inquiry, was persuaded by the Commission to take up the same office in the section of Territorial, Economic, and Political Intelligence of the American Delegation, and he at once succeeded

---

[1] The offices for the Delegation were secured at 4 Place de la Concorde on November 21. Colonel House, however, maintained "headquarters" for his Mission at his house, 78 Rue de l'Université, until the seventh of December, when he moved to the Crillon Hotel. The President was housed in the beautiful home of Prince Murat.

in changing our status before we had actually settled down to our task. The Inquiry was to have direct access to the members of the Commission, and the State Department officials were to form the secretariat of Mr. Grew's office instead of being immediately attached to the Commission. Naturally there was much appreciation, on the part of the Inquiry, of Dr. Bowman's success in bringing our staff so close to the scene of action. But at that date none of us, I think, expected to take any personal part in the negotiations themselves. It was not long, however, before the mere pressure of the situation brought most of us into the actual working of the Inter-Allied Commissions, where, instead of merely furnishing information to our own Commission, we were given the responsibility of shaping the terms of the Treaty, although theoretically these negotiations were never complete until approved by the President.

Dr. Bowman's success, therefore, on December seventeenth was the turning point in the organization of the Delegation and ultimately affected the structure of the whole Conference. From that time on he was consulted on all Commission appointments, and on the choice of experts to appear in the Council as advisers to the American Commissioners.

The reorganization had also an especial interest for me, for I was designated Chief of the History Division in it, while still retaining the position of Librarian. When Dr. Bowman told me of the situation which had opened up, I suggested to him that it would be much better if the Division were to be entitled "Social History" instead of history in general. Diplomatic history was taken care of in the field of international law, and political history was divided up among the different territorial sections. There remained, however, the field of economic and social history, the subject which I had been developing in my classes in Columbia University for some years past. Dr. Bowman discussed this with Professor Haskins and came back to tell me that it was Haskins himself who strongly urged that I have the Division of History without any qualifications. It later turned out, however, that it was to be social history, after all, owing to the nature of the problems with which I had to deal.

Such, in brief outline, were the origins and pre-Conference history of the organization of technical experts which President Wilson took with him to Paris. Colonel House himself had preceded the President, having gone over before the close of the War to take part in the negotiations for the Armistice. Absent or present, however, the Colonel was always, in the mind of each and all of us, the "Chief." It would be an utterly incomplete and even misleading narrative which would fail to recall this sense of his leadership, felt not only by those who knew him best but even by those working on his staff who never had more than a fleeting glimpse of him at the rarest of intervals. Nor have the intervening years in any way dimmed this sense of his leadership in those eventful days. This seems to me all the more remarkable in view of the fact that our relationship with Colonel House was so largely impersonal. He was for most of us the symbol of the Wilsonian program, and it was this symbolic figure, rather than an individual whom we hardly knew, which remained the unquestioned center of our organization.

It goes without saying that there were both advantages and disadvantages in the remoteness of our contact with Colonel House. Neither he nor President Wilson could have had any idea, when they called together a little group of a half-dozen scholars to study the terms of peace, that it would grow to the dimensions of a small State Department itself. The problems of administration which this involved were, in their way, not unlike those which Colonel House was loath to assume in the conduct of public affairs. Therefore, while he accepted the logic of events with that keen sense of reality which gave such sharp outline to his idealism, he must have been somewhat embarrassed with the very success of his organization. His position at best was extremely difficult, as the personal adviser and almost the *alter ego* of the President, but it was one thing to be a more or less unofficial Secretary of State, and another thing to have a staff that in any way tended to become a substitute for the permanent staff of the Department. It was not unnatural, therefore, that he should revert at times, even during the Peace Conference, to that kind of personal consultation with Dr. Mezes which tended to cut across organizational lines, a situation which Dr. Mezes, in his turn, accentuated by his method of consultation. When the crisis over Fiume was at its height, and the territorial experts of the Inquiry learned that Dr. Mezes had given advice contrary to their findings, they appealed directly to the President, basing their appeal upon his charge to them on the voyage over. The President, in turn, accepted very largely their point of view. It was Dr. Mezes' action which was directly responsible; but behind it lay the anomaly of a dual situation which had never been cleared up in his own mind. The Inquiry staff had by that time become a working part of the American Delegation as a whole, a fact which he apparently did not fully realize.

It is a tragic fact that the only relationship which this incident strained to the breaking point—when other pressures were added to it—was that between the Colonel and the President; for it is quite clear that, whatever other factors entered into it, the estrangement dated from that time. So far as his staff was concerned, Colonel House remained, throughout the Peace Conference and after, the same symbol of leadership which he had always been, in the practical task of reducing the principles of a Wilsonian peace to the needs of a world that was so largely unprepared to accept or apply them.

Would the battle have been lost if the major strategist of world politics had been kept at his post? That is a question which history cannot answer but which historians will be forever asking.

CHAPTER II

THE WILSONIAN PROGRAM

BEHIND Colonel House stood President Wilson.

It is not too much to say that future generations will never be able to know what Woodrow Wilson meant to the world throughout the year 1918. At a time when the moral forces of humanity were surrendering to bleak despair, he summoned them again to action. When the war had become mere meaningless carnage, he stated the purposes of nations in terms which won homage both sides of the front. In the darkest hour of disillusionment, he rallied the forces of civilization from their helpless involvement in universal destruction to a task not of rebuilding the outworn structure of the past but of creating a world community of which mankind had until then hardly dared to dream. Never before had any single individual in secular history been able to exert an influence like this. It was a world leadership, for which he himself had not been ready in the earlier years of the war, and from which, by heredity and training, his mind at first had sought to escape by insisting upon America's isolation and tradition of neutrality. Even from that distance, however, and even while claiming pride in America's aloofness from the struggle, he had made himself the exponent of the submerged peace forces of the world and had upheld with persistent tenacity the power of the idea against that of brute force, securing from the belligerent governments statements of their war aims which their own peoples had been unable to extract from them. But it was not until America entered the World War that the real power of his genius struck home with full force and effect. Even though subsequent events might falsify the ideal for which he stood, it was then the one flashing beacon in an almost universal night.

Cynics who, through the early years of the war, while America was still neutral, mocked at Wilson's phrases, watched with amazed bewilderment the effect of those embattled words during the period of our belligerency. When the Allies, in their distress, were ready to barter their very cause for mercenary troops from the Orient to the Mediterranean, and the war was becoming meaningless except as the collapse of civilization, Wilson recalled the moral purposes at stake, and he alone restated them for all the world. The phrase, "to make the world safe for democracy," was destined to be battered by the war itself and by the cynicism of succeeding years into a thing of cant and hypocrisy, but the historian must recognize the fact that it was a better, soberer and more valid slogan of crusade than any other which has ever animated so many diverse forces as in 1917. Compared with it, the "Liberty, Equality and Fraternity" of the French Revolution was vague and undefined, however vibrant its appeal to a Europe that had not yet had experience in responsible government. The war continued to be fought for other things than the inspiration of such a message, but without it the intervention of America would not have brought that temper and undivided strength which it carried into the battlefields of Europe. The German military and naval heads, unmindful of Bismarck's warning of the power of the moral "imponderables," and utterly miscalculating our capacity for action, employed their last full measure of force on land and sea and by unlimited submarine war and on the thin front by Amiens all but conquered; but our armies had been preceded by the force of Wilson's words, which shared with the blockade in the overthrow of Habsburgs and Hohenzollerns. At the close of the war the name of Woodrow Wilson stood out alone above all others in the world.

But it was one thing to secure the adoption of a program by nations at war when the immediate ends to be attained by its adoption were so obvious as to silence the opposition of all but the most belligerent and reactionary elements of public life; it was another thing to translate these principles into a working program for the confused counsels of peace-time politics. Yet the only hope for the permanent establishment of peace on the Wilsonian terms lay in securing co-operation, first on the part of the Allies, and then upon that of the Central Powers, to make these terms substantially their own. Neither Wilson nor House expected to find a full measure of this co-operation in the war-time governments of Europe; their faith was in the outlook of the common man, a faith which linked their ideals with those of the American and the French Revolutions through Jeffersonian democracy. In any case, Wilson was always on his guard when dealing with his European colleagues. Indeed, the records show that he even distrusted them unjustly at times; it is an utterly wrong perspective of history which presents the American participation in the Peace Conference as the only liberalizing agency there. No one nation has a monopoly of the ideas of progress. There were those in the American Delegation who interpreted the "new freedom" in terms of reactionary nationalism and whose concern in democracy failed to include that of the Central Powers. On the other hand, there was liberalism to be reckoned with in French and British opinion. France, it is true, was represented at the Peace Conference by Clemenceau, with Foch in the background. But when the Delegations really came to know each other, they discovered men like M. Fontaine, a true citizen of Europe, who framed the program for France in Part XIII of the Treaty, and some French colonial experts, who, while they held a different theory of colonial administration from that of the British, were proud of a tradition of successful local government. Other elements were there as well, representing the traditional liberalism of the Third Republic, based on a sincere regard for "the rights of man and the citizen." Still larger was the proportion of those in the British Delegation who were in agreement with the fundamentals of the American position. Although Lloyd George had fought his December election with the slogan that Germany must pay to the last pfennig and that the Kaiser should be tried, the British Delegation was largely composed of statesmen sincerely bent upon making a peace which would be a lasting bulwark against the recurrence of European wars. This applies to Lloyd George as well, in spite of his pronouncements in the election campaign. Indeed, when the treaty began to take concrete form in the shape of boundaries and the terms imposed on Germany, it was Lloyd George who, on more than one occasion, upheld the cause for moderation even against Wilson himself. At the very last, the protest against a "Punic Peace" reached such dimensions in the British Delegation and the Ministries in London as to threaten the disruption of the Conference itself.

Nevertheless, the program set for the Conference of Paris was that of President Wilson. If it was difficult to translate these principles into terms suitable for the conditions imposed upon the great Powers by the war and by the conflicting interests of their past history, it was still more difficult to set up new states to do this untried thing. For the liberated peoples did not bring to the understanding of this program of neighborliness and co-operation among nations anything of that experience in government which the older nations could contribute. Never was the adage more perfectly exemplified that "servitude is the worst of all schools for freedom." "Self-determination" was already shaping itself in flamboyant supernationalism and revelling in the oppression of the conquered. So unlovely were some of these exhibitions of vindictiveness that, had Wilson been the sentimental politician which his enemies have charged, he would have been tempted time and again to deny his major thesis of Jeffersonian democracy and frankly stop the processes of emancipation. For not having done so he earned the undying enmity of those of the ex-enemy states which had applied his philosophy to their own emancipation but not to that of their neighbors. By revolution they had overthrown imperialism at home, but their newly freed democracies felt cheated of their birthright when Wilson held them to the test of granting freedom to those peoples whose enmity they feared when it could no longer be controlled in the accustomed way.

To these new states as well as to the old, Wilson presented a challenge which accepted nationalism but turned it against itself. Had Germany triumphed, the *pax Germanica* which it would have imposed upon the conquered would have resembled in some degree the *pax Romana*, a peace held down by garrisons in the danger zones of Europe, or at least a Holy Alliance with William in the place of Alexander. Wilson's conception was the opposite of this. There was nothing in it of universal empire, no effort to retrace the processes of history. Instead of this he accepted the historic heritage of the modern age, with all its diversity of states and governments, seeking only to prevent its trend toward international anarchy by applying a device familiar to American thinking, a "Monroe Doctrine for the world," which would give a corporate guaranty against interference by reactionary and imperialistic powers. The supreme tragedy lay in the fact that it was his own country which led in the renunciation of this endeavor to apply its experience to solve the disorders of an unbalanced world.

It is easy now to pick out the flaws in Wilson's program. To secure agreement on the moral categories of the peace was so great an achievement as to make their embodiment in a treaty seem almost secondary. But to reduce a statement of policy to the terms of a contract raises a whole new set of problems. For treaties are programs which nations are left to work out when the original impulse is gone and later events are determined by the needs of the hour or the reassertion of ancient prejudices. Therefore the contract must be drawn with an eye to all the stresses to which it will later be subjected, whereas the general statement of policy need embody only the outstanding motive forces of the time. There is no doubt that the President tended so to concentrate upon fundamental principles that his critics, and among them his own Secretary of State, Mr. Lansing, have claimed that he was never properly aware of the nature of this second and more practical side of the peace settlement. The evidence which Mr. Lansing adduces for this is chiefly the fact that at no time did the President turn over to the State Department, or the American Commission as a body, this problem of the application of principles to practical politics which, in the normal course of events, it would have been the function of a State Department to negotiate. But Mr. Lansing's memoirs also furnish adequate evidence that had the task been left to him it would never have been fulfilled. This judgment has no invidious implications, but stands on the record itself. The treaty to be made was one for which no precedent existed, and the negotiation of it could not be solved by invoking precedents or dealing according to the accustomed routine of diplomacy. There was only one way to succeed in a task so vast and so intangible as that which lay before the President, and that was to direct and oversee the operations himself. There can be no doubt that President Wilson secured more of a Wilsonian peace than others could have secured for him. If, even with all the power of his prestige, his force of will and unflinching purpose, he ultimately accepted terms that history has harshly judged, the explanation is to be found in the fact that a new type of political strategy was required to meet a situation unparalleled in the history of politics, and that this strategy had to be improvised at a time when the whole world was impatiently clamoring for the speedy settlement of a war that had dislocated the structure of civilization.

Mr. Lansing's criticism, however, does touch the weak point in President Wilson's leadership; for it is certainly true that he placed too much confidence in the power of moral ideals and in his own ability, single-handed, to secure their acceptance in sufficiently tangible form to become the real basis of the Treaty. He is also right in pointing out that leadership of this personal character did not sufficiently mobilize behind it the support of the American Delegation, from the first days of the Conference. The making of a peace to end a world war called for a technical staff as far-reaching in its competence as the war government itself. Just as the World War transformed the existing organs of administrative and executive action in every country, producing war cabinets, boards, and bureaus that extended and in part supplanted the peace-time organs of government, so the making of a treaty in which the issues of the war were to be settled called for a similar far-reaching series of commissions and committees to adjust the infinite detail of conflicting demands in a settlement that extended over the whole sphere of economic as well as political life.

If the President relegated this technical organization to a secondary place, it was because he felt that the task of leadership which he had assumed during the war was not to be laid down at the Armistice. It involved a continuing responsibility until his program had been accepted in a post-Armistice, pre-Treaty agreement, a *modus vivendi* which should serve as a directive for all subsequent negotiations. It was this conception which dominated throughout the earlier weeks of the Peace Conference, and the fact that he carried this revolution in diplomacy thus far may yet be held to his credit when the full history of the Peace Conference comes to be written. It may be that Wilson's conception will be recognized as more profound than his contemporaries guessed, for subsequent events have made still more clear the distinction which he drew between the fundamentals of attitude and policy on the one hand, and the detailed operations of government in the ordinary business of furthering welfare and securing justice on the other. The progress of civilization is measured by the transfer of a nation's interest from the field of sovereignty, of prestige which thrives on conflict, to that of practical means to an end in the normal conduct of daily life. Wilson saw no hope for the second of these, so long as the first remained under the domination of that militaristic spirit which had, throughout the centuries, made it the center of the drama of nations. He therefore concentrated all his effort on the major revolution which would substitute for a world based upon war, a régime of pacific settlement of international dealings, in which there would be place for the undramatic and homely arts of peace.

It is, however, a highly superficial view of Wilson's statesmanship which presents him as a mere doctrinaire, incapable of appreciating the intricacies of economics or politics. This was the picture painted of him by that cleverest of journalists among the economists, Mr. John Maynard Keynes,[1] whose attack upon Wilson as a Presbyterian theologian, naïvely unconscious of the elements of his problem, was eagerly accepted as a historical document by a Congress that had forgotten the fact that the chief financial reform in a century of American history—that of the establishment of a Federal Reserve system—had been successfully carried through under Wilson's presidency. Not only was Wilson aware of the need of careful detailed work in the drafting of the final treaty, but he was the first of the heads of Delegations, as the narrative later will show, to set going an international co-ordination of the work of experts. He did not, however, propose to begin with them. The policy had first to be determined and that was a task for statesmen; the work of the technicians was to test the proposals submitted to them, to apply and, if need be, adjust and modify the blueprints of the new era. There can be no doubt that fundamentally the President's method was a sound one. One of the chief lessons of the Peace Conference—a lesson enforced by every year that has followed it—is that experts should not displace statesmen in the determination of great issues. Wilson's method, therefore, of subordinating the specialist, with his limited range of interest, to the wider outlook and direction of those who saw the problem as a whole, was a sound one, and had it been followed through consistently, this plan of work, for which he has been so much blamed, might well

---

[1] *The Economic Consequences of the Peace* (first ed., 1919). This volume, which had a phenomenal sale in the United States, contained a brilliantly written but utterly irresponsible diatribe against President Wilson. The alleged purpose of the volume was to secure American co-operation in a pooling of war debts and a financial liquidation of the war. It would be hard to find in the literature of controversy a work in which the author has so completely ruined his own case as in this instance. For the caricature which Keynes drew of the unscrupulous scheming of dishonest claimants was sufficient to deter any honest-minded American from ever having anything to do with such a world of tricksters as he made out the leaders of the Conference at Paris to be. To judge from the comment at the time, few of the many readers of that book read beyond the opening pages to study the statistical and financial details which were supposed to form the heart of the appeal to American common sense.

have turned out a treaty which would have offered much less chance for criticism.

Unfortunately, however, the plan was imperfectly applied, chiefly because of the peculiar weakness in Wilson's own method of work, which was also the source of its strength: the intense concentration on one subject at a time, which he himself referred to as the working of a "one-track mind." Instead of organizing the Peace Conference from the start, with the technical staff assigned its function and aware of its proper relations to those who were responsible for policy, the structure of the Conference had to wait until the heads of Delegations could have time to prepare their strategy. It thus seemed for a time as though the experts—at least those of the American Delegation—were not so much subordinated as ignored, with the result that as the problems were too intricate to be solved without the assistance of technicians, there tended to be an undue surrender to them in the later weeks of the Conference. Instead of keeping the balance steady throughout the whole period of negotiation, it swung from one extreme to the other. This fact, which is, in my opinion, more responsible for the faults in the Treaty of Versailles than is commonly appreciated,[1] calls for a detailed study of the technique of the Conference, which the historian will be able to supply only when he is able to secure access to all of the original documents. In the following chapter, however, the main elements of the problem are outlined in so far as they revealed themselves at the time.

[1] In his volume on the Peace Conference, Secretary Lansing lays the blame for the failures of the Conference upon "the lack of an American program," to which he devotes a whole chapter. An analysis of his criticism, however, shows that he was thinking of the weakness in the method of negotiation and the structure of the Conference, rather than in the substance of the American program.

CHAPTER III

THE ORGANIZATION OF THE PEACE CONFERENCE

PRESIDENT WILSON brought with him no fixed plan for the structure or procedure of the Peace Conference. His idea of how the Conference would set about its task was indicated in a note which he wrote to Secretary Lansing on October 29, commenting upon a plan of Dr. Mezes which Secretary Lansing had laid before the President after the Cabinet meeting the previous day. This plan was in the nature of a diagram of the proposed personnel for the Peace Conference. The President found Dr. Mezes' scheme somewhat too ambitious and asked the Secretary to have a simpler one worked out, and to explain to Dr. Mezes that the Peace Conference itself would most probably deal with nothing but the main territorial, political, and racial questions, and that it was practically certain that other questions, such as those dealing with finance and trade, would be delegated to special conferences or commissions. The President was of the opinion that Dr. Mezes should take with him only the men and materials which would be of service in dealing with the main questions at the Peace Conference. The State Department itself would in the meantime work out a minimum personnel and organization.[1]

That this remained the picture in the President's mind of the arrangement and method of the Conference is borne out by his talk with the members of the Inquiry on board the "George Washington,"[2] the one and only occasion upon which he fully opened his mind to the technical staff as a whole. A close study of this interview shows, however, that the President, in laying before his staff the general lines of policy along which they should be preparing to support the American case, found himself carried along at the

[1] It is clear from this that the President had then in mind the plan to divide the work in Paris into two parts: the preliminary peace, which should embody the fundamentals of the new era; and a series of detailed settlements to be left to those competent to deal with them, experts and technicians, rather than politicians, working in an atmosphere that by that time would have been partially freed from the poisonous hatreds of a war which had been the negation of most of their constructive activities.

[2] See below, pp. 74 ff.

close of his remarks to an assignment of a duty which distinctly did not belong to it. It was this ringing sentence, "Tell me what's right, and I'll fight for it," which already showed how difficult, if not impossible, it would be to draw the line between technical and political advice. This difficulty was bound to come to the fore in the application of principle to practice, especially in those cases where the principles themselves depended upon the facts in the possession of the technical commissions, as, for example, in the re-casting of a colonial system to one of mandates, which called for adaptation to varying conditions in different parts of the world. It was this difficulty, and not any plotting on the part of Wilson's colleagues, as has been charged, which ultimately led to the change of method in the Peace Conference, by which the making of a preliminary treaty was abandoned for the preparation of a final text.

The President's point of view that the most important thing in the Peace Conference was the coming to grips with the problems themselves, rather than the Peace Conference procedure, was reflected in the preparations made for the Conference by both the State Department and the Inquiry. It not only seemed a common-sense point of view under any circumstances, but in view of Wilson's leadership in the statement of war aims, through his Fourteen Points and other similar utterances, it was almost inevitable that the chief preoccupation of the American Delegation should be to translate into definite terms the bases of peace which the President had laid down. Had the State Department been fully functioning during the closing months of the war, the plans, or rather blueprints, for the organization of the Peace Conference which it drafted would have had to be taken into account by the other governments at that time, quite as definitely as the program of settlement. Moreover, this was a task for which it was best qualified. No one, certainly no inexperienced outsider, could be so well prepared for planning the procedure of negotiations as those schooled in its use; for however much the old diplomacy might be criticized for the content of its work, it was at least a master of form. But throughout the War, the State Department had been so definitely subordinated to the President that apparently it exercised little influence upon the structure of a conference, most of the preparation for which had been made by outsiders whose conclusions were often not even communicated to the Department in the course of their work.

If there were reasons for the State Department's failure to produce plans for the Conference which could have imposed themselves upon it from the start, the Inquiry had further alibis to plead as well, not only in the fact that it was not a regular department of the government, but also in the unprecedented scope of its problems. Vast as had been the political displacement of the Napoleonic wars, they had left no such problems in economics or in world organization as those with which the Conference of Paris would have to deal. Looking forward to that conference through the closing months of the war, we were confronted by so many unsolved questions in a world which seemed then to be breaking loose from the very mold of precedent itself that even the researches in history tended to concentrate more upon imponderable shifts in public opinion and the trend of calculable policy in both the old and the new state system of Europe than upon the mere manner of the meeting of plenipotentiaries. In the material which we prepared there were some studies of procedure in past peace conferences, such as those of Utrecht and Berlin.[1] But we turned out no such manual on the technique of conferences as that in which Sir Ernest Satow presented to the British Delegation a masterly summary of the methods and procedure of diplomatic conferences of modern times.[2] From the wealth of experience surveyed in this short but comprehensive digest, conclusions could be drawn as to both the structure and the functioning of the conference which was to close the World War.

Although the Inquiry, throughout most of its existence, dealt primarily with problems and policies, nevertheless those in charge of its program discussed from time to time the organization of the American Delegation at the Conference, and from the summer of 1918 on, the problem was definitely taken up at the meetings of its Research Committee. This Research Committee was created by Dr. Bowman in the first week of August, 1918, to co-ordinate the

[1] This was the work of the section on Diplomatic History which I organized in the summer of 1918. The State Department printed some of this material. Little work was done on the Conference of Vienna, because the British turned over to us the excellent study of Professor C. K. Webster, which was much used by us. Our program was complete, but it was insufficiently co-ordinated with practical measures for the forthcoming conference. This would probably have been corrected if Colonel House had remained in America; but during the vital weeks of October and November our chief was in Europe.

[2] This volume, entitled *International Conferences*, was published in the series, "Peace Handbooks" (British Stationery Office, 1920).

STAFF OF THE INQUIRY AT THE PARIS PEACE CONFERENCE

Sitting (left to right): Charles H. Haskins, Western Europe; Isaiah Bowman, Chief of Territorial Intelligence; S. E. Mezes, Director; James Brown Scott, International Law; David Hunter Miller, International Law. Standing: Charles Seymour, Austria-Hungary; R. H. Lord, Poland; W. L. Westermann, Western Asia; Mark Jefferson, Cartography; Colonel House; George Louis Beer, Colonies; D. W. Johnson, Geography; Clive Day, Balkans; W. E. Lunt, Italy; James T. Shotwell, History; A. A. Young, Economics.

work of the Inquiry. It consisted of Professor Haskins, Chairman; Professor Young, Secretary; Dr. Bowman, Ex-Officio; and myself, as Editor. As the whole purpose of the Inquiry was research, this committee was the co-ordinating center of the working organization throughout the months of August and September, and was only terminated after the departure of Colonel House for Europe, about October 20, when Dr. Mezes disbanded all committees, stating that the Inquiry was henceforth to be placed on a Peace Conference basis. While the plans of the Research Committee for the organization of the American Delegation at the Peace Conference were tentative, they were reduced to the form of blueprints, and as these will show better than any detailed description our conception at that time of the interworking of all the varied organs of government which should be represented in some way or other at the Peace Conference, one of these plans is reproduced in an Appendix. A second chart, showing how the Delegation was organized at the Peace Conference, is sufficient comment on what happened to our planning.[1]

The plan which Dr. Mezes took to Washington in October differed from this in that it discarded the structure of the Inquiry. He proposed taking to Paris, under his personal direction, a number of the specialists on the Inquiry staff, along with the material which it had accumulated. Secretary Lansing was as much opposed to this plan of Dr. Mezes as the President, if for other reasons; but, when the President finally put into his hands the organization of the American Delegation to Negotiate Peace, he turned to Dr. Bowman and carried on the final arrangements with him. The elaborate details on the blueprint of the Research Committee were not carried through. The main lines of our planning were to be realized, however, before the Preliminary Peace Conference was over.

A study of this plan will show that it was in harmony with President Wilson's conception that the preliminary work of the Peace Conference—that of securing "unity of aim" among the Allied and Associated Powers—was to be provided for not only before the meeting with the Germans but after the negotiations with them had begun. In short, *it was to be a negotiated peace.* The American Delegation should be organized with the two aims in view of securing harmony among the Allies and coherence in negotiation with the

[1] See Appendix VII.

Central Powers. But the blueprint had to do with the organization of the American Delegation and its staff, more especially the relation of the technical advisers to the negotiators. It did not deal with the Peace Conference as a whole, although a study of the plan shows that it was based upon a very definite conception of the program and procedure to be followed at Paris. Moreover, the blueprint would undoubtedly have been completed to include the whole international organization if Mr. Miller had not left for Paris, taking his staff with him. There he and Professor Manley Hudson immediately set to work to study the proposals of the French and British Foreign Offices. Mr. Miller's Diary, through the latter part of November and the first of December, shows how keenly he and Colonel House were interested in adapting these plans to American needs. But there is no evidence available to show that these reached the President.

The French plan was delivered by Ambassador Jusserand to the State Department on November 29 and a copy of it was transmitted to the President, on December 2, just before sailing.[1] So far as is known at present, this slight summary of the program and structure of the Conference is the only one of its kind which the President had with him prior to his arrival in Europe, apart from communications from Colonel House, telling of the moves then under way in Paris and London. Its authors had examined the precedents of the great conferences of the nineteenth century, those of Vienna, Paris, and Berlin, and proceeded upon the assumption that on the arrival of President Wilson in Paris in the middle of December, the four Great Powers would be able "to agree among themselves upon the conditions of the peace preliminaries to be imposed severally on the enemy without any discussion with him." These would cover the territorial settlements and related subjects; but then would come up the question of "the representation of the several belligerent, neutral and enemy states at the Peace Congress," in all its complexity. The labors of the Congress would be twofold: the settlement of the war and the organization of the Society of Nations, the latter to await the completion of the former. The memorandum then outlined the procedure for dealing with these and went on to list seven territorial commissions and also seven committees on gen-

---

[1] This document was published by Ray Stannard Baker in *Woodrow Wilson and World Settlement* (Doubleday, Page, 1922), III, 56–63.

eral questions.[1] It ended with the pious suggestion that "the Congress, finally, could place itself, as has sometimes been done in the past, under the invocation of some of the great principles leading to justice, morals and liberty, which would be proclaimed at its very opening and even before fixing the procedure," a declaration pointed up by specific reference to the rights of the Allies and the violations of law and humane principles by the enemy.

If this document was the best that the Quai d'Orsay could do, it might very well strengthen rather than lessen Wilson's distrust of the sincerity of European governments which he expressed in his interview on the "George Washington." It was not until January that M. Clemenceau, using M. Tardieu much like a Colonel House, mobilizing the French experts for effective service, submitted a plan of procedure worthy of the name.[2] But by that time the Preliminary Peace Conference was already taking shape under the pressure of the force of events.

It is not necessary to follow in detail the studies that were taking place in London; for the situation, so far as the American Delegation was concerned, was summed up by Mr. Miller in a cable from London to Colonel House in Paris, dated December 6: "Conference with Tyrrell and Crowe convinces me that no program of procedure for interallied conferences can be agreed on in advance and that it will be necessary for the President to have his own program of subjects to be discussed and of the order of discussion."[3] Lord Tyrrell and Sir Eyre Crowe as heads of the Foreign Office undoubtedly reflected the attitude of the British Government; but the statement gains added importance from the fact that it was made on the

---

[1] This list of technical committees throws an interesting light on the French conception of the scope of the Conference. It was as follows:

1. Committee on Jewish Affairs.
2. Committee on the international river navigation (Rhine, Danube, Scheldt, Elbe) practice of the society of nations.
3. Committee on international railways (railways of the 45th parallel from the Adriatic to the Baltic, Bagdad trans-African railways from Capetown to Cairo and from Capetown to Algiers).
4. Committee on public law (free determination of the peoples combined with the rights of the ethnical and religious minorities).
5. Committee on international labor legislation (a very important question, the initiative, management and settlement of which must be left to the Socialists).
6. Committee on law relative to patents and trade-marks.
7. Committee on punishment for crimes committed during the war.

[2] Cf. André Tardieu, *La Paix* (Paris, Payot, 1921), pp. 95 ff.; English translation, *The Truth About the Treaty* (Indianapolis, Bobbs-Merrill, 1921), pp. 85 ff.

[3] Cf. *My Diary at the Conference of Paris*, I, 36. Printed privately for deposit at authorized reference centers.

occasion of a preliminary "conference of Premiers," called to reach agreement upon this very question of the organization and procedure of the Peace Conference. M. Clemenceau and Signor Orlando were present, but Colonel House was seriously ill in Paris and sent Mr. Miller in his place.

If the fact that the chief political adviser and the chief legal adviser of the President were both absent from America during the month of November, and that they were in close touch with the other governments, had rendered it difficult to proceed with detailed planning this side of the Atlantic, on the other hand, neither Colonel House nor Mr. Miller could take any positive steps in the matter, especially in view of the fact that the President had turned over to the State Department what must have seemed to him the more or less routine problem of organizing the American Delegation. Thus a combination of circumstances reinforced President Wilson's own natural inclination to put substance ahead of form, and the issues confronting the Peace Conference ahead of its procedure.

After the President's arrival in Europe the political situation made matters worse. Both the French and British Governments had been carried on under war-time executives and felt the need of securing a new mandate from the people before engaging upon peace negotiations. Wilson was powerless to withstand this request for delay and, during the first week of his stay in Europe, found himself in the unfortunate position of a guest of the Allied and Associated Powers. The contacts which he established by his visits to France, England, and Italy, by the unparalleled enthusiasm of his reception, gave him a delusive sense of the power of European public opinion to force acceptance of the fundamentals of his philosophy upon reluctant governments; but this popular support was soon submerged in that rising tide of nationalism which was the inevitable outcome of the war itself; so that when the British election was over and the British Delegation arrived in Paris in the closing days of the year, there was still no clear plan of conference organization. The major issues had not yet been solved as to whether the preliminaries of the peace arranged between the Allied and Associated Powers should be carried to the point of a final draft of the Peace Treaty or whether it should only prepare the outlines for the real Peace Treaty itself, to the making of which the enemy states would be invited.

This period of hesitancy and uncertainty was a tactical victory for those elements at the Peace Conference which were skeptical of or opposed to the American program. President Wilson's program was now confronted with the stern realities of embattled Europe, and there was as yet no adequate provision upon the ways and means for making that program articulate in the terms of international agreement.

As a matter of fact, however, the real origins of the Peace Conference organization took shape not from any formal schemes of previous planning, either French or British, but from the developing needs of the negotiators, and resulted in a compromise between foreign office proposals and the still existing war-time organization of the Allied and Associated Powers. The thread of pre-conference history runs back to the Mission of Colonel House to Europe in 1917, which established American participation in the conduct of the war. This Mission was Colonel House's first official position as representative of President Wilson in negotiations with European governments. It was October 28, 1917, when, accompanied by representatives of the various branches of the American war government, he sailed to Europe to co-ordinate American policies with those of the Allies. In this Mission, in addition to the heads of Army and Navy (Rear-Admiral Benson, Chief of Naval Operations, and General Bliss, Chief of Staff) there were as well the Chairman of the War Trade Board, Mr. Vance C. McCormick; the Assistant Secretary of the Treasury, Mr. Oscar T. Crosby; Mr. Hoover's assistant in Food Administration, Dr. Alonzo Taylor; accompanied by such legal experts as Mr. Thomas N. Perkins of the War Trade Board, and Mr. Paul Cravath of the Treasury. But before this co-ordinating body reached Europe, the catastrophe of Caporetto had forced the governments of France and England to co-ordinate with Italy, and on the very day that Colonel House landed in England, November 7, 1917, Mr. Lloyd George, M. Painlevé, and Signor Orlando had signed an agreement in Rapallo creating "The Supreme War Council." Colonel House's Mission therefore stepped into a situation which already furnished the skeleton of an organization for closer political unity and military co-operation between the Allies. The first meeting of the Supreme War Council was held in Versailles on December 1, 1917; the real working body, however, was the Inter-Allied Conference, which Colonel House's Mission stimulated into action, composed of the technical heads of the various administrations. From then on there grew up a steadily increasing net of inter-Allied war controls which, by the end of the war, constituted something approaching an international government of the "crisis" variety.[1] The wide scope of these inter-Allied activities, which included practically the whole economic life of the countries concerned, made the situation at the close of the war a very different one from that of normal peace time. Had the Supreme Council, composed of Prime Ministers or their representatives and representing the political sovereignty in each country, been continued as a sort of "Aulic Council," to quote General Bliss's comparison, there would have existed at the close of the War a kind of Inter-Allied War Cabinet like that which actually came into being in London for the whole British Empire. Colonel House, however, soon returned to America, and the Prime Ministers found their chief tasks at home, leaving the various Inter-Allied Boards a relatively free hand in their own particular fields.

As these tasks had been definitely directed toward the single aim of winning the war, and the membership of the Inter-Allied Boards was so largely made up of business executives and technical experts, there was less of a foundation to build the Peace Conference upon than seemed to be the case at first sight.[2] The plans of British socialists to transform the war-time organization into a really governing league of nations came to nothing. Nevertheless, when the Peace Conference began, the first meeting, that of Sunday, January 12, although an informal meeting of the heads of the four Great Powers, was substantially the Supreme War Council called together for a strategy of peace. The Council of Ten, to which this gave place, when Foreign Ministers sat alongside the President and the Prime Ministers, was the continuation of this body, and it retained its practical authority as a sort of cabinet for the Allied and Associated Powers until the Council of Four came into being

[1] The student of these international war-time bodies will find a statesmanlike survey and estimate in *Allied Shipping Control,* by J. A. (Sir Arthur) Salter, in my "Economic and Social History of the World War" (Oxford University Press, 1921). The application of these experiments in international administration to a League of Nations was suggested by L. S. Woolf in *International Government* (New York, 1916). More recently the problem has been treated with penetrative judgment by Sir Alfred Zimmern in *The League of Nations and the Rule of Law* (London, 1936).

[2] The plan of organization prepared by the Research Committee of the Inquiry had been prepared with due regard to these inter-Allied organizations. Professor Allyn Young drew upon his former connection with the War Trade Board to secure a complete list of these bodies, and a statement of their relations to each other.

after the middle of March. In the meantime, the Commissions which were appointed to deal with the special problems of the Treaty grew to resemble, both in number and function, the inter-Allied war-time commissions, for their first task was the apportionment of rival claims among the Allies themselves, as had been the case in war-time administration. The general conference, consisting of the plenipotentiaries of all the Powers, met only to ratify the conclusions reached in these executive and fact-finding bodies. This Plenary Conference met only six times before the signing of the Treaty.

Such, in broad outlines, was the organization of the Paris Peace Conference. The Quai d'Orsay followed up its original plan with a comprehensive scheme for procedure, but its program, which listed some eighteen major topics, was not accepted by President Wilson or Mr. Lloyd George, both of whom wished to concentrate upon an order of priority which would permit a more rapid demobilization and return to the more normal conditions of peace-time business. It may be that there was also a fear that the creation of so diverse and widespread an organization would result in the Conference speedily getting out of hand, in view of the fact that there was such wide conflict of opinion and interest among those who would be represented on the Commissions. Above all, it would be more difficult for the Great Powers to keep their control of the situation, a control which they rightly felt belonged to them by reason of their incomparably greater losses and effort in the war. In any case, the first phase of the Peace Conference was so tenuous as to make little progress with any but those topics which interested the three real leaders, President Wilson, Mr. Lloyd George, and M. Clemenceau who, at the opening session, was elected president following the usual diplomatic practice of awarding this honor to the country within which a conference meets.

It was the pressure of circumstances rather than design which produced the ultimate organization by which the Treaty was drafted. The turning point is that noted in my diary on January 29, when President Wilson, after a session of the Ten on the question of colonies, in which there had been disagreement over facts as well as policy, expressed his impatience of the waste of time at that and previous meetings, and asked the American experts there to iron out their technical differences with the British specialists so as to bring an agreed body of facts for the discussions of policy. It is to President Wilson's credit that it was his initiative which was largely responsible for thus changing the work of experts from that of preparing the case for their own Delegations to that which might be termed the diplomacy of fact-finding. Once begun, this international co-operation spread, both as to subject matter and the nations concerned. From that time on, it became more and more evident that the task in hand had passed beyond the agreement on broad principles around which, or in harmony with which, the details would be subsequently grouped, into a statement of these principles definitely stated and exactly applied in the form of contracts between nations. This apparently slight structural change, begun in the first week in February, marked the beginning of the second stage of the Peace Conference; although it was not for another month that the full implications of this shift in the method of work were ratified by a formal recognition that instead of preparing a preliminary peace to be followed by a detailed treaty, the Conference as a whole should concentrate upon the making of a final text.

As this last phase of the transformation took place during President Wilson's absence in America, the charge has been made that it was due to the Commission's betrayal of his leadership while he was not at hand to defend his point of view. It would even seem that President Wilson himself came to share this opinion and that it had much to do with results, both personal and political, which are too well known to call for comment here. A study of the inner working of the Conference seems to point to a quite different conclusion. But so vast and complicated was the task that it is doubtful if even at the time the chief actors were fully aware of the way in which these subtle forces of reality, the necessities of the situation itself, really determined the event.

It is at this point that we begin to see the effect of the organization of the Conference upon its program. Once launched upon the study of detail, it was unreasonable to expect that all this labor would be spent upon a preliminary document, embodying only the tentative views of the Allied and Associated Powers, to be presented to the Germans, when the time came, as a mere basis for further negotiations, which in turn might undo the work of the whole winter. The preparation of a detailed provisional text created a situation which could not easily be changed and a text which could not readily be done over again. In my opinion this was hardly less decisive for the making of the treaty than the strategy of its leaders.

The significance of the change, however, was not, so far as I know, understood by anyone at the time. Nor has it been fully appreciated to the present day. This is all the stranger in view of the fact that the chief criticism of the Conference of Paris was that it undertook this very task of making a completed text without the participation of the ex-enemy States. To work upon the final text in the absence of Germany was to lose the perspective of Europe as a whole, because, in the very nature of things, the facts even if established were seen only from one side. As the draft treaty grew into a completed statement, it became not only harder and harder to change, but in the mass of detail which it covered it reached so deeply into the economic and social, as well as the political life of Europe, that only those who knew the conditions in the countries across the Rhine could adequately judge of the effect which the treaty would be bound to have upon the public opinion of succeeding years. In short, the shift from a purely preliminary peace to the detailed document that was finally produced called for collaboration from the ex-enemy governments if the treaty was to register a lasting peace.

It is in an analysis of this elusive page of the history of procedure that the future historian will find the clue, hitherto missing, to the reason for the difference between the Fourteen Points and the Treaty of Versailles. There were, of course, other reasons for the nature of the output than the method of work. The psychological effect on those who had been Allies and Associates in the war, of continuing to work together for a common purpose tended to accentuate their own community of interest. There was also the fact that the Fourteen Points themselves could not be applied without a vast disruption of the old state system of Europe, and with the possibility of bringing economic and political chaos to much of Eastern and Central Europe. It was simply impossible for the Fourteen Points to be applied, even by those who accepted them theoretically, without creating grievances. This tendency, however, was bound to be accentuated if there were not present at the making of the treaty those whose interest it was to keep the program as closely as possible to its original terms.

In any case, the explanation which has commonly been given by

Wilson's enemies of the difference between the Fourteen Points and the final settlement is altogether too cheap and superficial to explain what really happened. It was not simply a case of an idealist yielding point by point to the pressure of a grim, cynical realist like Clemenceau. For the points in the Treaty against which most of the criticism is now directed were honestly recommended to President Wilson by his own experts as the logical and inevitable consequence of an existing situation and of the historical forces which had produced it. This was especially true of the Polish settlement; but it was also the case in the settlement of Germany's western boundaries. The insistence of the French upon their own claims and those of their allies undoubtedly accounted for much in the Peace Treaty, but the real fallacy lay in the fact that when the Allied and Associated Powers shifted over from the task of making the broad outlines of a preliminary peace to that of shaping a final treaty, they did not at that time proceed to assemble the real Peace Conference, that which would include both victors and vanquished in the World War.

CHAPTER IV

THE TREATIES

I⊤ is not too much to say that the Peace Conference never met. The Conference of Paris was a meeting of the enemies of the Central Powers, which dictated treaties for each of the ex-enemy States and hardly listened at all to their protests against the conditions imposed upon them. To the post-war generation in every country this fact seems now almost as incredible as it did to the leaders of liberal Germany at the time. They had dared to hope that a peace based upon the Wilsonian program would offer the new German Republic an opportunity to co-operate to the full in building the structure of a world community. Instead, they were not only rebuffed in their efforts to negotiate but the members of their Delegation suffered the personal humiliation of ostracism in their retreat at the Hôtel des Réservoirs at Versailles. For this treatment the French Government was immediately responsible. But the responsiblity rests as well upon a war-worn public opinion in England and America, benumbed by suffering and exhausted by both the effort of the war and the long strain of overwrought emotions. There was no wide movement of opinion against the treatment of the ex-enemy Delegations, only ineffectual protests from quarters that were, rightly or wrongly, suspected of pro-German sympathies. In the United States, the opponents of Wilson attacked his conduct of negotiations on other grounds. Had Senator Lodge, by some miracle, been on the American Delegation in Paris there is no reason to believe that this blunder of the Peace Conference would have been corrected.

A dictated peace was accepted by all who had lost confidence in Germany's good faith, and that included the great majority of Americans as well as of the English and of the French. If, as Clausewitz phrased it, war was the continuation of policy, diplomacy was, so far as the conflicting aims of the contestants were concerned, the continuation or summation of war. Military leaders were afraid that what was gained on the battlefields would be lost at the council table, and both the "Khaki Election" in Great Britain and the attitude of the French Chamber showed that these apprehensions were widely shared. The debates in the American Congress, while upon the whole maintaining the high note of disinterestedness in material gains, showed no lack of stern purpose to carry through the "Great Crusade" to its appointed goal—that of democracy triumphant without a doubt, and so recognized in Berlin. General Pershing had not been bluffing, as the French thought, when he had stood for the march to Berlin so that there should be no question as to who had won the war in the field and therefore no question as to who should determine the nature of the peace.

Whether the peace was to be dictated or not, it was necessary for the Allied and Associated Powers to work together and to accept a common program. The winter months showed how difficult this was and what rifts might easily disrupt their forces. The discontent of Italy and the breach between China and Japan, which had such a strong reaction in Washington, were but indications of what might happen more generally. The narrative which follows shows how serious the divisions became within the delegations of the United States and Great Britain. It was chiefly to prevent the delegations of the Central Powers from exploiting this situation that they were kept so carefully isolated from the Conference to which they had supposed that they were invited. Conscious of how French diplomacy itself had divided the Allies opposed to it in the Congress of Vienna, the Quai d'Orsay saw to it that no German Talleyrand would have access to the counsels of the Allied and Associated Powers.[1] Held off like prisoners from even social contact with former friends, the delegations of Germany and Austria and Hungary were held in strictest quarantine and under police supervision in their separate quarters in Versailles and St. Germain. When the real treaty-making should have begun, in the exchange of views over the detailed proposal of the draft treaty, the task was declared ended, and the signature of Germany was procured by the threat of an occupation of Berlin; the Allied armies were moved out beyond the bridge-heads of the Rhine, and were ready at a mo-

[1] Yet the German secret service was not inactive. So slight a detail as my own assignment by Colonel House to Labor problems, known at the time to only three or four in Paris, was wirelessed to Berlin from Lyons at once, a fact revealed by chance many years later.

ment's notice to force the issue.[1] There was nothing for Germany to do but to accept. Nevertheless the German protests even under these circumstances did bring a certain measure of alleviation, enough to show how much more could have been attained had there been a fair chance at negotiation.

Unfortunately for the Germans, their former government had only too recently used its victories on the eastern front to dictate the terms of peace to Rumania and to Soviet Russia. The rattle of the saber and the banging of the fist of General Hoffmann at Brest Litovsk reverberated at Paris, and the plans to exploit the material resources of Rumania furnished a precedent for the hard-pressed Allies to recover what they could from Germany by following her example. We have now forgotten how much of the territory of the Allies was open to the war-time exploitation of the Central Powers and how great was the need of those who had suffered by invasion. But while the fields were still desolated and the cities mere heaps of ruins, the prospect of making the Central Powers pay opened up a prior problem which had to be settled by the recipients: that of the fair apportionment among themselves of the spoils taken from the vanquished. The extent to which the self-interest in this partitioning of expected benefits could go was registered in the attitude of so liberal a statesman as General Smuts toward extending reparations to cover pensions and allowances. The claims of the new countries and the newly enlarged ones which had been cut out of the monarchies that had disappeared were so hard to reconcile with each other and with those of their great allies that the added task of inducing the Germans to agree could only be taken on after preliminary differences had all been ironed out. And that created a situation which had not been clearly foreseen; namely, that a detailed text had been created which by the mere fact of its existence forced its way to acceptance as final. For no one wanted to do it all over again.

But the faulty organization of the Preliminary Peace Conference, noted above, had left its traces on the text. When the Treaty was finally put together it was evident to any fair-minded person that it was more than any country should be asked to bear, although—in spite of their critics—the majority at least of those who drafted its clauses were fair-minded men, as fair-minded and as

[1] See below, pp. 377 f.

liberal as could be found anywhere. But it had not been put together in time. The fault lay not so much in this or that single section of the Treaty, for in most cases these sections contained provisions that were not without justification and were not merely the embodiment of vindictive and arbitrary power over a helpless victim. What was wrong with the Peace Treaty was that, when all the sacrifices were added together, the whole was greater than the sum of the parts. It was impossible to accept because impossible to fulfill on the part of the citizens of the conquered nations and still maintain a decent standard of living. Since Germany had to take the Treaty as a whole, it, therefore, had every right to regard the cumulation of injury as vitiating all parts. Yet, had there been a negotiated peace, much of the Treaty would still have been kept.

The failure to see all this at the time was directly due to the fact that the organs of the Conference, as they finally developed, were never properly articulated with each other or with the directing heads. Covering so vast a field, which included almost all the conditions of life of all Europe and of much of the colonial world outside, the Treaty was prepared in more than a dozen different commissions, each working at its own task and each task large enough for a full-sized treaty of its own: territorial questions, economics, conditions of trade, the safeguards of minorities and nationalities, and all the problems arising from the devastation of the war and the menace of its recurrence. It was only when these separate sections were finally put together that the makers of the different parts of the treaty became aware of the nature of the whole document; and that was not until the Germans had been already summoned to Versailles.

So far as the American Delegation was concerned, it was again a fault of organization which was chiefly responsible for the fact that it was only at this late hour that the full nature of the Treaty was appreciated. The work of American representatives on different commissions was not co-ordinated as the Conference progressed. No effort was made to keep anyone below the rank of the five plenipotentiaries informed of the steady progress of events. Each specialist was supposed to work on his task without regard to what his colleagues were doing in other fields. It was even regarded as a somewhat illegitimate interest for any of the so-called technical experts to inquire about anything not in their own field. This did not prevent an exchange of gossip, however, especially at lunch and dinner or in casual meetings from time to time.

The shortcomings of the American organization can best be seen by comparison with the way the British Delegation was organized. The British Empire Delegation was a co-ordinated whole. Not only did they prepare their work beforehand more carefully than the Americans, but at the close of the session of each commission their secretary took his record to the office of the General Secretary, Lord Hardinge, one of the most experienced of English diplomatists, under whom a narrative was edited into a few pages of mimeographed text; and this account of the day's work, prepared after five o'clock, was ready on the dressing-table of each member of the British Delegation before dinner the same day. The result was that when the members of the British Delegation discussed the day's work together in the apparent casualness of the dinner hour, they were well informed as to the whole day's work in all departments. The American parallel to Lord Hardinge was, if my memory is correct, a typewriting clerk, and the minutes supplied him were casual and imperfect records. The result of this haphazard method was that the gossip of the day tended to concentrate upon dramatic points and to lose anything of that precision of outline which was supplied the whole British Delegation.

This inadequacy in organization was at least partly responsible for the failure to realize the nature of the whole Treaty until it had been put together. Even then it is doubtful if the woods could have been seen for the trees had it not been for Mr. Arthur Sweetser's fine journalistic effort in preparing the short summary of the whole document which was distributed to the press.[1] Although I have not mentioned the fact in my Diary, I distinctly remember Mr. Sweetser's own dismay as he went over the document with me before publication, and we saw how heavily weighted it was with the menace of future trouble. But it was Mr. Sweetser's own fellow craftsmen, the journalists, who were responsible, far more than has been realized, for the fact that the Peace Conference did not even at that late date begin over again and give mature consideration to the readjustment of the demands made upon Germany. Not only were the American journalists tired of the whole proceeding and anxious to see it ended and get home again, but they had by this time

[1] On May 7.

created such a current of feeling against what the American Delegation had done that there was no public understanding, let alone any public support, of such a wearisome task as that which should then have been undertaken. This maladjustment of the American newspaper men at the Paris Conference is a larger historical fact than has yet been recognized. It raises a point which has not been sufficiently considered in the history of democratic diplomacy. From the purely journalistic point of view, that is, from the standpoint of news, a conference is a success when it breaks down or its leaders disagree. Mere agreement lacks dramatic appeal.

Not all the faults in diplomacy, however, were on the side of the Allied and Associated Powers. The German Delegation also was responsible for the fact that the terms submitted to it were not recast or modified in more liberal terms. As has been indicated, when the British and American Delegations became fully conscious of the nature of the Treaty as a whole, there were protests which went so far as to threaten open revolt. This movement went farther in British governmental circles than among the American, for even the Conservatives were alarmed at the thought of the possible consequences upon subsequent relations of England with the Continent. The pressure to secure revision of the terms was therefore not limited to a negligible few. It was powerful enough to have secured a reconsideration of Germany's case if the German Delegation had known how to turn this situation to its own advantage. It was a situation which opened the door to German diplomacy to recover its lost ground. The French, however, had no reason to fear a Talleyrand in Brockdorff-Rantzau, for, instead of dividing the forces against him, he consolidated them by tactical blunders of the first magnitude. Instead of concentrating its attack upon those sections of the Treaty which were plainly intolerable, the German Delegation found fault with practically every part of it, and thus tended to consolidate in its defense even those members of the Allied Delegations who had been outspoken advocates of revision. Some of this fault-finding was obviously either insincere or trivial, and this scattering of the attack weakened it at those points upon which it should have concentrated. The explanation for this failure in strategy lies probably in the fact that the German Delegation was composed of specialists, each of whom had his task to perform, and whose memorandum was therefore embodied in the

German reply. The presentation of a case in diplomacy is, however, a different problem from the preparation of it, and in this case the direction was absolutely at fault.

It may very well have been that the precautions taken by the French against the diplomatic strategy of a possible German Talleyrand would have been so effective as to prevent a negotiated peace, no matter how perfect the German plan of campaign. But it is now well known that the revolt against the Peace Treaty which was gathering momentum in British and American circles had been anticipated as early as March by the British Prime Minister himself, who confided his doubts in a memorandum prepared in a week-end at Fontainebleau and circulated on March 25.[1] To weaken Germany down to the condition of almost a second-rate Power, which the French felt justified in doing, was contrary to that century-old principle of British policy, which was to maintain an equilibrium of power on the Continent. Moreover, the more sober opinion which prevailed in the Foreign Office was one of apprehension lest a Punic peace should bring war again into Europe when Germany should have sufficiently recovered its strength. There was no doubt of its ultimate capacity for recovery, no matter what the terms of the Treaty might be. Therefore prudence as well as a sense of fair play provided the German negotiators with more support for a revision of the terms of the Treaty than they seem to have appreciated. This phase of Peace Conference history has never been explored, and a full treatment of it would carry this discussion too far afield. Nevertheless, one is tempted to wonder what would have happened if the German Delegation had penetrated behind the façade of the delegations of "the enemy" and had by imaginative insight realized the differences and animosities which had at times so split the Conference as to threaten its very continuance.

Brockdorff-Rantzau had two speeches ready for the reply to Clemenceau when he received the Treaty. One was a short, formal statement, merely acknowledging the receipt of the document. The other was a strong protest against the proffered terms of peace. There can be no doubt but that he should have chosen the first of these alternatives, no matter what conditions were offered him;

[1] The memorandum was entitled, "Some Considerations for the Peace Conference before They Finally Draft the Terms," and was published as *Memorandum Circulated by the Prime Minister on March 25th, 1919*, in Parliamentary Papers, Cmd. 1614, Vol. 23 (1922).

because the second method tended to close the door of compromise. It was a door which could not be battered down, especially by an arm that had no strength left in it. The way to keep it open was by saying little at the time; for the one thing to avoid was to strengthen the support for the Treaty in the minds of its makers, which would be the inevitable consequence of a general attack upon the document as a whole. Yet the longer, not the shorter, speech was chosen; momentary satisfaction was gained at the cost of assured failure.

The work of the German Delegation in the succeeding days followed up this general protest by an attack upon the Treaty which failed to discriminate between those parts of it which were of vital interest to Germany and those parts which embodied general principles, such as the Covenant of the League of Nations or the Constitution of the International Labor Organization. It would be interesting to speculate upon what might have happened if their reply had been prefaced by a whole-souled endorsement of the Covenant and of all other provisions for international administration. Even the case for the Saar Valley might have been left for future diplomacy, in view of the fact that the settlement of that territory was but temporary and that the proposal to place it under the League of Nations was a challenging experiment in international administration. That is not to say that the alienation of the Saar Valley, if only for a limited number of years, could have been easily or lightly borne by the Germans; but the hard fate had to be faced of either choosing to yield with good grace some things which could either be retrieved later or mattered relatively little, or, on the other hand, of attempting impotently to hold everything and losing all.

Diplomacy, however, is not all a question of the substance of demands; it is, to a larger extent than critics realize, a question of manner. The stilted etiquette that had grown up in the relations of Foreign Offices with each other has a real historical explanation in the effort to avoid wounding susceptibilities that are quick to take affront because they involve, or are thought to involve, the attitudes of the nations whom the diplomats represent. It was because Brockdorff-Rantzau himself chose to affront these susceptibilities on the part of the Allied Delegations by the manner in which he received the draft treaty when it was presented to him that the Treaty was not revised more fundamentally than was the case—his failure to rise, the rasping and unconcealed hostility of his intonation, or that of his translator, and the implied defiance with which he repulsed the charges levelled against Germany.

By the bluntness of his words and the rudeness of his manner he played into the hands of Clemenceau, who had all along maintained that Germany, created by policies of "blood and iron," would understand only force as the basis of a European peace. There were those in the German Delegation who were sensitive to this disastrous blunder on the part of their leader, and the excuse was given that he was too ill and too overcome to be master of himself in so desperate a situation. I have it on good evidence, however, that he deliberately chose this manner to express resentment and defiance to the "Diktat von Versailles." It is only when one recalls how Talleyrand at Vienna divided the forces against France, that one begins to see how much was lost to Germany by the failure to employ on its behalf those qualities of imagination and penetrating insight which are the essential qualifications for political leadership, and nowhere more so than in the field of diplomacy.

The final judgment of history upon what was done or not done at the Peace Conference will have to take into account more than this analysis of the technique of diplomacy, however. For, what happened at Paris was but a single act in a much larger drama, one which stretches back to the Middle Ages and reaches forward through the era of science and mobilized industry to envisage new and untried forms of political and economic relationships within and among nations. The Peace Treaties had to deal with facts for which they were not responsible, but which, because registered in them, are thought of as their handiwork. For example, the fall of the Habsburg Monarchy took place months before the Treaties of St. Germain and Trianon were signed, and the documents in which the new sovereignties were recognized embodied, however blunderingly, the inescapable facts of war and revolution. It was impossible to draw this new map of Europe without doing injury to the vested interests of former governments and peoples. But it was also inevitable that the dispossessed would exploit the injury as a political slogan and a diplomatic weapon for years to come. Therefore, for the sake of all concerned, the new frontiers should have been drawn with at least equal consideration for the rights of the ex-enemy States. This could only have happened by a negotiated peace; for, however fair-minded the experts on one side of a dispute, they can rarely see the full merits of the claims of those on the other. Lacking the benefit of impartial debate, the Peace Conference made the inevitable mistake of yielding too much to the insistence of those able to present their case in Paris. In the adjustment of the German-Polish frontier, in the extent of the territories taken from Hungary, and in the extension of Italian sovereignty to the Brenner Pass, wrongs were perpetrated and gross injustices done. But neither Germany nor Hungary was without blame in such matters in the past, and to charge mistakes like these against the Wilsonian principle of "self-determination" is to ignore the lessons of history.

If the reaction to pre-war grievances played a part in the settlement, the continuing influence of the World War was still stronger. The winter of 1918–1919 was not only one of suffering for the Central Powers behind the barriers of the blockade, it was one of privation in France and Great Britain as well. As the Peace Conference was open to the winds of opinion, the voices that reached it were disturbing rather than helpful. So far as could be judged from the confusion of rumor and news, there was a hardening of spirit as the cost of the struggle began to be reckoned. There had not been time to do this when every effort was required for carrying on hostilities. But after the fighting ceased, in the first period of relief from tension, there came a new realization of what had happened. The War loomed again on the horizon, this time as a political and economic fact. Thus it was that those making the peace found that the breaking down of frontiers, far from increasing their freedom of action, cluttered the path of adjustment with new problems. This is but another way of saying that the war continued to dominate events throughout the whole period of the settlement and that this fact explains, more than any other, its failures and shortcomings. Too great a gulf had been blasted out between neighboring peoples, too much blood had been shed, too many homes ruined forever, for the surviving victims of such a costly victory to adjust themselves at once to the precepts of sound statesmanship and make a generous peace. If that had proved to be too hard a task for the Northern States in dealing with the defeated South at the close of the American Civil War, it was still more difficult when the belligerents were foreigners who had three times in a century invaded the soil of France.

And yet the fact remains that Lincoln would have done otherwise, and that the supreme attribute of statesmanship, magnanimity, was lacking at Paris. Wilson's sense of justice was, as has often been pointed out, of the stern, unyielding quality of the Covenanting Calvinist, more suggestive of the Old Testament than of the New. He accepted retribution for ill-doing as a part of the moral order of the world, and believed that it applied to nations as well as to individuals. It is a strange fact that one who abhorred as he did the rigidity of legalism in political dealings, should have been so rigid in his ethical outlook as to fail to see how far some of the items in the Treaties were from any generous or even fair construction of the Fourteen Points. There was always the saving qualification in his mind that the new dispensation, set forth in the Covenant of the League of Nations, would right the wrongs of the old; but he failed to see that the process of rectification could not be postponed without weakening and ultimately endangering the very existence of the League.

It has been customary for the critic of the Peace Treaties to pause at this point, putting upon Wilson's shoulders the responsibility for the "Punic peace." This means ignoring two main things: first that Lloyd George, Clemenceau and a number of lesser figures were joint authors of the Treaties, which were too vast for any one man to follow in the limited time of the Conference, let alone control; and, second, that some of the gravest mistakes, reparations, for example, were committed by others in succeeding years.

The action of Lloyd George at the Peace Conference, was, in some important respects, more liberal so far as Germany was concerned than that of his American colleague. But he was hampered throughout by the flamboyant nationalism he had displayed in the "Khaki Election" of December, 1918, in which he had received his mandate to come to Paris as head of the British Delegation. The temptation to use the written assurance of a man like Lord Cunliffe, Governor of the Bank of England, that Germany could pay the costs of the War, was too much for him. How different the history of the world might have been if he had gone to the country, risking defeat, on the appeal to avoid the costly and dangerous path of retribution! Would such statesmanship have triumphed? Perhaps not. But even in defeat it would have created a force for moderation which would have had a strong effect upon the negotiations in

Paris; while, if it had succeeded, it would have secured a treaty on which the structure of a League of Nations could strongly rest.

What should be said about Clemenceau? First of all, that he stood out against Foch and the militarists, and that the country which had suffered such tragic loss thought that he went too far to meet Wilson's ideals. This preoccupation of France with policies of security, its nervous, almost convulsive effort to prevent another invasion, its psychosis of fear, was a political fact from which there was no escape, except by treaty arrangements and collective security. Those who criticize France for it should recall that it was a heritage of the War, and that it was as much the condition of a continuing peace in Europe as the redress of Germany's grievances.

Wherever the fault lies, there were blunders and mistakes in the Treaties of Peace, with cruel consequences. But the responsibility for some of the worst of these rests at least equally upon some of those who were the most outspoken critics of the Peace Conference, those upon whom fell the responsibility for either putting the Treaties into effect, or, in case of rejection, of substituting something better for them. The blunders made concerning reparations were largely shared and perpetuated by subsequent governments, as unable or unwilling to face realities as the commissions which first grappled with these questions while the warring nations still had their armies at the front. As for the charge that Wilson's doctrine of "self-determination" was violated by including in the new frontiers remnants of peoples of foreign nationality, one can, without entering into the post-war controversies, point to the fact that the most far-sighted statesmen of Central Europe now look for the remedy for grievances not so much in a redrawing of the frontiers, as would have been the case in the past, but in an application of some sort of neighborhood accommodation—the theory of the "good neighbor"—which would give the mixed peoples in frontier areas something of that self-determination of their own local destiny that national states have reserved in the past for central governments. And that means building more, not less, upon the structure of the community of nations.

Perhaps the best defense for the Treaties of Peace is to be found in a comparison of them with the substitute treaties which the American Government subsequently signed with the Central Powers, treaties which embodied the conceptions of those critics of the Wilsonian settlement who were mobilized into action under Senator Lodge. These treaties keep for the United States all the rights and advantages which were granted to the signatories of the Peace Treaties, except where the League of Nations is involved. The only thing surrendered is the machinery by which redress of grievances could be assured and treaties modified by common agreement under the pressure of world opinion. It is at least not unfair to the architects of the Conference of Paris to recall how much better a task they performed than that achieved by those who denied the Wilsonian vision.

Still, making every allowance for ignorant criticism and partisan attack, the fact remains that the Peace Conference failed to meet the expectation of the liberal and progressive thinkers in almost every country. The challenge of today is to repair the bulwarks of peace and in the light of experience strengthen or, if need be, rebuild the League of Nations, with due provision for the varying needs of nations, so that somewhere in the world the forces of peace may be mobilized against that oldest instrument of politics—war.

Unless this is done, a new peace conference may not have enough of civilization left to restore its shattered fragments.

CHAPTER V

SOCIAL JUSTICE IN THE PEACE TREATIES

OF all the work done by the Paris Peace Conference, that with which this narrative chiefly deals will be judged by many students of its history to be the least interesting—the erection of a world organization for the problems of labor. There is nothing in it to excite political passions like the shifting of a frontier or the question of responsibility for the War. It had no touch of historical romance like the break-down of old empires, nor did it stir the imagination like the creation of a League of Nations. In the years following the Conference, it was obscured at first by the controversies over the political and economic terms of settlement, and by those arising over the failure of the United States to enter the League. But the International Labor Organization, dealing as it does with the homely problems of the welfare of the common man, has a universal constituency and a lasting cause to serve. It is the first creation in world affairs of an institution, participated in by workers, capital, and governments to deal with the problems that are most real to most people the world over, those that have to do with the day's work. Its name belies its nature; for it represents all interests, not merely those of labor. It is a world parliament limited in scope to the problems that affect labor but it acts in the name and interests of all. It might more accurately have been termed the International Industrial Conference or, better still, the International Organization for Social Justice.

There was a hint of this broader conception of the purpose and scope of the International Labor Organization in the preamble to its constitution, in the statement that universal peace "can be established only if it is based upon social justice." It must be confessed, however, that when we wrote those words into the text, we were not thinking of their far reach, but of a formula which would enable us to tie our institution into the structure of that new world order which the League of Nations symbolized. As I look back at it

54

now, I am led to the opinion that we stated the most fundamental of all principles in political as well as social polity. There can be no assurance of permanent peace in a world that perpetuates spoliation of the rights of others. Nations which permit this of their own citizens will all the more readily turn to exploit their neighbors. The institution which we founded does not deal with more than a fraction of this vast field of social and economic rights; but it lies at the point where world issues cross, and it is keyed directly to the dominant fact of contemporary civilization, the rise of applied science.

The story of how the I.L.O. came into existence at the Paris Peace Conference has already been told in a detailed and documented history, written and edited by those who took part in the negotiations.[1] The narrative which follows covers only parts of the negotiations, but they were the parts that were vital for success. The incidental comments that were jotted down at the time may serve to explain some of our difficulties. There is some need of this, because those who have not lived through the strain of confused debate and contrary purposes, which is always present when great issues are at stake, too often misjudge the event. They do not see why there should be difficulty in securing agreement when the facts stare one in the face. If they had tried their hand in the Paris Peace Conference, they might be less sure of their historical criticisms.

The I.L.O. has now justified our labors by its history. Instead of commenting here upon this achievement of succeeding years, however, it is more fitting that I repeat what I wrote in 1920, setting down problems of the Labor Commission while they were still fresh in my mind and basing on the few short months of formative beginnings a prophecy which is being fulfilled.[2] After pointing out that an official body limited to the realistic task of treaty-making could not indulge in the irresponsible exploitation of altruistic ideals, and that the past history of international labor legislation was almost negligible compared with the vast mass of domestic legislation, I reviewed the negotiations as follows:

[1] *The Origins of the International Labor Organization* (Columbia University Press, 1934).
[2] "Historical Significance of the International Labour Conference," in *Labour as an International Problem*, edited by E. John Solano (Macmillan, 1920), pp. 41–66. The casual reader of these pages, if there be any such, will probably find this extract hard going. But it is a contemporary judgment on an entirely new experiment.

The situation was certainly not promising, and yet the very difficulties of the case made the solution which was urged all the more remarkable. The British Labour Delegation to the Peace Conference made a proposal that instead of centering attention solely upon any specific claims of labour which might be inserted in the Treaty, there should be erected an annually recurring International Labour Parliament and an International Labour Office, which could keep pace with the progressive changing demands of the labour world, and so secure, not one single Labour Charter, but a never-ending series.

The idea was a large and fruitful one. So far as Labour was concerned, the Peace Conference of Paris would be but the first step in a continuous process; and the Treaty, instead of being a final document, was, in so far as it was concerned with industrial problems, but the first clauses of a document which was to be continued by future congresses through future treaties. It would thus be the beginning of a continuous co-operation on the part of Labour, Society, and Governments.

The contribution of the British Delegation, however, was much more than a statement of a policy—it proceeded to offer the details of a definite plan by which the policy could be realised, a plan which when first presented to the Commission on International Labour Legislation, was already elaborated in the articles and clauses of a proposed section of the Treaty of Peace, and contained most of the essential elements of the plan as later adopted. Indeed, from the standpoint of diplomacy, it is possible that the plan as first presented was too detailed; for it had not been whittled to fit all of the constitutional objections which participating governments were forced to raise against it, and therefore the first phase of the discussion tended to be rather critical and negative, because the larger principles underlying it were more or less taken for granted. But, on the other hand, this detailed plan of a constitution for Labour was a pleasing contrast to the unformed generalities which were all that a number of the other sections of the Peace Conference had to begin with; and, all things considered, it is possible that future historians may find in this well developed proposition the most original and suggestive experiment of all those which were advanced at a Conference at which the whole scheme of world politics was in discussion, if not on trial.

The distinctive contributions which marked the International Labour Constitution as original and of particular significance, are in the first place the recognition of non-official representation in an official international body, and in the second place the provision by which the action of that international body was to be related with that of the various governments. . . .

It was clear that some device would have to be found for the limitation of the powers of these non-official representatives, and yet it was necessary that that limitation should not be carried to the point of endangering in any way the reality of their work. As the Commission was warned more than once in the course of its proceedings, Labour was tired of words and empty and delusive promises and would not be interested in the erection of any institution which was devoid of power. If, however, power were to be given to men irresponsible to their governments, it was taking that power from the governments themselves. This brought one into a very dangerous dilemma, for if the power to make labour treaties were to be taken over by a body containing so large an element of unofficial representatives, what about the power to enforce the treaties? Should the governments be held responsible for carrying out propositions arrived at and agreed upon in the formulation of which they had been partly shut out? The result would be to make a government little more than a police force for the administration of regulations arrived at by these Industrial Parliaments; in short, there would have arisen something like a World State under the aegis of Industrial Democracy and the International Parliament of Labour would be the most august legislating institution in the world, over-riding government not only within itself but in the subsequent carrying out of its decisions.

This dilemma gave rise to a long discussion. The more revolutionary section of the Commission, represented especially by the brilliant Secretary of the French Confédération Générale du Travail, was strongly for proceeding at once with the bolder policy which would endow the International Labour Parliament with the powers of a genuine legislature and bind the constituent countries to the carrying out of its decrees. This point of view was apparently shared in greater or less extent by those qualified to speak for labour in all the continental countries—a fact of much significance in estimating how far towards industrial confederation the continental countries might proceed. Great Britain and the United States, however, and still more Japan, were reluctant even to consider such a revolutionary point of view, and stood out strongly against the notion that the time had come for the recognition of a world state, even where the impulse to common action was so strong. For the United States, which at best had come against its will into the arena of world politics, any such suggestion as that its government should abrogate its control of such domestic affairs as industrial legislation, seemed almost automatically to exclude it from participation in the scheme. Japan was equally reluctant from another reason, for its industrial problems were as yet so unlike those of Western Europe, that it could hardly be expected to place itself at the mercy of an international body in which it would have so slight a voice. Since there was no power to compel the representatives of any state in Paris to accept a parliament endowed with such prerogatives it was clearly necessary to find some device by which the Parliament of Labour should have sufficient authority to justify its existence in the eyes of Labour as a real force for securing legislation, and yet not set itself up as a super-government in opposition to existing governments.

It was this dilemma which brought forth the second and most ingenious contribution to the British scheme, namely that the power of the International Parliament be limited to secure the submission of its legislation to the legislatures or other competent authorities of the participating states. In the field of International Labour Legislation, the Foreign Offices and other bureaucratic intermediaries shall not interfere; no recommendations of the proposed parliament can be smothered in the files of a reactionary diplomatic official; they must be brought within a given time to the attention of Parliament or Congress or whatever law-making body the country may possess.

Beyond that, international compulsion cannot go towards securing the adherence of the participating Powers; so that all the World Parliament can do is to lay its conclusions before the highest tribunal of public opinion in each country, and leave it to that body to decide whether it shall adhere or not.

In the long history of political theory it would be hard to find an experiment more interesting and suggestive than this proposed delicate machinery for transmitting to Powers jealous of their reputation and their standards of social morality, the forceful suggestion of international co-operation in matters which have hitherto lain exclusively within their jurisdiction. On the face of it there is no derogation of sovereignty whatever; the International Parliament has no power to make legislation, but simply to suggest it. In reality, however, that suggestion, if passed by a two-thirds vote, comes to the various countries with an authority which somewhat resembles the device by which the British officials once governed the titular rulers of Egypt. It will be hard to believe that any state should be willing to write itself down as so backward in its ideals of social justice as to refuse to accept laws which are to be of otherwise universal adoption. The forces of progressive opinion will be given a leverage, by way of comparison and direct appeal, which should impel each state to go as far as possible towards meeting the demands of the yearly Conference.

In a word, the essence of the plan is to throw back upon public opinion in the various countries the responsibility for carrying on social legislation. By seizing upon this sound principle in the assignment of responsibility for passing legislation, it would be possible to exact from the participating states a degree of responsibility for such laws as they did accept, which otherwise could not have been exacted.

This brings us to the third main point in the British proposal, the question of the enforcement of International Labour Legislation, once it had been agreed upon. A long and very intricate section of the plan deals with this—too long and too intricate for the casual reader—and possibly it may be found to have gone too much into detail in a matter so intricate that it is impossible for us now to foresee just how it will work out. However that may be, the plan has the merit of frankly facing the difficulties of the situation and offering a number of alternative lines of action. The problem here is the most delicate of all. Can international action go so far as to interfere in the internal affairs of a sovereign state to pronounce upon the success or failure of its administration? That would be the recognition of a World State in the most sensitive part of government machinery—the power to enforce law; and yet it was the sense of every person concerned with it in the Labour Commission at Paris, that unless some provision were made to ensure the carrying out of the proposed legislation the whole enterprise would be rendered nugatory through the failure of those states to apply it for which it was more especially designed. International Labour Legislation would in the nature of the case be always minimum legislation. Its purpose would be to bring up the backward states to as near the standards of progressive countries as possible, in order that progressive states themselves should not be kept behind by the existence elsewhere of conditions permitting exploitation of labour and so causing unfair conditions of competition. Since experience has shown that these same backward countries might attempt to meet the situation by placing legislation on the statute books which was never intended to be carried out, the provision for overseeing the enforcement of labour legislation was of fundamental importance. Yet nothing can run more counter to the principles of national sovereignty as understood and applied throughout the world than this interference with the enforcement of law.

Here then was a further step towards the recognition of that limitation on sovereignty which is implicit in the concept of the League of Nations. It would have been a serious innovation to have permitted the government of one state to raise objections to the way in which the government of another state was carrying out its own laws in a field which had always previously been regarded as distinctly a home affair. But the British scheme went even further than that; it proposed to allow bodies of private individuals in one state to pass judgment on the way in which the laws of another state were being carried out, and to interfere in order to secure better enforcement, thus going a long way towards the breakdown of that conception of Sovereignty as absolute which was the ruinous doctrine upon which the old régime, before the war, was based. It was a bold and novel proposition, and if it were to be frequently invoked might conceivably accomplish as much mischief as good. But as drawn up, it is rather a negative than a positive provision. It stands in the background of the plan for international legislation with the threat of interference in the home life of the participants in case they do not behave. It is a recognition of the interests of all in the conduct of each of the governments of the world, and will be heeded without formal enforcement to the extent that the laws proposed have the general support of world opinion, and also to the extent of the vitality of the League of Nations, of whose constitution this is one of the most vital, if little recognised elements.

In the course of the debates in the Commission, it became more and more evident that while the plan was the product of the British delegates, the need for an international organisation was much stronger on the Continent than elsewhere. Labour laws, like labour movements, tend to break through boundary lines on the map, when those lines are drawn across a Continent so small and intricate as the Continent of Europe. Therefore the Continental representatives for the most part were in favour of making the scheme as rigid and binding as possible, and of frankly erecting a sort of International Industrial Super-State which should enforce both legislation and administration upon the various governments. The British proposal avoided the crucial point in the scheme for the creation of a Super-State by leaving untouched the power of the different national parliaments to pass their own laws; but it supplied all the mechanism for enforcement that the Continental representatives could desire.

The American representatives, however, were unable to agree even to this compromise, in the form in which it was originally presented. For even such a partial scheme as this was carrying them beyond the limitations of their constitution as well as against the traditions of their industrial history. In the President of the Commission, Mr. Gompers, the United States had supplied a delegate who represented the major force in American industrial history, the American Federation of Labour. The policy of this organisation had always been to "keep out of politics." While gladly availing itself of labour legislation, it had steadily maintained a policy of remaining aloof from purely political questions and of bringing the direct pressure of its organisation to bear upon either of the great political parties of the country as occasion demanded. It, therefore, had always regarded its proper sphere as distinctly economic. To participate in the international constitution might involve a break with its non-political traditions, for it implied concentrating upon legislative action in home affairs rather than upon direct action as in the past. However, the American Federation of Labour had already taken steps in this direction during the war, particularly since its Buffalo meeting in 1917, and indeed the genius of Mr. Gompers had already discerned the inevitable widening of the sphere of action of his Federation, so that while conscious of the momentous character of his decision as a possible turning point for labour policy in the United States, he accepted the situation to which the war had finally brought American labour, along with that of Europe, and lent his co-operation as far as it was possible.

But it was not possible to co-operate freely. The Constitution of the United States prevented that. Practically all the labour legislation of the United States is state legislation, and the States can have no relations with foreign governments. How then could the United States participate in the proposed international labour legislation if the country as a whole possessed no organ either for securing a uniform and universal adoption of the proposed international labour laws, or for the enforcement of these laws if they should be enacted, except in the very limited fields over which the Federal Government had unquestioned jurisdiction? These difficulties were laid before the Commission with great cogency by both Mr. Gompers and his colleague, Mr. Robinson, in the earlier sessions of the Conference, and for a time it seemed as though an impasse had been reached which made it impossible for the United States to participate in the plan. The country would find itself in an intolerable situation if it were to share in the passage of propositions through the international body, which it would have no way of either enacting into law through Congress or of enforcing through the Federal authority.[1]

To be sure, there were certain indications in American industrial history that the time was approaching when labour legislation would become more and more a national, and less a state affair. A way had been found for the national enforcement of a law to prohibit the use of phosphorus in matches; and another law had attempted to prohibit child labour under certain conditions by stretching the powers of inter-state commerce control to prohibit the commerce of articles in the making of which there had been child labour. But this child labour law had been declared unconstitutional by the Supreme Court as late as the summer of 1918, so that the supreme judiciary of the United States had declared itself, almost at the very moment at which the Peace Conference was held, as against any stretching of the constitution so that labour legislation could be undertaken by Congress through the inter-state control of commerce. On the other hand, the action of the Supreme Court in limiting the power of Congress to its traditional sphere, seems hardly likely to be final. No sooner had the Court pronounced its decision than the next Congress at once passed a new Child Labour Law which both Houses accepted simultaneously; and this time it proposed to go even further than it had before, and boldly enforce the law by its power of taxation.

The public opinion of the United States was obviously working towards the recognition of national labour legislation by way of Congress, in place of the old method of state action, and if the Supreme Court should again declare the new law unconstitutional, it is even possible that a constitutional amendment could be secured which would definitely place labour legislation within the power of Congress. But the representatives of the United States at Paris could not anticipate history, and although signs at home were more and more evident that the temper of the country would not stand any longer the obstruction which it had been meeting from a few backward states, such as North Carolina and Mississippi, in securing rudimentary principles of labour legislation, Mr. Gompers and his associates could not risk guaranteeing any such interpretation of American

---

[1] This is not the place for a detailed discussion of the legal questions involved in American participation. It is possible that it may yet be found that the constitutional limitations indicated above do not necessarily apply after all. A treaty becomes the supreme law of the land, and therefore it has been held that action by treaty involves any necessary extension of the field of Federal control to execute its provisions. A precedent already exists for thus overcoming divergent state laws by treaty action, in the case of a treaty protecting migratory birds which was made with Canada and is binding on the whole country, in a matter outside the reach of Federal legislative action. But it would have been hazarding much for the representatives of the United States at Paris to have based upon this precedent their assent to an international obligation to apply it in the manner proposed. Moreover, even if the legal argument should turn out to admit of acceptance of the scheme, there was much to be said against using it, if it should result in any enlargement of the control of the Senate, instead of that of Congress as a whole, over labour matters. Fortunately the alternative to a treaty, recommendation for legislative action, would not be open to this objection.

political tendencies in an international agreement. They had to take the situation as it actually was, with all the historic limitations of the Federal Government. They were, therefore, in a very difficult position, for were they to interpret the position of the United States Government in this International Congress as simply being one of traditional impotence they would be lending a leverage to the perpetuation of that impotence by allowing it to remain the basis of an international policy at a time when other governments were assuming the new obligations. Moreover, much depended upon the participation of the United States in the proposed world organisation. In the face of a Europe on the verge of revolution, the effect of American abstention would be to strengthen that conservative reaction which was a highly unsafe policy to pursue, and at the same time to lessen the effect of the participation of the United States in securing social justice in other lines.

The solution of the difficulty was found in a compromise. And the compromise, as so often happens, enlarged instead of lessened the scope of the proposed International Labour Conference. That body might present its conclusions to the participating governments in the form of recommendations for labour legislation, instead of simply as treaties to be adopted by them. At first glance this seems like enfeebling its action by permitting an evaporation into rhetoric, and so the American suggestion was interpreted by the continental representatives on the Commission who were anxious to endow the international organisation with the sanctions of a real government. They claimed that to allow the Conferences in the future freedom to vote mere recommendations instead of drawing up treaties, would tend toward weakened influence, and they feared that the recommendations would not carry sufficient authority to secure adoption in the different countries. On the other hand, it was pointed out by the American representative that the possibility of falling back upon recommendations when treaties could not be arrived at would give much larger scope for the work of the Conference, by enabling it to take action not only where technical difficulties stood in the way of treaty-making, but also in cases where public opinion had not reached the point of decision necessary to making treaty-contracts, although apparently moving in that direction. As a means for accelerating public opinion, the recommendation would, therefore, be the first step toward a treaty, and would keep the matter alive; whereas a rejected treaty would be difficult to recall. It was pointed out, in support of this point of view, that the history of labour treaties was a very slight one, that only two small matters already mentioned had been settled by general international contracts, namely, the prohibition of night work for women and the use of phosphorus in match making. If, therefore, the Labour Conferences were to be limited to this method of procedure—by treaty-making alone—they had no very large nor lasting history ahead of them. On the contrary, if their conclusions were to be submitted as recommendations for appropriate action by the different governments, they could be better adjusted to the variant conditions of law and custom, and so more sure of acceptance.

The American amendment to the British plan was, therefore, an addition to it rather than a limitation. This became apparent almost immediately when the question arose of the adhesion of Japan and the countries of newer or less industrial development. It will be unnecessary here to describe the further modifications in the plan which were made in order to secure the participation of those countries, but the point to be emphasised is that the difficulties presented by the United States Constitution carried the plan for the Labour Conference away from a somewhat narrow and legalistic conception of its possibilities, into an adjustable instrument for world legislation. The fact that that legislation would be to a large degree simply preliminary, and that it would have to overcome various obstacles in the different countries before it finally secured adoption, does not lessen the genuine character as legislation. The Labour Conference becomes a sort of preliminary legislature in which projects are shaped up for adoption, both immediate and indirect. This, after all, is all that can be accomplished in an international conference so long as governments make their own laws.

PART TWO

THE PEACE CONFERENCE
DAY BY DAY

The Voyage of the "George Washington"

Tuesday, December 3, 1918

My career as a Peace Conference official began at nine tonight. When I got out of the Tube at Hoboken and was dragging my parcels along with me through River Street a soldier challenged me, and then I discovered that the whole pier-front was closely guarded by troops. Pier 2 was at the far end of the street—as it is sure to be if you have a heavy lot of bundles. There my passport was waiting for me; and after twenty minutes or so an army officer came along and escorted a little group of us through to the ship. Of course, it was down at the other end of the piers, and we trudged along like very humble representatives of a great Republic, with our baggage jostling against our legs. The wharf itself had been turned into a series of reception halls by flags draped from the beams and bunting festooned along the walls of the passageway. At the gangplank our passports were examined by an army officer and our names verified. Then we went on board—to be met by a row of young naval officers, who at once challenged us again—and were listed as we showed our passports once more. A lieutenant then showed us to the executive officer, who turned us over to his adjutant, who again looked at the passports and then told us which rooms we had been assigned. Every aisle has a sentry pacing up and down it, and at every turn of the stairs a marine is posted, so that officers and men are eternally at salute. It is very military and the total effect reassuring, if a little bothersome.

When its former German owners named the ship "George Washington" to attract American passengers, they little thought that that would make it one day the flagship of our navy at the close of a war with theirs. For, apart from its name, the ship has no particular distinction. It is comfortable and large enough, but is not in the front rank of ocean liners. It is admirably fitted, however, for such a journey as this, a sort of ocean-going "Mayflower," or presidential yacht, with ample room for the official party and quar-

67

ters for several hundred more of the Expeditionary Force. Not much has been done to it, apparently, to fit it up for this voyage, beyond transforming the library into a working room for Military Intelligence with a large blackboard and maps, which fail to impress our geographers. The State Department has had the assignment of the rooms, but there are likely to be some changes before long.

Wednesday morning, December 4, 1918

The President has come on board. Secretary Baker came with him. He is a very unassuming, quiet-mannered man, and breakfasted with us instead of with the presidential party, but has now left the ship, which is casting off.

Later

As we slid out from the dock and headed south, the President's flag was broken out on the mainmast, and five destroyers, waiting in the river to escort us, fired the presidential salute of twenty-one guns. We replied, and the din was terrific. But that was only part of it. The river was full of craft; it looked as if all the tugs of the harbor had come to see us. The water was thick with them; and each one blew as long and loud a blast as it could. We could see people on the shores as well, especially at Battery Park, where there must have been ten thousand people or more along the sea-wall. Then we slowly pulled away from the crowded upper harbor, passing the Statue of Liberty, in procession, with two army airplanes playing around us. At the Narrows we were given a return salute from the guns of the old "Monitor," which was anchored at the open end of the net that had been placed there to block the channel against submarine attack.[1] As we passed through the gate in the submarine net, which brought us close to the Staten Island shore, we saw hundreds of school children waving flags, and that was the last clear glimpse we had of those on shore. At the tip of Long Island, on the east, there were crowds almost like those at the Battery, but we were already too far out to recognize those whom I knew were there, so we waved back a symbolical good-bye and turned to watch the pageant ahead.

Out on the lower bay the battleship "Pennsylvania" was waiting

[1] This was part of the war-time defense of New York harbor. An iron net was fastened to the shore by the Narrows to be drawn completely across the channel in case of need. An ancient battleship was stationed alongside, close to the forts.

for us, and the destroyers took up position before, beside, and behind us. There were eleven of them, a whole flotilla. Airplanes kept circling around us, much as in the river and bay, until we were almost out of sight of land, and a navy balloon from a guard ship looked down on us until another dirigible came up and gave us a final Godspeed, and then sailed off to the Long Island shore.

The President was on the bridge as we backed out into the Hudson, but went down to his quarters before we were out of the harbor. The ship is tossing lightly on heavy rollers from the southeast.

Saturday, December 7, 1918

There is little to record, even on a presidential ship. In spite of having every comfort that goes with such official state, the trip is beginning to be monotonous, one day like another.

During the first night out some of the destroyers left us. After a heavy blow which tossed them a good deal, only five were left in sight; and now we have only three. They seem to be headed overseas with us. One goes away ahead as if to announce us and clear the way, perhaps to spot any chance floating mine. Behind it is the battleship, then come the other destroyers, one on each side, sailing abreast our ship, about half a mile away.

We had very heavy wind and waves yesterday and today, but the ship cradles itself wonderfully in the water. It rolls slowly, and not too far, and we are so few that there is no need of anyone being ill.

I am saving the little newspaper sheet they publish on board. It is called "The Hatchet," supposedly with reference to its veracity. But it never comes to the test, for it has almost no news. Still it will give a better picture of what is going on than any diary I can write so it will have to tell its own story.[1]

Monday, December 9, 1918

We are now in southern seas and the air is as warm as June. We have windows wide open and sit out on the deck without overcoats or wraps and are too hot when in the sun, protected from the wind. We are said to be about 400 miles due west of the Azores now. We expect to get to Brest on Friday the thirteenth—a date to land on!

[1] Although trivial in themselves, these little newspapers have a certain historical interest in their record of the incidents of each day's happenings. A sample day's issue is therefore reproduced in Appendix I.

The rest is trivial gossip. I have a single room on the promenade deck. An armed sentry (a marine) marches up and down outside and salutes us whenever we appear. It is a little embarrassing, as we hardly know how to acknowledge his salute. Alongside my room is that of Colonel Ayres, Chief Statistician to the General Staff. I was very glad to see him and we have talked a good deal. He has told me many stories of the war.

The presidential suite is on the deck below, only a few feet away from the stairway. A guard is on duty at the door all the time. He, or another marine, follows closely behind the President whenever he takes a walk along the deck. Mrs. Wilson is not guarded. The President does not mingle indiscriminately with the rest of the party, although others join him from time to time. The presidential dining room is the small sitting room adjoining the bedroom. The Secretary of State, the Ambassadors and personal advisers of the President eat in the rear lounge. This leaves the main dining room free for the Inquiry and the lesser officials of various sorts.

The President has not called in any of us as yet nor paid any attention to our presence. But this aloofness seems to apply to his Secretary of State as well. It was only yesterday (as I am told) that he began to hold conferences with Lansing. We are all perfectly in the dark as to how useful we may be when we get across. Meanwhile we are taking it easy, although with some restiveness and grouching. But it won't be long before we'll all know about our job and be hard at it. I suppose the President is busy at his now.

After dinner

I have not been able to realize the romance of this trip anything like so much as the first trip over the Atlantic. I suppose this is one of the most historic voyages in the world's history, but it lacks the charm of the first time I crossed, when I used to stand on the prow of the little old "Etruria," a Cunarder of about six thousand tons, and dream dreams—day by day. This seems tame in comparison; though I may look back to it with a similar memory. Evenings, there are moving picture shows. I have gone to about half. One evening the President and Mrs. Wilson attended. It was Charlie Chaplin in "A Dog's Life," and Douglas Fairbanks in—I forget what. The President laughed heartily at Charlie. It was in the main dining room and he was only one table removed from where

I sat, but he shaded his face with his hand so I could not see him very well. Yesterday evening he went down to the sailors' mess hall to a "sing," and the boys sang very merrily—or rather, very seriously. And at the close he shook hands with eight hundred seamen. They are all young boys and they looked mighty pleased as they passed in line. We have eighteen hundred men to guard and look after less than a hundred "guests," as we are called officially. As a matter of fact, there is too much entertainment. We have two orchestras and a band. I never knew how tired one can get of orchestral music, even fairly good music, when it breaks out all afternoon as well as at meals. There is a beautiful glass-enclosed deck just out of my room where the orchestra plays on sunny afternoons, and it acts as a good conductor of sound. I get it all in my room.

In addition to "The Hatchet" every morning mimeographed sheets are distributed with additional items of news; but it seems incredible that on this particular ship there should be so little information as to what is going on in the world. Sport and sensational gossip are served up in undue quantities. This afternoon the crew gave a boxing match. Then at three-thirty one of the destroyers turned around in a half-circle and apparently made off for New York. I was standing on the upper deck beside the captain, and he explained that it would turn back to us from the horizon and when abeam drop some depth bombs for us to see what that looked like. It didn't take long for it to plough through the water back to us; and the bombs made only moderately large explosions, to everyone's disappointment. I suppose they didn't want to take any kind of risk, but we all voted it tame. The President was out to see it and was on the upper deck not far from where I watched it. He looks in fine trim. Everyone should be better for this trip. A wind is blowing up tonight, a warm wind from the southeast, off the coast of Africa, I suppose. We are nearer it now than America.

I nearly forgot to say that the Military Intelligence took our pictures this morning—not merely as a group, but individually, and then took films of us for a movie! The Committee on Public Information plans to give them out some day, when they get them back to America. They will be preserved in the war records in Washington as part of the history of the war. Then George Creel and I had a long talk, and while we were at it the Secretary of State and Mr. Henry White had a conference with Dr. Bowman and some of the rest of the group which was very successful, as the Secretary at last saw that we had some material which might be fundamental for him. He had been rather rigid before, but today thawed out and became cordial.

[It should perhaps be stated here that the five Commissioners of the American Delegation to Negotiate Peace were President Wilson, Secretary Lansing, Colonel House, General Bliss, and Mr. Henry White. Of these, Colonel House and General Bliss were already in Paris. Mr. Henry White had had long experience in the foreign service of the United States, having held the position of Ambassador to Italy from 1905 to 1907 and of Ambassador to France from 1907 to 1909. He had been the head of the American delegation to the Algeciras Conference during President Theodore Roosevelt's administration and had been sent on other special diplomatic missions. His long experience as a diplomat did not, however, wholly qualify him to represent the point of view of the Republican opposition.]

Tuesday afternoon, December 10, 1918

Today I saw St. Michael of the Azores and missed an interview with the President at the same time. Shortly after breakfast I went up on deck, and saw appearing out of a grey mist the bold headland of an island, just dimly outlined but only about five miles away. We sailed to the south of it and soon the island began to show little white specks of farm houses and streaks of white walls of village buildings along the slopes of the land above the cliffs, which were about like the Palisades of the Hudson for height in most places. The sky was overcast and a cloud hung over the island all the time, concealing its top, something like an ocean fog held up by the brows of the hills, leaving the sea and lower shore rather clear though not very definite at the distance at which we kept skirting it. The main town and port was ahead of us and we steamed close enough to see individual houses and the groves of cypress trees here and there along the hillside. The fields behind were green, with lines showing between them where hedgerows ran. The town had mostly yellow-walled houses, mellow like those of Italy, with square church towers reminding one of Spanish architecture. A few new chimneys of factories indicated where Americans (I suppose) had got in since the war made this one of our main *entrepôts* in the Atlantic. Three more American destroyers came out to meet us and have taken their place in line at each side and in front. A little Portuguese gunboat came steaming along about a quarter of a mile away, firing a salute, and I looked down on our gun deck to find our marines at the salute guns and soon we fired our twenty-one guns in reply; passing the harbor batteries a few minutes later we fired a second salute; that is the extent of our visit to the Azores! We never got within a mile of the shore, but we kept steaming along for over three hours, past headland after headland with quaint little villages nestling in the hollows between the hills and hillsides all cultivated right to the cliff's edge. The cloud lay low over the island all the time and only once was there enough sunshine to bring out the color of the hills and fields.

But seeing the Azores cut me out of the most important event of the voyage so far. The President chose this moment to send for a few of us, including me, to come to his cabin and have a very confidential chat, the first on the trip. Bowman sent his secretary, Storck, to find me. He hunted high and low for twenty minutes but failed in his quest, as I had gone up to the bow to see the guns they used at salute. It was no one's fault but my own, as I should have left word with my marine at the cabin door where I had gone. The President talked with some seven or eight of the group for an hour, and they got on splendidly. Everyone feels very much cheered and also begins to see a chance of being called on for really useful work at the big conference ahead of us. The President was very frank and very cordial, so they tell me. If I hadn't been watching the Azores fade out of sight on the northwest horizon, I should have a historic interview to record. However, my colleagues were properly sympathetic, and I hope it won't be the last chance.

After dinner I saw the President at close range as he sat watching the movie. He conceals his emotions very well, but he was very much absorbed in the emotional scenes and seemed to enjoy them rather intensely. The silhouette of his face against the sidelight across the room showed a very determined looking man. His front face is much more pleasant than his profile, which is very severe. He has a pleasant smile and his eyes are kindly. Mrs. Wilson sat in front of him and he was very attentive to her comfort. After the show Beer came to my room and we gossiped until midnight again.

[It turned out after all that this meeting was both the first and the last chance for members of the various divisions of the Inquiry to be called in together by the President for a discussion on the work of the Inquiry as a whole and its relation to the formulation of the Wilsonian program at the Peace Conference. Indeed there was only one occasion during the whole Peace Conference which bore any resemblance to this, and that was on the third of June, after the Draft Treaty had been completed and when the criticism of it had begun. As it is one of the most revealing incidents of which there is any record, with reference to Wilson's ideas of the Peace Conference before he came to grips with the actual problem of negotiation, the story that follows would be incomplete without a first-hand account of the interview. Fortunately the incidents of the day can be reconstructed both from Dr. Bowman's memorandum, which he dictated immediately,[1] and from Mr. George Louis Beer's Diary, which remains unpublished. These two agree point by point, although with slightly different emphasis.

The notes in Beer's Diary run as follows:

Chief specialists of our group had an hour's conference with the President today. Chief points emphasized were:

1. U.S.A. only disinterested party, and Allied Statesmen do not really represent temper of their peoples;

2. Peace must be based upon justice and Americans must use every endeavor to secure justice. We have no interest in specific boundary questions, but must see that the settlements are fair ones.

3. A League of Nations is essential, but its covenants are more important than its organization. Wants to go slowly. Disapproves of League to enforce Peace plan. Council of League should be ambassadors at some small place, Hague or Berne. Germany not necessarily to be admitted immediately. Possibly a probationary period. W. W. is heartily sick of balance of power. Emphasized economic boycott, including communications, as a weapon.

4. Common property will hold League together: e.g., German colonies. Evidently no idea of returning them. Their administration under mandate of League should be entrusted to some small state or several, e.g., Scandinavian, not to a large one for fear that in latter event mandatory may develop into owner.

Whole talk frank, witty and full of charm. Wilson convinced that Allies were beaten and that America turned tide and at Château Thierry

---

[1] Dr. Bowman's memorandum was published in David Hunter Miller's *The Drafting of the Covenant* (Putnam, 1928), I, 41-44, and in *The Intimate Papers of Colonel House,* edited by Charles Seymour (Houghton Mifflin, 1926-28), IV, 280-283.

saved the world. Talk demonstrated that he had not gone into details—
he frankly said so—and that he had not thought out everything. Firm on
broad general principles, but flexible as to their precise application. His
mind in that respect evidently open, and he said that he depended on us
for the facts. While he is in a fighting mood and is prepared to fight for a
just peace, he virtually said that absolute justice in any specific instance
was not attainable.

Beer was much disturbed about an apparent vagueness in the
President's reference to the League of Nations,—more especially on
the question of mandates. On the latter point the idea had been
thrown out that mandatory states should be chosen from among
those which had had no previous interest in the colony assigned.
Beer regarded this as a very dangerous and academic type of thinking, for he said that the President in his anxiety to secure an un-
biased and unselfish attitude on the part of the mandatory had
overlooked the point, which in Beer's mind was fundamental, that
colonial government requires experience both in the governing state
and in the colony on the part of its administrators. He was very
much afraid that if we approached the colonial problem from this
angle we should not be able to reach agreement on one of the fundamental questions before the Conference and that this might block
the whole peace settlement. As a matter of fact Beer's apprehensions
were unfounded, for the President showed as realistic a conception
of the fundamentals of government when he actually came to deal
with the specific issues of the Peace Conference itself as Beer or
anyone else could have desired. The incident, however, does show
what distances had to be traveled in the international orientation of
the next few weeks.

Dr. Bowman's memorandum retained not only the points which
the President discussed but also the flavor of the Wilsonian phrasing. The words underlined were actually written by Dr. Bowman
as the President spoke. The text is therefore literally exact in all
essentials.

MEMORANDUM ON CONFERENCE WITH
PRESIDENT WILSON [1]

December 10, 1918

After a few introductory remarks to the effect that he was glad to meet
us, and that he welcomed the suggestion of a conference to give his views
on the impending Peace Conference, the President remarked that *we would*

[1] Miller, *loc. cit.*

be the only disinterested people at the Peace Conference, and that *the men whom we were about to deal with did not represent their own people*.

He next mentioned the advisability of not leaving in purely political hands the question of the German indemnity, and went on to say that the matter should be studied by *a commission to determine the just claims of the Allies against Germany*, and that after such determination *Germany should be made to pay*. The President illustrated the difficulties of Allied action in imposing an indemnity by a reference to the Boxer question of a few years ago, and contrasted the attitude of the United States with that of Germany and the other European powers.

As for the form of Poland's government and questions like that of the disposition of Danzig, he would only say that he was in favor of their having *any government they damned pleased*, and that he was for imposing upon them *no other provision* than those which applied to individuals —the important thing is *what a person ought to have, not what he wants*.[1]

The President pointed out that this was *the first conference in which decisions depended upon the opinion of mankind*, not upon the previous determinations and diplomatic schemes of the assembled representatives. With great earnestness he re-emphasized the point that unless the Conference was prepared to follow the opinions of mankind and to express the will of the people rather than of their leaders at the Conference, we should soon be involved in *another breakup of the world, and when such a breakup came it would not be a war but a cataclysm*.

He spoke of the League to Enforce Peace, of the possibility of an international court with international police, etc., but added that such a plan could hardly be worked out in view of the fact that there was *to be only one conference* and it would be difficult to reach agreements respecting such matters; and he placed in opposition to this view of the work of the Conference and of the project of a *League of Nations, the idea of covenants*, that is, agreements, pledges, etc., such as could be worked out in *general form* and agreed to and set in motion, and he particularly emphasized the importance of relying on *experience to guide subsequent action*.

As for the League of Nations, it implied political independence and *territorial integrity plus later alteration of terms and alteration of boundaries if it could be shown that injustice had been done or that conditions had changed*. And such alteration would be the easier to make in time as *passion subsided* and matters could be viewed in the light of justice rather

---

[1] This last phrase seems to be contradictory of the previous sentence. As to this, Dr. Bowman wrote me [Mr. Miller] as follows, under date of December 2, 1924:

The President was making two points, first that he was in favor of letting them have a wide area of liberty in which to play with reference to their form of Government; second, that so far as their outside relations were concerned he also wished to meet them halfway, but in dealing with them he wanted to set up the principle that the nationalistic desires of a particular people could not be always or fully satisfied though he did feel that the Peace Conference could give each nation what it ought to have. In the form in which my memorandum casts his thought there is room for misinterpretation. I hope this explanation makes it clear.

than in the light of a peace conference at the close of a protracted war. He illustrated his point by the workings of the *Monroe Doctrine,* saying that what it had done for the western world the League of Nations would do for the rest of the world; and just as the Monroe Doctrine had developed in time to meet changing conditions, so would the League of Nations develop. In fact, he could not see how a treaty of peace could be drawn up or how both *elasticity and security could be obtained save under a League of Nations;* the opposite of such a course was to maintain the idea of the *Great Powers and of balance of power,* and such an idea *had always produced* only *"aggression and selfishness and war"*; the *people* are *heartily sick of such a course* and want the Peace Conference and the Powers to take an *entirely new course of action.*

He then turned to some specific questions and mentioned the fact that *England herself was against further extension of the British Empire.*

He thought that *some capital, as The Hague or Berne,* would *be selected for the League of Nations,* and that there would be organized in the place chosen a *Council of the League* whose members should be *the best men that could be found.* Whenever trouble arose it could be *called to the attention of the Council and* would be *given* thereby *the widest publicity.* In cases involving *discipline* there *was* the *alternative to war,* namely, the *boycott; trade,* including *postal and cable facilities,* could be *denied a state* that had been *guilty of wrong-doing.* Under this plan no *nation* would be *permitted to be an outlaw,* free to work out its evil designs *against a neighbor* or the world.

He thought that the *German colonies* should be *declared* the *common property* of the *League of Nations and administered by small nations.* The *resources* of each colony should be *available to all members of the League,* and in this and other matters involving international relations or German colonies or resources or territorial arrangements, the *world* would be *intolerable if only arrangement ensues;* that *this* is *a peace conference in which arrangements cannot be made in the old style.* Anticipating the difficulties of the Conference in view of the suggestion he had made respecting the desire of the people of the world for a new order, he remarked, *"If it won't work, it must be made to work,"* because the world was faced by a task of terrible proportions and only the adoption of a cleansing process would recreate or regenerate the world. The *poison of Bolshevism* was *accepted readily* by the world *because "it is a protest against the way in which the world has worked."* It was to be our business at the Peace Conference to fight for a new order, *"agreeably if we can, disagreeably if necessary."*

We must *tell* the *United States the truth* about diplomacy, the Peace Conference, the world. He here referred to the *censorship,* saying that he had arranged in the face of opposition from Europe for the *free flow of news to the United States,* though he doubted if there would be a similarly free flow to the peoples of other European countries; after a considerable effort he had secured the *removal of French and English restrictions on political news.* Thereupon he finished his reference to the frank conditions under which the Conference had to work and the necessity for getting the truth to the people by saying that *if* the *Conference did not settle things* on such a basis the Peace Treaty would not work, and "if it doesn't work right *the world will raise Hell.*"

He stated that we should only go so far in *backing* the *claims of a given Power* as *justice required* "and not an inch farther," and referred to a remodeled quotation from Burke: *"Only that government is free whose peoples regard themselves as free."*

The European *leaders* reminded one of the *episode in Philippopolis*—for the *space of two hours they cried,* *"Great is Diana of the Ephesians"*—to which the President appended in an aside, *"in the interest of the silversmiths."*

The President concluded the conference by saying that he hoped to see us frequently, and while he expected us to work through the Commissioners according to the organization plans of the Conference, he wanted us in case of emergency not to hesitate to bring directly to his attention any matter whose decision was in any way critical; and concluded with a sentence that deserves immortality: *"Tell me what's right and I'll fight for it; give me a guaranteed position."*]

December 11, 1918

This afternoon as I came out of the map room of the Military Intelligence for a stroll on deck, one of the men from the State Department came hurrying up to me with the news that word had come from the presidential quarters that I was sent for. Great curiosity! I hurried into the corridor and was accosted by each sentry in passing with the news that the orderlies had been hunting for me for twenty minutes. I went over to the presidential quarters and found that it was *Mrs.* Wilson who had sent for me! The mystery grew. Then I found that she was aft, in the lounge, playing bridge. On my way there I met another State Department official who told me it was George Creel [1] who had been asking for me—and the situation was less interesting. However, I found that Creel

---

[1] Mr. George Creel, Chairman of the Committee on Public Information—the American substitute for censorship during the war—was not a member of the Delegation to Negotiate Peace. The technical reason for his being with us was that he was on his way to inspect and close the offices of his correspondents in various countries, especially in Eastern Europe. There was always something touching in Wilson's friendship for Creel and the latter's absolute loyalty to his chief, but it would be hard to imagine anyone less qualified for the reticences of diplomacy than this impulsive, frank and unreserved representative of Western journalism, who, in spite of his lovable character, had made some of the bitterest enemies that plagued the official life of Washington in war-time. My own association with Creel and my knowledge of the work which he achieved as the government official with whom the American press had to deal during the war has convinced me that Creel served both his President and his country with competence and success.

had the message which the President had written to be given as a greeting to the President of France on landing and wanted me to turn it into French. There was nothing to do but to accept, and I got with Haskins for part of the job and went at it by myself for the rest. Before risking giving it back to the President, however, we turned it over to Ambassador Jusserand for his suggestions, and I have seldom seen a school theme more marked up than the corrected document that came back to us. The incident is not without its historic interest, for M. Jusserand, in conversation, made the point that Wilson's phraseology had become so familiar to French-speaking people that it was necessary to keep as closely as possible to the original English in order to give the flavor of Wilson's own speech.

When I saw Beer and told him I was translating the President's message into French, he was terribly disturbed. He thought it was for the French nation to read and the future historian to record! What they want to do with it I don't know, but I imagine it's just some family party idea and the President may not use it. When I told Beer so after leaving him an hour or so in suspense, he was much and visibly relieved.

There's not much news to record. Colonel Ayres and I have had long and profitable talks, and I've met Mr. White very pleasantly, but otherwise the day has gone quietly. We are sailing northeast now through tranquil seas along toward Brest, and are about six hundred miles off the coast of Spain. Tomorrow we shall be getting into the Bay of Biscay. The weather keeps wonderfully warm. But it is getting misty now, and we may soon strike the cold north again. I wonder what the President will do with my French? [1]

Friday morning, December 13, 1918

Last night after the movie, which the President seemed to enjoy, we sang "God be with you till we meet again" and "Auld Lang Syne." At 4 A.M. the engines slowed down. It is now 7:30 and I'm up on the upper bridge looking out over a rather smooth but grey sea, with about eighteen destroyers in a great horseshoe around us. One has already brought out a pilot, and away on the horizon to the east, just visible across the stretch of water, lie at least eight

---

[1] I never found out whether the President used this text on any occasion. There is no reference to it in the collection of his messages and addresses published in 1924.

of our battleships in line waiting for us. The sky is clearing and
we may have real presidential weather. Colonel Ayres says it will
rain at Brest, because it always does, but I doubt it today.

9:30

About an hour ago I was called upon by the State Department
to translate into English the message of the Mayor and Council of
Brest to the President.[1] I have just turned it in to Lansing. But
the aid of Haskins was back of it again. Here it is:

> Mr. President: I feel the keenest emotion in bringing to you the cordial
> welcome of the population of Brest.
> It is now some time since our city manifested its admiration of your
> great work by giving the name of President Wilson to one of its most
> beautiful public squares, and we have awaited with impatience the brief
> but solemn moment when we should be permitted to express personally
> our feeling of profound sympathy.
> The ship which brings you into this harbor is itself symbolic. Just
> as George Washington, champion of your liberty, once led the legions of
> your peaceful citizens who had become soldiers in the great cause of
> the independence of peoples, so under the same auspices today you bring
> to the tortured peoples of Europe the comfort of your powerful voice in
> the agonizing debates to heal our strife.
> Mr. President, on this soil of Brittany our hearts are one in hailing
> you as a messenger of justice and peace.
> Tomorrow the whole French people will acclaim you, and the peoples
> will thrill as one with enthusiasm for the eminent statesman who defends
> their aspirations for justice and liberty.
> The old city of Brest is eager for the honor of saluting you. It will
> remember this with pride. In order that our descendants may ever cherish
> the memory of this occasion, the municipal council of Brest has charged
> me to deliver to you this address. It attests our joy in being able to do
> homage to the illustrious representative of democracy who presides over
> the great republic of the United States.

Later

I'm up on deck again on the bridge, looking out toward France.
Six big battleships are now steaming alongside, each with a huge

---

[1] The correspondent of the Associated Press, Mr. Charles T. Thompson, in *The
Peace Conference Day by Day* (p. 6), describes the actual presentation of this address
after the landing at Brest, commenting that though the Mayor spoke in French, "the
President appeared to follow and understand, smiling and bowing an acknowledge-
ment as he heard himself greeted as the apostle of liberty, come to relieve the tortured
peoples of Europe from their agony." It is hardly to be expected that he should have
known that the President had seen a translation of the text some hours before.

flag at the masthead, and a whole fleet of destroyers. The sky is clearing and the sun shines against the ships in a cheery way. The sailors are busy with the ropes and winches getting ready to hoist the luggage from the hold. Everyone is going around smiling and whistling, or at least looking pleased at the end of the trip.

Here is a hydroplane flying around. It is very beautiful, glistening in the sun. I have been watching it pass up and down between the lines of ships. There are over thirty destroyers with us now. A fleet of French ships has just put in an appearance on the southeast, headed straight for us in a long line with flags flying. As they came out of the mist which hid that part of the horizon, they swung broadside about two miles off, and every ship in turn fired its twenty-one guns. The smoke lay thick upon the water. We haven't replied yet; I don't know why. I thought we always were supposed to answer salutes. We have not only our little 4-inch guns ready but our two big 5½ or 6 inch guns at the prow, and I suppose that soon we'll be holding our ears. Here's a dirigible French balloon—over at the north there's a lighthouse and houses on a rocky island still about five miles off, but no land ahead.

After lunch, 12:20

Just coming in to port. The land lies in mist, but one can see its outlines growing clearer on both sides as we steer into the channel. Airplanes are buzzing around coming quite close. The sun has broken the mist now, and the water shows up mottled gray and green.

Later (from notes on the train)

The battleships which preceded us took up a double line in the harbor, with the destroyers behind them and at their sides. We slowed down and came on majestically up to the first of the line. Then the President came up to the bridge, where I had been writing the previous pages of this account, and stood not ten feet away from me as he reviewed the fleet. (Later, he was on the top bridge for the last of it.) The guns on our ship gave their deafening salute as we nosed up to the great line. Then each of the battleships had its crew standing in a long line all around the deck, at attention, and as we passed, ship by ship the crews cheered, so that you could hear the voices distinctly across the little stretch of water. Then each ship's band played the national anthem, and we stood with bared heads.

When the last battleship had been passed, our ship dropped anchor. Then the fleet of destroyers passed in review before us, all the crews at salute. One after another in a long line they came up the alleyway between the big men-of-war and swung around us. If you have seen them battling big seas and crossing the whole Atlantic for a week, you know how to appreciate the men who sail these little craft—and who saved the war for us by destroying submarines. They are the real heroes of the sea.

The President, however, was not given long to view this pageantry. Down on the deck and in his stateroom, two delegations had already assembled to greet him, having come on board from launches as we were slowly entering the harbor. There were the high dignitaries of France, M. Pichon, Minister of Foreign Affairs, and M. Leygues, Minister of Marine, along with the heads of our Expeditionary Force and the civilians in charge of American interests in France, Generals Pershing and Bliss, Admirals Sims and Benson, Ambassador Sharp, and others. The greetings over, it seemed only a few minutes until the launches were cutting loose from the side of the ship, with the President and his party in one of them. As he left, the "George Washington" fired the presidential salute. It was the end of the voyage.

After the President's party had left, a second boat took the rest of us off. We swung in toward the shore, across about a mile of water, to the quaint old harbor, with its fishing boats—blue and tan sails—hauled up beside the rocky, inner basin, and the quainter fisher-folk, the old Breton stock, pausing in their work as we went by. The gray walls of the town rise from the harbor's edge, crowned by the old castle of the dukes of Brittany, as at Saint Malo. Breton sailors were waiting on the wharf to take our luggage to the special train which stood on a siding close by. The Commandant of the Port of Brest, in gold lace, was there in person to see that everything went well. It was a special train, a train de luxe—and very luxurious indeed. We were told that it would not leave for at least a half hour—it proved to be an hour and a half—so I went (with Haskins) up into the town for newspapers. I bought out an old lady, and then we went to the square they have named Place Wilson, a pretty corner on the walls above the harbor, with palms in the open. The architecture of the port is too regular, with slate-roofed stone houses stretching away, row above row, around the amphitheatre of the basin of the harbor. But here and there a touch of real grace broke the monotony, as in the tower of the customs house and the Renaissance entrance to the warerooms. The town was decked for a holiday. There were Bretons in their quaint costumes, mostly women, with white lace coiffes on their heads; the men were less frequently dressed in the national dress, although we saw some. But the streets were guarded with American soldiers! Nothing could ever be more incongruous. The explanation came as our train pulled out, for we passed miles of American encampments. There is room for a hundred thousand American soldiers at this one port of embarkation. As we passed we called out to the groups we saw. They were out in the muddy street and their feeling about those who were just landing in France instead of leaving was expressed by more than one comment, "Going to Paris? Hard luck." One fellow looked up surprised to see a train full of civilian Americans, and called out, "Real, honest-to-God Americans!" The boys want to go home.

We had a dinner with wines and good cooking. But it was served by waiters with war crosses on their breasts, assisted by very efficient women. The car attendant had three stars for additional citations. I was not the only one of our party who felt that it was wrong for him to be shining our boots. In spite of all our study of the war it is much more real already. The very atmosphere is different. Even in the crowds in Brest there was a noticeable preponderance of women, and most of them in black. There was a nice old woman selling papers, and I left her a franc for some copies of placards on the wall eulogizing Wilson.

These placards will be historic documents some day.[1] The first one that caught our eye as we turned the corner of a street—a red splash of color on a gray stone wall, with bold-faced type—was

[1] Mr. Frank Warrin made a rather complete collection of them for Mr. Miller, who, I think, had the intention of turning them over to President Wilson himself. In no other country, so far as I know, does the political placard play the rôle it does in France. One could hardly imagine Congress, in a moment of enthusiasm, voting to post any speech of any American statesman on the walls of the cities and towns of the country. Yet it would not be much of an exaggeration to say that the historian could at least illustrate all the great moments of French history from the placards posted on the walls of Paris and the cities of the provinces. In the light of the history of succeeding days, therefore, the eloquent tributes to Wilson to be found in the posters of France were doubly significant.

signed by a Radical Deputy of the City of Brest, calling upon "one and all, without distinction of party, all with uplifted hearts" to acclaim the statesman who had come "to found a new order on the rights of peoples, and to stop forever the return of an atrocious war which has been imposed upon us for the defense of our homes." Alongside this appeal was the green placard of the Federation of Labor (La Confédération Générale du Travail), which struck a more serious note, and gave a warning of the task ahead for those who could read between the lines:

TO THE FRANCE OF THE WORKERS AND THE PEASANTS!
TO THE WORKERS OF PARIS!

President Wilson is about to touch the soil of France.

President Wilson is the highest and the noblest representative of the great American nation whose cooperation has been decisive in the formidable conflict into which the peoples of all the world have hurled themselves for their interests and their rights.

President Wilson is the statesman who has had the courage and insight to place rights above interests, who has sought to show humanity the road to a future with less of sorrow and of carnage. Thus he has given voice to the deepest thoughts which stir the democracies and the working classes.

Now that German reaction and militarism have been vanquished, the democracies wish to have the curse of war forever banished, so that labor in its sovereign right may develop in peace.

For having affirmed these principles of action, for having placed them in the center of the stage of the world, PRESIDENT WILSON HAS MERITED WELL OF HUMANITY.

France of the workers and the peasants who have so often fought for liberty will thank President Wilson at the hour of his arrival among us.

For the task which remains to be accomplished, may President Wilson feel near to him the hearts of millions of men and women!

In the streets on the fourteenth day of December the workers of France will be assembled in force.

To President Wilson their presence will cry aloud:

For international justice, for the League of Nations, which will make all people equal in rights and duties—for the peace that endures.

Courage, we count on you, we are with you! [1]

The General Federation of Labor
of the Socialist Party (S.F.I.O.)

[1] The Federation of Labor made good this pledge, by continued support of President Wilson after actual negotiations were on; and its address to him was a welcome expression of support at a time when it might have seemed as if M. Clemenceau were the exponent of the attitude of all France.

The First Days in Paris—Fumbling

Paris, Saturday, December 14, 1918 [1]

I slept little on the train and was dressed as we drew up by the siding south of Versailles and looking out saw the great château. A hurried cup of coffee and a slice of bread made breakfast, and by the time it was over we were in Paris. As we stepped off the train, David Hunter Miller and Frank Warrin were on the platform, also Lieutenant Wanger, a cousin of Beer's who took us and a journalist friend, Bullitt, to the hotel. We hesitated a little at accepting the army car, but Lieutenant Wanger, a very jolly boy, assured us we were going to have "major-generals do our laundering," and all things on a similar scale! We were the first car out, the first of the Peace Commission to arrive.

Place de la Concorde! You can't imagine what a sight it was. Every part of the square not needed for street was packed with captured German cannon. We caught a glimpse in passing of the Champs Elysées, with miles of cannon on each side of the driveway. France's trophies.

As we came along, people were already hurrying in throngs to get good places to see Wilson arrive. His train had been run onto a siding out in the country (at Plouart in Brittany) to give him a night's rest, and he was due to arrive at ten.

Colonel House and his associates have already established themselves in the Hôtel de Crillon. After a survey of our quarters there we went up to the International Law Section (Mr. Miller's) of the office building to look out over the Place de la Concorde on the crowds which were packing every inch of space to wait for the coming of Wilson. We were at the windows at the corner of the Place and the Rue Royale up which the President was to come, so we had the best view in Paris of this historic sight.

The tribute of respect which Paris paid to Wilson was one that I never saw the like of and shall never see again. As one of the papers

[1] This description of Wilson's arrival in Paris is from a letter home.

85

put it, it was a "pious privilege" on the part of the populace of Paris to see the man who is in their eyes and in the eyes of most of the oppressed of Europe, the first moral force in the world today. The tribute was more than a casual one; it was obviously heartfelt. In spite of the size and density of the crowd, which moved in swirling eddies between the piles of cannon and the twisting, narrow files of the Garde Républicaine and the regular troops that were keeping the roadway open, there was almost no sound of voices loud enough to reach the third story of the building.

Already long lines of horizon blue poilus stretched away across the Place and over the bridge. In the crowds the dominant colors were the black of the women, and the blue or khaki of soldiers on leave—little else, except where a red turban of an African showed like a single point of contrast. Horizon blue is the most beautiful color you can imagine. It is a tender blue, like that on distant hills. And when you recalled that those poilus, slouching at ease in typical French soldier fashion, were the very men who had taken from the Germans the cannon which were parked up behind them in the great spaces of the square, you got a queer feeling in your throat just watching them there, waiting for Wilson, "Wilson the Just" (*le juste*), as they have called him in one big placard.

Soon troops of artillery moved into position at the angles of the square. People jumped up on the gun carriages, the soldiers helping them up. Looking down from our windows we could see the crowds converging down the different streets into the square like a solid black stream, filling the streets from side to side. The soldiers tried to keep a single trackway open for the President from the bridge over the Seine through the Place de la Concorde and on into the Rue Royale. But the pressure of the crowd was so great that the line of soldiers was moved in and out until the space which they were to keep clear was all indented and twisted instead of being a straight line held in place by an immovable row of soldiers. There may have been anywhere from fifty thousand to a hundred thousand people in the square before Wilson came.

Then guns started booming over by the river bank, a little to the southwest, by the railroad station of the Luxembourg, where Wilson's train arrived. We could see the smoke. The crowds began to strain against the guards. Over the river we soon saw the bright helmets of the Garde Républicaine, the same old splendid-looking

President Wilson and Premier Poincaré entering the Champs Elysées

The crowds from the windows of the Crillon

guards on very fine horses—the war has left some—and behind them, first a closed carriage, then an open one, and in it Wilson and Madame Poincaré. We saw him very well. He was bowing and raising his silk hat all the time. The people cheered wildly. Then Monsieur Poincaré and Mrs. Wilson—also cheered by the crowd, but less. Then files of carriages and soldiers, and it was over.

As for the crowd, it was out for all it could see and our well-decked quarters got much attention. It was a public holiday. Everything was closed up tight. All Paris was on the boulevards, and that afternoon [1] and night they were packed. I never saw more people. In the evening five of us took an army car and drove through the boulevards until we were finally unable to move, and then slowly turned off into a side street. A funny side to it was that in the shadow of the interior of the car, Beer was taken for Wilson in disguise by people in the crowd—not once but half a dozen times. They caught his profile; and then, as Haskins said, the rest of us looked like strong-arm men—with the exception of me, whom Haskins proposed for a counterfeit House. Soldiers and officers in the crowd were having their caps stolen (snatched from behind for souvenirs), and most were bareheaded; but they stayed on—sometimes, I'm afraid, following their caps. There was a good deal of rather more than cordial fellowship, but none of the boisterous quality of the New York crowd at the celebration of peace.

We edged our way bit by bit along the great boulevards till we came to the Boulevard Strasbourg, which cuts off at right angles, and turned down it to the river. In a few hundred yards we had gone six hundred years, through the silence of deserted streets, by the Palace of St. Louis over to Notre Dame, standing out massive and almost spectral in the darkness. There were only a few street lights at long intervals, except on the boulevards, and, even there they seemed to be only about half power. The side streets were almost pitch dark. We turned south from Notre Dame and up the hill of Ste. Geneviève by the old Roman road, the Rue St. Jacques, which still bears the mark of the Roman engineer, past the site of the church where Clovis was baptised, and swung around the Panthéon, which crowns that hill with its tribute to France's immortals—*Aux Grands Hommes la Patrie reconnaissante,* as the

[1] The Miller Diary (I, 44) has the following entry, "Conferred in the afternoon with Dr. Scott and Professor Shotwell." There is no record in my notes of this consultation because it was entirely overshadowed by the historic event of the day.

motto reads across the architrave above the pillars of its façade. There were no crowds here; it was absolutely still and quite dark. We turned the search light of the car upon Rodin's *Penseur,* standing out in front of the great shadowy mass of the façade of the church—and that was the last impression that I carried away from Wilson's day in Paris.

[The Hôtel de Crillon, American headquarters, has been one of the most aristocratic and exclusive in France. It is smaller than the Ritz or the Meurice, and its dining room is hardly larger than that of a provincial hotel. That is because its clientèle has been of the kind that does not entertain in public but receives and entertains in the private rooms above. It has been re-equipped since the Peace Conference days, but it was then distinctly a hotel of the old régime. Quaint old-fashioned elevators sauntered slowly from one floor to another, sometimes hanging half way between floor and ceiling until the water slowly gathered weight enough to balance the passengers. The rooms of the commissioners looked out over the Place de la Concorde. There were, however, no meeting rooms for conferences with the members of other delegations. This lack was not compensated for by the office rooms, which were in the building on the other corner of our block, for there we had our documents and were crowded for space. All in all, the arrangements were not satisfactory.]

Sunday, December 15, 1918

Today was spent opening the offices at Number 4 Place de la Concorde. Boxes containing the books for the Library and all the other materials from the "George Washington" have been stored temporarily, awaiting final assignment of office space, which is causing some heartburnings. The quarters assigned the Library are on the mezzanine floor of the Rue Royale and not large enough to work in, let alone to receive the pile of books that we have brought. These quarters are to be exchanged for larger ones in the center of the building, a sort of rotunda which, however, lacks outside windows and ventilation. It is also an alleyway for those who want to go to some of the offices around about it, and it will be hard to make sure that books will not wander from the stacks. I have a little nook to myself just back of the alcoves.

The event of the day is that President Wilson has asked us for information concerning the problems of the Dalmatian Coast. It looks as though we were really going to play a part, if only in the background.[1]

Monday, December 16, 1918

I began my duties as Librarian of the Delegation by a visit to the Bibliothèque de la Guerre, the library which has been established to gather every book, article, or scrap of paper that is of any importance for future historians of the World War. It is housed in a street that runs north from the Champs Elysées, and not far from the Hôtel de Crillon.[2] The Librarian is Camille Bloch, a historian whose volume on the care of the poor in the old régime on the eve of the French Revolution was one that I had reviewed at length in the *Political Science Quarterly* years before, and had sent him a copy of my review. It was a fortunate coincidence, for it opened the doors of French bureaucracy, and he set about getting the wheels started which would permit us to have free access to all their documents. I came back to the Crillon very well satisfied with the first contact with the French.

Then came the ceremony of Wilson's reception at the Hôtel de Ville, to which I had received an invitation. The drive from the Crillon to the Hôtel de Ville was through streets with crowds at least eight deep or more all the way on either side behind the long row of regular troops that guarded the driveway down the center of the street. The ceremony in the gilded hall of the Hôtel de Ville was stately enough, with the guards presenting arms along the corridors; but the unforgettable part, once more, was the silence of the crowds along the way. Except for the uniforms of the soldiers, the only color anywhere to be seen was black. I dismissed the army car at the door of the Hôtel de Ville, for I wanted to get the feel of the situation by walking back; and besides I distinctly felt that there was something wrong in my riding past the long line of those sorrowful, war-stricken people. If anyone wants to feel the full measure of the tragedy of war, he will find it here.

[1] The Miller Diary (I, 45) has the following entry for December 14 which shows that the President's first request for reference material, on the very day of his arrival, was for the text of the Treaty of London:

"A little after seven I had a message from Mr. Warrin at the office, by telephone, that the President wanted a copy of the Treaty of London. I at once went to the office, and after some difficulty a book containing the Treaty was found, which I delivered at Colonel House's office about eight o'clock."

[2] Subsequently it was moved to the Château de Vincennes, just outside the eastern gate of Paris.

The morning was spent in routine work, getting the material organized. At noon Colonel House himself received the heads of divisions, and cordially told us that he would be happy to be in touch with us throughout the whole conference. Our interview was delayed by Clemenceau, coming to call on the Colonel, and there were telephone calls during the course of the interview from the Italian Delegation.

In the evening Dr. Bowman called together a meeting of the heads of divisions and announced to us the reorganization of the Peace Delegation, which has been so unsatisfactory since the Armistice. The State Department and Military Intelligence have both been obliged to yield recognition to the Inquiry, which in future is to advise the Commissioners directly and not at second hand.[1]

Wednesday, December 18, 1918

At noon General Bliss received the members of the Inquiry. He has his own staff, however, to fall back upon, both in Military and Naval Intelligence, and has special officers detailed to him. That part of the hotel where he has his headquarters has a very military look, with sentinels walking up and down and a guard at the door.

Lunch with Beer and Lionel Curtis. Curtis brings news that a plan fostered by Beer will likely be adopted by the British Government.[2]

[1] See discussion of this above, pp. 15 ff.
[2] The blind reference to Curtis's plan has to do with an important article which appeared in the December *Round Table,* the quarterly magazine of that group which looked to Lord Milner as their political and intellectual leader. The article was entitled "Windows of Freedom," and it is one of the most eloquent statements of responsible idealism to be found in any of the literature at the close of the war. It had two main ideas. The first was that the League of Nations could not itself become a government in the strict sense of the word, therefore its organization should honestly register its limitations. There should be annual conferences with a permanent secretariat but no attempt "to govern the world." The Peace Conference must not be misled into attempting to write a constitution for the world or to create a "genuine government of mankind." The annual conference would "act as a symbol and organ of the human conscience, however imperfect, to which real governments of existing states can be made answerable for facts which concern the world at large." The second point was the one which Curtis and Beer were most concerned to further at Paris,—the establishment of mandates in the place of the old colonial system. But the British were already too heavily charged with responsibility for maintaining law and order throughout the world. "The Allies in Europe ought not to be made answerable to a League of Nations for the whole of the regions outside Europe now severed from the German and Turkish Empires. The future of the system depends upon whether America will now assume her fair share of the burden, especially in the Near East and even in German East Africa." This suggestion that the United States should assume mandates was largely due to the letters from Beer to Lord Percy and

Have just learned that Young has been placed in charge of the Economic Division of the Peace Delegation, with Colonel Ayres as his collaborator. They have been assigned the subject of indemnities. This is in line with the newly established policy of bringing the Inquiry to the fore as the real advisers of the Commissioners and the President. Young is happy and excited.

The mailing system has broken down. Letters from different parts of France are often one to two weeks late. In short, the confusion connected with all transportation matters seems as bad as can be. Of course, we have seen nothing of this. In fact, living here as we do, with absolutely no privations, I have come to see how diplomats are almost sure to lack the atmosphere of reality. We do not realize what the hardships of the war are. We have steam heat, coal in the grate, and a full menu with white bread—even if rationed on bread cards. There is some fresh milk, except in coffee, when it is the condensed Borden brand.

Each member of the delegation is allowed one guest a day at meals, so we co-operate in inviting outsiders.

As I had been all day long inside the walls of the hotel, I took a walk after dinner with Hornbeck across the Place de la Concorde to the river bank, and in the moonlight we looked back across the grotesque jumble of cannon to the hotel and the offices.

Thursday, December 19, 1918

A day spent in routine, working in the Library and talking things over with my colleagues. Lunched with Beer, Miller and Curtis to follow up Beer's plans. When he gets going on a thing like this he never turns aside from it until the last chance of success or failure has been exhausted. Dined with Miller at his quarters at the Hôtel Meurice.

Friday, December 20, 1918

Again a day of routine, except for a lunch with Max Lazard. Although a member of one of the richest banking families of France, he came out to Columbia University as a student in 1899 to live

---

Professor Coupland during the previous summer. Beer took Curtis to see Colonel House and General Bliss and recorded in his diary that "both were much impressed with views advocated and expressed no dissent." Curtis continued to work at the proposal with Lord Milner, Mr. Lloyd George and others; but though echoes of it occurred from time to time, it was not long before it was evident that neither section of the plan was being taken seriously.

with American students in exactly the way the poorest of them had
to manage. I met him first at a boarding house in Harlem that was
anything but elegant, the cheapest in fact that a student could find.
Then he went back to Paris to found or direct the Society for the
Prevention of Unemployment, and has been giving his life to philanthropic and moderately radical movements ever since. A first-class
witness for liberal French opinion, yet he cannot conceive of a League
of Nations with Germans in it for years to come. The war has
destroyed all confidence in Germany's good faith on the part of even
liberal France.

Saturday, December 21, 1918

The new quarters for the Library are ready at last. The books
and materials are unpacked and checked, and everything is in order.
Minister Wellington Koo, the Chinese Minister to Washington, had
called when I was out and sent word he wanted to see me. So I
invited him to lunch with a few of our staff.[1] We had very pleasant
reminiscences and then got down to the problems of China at the
Peace Conference, problems which will cause difficulty in the coming days.

Ray Stannard Baker tells me that he has been given charge of
the publicity work of the American Delegation. This means control
of the messages given the American press representatives, a censorship which will not be easy. But Baker's close contacts with President Wilson, who has full confidence in him, will probably enable
him to carry the day.

In the afternoon I paid a visit to M. Tardieu (the former French
High Commissioner at Washington, whom I had met before) in
order to have a conference with M. Dolléans [2] on Labor matters.
M. Dolléans is the author of a book on the English Chartist Movement, which I had reviewed at length when it appeared. This gave
us a good point of departure, but we did not get very far upon our
way.

Went with Dr. Mezes to dine at the Cercle Artistique et Littéraire,
a club at which we have the right of honorary membership. There I
met M. Gauvain, a well-known journalist who has for many years

---

[1] He had been a student in my classes in Columbia.
[2] Subsequently Executive Secretary of the International Chamber of Commerce.

been publishing almost daily articles describing European politics. These he has now republished in a long series of volumes. As I had used some of these in the preparations for the Peace Conference, we got along famously.

Sunday, December 22, 1918

No rest from our routine, Sundays or week days. The Library has been set up in its new quarters and the check-listing of books is still going on.

Monday, December 23, 1918

A day spent in the same routine of check-listing the books.

Tuesday, December 24, 1918

A long talk with M. Albert Thomas. I had written him to ask for the interview and received a funny little reply suggesting that I come to his office at half-past five at 74 Rue de l'Université. It added, "Do you speak French? Must I call in one of my friends to interpret for you?" Beer went along with me. We found him alone, and he talked freely and frankly on all kinds of questions. As Beer's interest was predominantly colonial, we covered that ground first. France, he said, was relatively indifferent in the matter of colonies. Its interest lay in Alsace-Lorraine, Morocco, and a reversal of the Congo arrangement of 1911. The French have given no attention to the question of a colonial tariff. With reference to Syria, the Treaty with Britain of 1916 must be revised. Syria should not extend around the Cilician coast. It should extend "towards Damascus," but with enough hinterland not to be simply a littoral. As for Constantinople, the British have an *"ambition cachée."* For his part, he thought that the one nation culturally and strategically best suited to be at Constantinople was France, as a mandatory of the League of Nations. This was said with a winning smile. Turkey proper should not be within the French sphere, but rather in the Italian sphere. Armenia should be turned over to the United States. The Armenians would naturally look to France, but America is in a better position to do things for the people there. Italy should not have the Greek sphere in Asia Minor.

Then we turned to the question of the League of Nations. M. Thomas is secretary of the French branch of the League of Nations

Society, of which M. Léon Bourgeois is president. He pointed out the difference between this and M. Buisson's League for a World State. M. Thomas had no clear idea as to who should be mandatories.

Discussing voting arrangements in the League, he fell back upon his experience with the Socialist International. At the meeting in Amsterdam in 1904 the representatives of Japan had blocked a decision of the Socialists of Europe. There they had arbitrarily decided that in voting power England, France, Russia, Germany and the United States should each have twenty votes, Italy ten, and most of the others three. The basis of the apportionment was on the output of the mines, etc.[1]

M. Pichon (Clemenceau's Foreign Minister) said in the commission of the Chamber today that there should be no relations with Germany except through Foch. Thomas was strong against this. The French must have right, *"droit,"* on their side, and there must be no protesting debates in the French Parliament as there had been in Germany after Alsace-Lorraine was taken from France.

In the making of the League of Nations it would be necessary to proceed arbitrarily, as universal agreement would be impossible. Every nation should have a right to enter. He did not mention how the representatives for the Leagues should be chosen.

Turning then to the economic situation of France, he spoke of its future budget of about $3,400,000,000, to be raised on an income of a little over a billion dollars a year. The balance could not be raised by direct taxation. The French were not accustomed, as the English are, to the method of direct taxation. State monopolies might be tried, as for instance in alcohol, sugar, petrol, etc. Graded taxation tends to limit the use of alcohol, as in Switzerland.

This is perhaps as close as we shall come to a program of the Socialist Party that follows in the magnificent traditions of Jaurès. But, as Beer and I said to each other in the cab coming home, Thomas will have no chance to determine the policies of France. It will be Clemenceau and his associates, Thomas' bitterest enemies, with whom we shall have to deal.

---

[1] This blind sentence is explained by Beer's note of the conversation, which reads as follows: "He spoke of various possible coefficients to determine this, and seemed to form a metallurgical one." This would indicate that Thomas was referring to the League of Nations and not to the Socialist Conference, but neither my diary nor a vague memory of the conversation throws light upon the idea which M. Thomas entertained.

Wednesday, December 25, 1918
Christmas Day.

Christmas can be lonely even at a Peace Conference. Paris and France celebrate New Year's rather than Christmas Day, and the city wears a dreary look. In the morning I took George Creel and Sisson of Creel's committee to visit old Paris. First we drove past the Tuileries Gardens to look at the splintered stone wall and the hole in the rose garden where a shell from "Big Bertha" had fallen. It gave one a much more comfortable feeling to have those German cannon parked in front of our hotel. Then on to the Palais de Justice, where I showed him the Prison of the Conciergerie of the Reign of Terror; then on to Notre Dame, where they were celebrating High Mass in the unheated cathedral that was as cold as Greenland. I suppose since the days of Jeanne d'Arc there never was a greater sense of deliverance in France; and yet, though the music was fine, the people looked sad and stolid and the cathedral dingy and dreary. The rich-colored glass windows have been temporarily replaced by pale yellow glass because of the explosions, and the cold gray sky outside sent no bright shafts of light between the pillars of the high altar. From Notre Dame we went across to the Left Bank, to the old parish church of St. Séverin. This was filled with parishioners of the real Latin Quarter—not the spurious modern one where the artists foregather, but where Latin was really spoken, in those narrow side streets below the hill of Abelard's Paris. The thing that interested Creel the most was to see the walls of the church placarded with little marble votive offerings from the students of the University, in recognition of help rendered at examination time. More than one read, *"Succès inattendu"* (unexpected success), showing a certain surprise when the miraculous intervention actually occurred! From there we drove up to the Sorbonne, the Panthéon and the old Roman arena.

We came home thoroughly chilled from the penetrating east wind. I never seem to have known such a wet cold, even in winter. It isn't really so very cold, but is icy and wet and freezes one's blood. As we shivered in our warm overcoats, I realized what it would mean to be a refugee, without coats or wraps, struggling along the muddy roads of France in such weather. Even now in the towns there is a shortage of both food and coal. It was cozy enough in the Crillon, but everyone was homesick and looked it. To cheer us up, the hotel gave us an American Christmas dinner, with oysters, lobster, turkey, plum pudding, pumpkin pie, ice cream, cheese, nuts and fruit, coffee, cigars—and French wine. I took only part of it, but some of the party ate right through!

Most of the rest of the day was spent at the Crillon, either in my room or talking with members of the group. General Bliss had a talk with Haskins, as the head of the section on Germany's western frontier, concerning Germany's future political, economic and territorial status. The General asked members of the Inquiry to come to him freely at any time for any sort of discussion. He indicated that he wanted to have the reports which we might be developing from time to time sent in to him so as to have all possible questions taken up in two- or three-page reports before Congress gets under way.

The President has gone to army headquarters at Chaumont, and then will visit England. The Commissioners have not held any formal session yet. The one problem already discussed is that of the Dalmatian coast.

Thursday, December 26, 1918

At ten thirty, conference with Bowman on naval strategy questions.[1] Luncheon with M. Aubert at twelve thirty.

In spite of the hardships from which France and the rest of Europe are suffering, Paris is full. It is almost like a watering place at the height of the season. The hotels and pensions seem to be crowded with rich people of all nationalities. They pay as much as five dollars a day for the poorest of rooms in servant quarters. Meals are exorbitant; even the soldiers cannot get a dinner at a cheap restaurant under six francs. At the stores eggs are fourteen cents apiece and meat costs twice or three times what it does in New York. The Parisian boarding-house keepers are making up for lost time. One result is a feeling on the part of the privates of the American army that is growingly anti-French.

[1] The Miller Diary (I, 58) has the following on this interview: "At the request of Dr. Bowman, who in Dr. Mezes' absence is acting chief of that division, I attended a conference at which he, Dr. Young, Mr. Haskins, Mr. Shotwell, and Mr. Beer were present. There was a somewhat general discussion of the bearing of questions of naval strategy on the questions of law which may arise in particular problems. I took the view that definite answers at this time were not possible owing to the possible or assumed change in the régime for the future, and that new principles could probably not be laid down by the Commission as to their attitude on such questions as strategic boundaries as this was a matter for consideration in each case."

Friday, December 27, 1918

Lunch with Dolléans. Members of group invited to luncheon at Cercle Artistique et Littéraire.

Saturday, December 28, 1918

Spent the day in my room. Symptoms of grippe. Beer of his own accord telephoned his friend, Dr. Sternberger, the head of the American Military Hospital in Neuilly—the largest in France—and had him come in to see me. Nothing to worry about.

Sunday, December 29, 1918

Spent day at Crillon. Dined with Miller in evening, also Mrs. Miller and Young. Discussed British elections, indemnities, etc.

December 27–29, 1918

[These three days for which my record is so slight were busily spent by members of the Inquiry in finding their way within the new organization of the Peace Conference Delegation and getting their bearing on the problems which seemed likely to arise. In my own case, this meant having the Library adequately set up, the History Division re-established, and the exploration of a definite field of my own in International Labor Legislation.

The first request of the President from the technical staff was in the field of Diplomatic History. He had already begun his conferences with Sonnino and Orlando and at once called for material on the Italian question. It is important to note that this question, which later almost wrecked the Conference and played so large a part in causing the break between President Wilson and Colonel House, was the one on which the Inquiry staff was first busied. The President's preoccupation with this problem was reflected in the activities of the other Divisions of the Delegation as well. Mr. Miller was also at work on it and Naval Intelligence was calling for material. On December 25 Mr. Miller had a long discussion with Count Macchi di Cellere, the Italian Ambassador at Washington, which is summarized in his Diary.[1] On the twenty-sixth he noted that he asked me to get him for Admiral Knapp some material on the Adriatic question, and on the twenty-seventh he had a conference

[1] The Miller Diary, I, 55–57.

with me in the afternoon regarding my file on the Adriatic questions
and the Slav attitude generally. For my part, the problems of Labor
opened a field which I might make my own in the American Delegation, as none of my colleagues was interested in it. The position of
Librarian to the Delegation could be regarded as a side issue as
soon as I had the Library all set up and could leave the actual running of it in the hands of assistants. In the reorganization of the
Delegation which Dr. Bowman had effected, I had been designated
Chief of the History Division. This position was difficult to define,
for it was obviously nothing more than a parallel to the position of
the heads of the other sections under Dr. Bowman's general direction. The work of the Diplomatic History section was taken care
of for the time being both by International Law and by the researchers of the Territorial Division; although when the Conference really got under way in the last week in January it had to be
reconstituted. There was one field of history, however, which was
not delegated to experts, that which had to do with both the policies
and outlook of Labor and its economic demands. The ominous
threat of revolution from the other side of the French frontier hung
over Europe at this time. British Labor, while not revolutionary,
was insistent upon recognition, while in France the most sincere
support which the Wilsonian ideals had evoked came from the
French Trade Unions—the Confédération Générale du Travail—
under the leadership of M. Jouhaux, and from Socialists like M. Albert Thomas who cherished the traditions of Jean Jaurès. The
problem of securing recognition for Labor at the Peace Conference
had not, however, entered seriously into the plans of the American
Delegation. In the course of the work of the Inquiry in New York
I had mentioned the subject to Professor Young, but apart from
the fact that I had my lectures in Social History in Columbia University to fall back upon and had taken with me from my own
library Métin's manual on international labor legislation, *Les
Traités ouvriers. Accords internationaux de Prévoyance et de
Travail*, no special preparation had been undertaken in this
field.[1]]

[1] The detailed story of the origin of the International Labor Organization and the
negotiations concerning it is told in the volume, *The Origins of the International Labor
Organization*, in the series "The Paris Peace Conference: History and Documents,"
published by the Columbia University Press, 1934. As this was to be so largely the
field of my own activity, the narratives in that documented account will supplement,
for the historian, that in the pages which follow.

Monday, December 30, 1918

At 10:30 A.M. I set out with Young for a visit to M. Justin Godart, whom I found in his library in a quaint little room up more than one flight of stairs at the back of 9 Quai Voltaire. M. Godart is Deputy from Lyons, and his interest in labor is, as he made clear, rather philanthropic than political. He is not associated with the Socialist party. As *rapporteur* of the Commission of Labor of the French Chamber of Deputies he presented the only published report before the French Parliament on the subject of international labor legislation. He did not, however, give me the impression of having a deep and continuing interest in the subject, although he was interested in the limitation of the hours of labor of women and children. He stated that little had been done in international labor legislation since 1910, when Métin's book appeared, except the conference at Leeds. Young and I came away from the interview with the feeling that not much more was to be got from that quarter.

Noon—Westermann and I lunched with Herbert Adams Gibbons, Nubar Pasha, Hovhannes Khan Massehain (former Persian Minister to Berlin), and an Armenian with a London monocle and point of view. The purpose of the conference was to discuss Armenian national claims. Nubar Pasha and the monocle monopolized Westermann. No new developments or valuable information. A lunch fit for Lucullus.

4 P.M.—An interesting conference with an American Commission which has just reached Paris after a survey of conditions in India, Persia, and Mesopotamia. The chairman of the Commission, President Judson of Chicago University, was strongly for the British in Persia and Mesopotamia. The other members of the Commission are A. V. W. Jackson, of Columbia University, whose learning seems to be even more recognized in Persia than at home, Dr. Post, and Mr. Wertheim. Dr. Gray,[1] acting as Beer's secretary, took careful notes, and so did Westermann.

Had Albert Thomas for dinner, and most of the Inquiry group joined us in the subsequent conversation with him.[2] In the Cham-

---

[1] Dr. Louis Gray subsequently edited Beer's papers, but only those dealing with the African problems have been published.

[2] Beer's Diary has the following note: "In the evening Albert Thomas dined with us and was very charming. I talked freely to him about what I consider to be the dangerous attitude of French statesmen, e.g., Clemenceau and Tardieu, and explained the need of not 'froisser l'idéalisme américaine.' He agreed with me, and said most Frenchmen did not understand American and British idealism."

ber today,[1] M. Thomas had been attacked by Clemenceau in such
brutal fashion that he confessed to be suffering still from the Tiger's
claws, "*les griffes du Tigre*." Clemenceau let himself go in this
speech in the Chamber in other ways as well. He referred to Wilson
as a man of noble "*candeur*," which in French is not candor but
something like simple-mindedness. There were cries of "Shame!"
for that was going too far.[2] Thomas' main interest is the League of
Nations, but he finds little interest in the question in France, and
admitted that if there were a general election there would be a
Socialist defeat. The menace of the frontier is the background of
French history, and France is still seeking security. This must at
all costs be assured. He spoke of the value to the French of a
formula, like the Declaration of the Rights of Man; some similar
formula for the League of Nations must be found and emphasized.
We should get the ideal clearly stated. The British have less difficulty than the French in visualizing the concept, because they see in
their own Empire a virtual league of nations. His own party especially, the Socialists, had been too much preoccupied in fighting
local battles to have any well developed program. He felt obliged to
admit that Clemenceau's realism and patriotism are the embodiment
of contemporary French sentiment.[3]

Then we turned to a discussion of economic problems in some
detail. The great weakness of France is lack of coal. The "dis-
annexation" of Alsace-Lorraine will increase the coal deficit because
of the local consumption of coal in the factories and the iron mills.
The deficit will reach forty-five million tons. He does not want the
annexation of the Saar Valley, but thinks that the League of Nations
can arrange for an international control that would make Germany
pay France in coal.

[The shortage in coal was especially felt by France during the
winter and the long cold spring of the Peace Conference. The
hardship was especially felt when the influenza was sweeping over
Western Europe, and France was obliged to import its coal from

---

[1] *Journal Officiel du Chambre des Députés*, 11 législature, session ordinaire de
1918, pp. 3733–3734.

[2] The incident escaped official record, for in the *Journal Officiel* "candeur" was
changed to "*grandeur*."

[3] This recognition of the legitimacy of Clemenceau's leadership at this time, coming
as it did on the very day when Thomas had suffered from Clemenceau's personal
animosity, is a good instance of Thomas' own statesmanlike detachment of personal
feelings when judging a political situation.

England, owing to the wanton destruction of the French coal mines by the Germans. The British coal industry was still under government control, and during the shortage maintained an export to the Continent at sufficiently high prices to make a net gain to the British exchequer which the miners calculated at £60,000,000.]

Tuesday, December 31, 1918

Lunch at the Crillon with Max Lazard, Miller and Beer. Lazard unable to see how France can enter a general league of peace. Germany must be put on probation.

Letters home.[1]

Wednesday, January 1, 1919

Morning spent at the archives; problem of rearrangement considered.

Afternoon—Conference of department heads. Assignment of presidential job. Work to be completed in ten days.

Late in the afternoon there was a reception at the Crillon by Mrs. House, Mrs. Lansing, and Mrs. Grew. I was unable to attend.

Evening—Walk on the boulevard with Bowman and Young. Dropped in to the Théâtre Fursy, a small variety theatre hardly larger than a transformed shop. The program consisted mostly of political satires in the form of original ballads or other verses, *Les Chansonniers de Paris*. It was reminiscent of the jongleurs and troubadours of the Middle Ages, and the humor was of the same kind. The Americans were not spared, but it was too funny to be malicious. There was a long poem of the *"permissionaire,"* the poilu who had a few days leave of absence from the front and whose train never reached the station.

[The conference referred to above met at Dr. Mezes' call. He explained that the President wanted our conclusions with reference to every problem. Everyone present was much impressed with the

---

[1] A passage from one of these—written just at midnight to my daughter—gives a glimpse of the underlying mood in which our work was done: "The old year is ending, the most tragic in the world's history. Millions of the best and bravest died to make such a year of death impossible again. And now it falls upon us to realize the great ideal and in the treaty to be made to secure for the world happier years for all people and all time to come. You know how much they are expecting of us now. The happiness of future years for many of them is to be settled shortly here in Paris. That is a great responsibility for anyone connected with the Conference. And I want you to know that the American Mission in Paris is facing its work this New Year's Eve in the spirit which reflects the responsibility."

possibilities which this direct call upon us opened up.[1] It was decided to prepare a clear statement of the problems and the recommendations which each division of the Inquiry could shape up at the time. Dr. Bowman was to have charge of the preparation of these summaries of the studies and conclusions of the Inquiry. When finished they were assembled in a highly confidential collection consisting of two main parts, the territorial and labor reports on the one hand, and the colonial on the other. It did not include the proposals for the League of Nations. The preparation of these documents was the chief work of the days following. It was the foundation work of all our later activity in the special fields to which we had been assigned.

As the Miller Diary shows,[2] he and Dr. Scott were also at work at a similar task. Secretary Lansing, on December 27, had requested a "skeleton treaty which would indicate the various subjects to be taken up in the treaty and the difficulties connected therewith." On January 3 he followed up this request by directing the preparation of a full draft treaty along the lines of this skeleton draft, and Dr. Scott and Mr. Miller were working on this under Secretary Lansing's direction while we were working on our draft for Dr. Bowman. Mr. Miller in addition was working on the "Draft Agreement for a League of Nations." Military Intelligence was similarly at work on military problems, frontiers, etc. Thus the whole technical staff of the American Delegation was settling down to its tasks by the opening days of the new year.]

---

[1] Beer, however, notes in his Diary that in the evening Bullitt told him a story of the origin of the request, which shows how hard it is to know whether one is dealing with realities. Bullitt stated that he wanted to have our ideal solutions, looking toward a Bolshevik revolution when the world would be a clean slate on which to write, and he pressed his request upon Colonel House, who finally yielded. Beer told me of this interview and expressed his doubts as to whether the President really wanted the memorandum or would read it when it was finished, but agreed with me that whatever the original stimulus for the request, it was our task to tackle the problem for all we were worth and to do the best we could.

[2] Miller Diary, I, 60–66.

Shaping Labor Problems

Rearrangement of the Library.

Work on "social history" undertaken.

[This was a preliminary study for a statement on international labor legislation. I worked at it with Dr. Slosson both in the Library and in my room. By a coincidence of which I had no knowledge at the time, this was the very day that Mr. Phelan of the British Labour Ministry arrived in Paris to secure office space in the British Delegation headquarters for a section on Labor. His coming was the result of a decision of the British Cabinet a few days before that the question of Labor at the Peace Conference should be given separate recognition in the British Delegation apart from the section on the League of Nations.[1] I had no knowledge, however, of this fact when I began work on the American memorandum for labor legislation, and my contacts with the French so far had given little indication of any serious offering from that quarter. The past history of international labor legislation, apart from the Franco-Italian treaty, was slight enough in any case, limited as it had been to international agreements restricting the night work of women in industry and forbidding the use of white phosphorus in matches. My memorandum was therefore begun with a purely American background.]

Friday, January 3, 1919

Work in the Library. Took up with Warrin, Miller, and Bowman the possibility of the Conference dealing with the question of child labor. All favorable, though not much interested.

[A glance at the memorandum which I prepared on that day will easily explain my colleagues' lack of interest in it. In view of what subsequently developed, it must be admitted that there is a certain naïve quality in this first document prepared within the American

[1] Cf. January 7.

Delegation on questions of labor. It was far removed from the proposals which were being shaped at the same time by the British and French Ministries of Labor, and still farther from the plans of the international trade union movement. It should be said, however, that the memorandum was not prepared for submission to the Commission, but for the sake of discussion with my more immediate friends in the American Delegation.

In spite of its apparent simplicity, however, the proposal was one which had a great weight of legislative history behind it. It had been the conditions of child labor, even more than those of women in industry, which in the days of the Chartists had called for the first social legislation in England to curb the evils of the factory system. The Parliamentary reports on which Karl Marx had based his attack on capitalism in *Das Kapital,* dealt largely with this situation; yet it was the one aspect of social reform which most clearly avoided the question of class warfare, based as it was upon humanitarian principles.

Although, in the following months, negotiations on labor questions proceeded along an entirely different line than that of presenting problems for specific reforms to be embodied in the Peace Treaty, building up instead a permanent organization to deal with the changing and developing programs for labor legislation in the future, nevertheless I did not lose sight of this interest in child labor legislation, and in spite of a feeling in the Labor Commission that this was not a pressing issue like the eight-hour day, I had the satisfaction of carrying it through on to the program of the first International Labor Conference, that held in Washington in the autumn of 1919. The text of the memorandum follows.]

MEMORANDUM ON LABOR LEGISLATION

The main interest in the Peace Conference seems to be centered upon divisions of territory, possession of colonies, popular self-determination and self-government, and upon such economic topics as indemnities and questions of trade.

All of these subjects are, to a large degree, nationalistic in character. They call for maps, on the one hand, or statistics on the other.

But there is a whole series of questions which lie outside these, and which are of vital interest to as many people, although not so definitely before us—the questions which are associated with labor, with the demands of the great masses who are suspicious of this assemblage of diplomatists. Just now, a wave of national feeling has smothered the most notable signs of this aloofness, as the English election shows; and Albert Thomas says (privately) that if France were now to have an election the Conservatives would sweep the country, and he and most of his Socialist comrades would be driven out of public life. But this national wave will not last; and in any case it must not be permitted to be made the cloak for conservative or reactionary policy. Moreover, the unreconciled, rebellious section of the population will turn to anarchism if we do not move honestly along the lines of social legislation at the Peace Conference.

To meet this situation we have only to build upon policies already planned. There have been more international congresses of Socialists than of any other class of men. But the trouble is that their programs are so thoroughgoing and revolutionary that they carry us too far. In the next place they raise the problem of internal government of States, of peoples' rights to settle their own home matters, and hence any effort to establish the dream of the Socialists' revolutionary State is not only impossible at this Conference, but the mere fact that such dreams exist blocks the path to practical progress. Socialism is worse as a name than in practice, in the eyes of most liberals.

Therefore, little real guidance or direction is to be had from an analysis of Socialist programs. The survey must be wider so as to give a genuine outlook into the whole history of democracy. Now, there is one demand for reform and supervision, which has antedated all others and comes right down to the present. It does not awaken class problems; it goes to the very root of social deterioration from industry—Child Labor. The Peace Conference must forbid child labor.

The Congress of Vienna banned the slave trade. The Congress of Paris-Versailles must save the children. For the future upbuilding of democracy this is essential. Singly, nations cannot be allowed to depend upon themselves; they are too near exhaustion and are calling on their children to help. Little boys of seven or eight are dragging great carts through the streets of Paris—little boys with a strip of black on the arm. They must not be permitted to lack the education which would make free men of them. France alone cannot deny herself their labor, if Germany is using them, for she would lose the industries they make possible. Belgium and Italy need even more the moral and joint support of the League of Nations. Fortunately England, by the great Education Bill of last winter, has laid down a program for us all. Unfortunately, the United States Supreme Court, by its decision of last June, declared the child labor law there unconstitutional—having regard to southern mill-owners. That one decision now stands in our way like a mountain, for it makes it difficult for the United States to take the lead. Besides, the only way to enforce the legislation would be the way the American law attempted it, by control of commerce—forbidding trade in articles made by children. We'll have to do some tall fighting to get it repealed!

Think what it means to put into the acts of this Conference a charter
of liberties for the children of the world. They, alone, are not citizens
of any one nation with obligations, they are the wards of us all; and the
strength of the moral forces of the League would be placed at the one
common task of ensuring their liberties. The one hope of democracy is
education; it has no safety but through intelligence; here is a guarantee
for the future, as well as a security for the present, through the association
of the great Powers and the progressive minor peoples in a single purpose.

Saturday, January 4, 1919

Had as a guest at lunch Patrick Gallagher of Dublin, Man-
chester, New York and the Far East, an irrepressible and lovable
Irish journalist, one of Beer's friends and admirers. The talk centered on the politics of the Far East, and Hornbeck listened in with
much interest. Somehow the politics of the Orient took on a different quality in a strong Irish brogue.

In the afternoon a call from Austin Evans, who has been at the
front in the French Y.M.C.A., "Le Foyer du Soldat," and has seen
hard fighting in the front line. It is a long way from medieval history, but that was once my field as well. I found him rather
reticent about his experiences at the front but anxious to secure help
in the movement to educate the soldiers, who are restless from
inaction.[1]

Lord Eustace Percy called to see me because someone had told
him that I was working on labor legislation. He had been in touch
with the preparations of the British Foreign Office, and in his
capacity as liaison officer between our Government and his offered
to put me in touch with Mr. Phelan, the labor expert who had just
arrived.

Evening at the Cercle Artistique et Littéraire. Max Lazard and
Dolléans offered further co-operation on the French side of the
labor problem. I met also Professor Lichtenberger, the French
authority on Germany, and several others whose names escape me.

Sunday, January 5, 1919

Morning—Working on social legislation.

Lunch furnished me with my first glimpse of a restored French
mansion of the old régime in the aristocratic Quartier St. Germain,

---

[1] Professor Evans of Columbia University. I found out later, not from him, that
he has been given the *Croix de Guerre* for bravery under fire.

an imposing building which had formerly been transformed into an apartment house and was rearranged about four years ago as a private dwelling. It is the home of M. Aubert, the close friend and the right-hand man of M. Tardieu when he was High Commissioner to the United States. There were present besides M. and Madame Aubert and M. Tardieu, M. de Martonne, a savant who has gone into diplomacy, two journalists, MM. Gauvain and Comert, the latter a most attractive young man with almost perfect command of English. Our group was represented by Bowman, Young, Haskins, and Beer. The life of the party, however, was Wickham Steed with his gossipy stories of high politics. The gardens behind the house abut on those of the Austro-Hungarian Embassy, one of the best private parks in Paris, now shabby from four years' neglect. Steed's knowledge of the Habsburgs came in quite apropos. Madame Aubert told him he looked like Van Dyke's "Charles I."

Late in the afternoon I had another visit from Max Lazard, and we discussed child labor and similar problems.

At dinner we turned back again to the question of the Far East with Gallagher, Beer and Hornbeck. There was the Japanese problem of Kiaochow, the British interests in Hongkong, and the far-away romance of Tibet.

A strange variety, but not more so than the problems that must be dealt with in the treaty that lies ahead.

Monday, January 6, 1919

Spent the day in the Library getting it in shape to turn over to others.

Beer had a visit from Lord Eustace Percy, who told him of British proposals for the settlement in the Middle East.

Tuesday, January 7, 1919

Spent much of day at Library.

Lord Eustace Percy and Mr. Phelan, of the Intelligence Division of the British Labour Ministry, called to talk over labor legislation. Phelan offered British co-operation in regard to materials. Substantial agreement reached.

Dined with Lionel Curtis, Wickham Steed and Beer. Steed told a story of the negotiations that lay behind the Pact of Rome. Sonnino had played a perilous part in European as well as Italian

politics owing to the fact that down to the defeat of Bulgaria he had
maintained his belief in the invincibility of the Central Powers.
This leaves Sonnino in a weakened position at the very time he
needs all the support he can get for Italy's claims. Italy has come
to the Peace Conference poorly equipped and in a weak strategic
position. The French in Syria came in for criticism. Curtis is for a
pan-Semitic country based on the influence of Colonel Lawrence.
Steed is for practical politics as compared with Curtis and ready to
recognize existing pressures and realities. Steed told of how Sonnino got Chamberlain to consent to admitting the legal right of
establishing the Italian language in Malta. Chamberlain had made
a *faux pas* by commenting adversely on the Jews, not realizing at
the moment that Sonnino was Jewish. Steed kicked his shins under
the table to remind him. Venizelos is asking Italy to do with the
Dodecanese what the British are ready to do with Cyprus. Steed
tells the story as he told it to Sonnino. He also is authority for the
statement that von Bülow admits that the *Einkreisung* (the encircle-
ment of Germany) is a myth. The talk then drifted as far as
Morocco with speculation as to the possibility of a French-English-
Spanish deal.

[The discreet reference above to my first meeting with Mr.
Phelan registers an incident which turned out to be the starting
point for my active participation in the negotiations with reference
to the labor section of the Treaty. From the very first the British
were ready to lay all their cards on the table and I was given a
chance to read over the documents which they brought with them.
With the customary efficiency of the British Civil Service they had
gone much farther than merely to outline a program of labor
clauses for the Peace Treaty. The problems of labor legislation, as
they pointed out, could never be wholly settled at any one time
and would need for future development the erection of some sort
of international organization, capable of carrying on the work
from year to year. My own tentative beginnings, as indicated in
the memorandum on child labor, had not gone beyond the idea of
having the League of Nations assume this continuing responsibility.
This had also been Lord Percy's point of view and would seem to
have had some support in the trade union circles with which Sir
Eric Drummond had been in contact. On the other hand, the

officials of the Ministry of Labour and Home Office had combined to propose a definite international labor organization which would eventually form part of the organization of the League of Nations but would be set up at once without waiting for the full establishment of the League. None of this inside story of the formation of the British program was known to me at the time. But Mr. Phelan argued effectively that the League of Nations would not be able to mobilize as efficient instruments for actually securing social legislation as a body especially appointed for that purpose.

This way of thinking was in harmony with the past history of international labor legislation and not out of keeping with my own idea of a League of Nations which should provide for special conferences to deal with a given number of outstanding international problems such as mandates, minorities, disarmament, trade conditions, etc. The preparatory materials of the British Government, which, as Phelan described them, already were fairly extensive, were to be placed quite freely at my disposal in shaping my own memoranda on this subject in the future. It will be recalled that Lord Percy's assignment as a member of the British Embassy at Washington had been to further this co-operation in British and American preparations for the Peace Conference.[1] Now, in the fulfilment of his work as liaison, he forced the pace somewhat on the Labour and Home Office officials, who, having sent Mr. Phelan ahead of them to secure working offices in the British Paris headquarters, had not been aware of the extent to which the American and British staffs were co-operating in matters like this. It is true that the co-operation which Percy brought about was practically all on the British side, as I had prepared no such documentation as they.

In the weeks and months that followed, Mr. Phelan and I were destined to work together intimately and at high pressure in the negotiations which led to the creation of the International Labor Organization, and I found him a loyal colleague, fertile and creative of suggestion, one who was never lacking in the understanding of the difficulties confronting the American Delegation, perhaps aided in this by his Irish sense of humor. The International Labor Organization owes more to him than will probably ever be widely known,

[1] See above, p. 11 n.

for both as planner and negotiator he worked impersonally in order to work effectively. The immediate outcome of the talk with him was that I set about the preparation of a more serious and enlarged study of the problems of social legislation, the result of which was summarized in the memoranda of the following days.]

Wednesday, January 8, 1919

Tea with Miller and Phelan in afternoon. Discussion of labor points, Miller agreeing. Phelan has been in Russia and is alarmed over the labor situation in Europe. He says that we are by no means out of the woods. There may be a terrific upheaval in Italy, and heaven knows where else. It is bad enough in Berlin.

[Mr. Miller's Diary throws light on this discussion with Phelan but is certainly inaccurate in the statement that Phelan placed the emphasis on child labor and the labor of women; for these two matters were not to the fore in the British program which Mr. Phelan had then in his possession.¹]

8 P.M.—Dinner with Lord Robert Cecil. League of Nations. The British plan for it is to arrive by airplane. Elimination of war the first object: machinery for arbitration, etc. Arbitration machinery, supplemented by economic and other existing international organization, to be brought under its authority in so far as possible, but purely war institutions not an adequate basis for a peace structure, e.g., Inter-Allied Purchasing Commission.

[This bare note of the subject of our conversation is highly interesting if one reads between the lines, which is not difficult to do. A letter written home next day gives some further incidental details. A comparison of the two accounts will show how the actual

---

¹ Mr. Miller's account runs as follows: "I had tea with Professor Shotwell and Mr. Phelan. Mr. Phelan is one of the secretaries of the Labor Department of Great Britain and his own Division will probably be under Lord Robert Cecil in the British Delegation at the Peace Conference. He has studied the labor movement and Bolshevism apparently with great care and wanted to have some international agreements for the benefit of labor, particularly in regard to child labor and labor of women, as he thought this would block the effect of the Socialist Conference at Lausanne by turning them toward constructive lines rather than merely critical ones. I thought his purpose was largely political from the point of view of the Coalition in Great Britain but I told him that I was personally sympathetic with the idea but that the question of policy would have to be determined; that is, whether any such provisions are to go in the Peace Treaty, and that presumably this would be determined at Inter-Allied conferences. I think that Mr. Phelan takes too serious a view of the Bolshevik movement, as he said that it nearly succeeded in Sweden, or at least that there was nearly a revolution there. He also spoke of the munition strike in Great Britain in the Spring of 1917 as having nearly brought about a revolution." Miller Diary, I, 68–69.

matter of discussion was left out of letters home at that time and news was limited to descriptions of externals.

"Last night Beer, Young and I were invited by Lord Robert Cecil, British Minister of Blockade during the war, and now head of the British 'League of Nations' section of their Delegation here, to dine with him and Lionel Curtis, the brilliant young (40 or over) statesman of the 'British Commonwealth' plan of British federation. It was a quiet dinner in Lord Robert's room, and the only other person present was his private secretary, Captain Walters.

"We took an army car and got there at 8. The British have taken two big hotels, the Astoria and the Majestic, and they have a group of very solemn butlers and detectives at the door to look you over—or look over you, as they mostly do—with British imperturbability and in a calm, quiet, efficient manner. There was some reluctance to taking us up to Cecil's rooms, which made the butler apologetic when he discovered that it was all right. Cecil is a very tall man—six feet three or more. When he sits down he slides into the chair and lets his body get under the table, so as he and I sat opposite and looked across at each other, we were both comfortably fixed with our eyes above the tablecloth. After all, Lincoln used to like to sink to his shoulder-blades, so why shouldn't we! He has a massive forehead with a curiously thick shock of brown hair back of it. In some ways he reminded me of Moberly Bell, of the *Times*, especially the play of a smile on a rather stern face—the sternness entirely contradicted by kindly blue eyes. A modest, quiet man, very serious and very thoughtful, religious in tone, but not without a keen sense of humor. His father, the Marquis of Salisbury, had a much heavier face, to judge by his pictures. His secretary, Captain Walters, is a very lame young veteran, with the quiet manners of England at her best.

"We had a simple English dinner, served by English girls—for the British haven't left a single Frenchman in their building, having brought over servants and all—the simple fare being as elaborate as the Crillon menus, with champagne and port in addition! It may have been that which made the subsequent conversation so entertaining. But in any case we handled the League of Nations and settled derelict peoples' fate to our mutual satisfaction. There is no time like this for political philosophy. Coming home Young agreed with Beer and me that the English were 'all right.' "]

Thursday, January 9, 1919

Working all day on labor legislation. In the evening Phelan dined with me along with Haskins, Beer and Young. Young insists on connecting labor clauses with equality of trade conditions, to which Phelan objects. Inconsequential discussion. After midnight —read the papers.

Friday, January 10, 1919

Labor legislation still to the fore.

In the afternoon Dr. Herbert Putnam, Librarian of Congress, called on me at the Library. Most cordial and helpful.

Evening—Dined with Miller at the Crillon and had him up to my room afterwards to talk about social legislation. He advised taking the matter up with House. He described his draft of the proposed treaty.

Midnight—Walked with Beer along the Seine on his return from evening with Lords Cecil, Percy and Hardinge, and Louis Mallet. It has rained a lot, so the Seine is in flood. It is right up to the arches of the bridges now and still rising. We are not affected, but the city will lack coal soon, they say. Traffic on the river is stopped. Today, however, has been mild and beautiful and tonight the sky is clear. It is not at all cold. I doubt if there has been a heavy frost. The grass is green in the parks and there are even some flowers out in bloom. We may get real winter soon, though, for Paris is not a warm place in winter.

Beer repeated a story about diplomatic phraseology which Lord Robert had told. He said that there was a story current in the Foreign Office about his father, that when Lord Salisbury wrote a despatch he then called a secretary and said, "Now turn this into diplomatic jargon."

Began memorandum.

Saturday, January 11, 1919

Completed preliminary memorandum on social legislation. Dr. Mezes will get it to Colonel House next week.

[This document is short enough to quote. It also shows the effect of contacts with the French but does not as yet deal with a permanent organization, except as a bureau of the League of

Nations with "a periodic conference connected with the central organs of the League."]

INTERNATIONAL LABOR LEGISLATION

The working classes of Europe are expecting some pronouncement on Labor at the Peace Conference. To ignore this hope would be to invoke the consequences of disillusionment.

Fortunately, the situation is not so difficult as might seem; for the programs which have been suggested to the Conference by Labor prior to the close of the war are, for the most part, modest. Labor has been content to leave their extension to the League of Nations.

I. *Labor and Socialist Programs*

An analysis of the various programs of Labor and Socialist Conferences held during the war reveals the significant fact, of which Labor may be justly proud, that, in their statement of peace aims, the demands for class betterment were subordinated to those of general social and national justice. The program of the British Labour Party, for example, or that of the Inter-Ally Socialist and Labor Congress held in London in February, 1918, dealt primarily with international politics, such as the boundaries of new States and equality of trade opportunity, and only secondarily with the needs of international guarantee of labor conditions.

But it must not be imagined from this that the expectation of a recognition of these needs by the Peace Conference is any the less real. Indeed, in the present temper of Europe, the social problems may really be the fundamental ones; and the attitude of trust in America a rather perilous diplomatic asset.

Of the various programs thus advanced, the most important is that of the International Conference held at Leeds, England, July, 1916. Its recommendations were again unanimously adopted at Berne in October, 1917, by the labor representatives of the central and northern Powers, and have finally (December, 1918) furnished the basis of a proposal which has passed the French Chamber of Deputies as the scheme of labor legislation to be recommended to the Peace Conference.

From this program, which comes nearest to claiming international sanction, the following points may be taken as a basis for international action by the Peace Commission:

1. Prohibition of child labor.
2. Regulation of the conditions of labor, especially for women and young persons.
3. International agreements to safeguard migratory labor.
4. Organization, under the League of Nations, of an international bureau to study labor problems and a periodic Conference connected with the central organs of the League.

These four points—with their implications—cover the more essential elements in the Leeds program, with the exception of a demand for a limitation of the hours of male adult labor.

II. *Precedents Already Established*

The points which are here proposed for international treatment are already the subject of joint international conventions by the European Powers, with the exception of that referring to a League of Nations.

Beginning with the Berlin Congress of 1890 a series of joint international conventions have been drawn up among European states, dealing with such matters as social insurance rights of immigrants, savings banks, prohibition of yellow phosphorus matches, regulation of dangerous or exhaustive industries, night work for women and young persons, etc. By means of these the legal condition of labor in the more backward countries has been brought nearer the uniform standard established, a delay of a few years being allowed for adjustment.

The International Association for Labor Legislation, with its central office in Switzerland, and branches in each country, could be recognized as furnishing the basis of the permanent bureau of the League. This association is largely responsible for the existing body of international labor law, and the calling together of the congresses.

The First Phase of the Preliminary Peace Conference

Sunday, January 12, 1919

The morning began with a search for documents in the office. Then I paid a call on Frank Warrin, who is sick in bed with inflammatory rheumatism. I stayed with him through lunch and we talked away until about two o'clock, when Mr. Miller called. Miller described his evening with the British—Colonel Lawrence, Sir Valentine Chirol, and Lord Cecil. Then Miller took me along to his apartment for a talk on the way things are going. And when we finished it was after three.

I crossed the Place de la Concorde to the river, and over at the river bank stayed looking at the crowds and the sky and the river for nearly an hour. It was very lovely. The sky of Paris has been wonderful this winter, whenever the rain stopped, for the sun breaks through the mist with the softest light imaginable and there is a gracious quality in the scene which is lacking in New York. I never felt it in past visits to Paris as I have noticed it this time. It is as if, to use Whistler's term, nature were really looking up—to all the Corots. There was a group of three musicians on one of the *quais*, a girl with a violin, a man with a guitar, and another girl to sing, and quite a crowd gathered to hear the song they were selling. The girl sang beautifully and there were many buyers who joined in learning the songs, a good many soldiers and some women in black. It was almost like a religious group. They sang of the *nouvelle époque* and the great *épopée* and the liberation of France. And behind them the swollen river (it is still nearly up to the bridge arches) caught the reflection of the setting sun. One didn't need the dome of the Invalides in the background, with its reminder of Napoleon, to be in touch with history. For the crowds were waiting to see Wilson and the other plenipotentiaries, Lloyd George (who came last night), the Premier of Italy, and the Slavs and the rest, come back from the opening session of the Conference.

There were quite a number of little children in the crowd, about the size of some I knew in Paris years ago, when they liked the Punch and Judy show better than anything else in the city. They had bare knees in the cold January weather and were running hoops up the Champs Elysées, just the way it used to be. There was the old gingerbread woman, and the little lad with a drum, and the nurse scolding the girl who got mud on her dress—and the next wish I had was to turn back the clock for seven years and—

Evening—At that point I stopped writing, dressed in street clothes, called for a car at the door and told the chauffeur to drive up the Boulevard Raspail past Montparnasse, to a quiet street of studios where Mr. Edwin Scott [1] lives. He met me at the door, and kept me for tea, which was their supper—just tea, johnny-cake and syrup. There is no bread just now in parts of Paris. A French woman, wife of an artist, was there too. She has a family of young children and they moved to the country to get eatables. But eggs are fifteen to eighteen cents each. She says the hens won't declare an armistice, but keep on thinking it's war still. It will take months before Europe can be supplied with a stock of things necessary for the merest comfort. I was surprised, for instance, to find the other day that in the Bon Marché they had only one pair of gloves my size and it was a miscut pair which the salesman apologized for. The same was true of other staple articles of clothing.

The Scotts say that what is making Paris so full just now is not the Conference but the refugees. There are many from all the devastated regions. They described how a shell from a Bertha had fallen in the garden back of their Paris studio, showering earth over it and others nearby. The aviators had dropped bombs on the Boulevard Raspail, destroying a big house almost opposite. He said he had done very little during the war. It was impossible to concentrate, and besides, the alarms and the cannon kept them awake nights, and no real rest was possible.

I don't know what England is like, but Dr. Putnam, Librarian of Congress, says that it is cold and dreary there in the hotels. They have a little fire for a big room and none in the private rooms, and there is a great scarcity of food. So it looks as if this were not the right side of the Atlantic in the winter.

[To the historian of the Peace Conference the entry for this day

[1] An American painter who had lived nearly all his life in Paris.

will show how far away from great events one may be, even when they are happening close at hand. This was the day on which the Supreme Council of the Allied and Associated Powers held its first meeting for the purpose of organizing the Preliminary Peace Conference. In a letter home written next morning, I said: "Yesterday afternoon, as the papers will have told you, the first meeting of the Allied Powers took place. I suppose the whole world knows as much about it as we do, however, for only those present could tell what happened and they won't." The Miller Diary makes no mention of the meeting at all. In form and membership it was the same as the Supreme War Council, indeed, it began its meeting on this occasion as the Supreme War Council, passing over into the Peace Conference organization by simply having the military advisers withdraw. Next day the Japanese representatives were admitted to it. Consisting as it did of two representatives from each of the five principal Powers, it soon became known as the Council of Ten.[1] As Mr. Lansing has pointed out, the transition from the one body to the other was thus made almost imperceptibly.[2]

The first meeting of the Supreme Council as an organ of the Peace Conference was held at four o'clock in M. Pichon's room at the Quai d'Orsay. The points discussed were the procedure of the Peace Conference, on which Miller and Scott had been working; the representation of Montenegro; renewal of the armistice with Germany; the representation of Russia at the Conference; technical advisers; Japanese representation at the informal conversations. No news of this, however, was given to any of us on the Inquiry.]

Monday, January 13, 1919

A rainy Monday morning, not very propitious for the first week of the Conference. Whole day in the Library arranging new books.

Evening—Beer wants me to write an article for the *Round Table*. Went to Bowman's room with Young and Beer. Bowman tells of Lord's work on Poland which Lansing gave to the press.

[1] This term, "Council of Ten," was later applied to another body consisting for the most part of Foreign Ministers after the formation of the Council of Four.

[2] Robert Lansing, *The Big Four and Others of the Peace Conference*, pp. 12–15. The way in which the Supreme Council of the Peace Conference grew out of wartime organizations has been described above. Mr. Lansing suggests that possibly M. Clemenceau postponed the meeting of the Peace Conference until the meeting of the Supreme War Council in January, when it was called together to extend the Armistice, "as it would form an easy stepping-stone for him to assume a general direction of the proceedings."

As Young is fully occupied with reparations, he suggested that I should have full charge of labor problems for the Inquiry.

Tuesday, January 14, 1919

Breakfast with Young, Westermann and Bowman in Bowman's room. Young troubled over what may happen to his Division of Economics now, after the arrival of John Foster Dulles and the men who worked with Gay at the various "controls," War Trade Board, War Industries Board, etc.[1]

Today is fair again after much rain, and the weather continues mild. Dr. Putnam and I called on the British Delegation to talk about getting British documents. I have a courier daily to Switzerland and one to Holland upon whom I rely to get me books from the frontier and beyond, and we already have agents in Vienna and Berlin, as well as in Poland. Dr. Putnam lunched with me and gave me carte blanche as to periodicals.

Dictate letters. Call on Warrin.

Dinner at Max Lazard's to meet M. Grunebaum-Ballin, a specialist on merchant marine and a syndicalist, and Professor Mantoux, the official interpreter of the Conference.[2] M. Mantoux is one of the few Frenchmen I have met who not only speak English with hardly a trace of accent but have a real sense of the nuance of English and American phrases. He was a professor in London for some years, and his doctoral dissertation for the Paris doctorate on the Industrial Revolution in England in the Eighteenth Century is a work which still remains unique in that field, although it has become so rare as to be practically inaccessible. He was surprised to know that I used it as a text book in my Columbia class in Social History.

Madame Mantoux made the penetrating remark that the difference between French and British attitudes towards the questions of the day is due to the fact the French are patriotic, the British public

[1] The reference is to Dean E. F. Gay, of the Harvard Business School, who had made for himself a strong place in war-time Washington administration. He and his associates had not been connected with the Inquiry, however, and Young was now worried for fear his Economics Section might lose its place in the Peace Conference organization through the influence of those who had been so important in the economic management of the war. Fortunately, Dulles and Young were too much in agreement and of too large caliber for anything but the happiest of personal relationships.

[2] Professor Mantoux is said to have kept a diary. If so, it should be, next to that of Sir Maurice Hankey, Secretary of the Ten and then of the Four, the most intimate story of the Peace Conference.

spirited. Patriotism does not necessarily extend to the realm of tax paying.

Wednesday, January 15, 1919

Morning was spent in work at the Library, ordering books and periodicals. Fruitless attempt to arrange for the entrée into the French Foreign Office Library, for the preparation of a guide to the *Yellow Books*.

[This was with reference to a question which had arisen during my work on diplomatic history in the Inquiry. We found it hard to work with the French *Yellow Books*—the publications of the French Foreign Office—because of the lack of any system either in their appearance or their numbering. The consequence was that it was difficult to know what official publications existed on any given subject. The reason for this irregularity was that the Foreign Office publications were called for at irregular intervals, or sent to press when there was occasion for their use rather than when the event itself occurred. Sometimes it was even difficult to know whether a report for a commission was open for public consultation or not, as I found on inquiry at the Imprimerie Nationale. As a part of the documentary preparation for the Peace Conference I had had an index prepared by Miss Isadore G. Mudge, Reference Librarian of Columbia University, of all the French documents then available to us in America. I had hoped to secure the co-operation of the French Foreign Office to make this list complete, but ran into unexpected obstacles and was never able to finish the task. The value to the student of French diplomatic history of a guide of this kind would have been considerable.]

While arranging for the detail to the Library staff of Mr. Roger Howson, of Columbia University Library, from Adjutant General Headquarters of the Twenty-seventh Division, ran into Wickham Steed, who was patiently waiting for a chance to get a pass into the Crillon so that he would not be turned back at the door by a new, young detective, as had happened to Clemenceau and to Lord Reading! Steed took it in good part. He referred himself to the project which I had mentioned to him before, of having the British Foreign Office thrown open to an American scholar to analyze the documents there relating to British foreign policy right up to the War. Steed said that he would take the matter up with Lord Hardinge and bring Hardinge and me together.

Had lunch with Dr. Putnam, who is leaving for southern France, having stated to me that he places no limit on my demand for books and periodicals. He is returning in ten days or so. With unlimited funds, the temptation is to overdevelop the Library, and the need of a trained librarian like Howson becomes imperative.

Afternoon at the Bibliothèque Nationale to work on one of our propositions. It was strange to drive up to the old library in an American army car. The *administrateur* to whom I referred for a ticket, when he saw my name on the card, seemed to think that formalities were unnecessary in my case, as the Chief Librarian had apparently impressed upon his bureaucratic mind the rareness of the privilege which I enjoyed for the first week of the Conference of entering the Bibliothèque Nationale on my own visiting card. The Salle de Travail has not known there was a war. The same old attendants, slightly more bent and whitened, the same collections of medieval texts, and the same delay in getting books. I asked the man at the desk, after waiting twenty minutes, if he could hurry a book along. He asked how long I had waited and when I told him, he said, "Oh, well, then, wait twenty minutes more before bringing a complaint."

At four o'clock I came back to change hastily for Mrs. Wilson's reception in the French "White House."

Sentries presented arms each side of the doorway, a French officer took our cards, and two high functionaries in red breeches gave us the check for our coats, while two or three more lined the stairway to the reception room. The rooms of the Murat Palace have costly paintings and the ceiling is filled with original frescoes, but the most distinctive note of decoration is that afforded by the electroliers which give an indirect lighting through a mass of crystal and twisted bronze.

These lights are multiplied by huge wall mirrors, so that one can hardly tell how many rooms are real and how many only reflection. The chairs were deftly placed so as to put us in line for the third door to the right, where Mrs. Wilson stood waiting for us. She was dressed in a low-necked gown with a long train, and her hair was artistically arranged. A few cordial words of greeting, and we were in the room beyond. The party was not a large one, which made us feel

all the more at home—meaning that we of the Inquiry herded together and exchanged commonplace remarks to show that we could
have said something to someone else. A hint from a nice young
captain carried us into the adjoining room, where some five or six
new butlers were serving tea and other things from a buffet. After
a cup of tea we started home, and as the car had not come back for
us in time, Farabee, Hornbeck and I walked back to the Crillon in
the rain.

Seven-twenty found Mezes, Bowman and myself in a car headed
for the Majestic Hotel (the British headquarters) to dine with the
representatives of the British Labour Ministry, who are here to
arrange for clauses in the treaty of peace guaranteeing the international recognition of social legislation. The Englishmen were Mr.
Harold Butler, the Assistant Minister of Labour; Mr. Phelan,
head of the Intelligence Service of the Labour Ministry; and Mr.
Philip Baker, of Lord Robert Cecil's party on the League of
Nations.

The dining room of the Majestic is at least twice the size of that
of the Crillon; the tables are not crowded so close together, and the
service moves with British precision. The scene at dinner was the
most remarkable I have ever witnessed, and I suppose I shall never
see another like it. At different tables sat the delegations of the
different parts of the British Empire. Behind me was Australia, with
Premier Hughes, whom we had met in New York, and his colleagues.
Next to Australia, but separated by a wide strip of carpet, was a
large round table for the Indian Empire, with the new Indian Under-
Secretary, Sir S. P. Sinha, and the Maharajah of Bikaner, and others.
Farther down that side of the room another young Empire was presided over by Sir Robert Borden. I did not know personally the
other Canadians at his table. Next to the Canadian table was a large
dinner party discussing the fate of Arabia and the East with two
American guests, General Bliss and George Louis Beer. Between
them sat that young successor of Mohammed, Colonel Lawrence, the
twenty-eight-year-old conqueror of Damascus, with his boyish face
and almost constant smile—the most winning figure, so every one
says, at the whole Peace Conference. I was to have met him this
week but the meeting has been postponed until Monday. At the same
table sat Sir Valentine Chirol, the best informed man on European
politics, Lord Robert Cecil, and Lionel Curtis.

Across the dining room was a similar row of tables and at the one nearest me sat two men whose faces I knew from their pictures, Sir Louis Botha and General Smuts. Both were turned so that I could see them, but I didn't know the men they were with. At the next table, however, was Lloyd George, with Lord Reading at his side, and Balfour. The rest of the table I didn't know. Lloyd George is a very well preserved middle-aged man, and even Balfour is not so decrepit as the pictures have made him out to be. I saw him close at hand later, and he might pass for a man of less than sixty. They says he plays tennis every morning all the year through and cannot be got down to work before half-past two in the afternoon, so it is very difficult to get details to his attention. The story goes that a memorandum on Armenia was handed to him last night and he read a page of it, and then dropped it on the floor and kicked it into the farthest corner of the room, with the remark that as long as he was at this Conference he was not going to read any more memoranda, that he knew now all he wanted to know about the Armenians or anyone else; dismissed his secretary and went to bed. But this is mere anteroom gossip.

A glimpse of Lloyd George's young daughter, a comical little replica of her daddy and aged about sixteen, with her hair hanging down her back and her ruddy little face smiling up at the master of the British Empire, was the most pleasant incident of the evening that caught my eye.

We discussed the Labor program until late and then, as our car had not come, walked home along the Champs Elysées, with its long row of battered cannon, the sinister reminders of the war that brought us all here.

At the hotel I met Beer, who had just come in with General Bliss, and he came along to my room and we discussed Imperial politics until after midnight. The General had had a pleasant evening with the British, but the complexity of the problems of the Conference is commencing to tire out the Commissioners. I am afraid they may pull out before some of the most important items are settled—or get like Mr. Balfour.

At 12:30 I start reading the morning papers, the London *Times* and *Le Temps,* to keep up with the busy world.

I forgot to note that the planks for the League of Nations, as Cecil has the plan now, are about as follows:

(1) International tribunals, such as The Hague, for the enforcement of international treaties, etc.

(2) Freedom of the seas by way of equality of trade conditions.

(3) Free passage to markets, etc., by international railways, open ports, international rivers, etc.

(4) Control of the trade in arms, opium, liquor, etc., with backward peoples.

(5) System of government of backward peoples through States mandatory of the League.

(6) International labor legislation to be maintained through international commission and possibly periodic conferences.

[The inadequate reference in my diary to this first detailed discussion of the labor program with the British can be supplemented by the following passage from a memorandum of the conversation made by Mr. Phelan.

The American representatives are in complete sympathy with the British view that the Conference should provide the opportunity for a discussion of these questions at an early date by means of what Dr. Shotwell terms a "committee of reference," the duty of which would be to make recommendations concerning the form of the permanent machinery, and the constitution of an international commission, and possibly also to suggest some definition of the area over which the deliberations of the commission should be directed.

As regards the best method of securing a strong and effective body of international public opinion, Dr. Shotwell was of opinion that the Peace Conference should base its actions on a recognition of the existing body of international labour agreements and should declare itself in favor of the development and extension of these in the future. In this way it would be regarded as building on precedent rather than launching any new and utopian scheme, and would be sure of more support both from conservative elements in Europe and from many elements in America, which though possibly uninterested in or doubtful of the effect of international labour legislation, could not remain aloof from a general approval of a system of agreements which had already in Europe produced demonstrably good effects.

Dr. Shotwell further put in a strong plea for a recognition of the right of the child to a special place in the pronouncements of the Conference in relation to measures for securing the general welfare of mankind. Other labour legislation he argued was definitely a question of class, but the consideration of child welfare in a general way, beyond mere prohibitions of excessive hours or unsuitable industrial processes, etc., was a matter not of class but of progress. In particular he suggested that the responsibility which the League would in all probability assume for the tutelage of backward states must include responsibility for the education and welfare of the children in those states, and that on the success of these measures would depend in a large degree the future of the new and at present undeveloped states and the general security of the world. He argued that a plea of this kind would obtain a general response from the common sense and common heart of all humanity, and thus again help in securing that international public opinion without which full vitality cannot be infused into the work of the League. This general consideration for the welfare of the child should go side by side with the questions of international labour legislation and be co-ordinated with industrial measures, but, in view of its wider appeal and importance, it should have special mention possibly under the pronouncement dealing with backward races.

With these views of Dr. Shotwell there was general agreement. The necessity for a permanent bureau to act as the secretariat of the International Commission and to collect and classify facts was generally accepted. Some discussion also took place as regards the difficulties arising out of the form of the U. S. Constitution in the way of concluding agreements on treaties of certain kinds, but the opinion was expressed that so far as concerned agreements of the kind likely to result from the recommendations of an International Labour Commission such difficulties would not prove insuperable.

The character and strength of the representation of the various States on the Labour Commission was also mentioned and it is proposed to resume the discussion on this and other points at an early date.

I did not appreciate at the time the speed and precision with which my British colleagues were working. It subsequently appeared that the War Cabinet had that very day finally discussed and agreed to a "Joint Memorandum" of the Ministry of Labour and the Home Office on International Labor Legislation which sanctioned the creation of a Commission at the Peace Conference for Labor Legislation. Lord Curzon, Foreign Minister, telegraphed to Mr. Balfour in Paris a summary of the Cabinet decision and that night the Right Honorable George N. Barnes, representative of Labor in the War Cabinet, crossed over to Paris.]

Thursday, January 16, 1919

Bibliothèque Nationale. Introduced Slosson to work there.

Evening—Dinner with Beer, Mezes and Hornbeck, and Sir Valentine Chirol, Lionel Curtis, and Philippe Millet of *Le Temps*. Millet speaks English so well that Mezes took him for an Englishman, and even at the end of the evening Millet had to remind him that he was "only a poor Frenchman after all." Beer and Curtis waded into

Millet on French foreign policy. Millet reacted very strongly but had some caustic comments to make about the French Foreign Office. Chirol, in a reminiscent mood, told his memories of Bismarck's days in Berlin and especially of the man who pulled the wires in the German Foreign Office and to a large degree controlled its policy, Holstein, *"L'éminence grise"* of Wilhelmstrasse. Holstein once said to Chirol that William II would either lose his crown or die in the madhouse. Holstein had secret correspondents in the European capitals and kept spies watching the German ambassadors. Everyone was afraid of him. Von Kühlmann's share in ruthlessly forcing the Brest Litovsk treaty upon Russia makes impossible his being sent as an envoy to the Peace Conference, where he would have been a powerful figure. Chirol said that Lichnowsky's tribute to Kühlmann was due to the fact that he did not want to show how much he had been taken in. Beer and I told Chirol that he should write his memoirs for the public, especially the history of the Entente diplomacy.

A cable from Professor John Bates Clark, Director of the Division of Economics and History of the Carnegie Endowment, announced my reappointment as editor of the *Economic and Social History of the World War,* which the Carnegie Endowment propose to publish. It is the same plan which I was offered two years ago. It will involve spending at least three months of every year in Europe.

Friday, January 17, 1919

Routine library work. Bibliothèque Nationale. Find it of little use for reference work in recent European history, especially if one is in a hurry. Drive to London *Times* office to consult their files. Hoped to profit from the use of the detailed cumulative index, which I had started when I was on the *Times* in 1905, with Mr. Moberly Bell, the General Manager, as a substitute for the old Palmer's Index. For ready reference it might prove invaluable now. But the Paris office gets along without such devices, just as Mr. Buckle used to when he was editor of the *Times.* The reference shelves just back of his swivel chair contained the Greek classics! Chirol's library at the office of the *Times,* when he was foreign editor, used to be almost as antiquated in the field of European history—the Victorian classics and the old masters. One of my tasks in London had been to get him to give these up in exchange for recent works. In the

Paris office I found little but the more recent numbers of the *Times*, and these unbound. Wickham Steed tells me that there is a historic reason for this. The accumulation of old files threatened to drive De Blowitz [1] out of his apartment, so he gave them to the Bibliothèque Nationale.

Evening dinner guest, Professor Gaston Jèze, professor of law and specialist in economics. During the war he had had charge of contracts for munitions, etc., and he described the liquidation of war material. Quite outspoken in his criticism of waste. He came as Lybyer's guest, through an introduction from Garner,[2] who had translated some of Jèze's books.

Afterwards Young came to my room and brought his memorandum on the economic propositions to be put in the Treaty. Discussed them in detail till after midnight, especially the French Moroccan claims and those of the British colonies and Dominions. Young's figures are far under the French claims. After midnight read the morning papers.

Saturday, January 18, 1919

In the morning routine library work with a vist to the Bibliothèque Nationale, where Slosson is hard at work.

Afternoon—First meeting of Peace Conference in plenary session. In the scramble for tickets, the State Department won out! Very little chance for the Inquiry group and none for me. Learning that journalists could get in at the last moment, I walked across to the Quai d'Orsay with Frederic Howe, who explained that he represented some mythical magazine at moments like this, although really Commissioner of Immigration at New York. Unhindered, I entered the courtyard by the first gate and got up the steps to the main entrance, at the east of the building, and from there watched the statesmen arrive. A single company of soldiers on the Quai along the other side of the street, and another company in the courtyard with a trumpeter's band and kettledrums blare out a note of welcome for a big automobile from which emerges Woodrow Wilson. Camera men turn their films busily while Wilson takes off his silk hat and smiles to the crowd. Almost no cheering and very few spectators.

As there was no way of getting in, I came back at once. Paris

---

[1] The famous correspondent of the *Times* in Paris in the early years of the Third Republic.

[2] Professor J. W. Garner of the University of Illinois.

busily at work in the streets and on the river, where tugboats were making up for time lost during the flood by hauling an extra number of barges under the bridges. While the statesmen were planning the program of peace in the building alongside, I joined the crowd that lined the river bank watching the boatmen. Compared with the work of the Conference theirs seems ever so much more real; perhaps in terms of the long reaches of history it is.

About five o'clock I had an urgent telephone call from Ray Stannard Baker, in charge of American publicity work, that at this first meeting of the Peace Conference, to the surprise of the American Delegation, Clemenceau announced that next to placing responsibility for the war and for crimes committed in it, the third item on the agenda was labor legislation, on which I have been working, and which, only at three o'clock this afternoon, Dr. Mezes placed in my hands.[1] Great panic in the newspaper world, as no one knew what was meant; so with the assistance of Frank Warrin, I prepared for Arthur Sweetser, of Baker's staff, a detailed story of Labor's demands which is to be given to the press.[2] Finished about midnight and continued legal study of the situation with Warrin until about one.

[It was not only this one point of the announced program of the Peace Conference that puzzled the journalists, but the fragmentary and apparently hastily improvised program of the meeting as a whole. It gave the impression that somehow or other things behind the scene were not going well, and the inference was quickly drawn that the meeting had been staged more to distract public attention from the real progress of negotiations than to furnish a proper clue as to what was actually taking place. The three points mentioned first on the "Order of the Day" were those which engaged no vital interests of the Allied and Associated Powers, and therefore could be undertaken without fear of undue disagreement. But on territorial, financial, and economic questions it looked as though the small Powers were to have to plead their case with the great Powers, and this meant that the storm signals were already set. Although

---

[1] I have no notes of my interview with Dr. Mezes at which this took place. Mr. Gompers was landing in England on this day and did not arrive in Paris until the twenty-second or twenty-third, and spent the first days of his visit with the French labor leaders (M. Jouhaux and other members of the Confédération Générale du Travail).

[2] This document is the first statement given to the United States on the question of International Labor Legislation, then so suddenly sprung upon the world. As it is a relatively complete survey of the whole subject in about the shortest possible terms, it is quoted in Appendix II.

the program announced that the question of the League of Nations would be the first to be taken up at the next session, the way in which the announcement was typed in at the bottom of the page seemed almost to suggest an afterthought. This impression of haste and improvisation was accentuated by the fact that the program itself was not printed, but only mimeographed, as if done at the last moment. The document itself is short enough to quote.]

PEACE CONFERENCE

Programme of Arrangements for the Opening Meeting on Saturday, January 18th, 1919, at 3:00 P.M.

1. The President of the French Republic arrives at 3:30 P.M., when all the representatives are in their places.
2. Speech by the President of the French Republic.
3. The President of the French Republic shakes hands with all the delegates in order.
4. M. Clemenceau takes the chair provisionally.
5. Definite election of the President of the Conference. President Wilson will propose; Mr. Lloyd George will second; M. Sonnino will also second.
6. The election of Vice-Presidents, one for each of the other Great Powers, United States of America, the British Empire, France and Italy.
7. Proposal for the appointment of a Secretary-General.
8. Proposal for the appointment of a Secretary for each of the Great Powers, with the right of substitution.
9. (a) Each delegation of the Great Powers will nominate, in addition, a member of a Drafting Committee.
   (b) The President will invite each *Delegation* of the Great Powers to nominate a plenipotentiary to constitute a Committee in order to verify the credentials.
10. *AGENDA.*
    (a) Placing of the Regulations on the table of the Conference.
    (b) Questions on the Order of the Day for the present meeting:—
        (i) Responsibility of the authors of the war.
        (ii) Responsibility for the crimes committed in the war.
        (iii) Legislation in regard to International Labour.
        All the Powers will be invited to present Memoranda on these three questions.
        The Powers with limited interests will also be asked to send Memoranda on the questions of every kind, territorial, financial, economic, etc., which particularly interest them.
        (iv) The Society of Nations will be put at the head of the Agenda of the second sitting.

Sunday, January 19, 1919

Slosson and I working on labor questions in my room.

Breakfast with Sweetser at which I read over his mimeographed account of what I had prepared for the press. This was then passed to the Commissioners and given to the press in the afternoon for cabling home.

Baker brings in M. Léon Jouhaux, of the Confédération Générale du Travail, who had drawn up the program of Labor of the Leeds Conference of 1916, which has been taken over largely as a basis for suggestion by the Chamber of Deputies. A man in early middle life, looking like Ebert, forceful but rather quiet, letting the other man do the talking, but able to express himself with moderation and clarity.

[This characterization of M. Jouhaux hardly does justice to that vigorous trade union leader and orator who has dominated the Confédération Générale du Travail for more than a generation by the spell of his dynamic personality.]

Lunch with Baker and Warrin. Baker turns over to me the address which the Confédération Générale du Travail has prepared for Wilson, and Warrin and I spend the afternoon translating it.

Dinner with Miller at the Hôtel Meurice. Discussion until 11 P.M. about what has been done so far at the Peace Conference. Arranged to swing the Division of History more closely to that of International Law, in order to have the documentary material more available for consultation during the actual work of negotiation.

[I had been short handed in diplomatic history after all, and had succeeded in having Professor Frank Anderson, of Dartmouth College, cabled for to join me and take over that part of the Division of History. I had a personal satisfaction in this, as Anderson worked with me in the summer when I transferred the Division of History to Columbia University Library, and he, with Professor Hershey, drew up lengthy studies and memoranda. The State Department, however, at first barred his coming.]

Monday, January 20, 1919

Stayed in my room all day with a slight cold. Lunch with Colonel Cox from General Headquarters.

Dinner with Feisal and Lawrence—His Royal Highness Emir Feisal, son of the King of the Hejaz and Sherif of Mecca, and

Colonel Lawrence, of the British army, the conqueror of Damascus. It was a small dinner arranged by Beer. The other guests were Bullitt, the young journalist who clips the day's news for the Commissioners and sometimes edits it orally for them; Bowman; Westermann (as the specialist on Turkey); and two lieutenants, Wanger and Osborne, who work with Beer.

The Emir wore a long black gown with sleeves, like a professor's gown, with no embroidery except on the shoulder, where there was a network pattern of thread of gold. He wore over his head a light silk cloth that hung down to the shoulders and was tucked away inside the gown in easy folds. Around his head, on top of this simple substitute for a turban, were two rows of large, white braid, bound together by a single gold string. The effect was singularly like a crown. His face was one of the most attractive I have ever seen, beautifully shaped, with clear, dark eyes that struck us all as being those of a man who, although he has been facing constant danger for many years, retains an irresistible sense of humor. He carries a golden dagger in his girdle, which is woven of gold thread, and when someone remarked on it said that the Parisians said he was only half civilized because he carried a dagger—but their officers carry swords! This descendant of Mohammed was cracking jokes all evening, even in the midst of his most serious argument for the Arab cause. When he was asked what his right title was, he said that the Western Powers were imagining that they had conferred a favor on his father by calling him king; but his father was only amazed at their impertinence, seeing that a man who was the descendant of the Prophet and Sherif of Mecca bore so proud a title that it could not matter to him whether men called him, in addition, King, Emperor, President, or Donkey. His ancestors had been Sherifs of Mecca for 900 years, and no other title in the world compared in splendor. One hundred and eighty million Mohammedans share his view. Later, when he was presenting the Arab case, he interjected: "You know that out in the desert we often tie the camels head to tail in a long row, and then we put a little donkey at the head to lead the line. Lawrence has been that little donkey." But here were present not one American donkey but seven! What might they not be able to do for Arabia! If they would go out to Arabia they might see for themselves the justice of his demands. Then there would be statues erected to them all over Syria! Noting that we were seven, he recalled the Arab proverb: "When seven agree, the world will become heaven or be utterly destroyed."

His story of the Arab independence movement kept us till about midnight. Colonel Lawrence had to do all the translating, for when they were together in the East, as Feisal jokingly said, Lawrence was so set on learning Arabic that he couldn't be got to talk English, and as he, Feisal, distrusted and disliked the French and so would not learn their language, there was no way to talk except through Colonel Lawrence. But all the same he caught on to what we were doing, and when Bowman asked for his autograph on the dinner card he remarked that everyone of us wrote backwards and he alone wrote forwards. He asked for Bowman's dinner card in return, and then, bubbling with laughter, asked for a fountain pen and wrote just above his name a line of Arabic and showed it to Lawrence, who said that it read, "I agree to all of Feisal's demands."

Lawrence came in the uniform of a British colonel but wore his Arab headdress to keep his friend company (they wore them through the meal and all the evening.) His veil over his explorer's helmet was of green silk and hung down over his shoulder with a tassel or two of deep red. Around his head was a similar double strand of big, corded braid, as in the case of Feisal's, about three-quarters of an inch in diameter and looking much like a crown. He has been described as the most interesting Briton alive, a student of medieval history at Magdalen College, where he used to sleep by day and work by night and take his recreation in the deer park at four in the morning—a Shelley-like person, and yet too virile to be a poet. He is a rather short, strongly built man of not over twenty-eight years, with sandy complexion, a typical English face, bronzed by the desert, remarkable blue eyes and a smile around the mouth that responded swiftly to that on the face of his friend. The two men were obviously very fond of each other. I have seldom seen such mutual affection between grown men as in this instance. Lawrence would catch the drift of Feisal's humor and pass the joke along to us while Feisal was still exploding with his idea; but all the same it was funny to see how Feisal spoke with the oratorical feeling of the South and Lawrence translated in the lowest and quietest of English voices, in very simple and direct phrases, with only here and there a touch of Oriental poetry breaking through.

Among the experiences which Lawrence recited none was more

interesting than his description of what the motor car and the airplane have done to the desert. He got in his airplane out east of the
Jordan one morning, crossed over to Jerusalem to see General
Allenby, flew down to Cairo to lunch with the Sirdar of Egypt, then
on to Alexandria for a call and back to Jerusalem for afternoon tea
(it once took forty years to make the Egypt-Jerusalem trip), and
had time before dark to write out his dispatches and plan the next
day's campaign, having flown a thousand miles in one day in addition to the day's work. He says that after airplaning in the desert
one doesn't want to fly anywhere else. One can land anywhere at
any time in safety. The British have established a three-day route
across the Arabian desert from India to Cairo, with one stop at an
oasis for lunch in the Arabian desert, passing the night at Basra, and
making only one more stop en route to Delhi. He explained the
change in desert fighting which the airplane has brought about. The
Arabs have to come to water holes, with their camels; an airplane
with a machine gun sets out for each water hole and settles down
to wait. . . .

Automobiling also is a rare sport and there are two ways of doing
it. One is to have a Rolls-Royce and put it through at fifty miles
an hour, so that it just catches the tops of the dust bumps and
almost goes like an airplane. The other way is to have a series of
Ford cars stretching across the desert, so that as soon as one breaks
down another can be taken. Either one beats camel riding. Feisal
invited us all to come to within ten miles of Mecca to visit him. His
father wouldn't mind our coming all the way, but some fanatics in
India would think that the Sherif was an unbeliever too, so he
guesses it would be best to meet us some miles out from the sacred
town. The story of his demands, the serious part of the evening, is
being jotted down by Westermann in another chronicle, but Feisal
completely won his audience.

Tuesday, January 21, 1919

A visit in my room from Dr. C. T. Wang [1] who, although technically in rebellion against the Chinese Government, has joined the
Chinese Delegation. Nothing could be more typical of China.
Formerly head of the Chinese Senate in the short-lived experiment
of a Chinese Parliament, he had joined his Cantonese friends in

[1] Later the well-known Foreign Minister of the Chinese Republic through some
of its most critical years.

revolt against the *coup d'état* of the Peking Government. A convinced republican, he came over to the United States during the war
to carry on propaganda against the Peking Government. I met him
first in the apartment of Francis Sayre, President Wilson's son-in-
law, and he visited me once or twice in my own house as well. He is
working with those who are his enemies in China; but the incongruity of the situation seems less evident to them than to us. The
Chinese Delegation is at least united in opposition to the Japanese in
Shantung and also in the expectation that the United States will not
let China down. Dr. Wang left a document with me for later discussion. I arranged to take it up with him, Miller, and Hornbeck at
lunch tomorrow.

From China to Yugoslavia! Dr. Bogumil Vosnjak came to discuss
the Slovene question and to renew his acquaintance from New York
days. He will supply us with the official documents, particularly
with reference to a plebiscite which has been held in the country of
the Slovenes and which shows a great growth of Yugoslav feeling. A
copy of a second plebiscite taken in the districts bordering Italy
will be on hand, to try to meet Italian claims.

Lunch with Mantoux, the official interpreter of the Conference,
whom Beer and I met the other evening at Max Lazard's. He
described interviews between Lloyd George and the French, but
nothing very essential came out.

Dinner with Barry of the Associated Press, a young man who
spent three years with Hoover in Belgium. He was then with the
Italians for eight months. Now he comes back from a journey across
the Balkans to Constantinople from which he went to Odessa. That
part of the world is still so isolated as a result of the war that we
eagerly seize the chance to talk to any returning traveller.

During the day we finished and sent in the memorandum on international labor legislation. The whole series of memoranda, of which
this is one, is now finished, and all will go in together.

[This series of short general statements by the heads of the
Divisions of the Inquiry was the answer to President Wilson's request of January first. Each memorandum was kept down to the
merest skeleton of an outline so that the whole body of material
would not be too long for the Commissioners to have at hand for
ready reference. Gathered together by Dr. Bowman, the typewritten
pages were bound in a black cardboard cover. Only enough copies

of this text were typed to give one to each of the Commissioners and to have the necessary extra number of reference copies kept under lock and key in the office. The collection was known as the "Black Book" to those who were aware of its existence.[1] Later an additional companion collection was prepared, with red typed headings and a red binder, to include suggestions not incorporated in the "Black Book," especially covering colonial matters. The "Red Book," along with the "Black Book," furnished the final statement of the Inquiry. Prior to the actual negotiations, they represented the findings of the American specialists which they recommended to the Commissioners for insertion in the Treaty. In the succeeding weeks there was naturally some modification of these views, but the "Black Book" and the "Red Book" will remain for the historian the central statement of the work of the Inquiry and its contribution to the Peace Treaty.

My own memorandum, reduced to three short pages of typewriting, was buttressed by a comparative survey of the minimum age of employment in various countries and in the States of the Union, as well as by a tabular comparison of provisions for preventing night work by women in industry. The memorandum follows.]

RECOMMENDATIONS RELATIVE TO LEGISLATION IN REGARD TO INTERNATIONAL LABOR

I. *Existing International Agreements:*

The body of general international agreements existing between the European Powers with reference to Labor Legislation should properly be made the starting point for action by the present conference. From these covenants the following recommendations are suggested for immediate adoption in the Treaty of Peace:

1. The prohibition of the employment in industrial labor of children less than 14 years of age.
2. The imposition of proper restrictions upon the night labor of women and youths less than 16 years of age.
3. The application of domestic protective labor legislation to resident and migratory aliens.

II. *Relation to the League of Nations:*

Future development of International Labor Legislation should be provided for in the structure of the League of Nations, as follows:

[1] Its official name in Paris was "Outline of Tentative Report and Recommendations Prepared by the Intelligence Section, in Accordance with Instructions, for the President and the Plenipotentiaries, January 21, 1919."

A Periodic Conference upon the international aspect of labor legislation in general, and

A Bureau to serve these periodic conferences by the study of such aspects of labor legislation, and by the compilation of statistical, experimental, and other information.

Comment on the Proposals for Legislation

I. There exists a small but important body of general treaties by which the European Powers, through joint agreement, have mutually bound themselves to certain measures of labor legislation. These general European covenants should now be made universal. The experience of Europe has definitely established that such international action is effective in raising the level of the standards of civilization, as the following facts indicate:

1. *Child Labor.*—In 1890, when the series of International Labor Conferences was inaugurated at Berlin, twelve of the fifteen European countries which had laws protecting child labor permitted children from nine to twelve years of age to work in factories. In 1918 twenty-three states in Europe had enacted child labor laws, and thirteen of them, including the chief industrial nations, had made thirteen or fourteen the minimum age of employment.

2. *Labor of Women and of Young Persons.*—Prior to 1906, when the Berne Conference recommended a nightly rest of eleven hours for women in industry, there were no laws on the subject in fifteen European states, and only one required as much as eleven hours. As an immediate result of the Berne conference, nearly every European country has enacted into law the eleven-hour nightly rest for women and young persons.

3. *Migratory Labor.*—The need of international agreement with reference to the labor of aliens has been keenly felt in Europe. It has two aspects: the protection of the immigrant and the protection of the native from his competition; both of which are met by insisting upon his participation in social legislation, either of his country of origin (by reciprocal agreements) or his country of residence. Such legislation would make universal the application of existing laws.

Comment on
International Labor Conferences and Bureau

The League of Nations should have a periodic Conference for international labor problems similar to those for colonial or economic problems. The composition of this conference would be determined by the governments of the various countries; but it should include some representatives of Labor, as has been the case in the Berne Conferences.

Such conferences would assume much the same functions as are implied in the proposed Labor Parliaments referred to in the programs of the Labor leaders. They should work in close articulation with the Secretariat of the League of Nations.

The Bureau for the study of Labor Legislation could be based directly upon the existing organization known as the International Bureau for Labor Legislation, which has its central office in Switzerland, but which has affiliated with it various national Committees, such as the American Association for Labor Legislation. Indeed, this admirable organization can be taken over and made responsible to the Secretariat of the League of Nations. It has a long and successful experience upon which to build.

Wednesday, January 22, 1919

Moved to room 426 Crillon, on the sixth floor facing south, a lighter and better room, with better air. My cold is gone. There are four army doctors with offices installed in the Crillon, waiting to spray our throats or noses. Patients are more than welcome, for if no one calls they cannot stay at the Peace Conference. So far they need have no worry on that score. There seem to be millions of throat germs going around, and a number of diplomats have lost their voices altogether. This old world is badly germ-ridden. It is soaked with disease. The cost of living is atrocious. People are underfed and live in underheated houses. The long strain of the war is showing, too, in both health and morale. Things that should be done don't seem to matter. This is a poor place for anyone to live in who can escape it, and everyone says privations in England are worse.

Luncheon with Wang, Miller, and Hornbeck. The subject was the program of the Chinese Delegation with reference to the denunciation of the treaties with Germany and Austria. He wanted this done at this stage of the negotiation so as to establish a precedent for the treatment of Japan later. He developed the story of the Chinese international history as follows:

After the defeat by Japan in 1894, the Chinese decided to learn what was wrong with the oldest of civilizations. About a hundred thousand students went to Japan, many more than those who left for America and Europe. These returned students have been the directing minds of China, but they differ according to their training. Those who have been in Japan are for a monarchy, or at least for Oriental political methods, and these have been in control at Peking, while the liberal element is in the south. Hence the civil war which they are just patching up. China now wants to begin to free itself from foreign control by getting rid of jurisdiction of foreign governments, making a start with Germany and Austria, its late enemies.[1]

[The document which Dr. Wang had left with me the day before came up for technical discussion. It was a well thought out plan to take the first step towards the abolition of extraterritoriality in the treaties with ex-enemy Powers and then proceed to deal with those which had been technically its allies. The document in which this proposal was set forth is short enough, covering only two pages of typewriting, and, in view of later events, interesting enough, to quote in full. The casual element in negotiations of this kind is shown by the unfinished text of the tenth point in the Chinese program, which I added in ink in the course of our conversation; nevertheless, it resulted in Article 131 of the Treaty of Versailles, which restored the famous old astronomical instruments to Peking.]

ARTICLE OF PEACE PROTOCOL REGARDING THE REPUBLIC OF CHINA

I. *General Preamble*

Due provision for the future being even more important than reparation for the past, a just respect for the opinions of mankind, as well as world-wide desire really to unite the peoples of all the earth in a peace of victorious justice, of enlightened, common interest and of mutual benefit, requires that Germany and Austria-Hungary shall renounce absolutely and forever all rights and advantages, both public and private, deriving their authority or inspiration from the treaties entered into be-

[1] Mr. Miller's Diary (I, 88) gives a clearer account of Dr. Wang's conversation: "Mr. Wang discussed a paper [Document 215] of which Doctor Shotwell had sent me a copy, which was the Chinese idea as to the Treaty so far as relations between China and the enemy Powers were concerned. Mr. Wang's idea was that the rights of Germany and Austria-Hungary should cease and that they should not have the same privileges as other Powers of extra-territoriality, etc., but that they should have to make a commercial treaty, if they wanted to, with China on China's own terms. Hornbeck's idea was that there should be equality but that Germany should not be able to block China's progress toward release from the limits on her sovereignty. I suggested that China might properly present her whole case rather than simply the part of it which related to Germany and Austria as the matter was bound up with her relations with Japan and the Allies in the West."

Mr. Miller also notes that at lunch I handed him a memorandum on the treatment of Napoleon, Document 216 of the Miller collection, in connection with the problem of the treatment of the Kaiser.

It is interesting to recall that it was during these days that the work on the drafting of the Covenant got definitely under way. It was on January 22 that Wilson proposed at the Council of Ten that the drafting of the League Covenant should go to a small commission of the Great Powers. See Miller, *The Drafting of the Covenant*, I, 83.

tween the government of China and the imperial governments of Germany and Austria-Hungary, especially the treaty of Tientsin of September 2, 1861, between China and Germany, the treaty of Peking of September 2, 1869, between China and Austria-Hungary, the treaty of March 6, 1898, between China and Germany (commonly known as the Kiaochow Convention and the Railway and Mining Concessions), and such parts of the protocol of September 7, 1901, conveying or authorizing any rights whatever within the sovereign domain of China to either the governments or all and sundry beneficiaries of the governments of Germany and Austria-Hungary.

Furthermore, all agreements, concessions, conventions, protocols, and treaties, being the offspring of the acts of war committed upon China by the imperial government of Germany, and contrary to the spirit as well as to the letter of the policy enunciated in the note of September 6, 1899, addressed by the Secretary of State of the United States of America to the governments of all the Powers, and duly and fully accepted and affirmed by them, shall be and they now are denounced and abrogated.

For the purpose of giving full effect to this article of the protocols of peace, the Allied and Associated Powers do hereby assure to the government and people of China their rightful place in the family of nations, complete and actual preservation of Chinese sovereignty and of the entirety of the domain of China, and full and complete retrocession of all rights, claims, concessions, or undertakings whatsoever, obtained by the governments and nationals of Germany and Austria-Hungary, which are hereby declared to be subversive of universal interest in world peace. Such assurance must and shall provide for complete recognition of the sovereign rights of China in accordance with the expressed will of the government and people of the Republic of China and of the associated interest and sympathy of enlightened humanity.

II. *Programme*

1. Abrogation of the "Most Favored Nation" clause.
   (Tientsin treaty with Germany, article 40.)
   (Peking treaty with Austria-Hungary, article 43.)
   (Yen's suggested draft, article 10.)
2. Restoration of the leased territories of Kiaochow and cancellation of all railway, mining and other rights.
3. Restoration of German and Austria-Hungarian concessions.
4. Recognition of the annulment of extraterritorial rights hitherto enjoyed by the subjects of Germany and Austria-Hungary.
5. Recognition of the annulment of the right to install postal and telegraph offices by Germany and Austria-Hungary.
6. Recognition of the annulment of the portion of indemnity required of China to be paid to Germany and Austria-Hungary in accordance with the Protocol of 1901.

7. Recognition of the annulment of the right for Germany and Austria-Hungary to quarter troops upon the territory of China.
8. Recognition of China's taking over of
   (a) arms, munitions, barracks found in the territory of China upon the declaration of war with Germany and Austria-Hungary.
   (b) ships, wharves, pontoons, etc.
   (c) public buildings and establishments other than diplomatic, consular and philanthropic.
9. Acceptance of reparation and restitution for damages done to, and expenses incurred by, China.
   (a) Properties, moveable and immoveable, destroyed or damaged.
   (b) Care of prisoners of war and other interned subjects.
   (c) Other claims in accordance with the principles to be adopted by the Peace Conference.
10. Restoration to China the looting of Peking in 1900.

Thursday, January 23, 1919

Professors Anderson and Notestein arrived with messages and letters from New York. Anderson is to be in the Division of History, and I spent the morning with him planning work. Notestein is assigned Germany as his territory—an impossible field for effective research today. Lunch with Austin Evans of Columbia, who asked for assistants in the educational scheme, and I recommended Harold Crandall, a former student of mine, who had called the day before to ask the chances of getting released from his present job of buying lumber for the United States army, which no one either buys or sells any more. He had just come in from travelling in the south of France, two days of solid misery in unheated trains. Bayonne was as cold as Iceland.

Ray Stannard Baker's publicity office asked help in framing a statement on questions of international waterways, as it previously had on labor, and Anderson spent the evening working with Sweetser preparing a statement to be cabled through to the American press. My own time given to labor problems.

Tea in my room with Phelan, Butler, Assistant Minister of Labour, and Sir Malcolm Delevingne, of the Home Office, who had just come from the French Ministry of Labor with news as to what Clemenceau is proposing to take up on Saturday at the plenary session of the Conference. The British proposal is to make sure first of an organization for future international labor legislation and not to insist on any one provision in the present preliminaries. This, under the circumstances, is better than my proposal to have three main international agreements now, leaving the future development for periodic conferences under the League of Nations.[1] Young and I prevailed upon Dr. Mezes to see Colonel House and acquaint him with the new situation, which he did. The Colonel expressed his appreciation and sent back his thanks, for the plans in hand for Saturday were unknown to him until we sent him word.

[This conference with the British rounded off the first phase of my work in labor legislation. While I had been preparing the statement for the Commissioners, the British labor section had been shaping up their suggestions in the form of a Draft Convention for actual negotiation. The French also had been busy preparing their plans. Clemenceau's request at the first plenary session for a memorandum from each of the delegations was met with what at first sight seems to be almost incredible speed. The summary of the French plans was sent in to M. Pichon on the twentieth, and the British Empire Delegation received a statement of the British proposals on the twenty-first, the same day that my own memorandum was sent in to Colonel House. But behind this apparent improvisation there had been long and careful preparation; the British plan was the most complete, with draft clauses ready for actual negotiations. The gossip which the British brought along was that a Commission for International Labor Legislation would actually be set up at the plenary session on Saturday. I therefore continued the preparation of material for the use of the American Delegation and our representatives on the Labor Commission, whoever they might be.]

Dinner at the Majestic to meet those representing the Empire of India. Beer, Bowman, and I were guests of the Maharajah of Bikaner; the Secretary of State for India, Mr. Montagu; Lord Sinha, Assistant Secretary for India and representative in the House of Lords; Lionel Curtis; Sir Dunlop Smith, brother of Sir George Adam Smith, the archeologist, a typical soldier of India, with a Scotch accent direct from the heather; and another belted knight, who represents England in an Indian State of some four million inhabitants, the name of which I did not get. At another Indian table next to ours the Maharajah proudly pointed out his

[1] Cf. January 21; the "Black Book" proposal.

son and heir, the boy being about twenty and the Maharajah only thirty-eight. Lloyd George and his gay little daughter were present, as before; and Borden and Smuts and those from the other Dominions were seated around at the various tables, as usual.

I sat next to the Maharajah, who has all the easy manner of an English gentleman. It was a new experience to sit beside a king and to listen to his description of his royal progresses from village to village in his little State, dispensing justice, at least once every three years. In the years intervening, apparently the head men in the village democracies settle local questions, much as with us. He was very proud of the railway he had built and of the progress of his State. He amused himself initiating me in the use of Indian red pepper, of which two grains are strong enough to season a whole oyster. He had brought his own little box of red pepper along. The cooking was English in everything except that no beef was served, as the sacred cow must not be killed in India, a prohibition which Sir Dunlop Smith assured me was as wise in reference to the Hindus in saving cattle as the Mosaic prohibitions were in the food of the desert people like the Bedouins. I should add that the Indians dress in the uniforms of British officers, and the only signs of distinction are the orders across their breasts.

After dinner we went to another room in the hotel, down a long, unlighted corridor. The British are not burning fuel as we do at the Crillon, and the room was so cold that I had to return for my overcoat and sit with it draped over my shoulders, oriental-wise, the rest of the evening. We had hardly got going in our conversation when the telephone rang and another Indian dignitary was announced, the famous Aga Khan, leader of a sect of Mohammedans from India to Central Africa and through the wild sections of Central Asia. He is the modern descendant of the old sect of the Assassins, and has unlimited authority although no territory. He is believed to be more than a prophet, a divine incarnation. The Aga Khan lives most of his time in Paris. He is said to have a tremendous hold on his fanatical followers, however. When those in the Afghan frontier rose in rebellion during this war and were making much trouble, the Indian Government tried to find the Aga Khan, but he was off in Paris, so his mother issued a document with a seal on it as big as a saucer and sent it back to the British, who got it through to the hillsmen, and they came in next morning with ropes of grass around their necks, and holding out the rope-ends offered them to the British officers, saying, "Take us; do what you want with us."

The Aga Khan has written a book called *India in Transition,* which is a first-class survey of modern India. He engaged Montagu in serious controversy on Indian education, insisting that if Britain would lessen its army of occupation, India could afford a better school system. Money should be spent for primary education instead of for fine college buildings. Montagu asked about education in the Philippines, and Bowman and Beer put me up as the American specialist on the subject! I managed to scrape together every item of information my memory contained; unfortunately the psychologists tell us that the functions of memory and imagination are substantially one. Once I tried to shift the conversation to another subject, that of the education of the "poor whites" in the South, but I found that His Holiness had traveled there and knew more about the situation than I did. It hardly seemed fair. It was half-past twelve when we got home.

Beer tells me that while I was talking to the Maharajah, he had an important conversation with Montagu and Lord Sinha, both of whom strongly support his idea that German East Africa should be placed under India as mandatory.

Friday, January 24, 1919

Work with Anderson in the morning; the Division of Diplomatic History gets under way. Rivers, railways and ports to the fore.

In the evening I took Bowman to dine at the Majestic with the Right Honorable George Barnes, Sir Malcolm Delevingne, Mr. Butler, and Mr. Phelan. We dined in the same large dining room, with our friends of the Empire of India slipping past me to their places, and Lloyd George's little daughter meeting us once more in the corridor. There were fewer in the room, however, as it was a gala night at the opera. I had hardly got started with the first course when a group of English officers came in and took the corner table facing me, and the man whose face was turned directly my way I recognized at once as Sir Douglas Haig. He is not a very impressive general. He is, like so many of these soldiers, prematurely gray, and his bearing is rather that of a quiet, thoughtful man than of a man of action. He seemed to be a little tired and to lose interest in the conversation at his table, but when an American general, whom I did not recognize, joined the group he became quite animated and they evidently exchanged good stories.

As for our own dinner party, I found Mr. Barnes a straightforward, intelligent man, of a substantial, wholesome type, whose strength is rather moral than intellectual. He has none of the fire of Kier Hardie, but he has been fighting labor battles for almost half a century and is now sixty years old. He and Sir Malcolm, who sat at my right, have been appointed the British Commissioners on international labor, and they were kind enough to hope that I might be appointed to work with them from the American side, as we have got along well together. But no such luck. After dinner Sir Malcolm talked interestingly of his experiences in past international labor conferences. He represents the Home Office as well as that most competent body of public officials of which any government can boast, the British Civil Service, and, as the British representative in the pre-War conferences, has a mastery over the whole subject in its Continental as well as its British background. In temperament the very opposite of Barnes, he is quick and keen in discussion, downright and direct in critical comment, but shows a courtesy and regard for his chief which is distinctly pleasing. Mr. Butler has the quiet Oxford manner, but when he intervenes it is always to the point. They would be great colleagues to work with on a constructive program such as they have brought with them. They are intent upon heading off premature legislation now and concentrating everything on the instrument of the League of Nations. Home by 11 P.M. Exchanged views on problems with Beer till midnight.

[It is to these men, along with M. Fontaine, who spiritually belongs with them, that the International Labor Organization owes its very existence. My friendship with them, forged as it was in the heat of discussion and argument in succeeding weeks, was one of the richest rewards of the Peace Conference days. But it has the one disadvantage that it makes the expression of my regard for them and their work more difficult. To the documentary history of the International Labor Office will have to be left the full story.[1] The discriminating historian will detect in its impersonal narrative their varied contributions in that historic task.]

[1] Cf. *The Origins of the International Labor Organization.*

Morning in my room straightening up.

Afternoon—The second session of the Peace Conference met at three o'clock, the session at which Wilson made his great speech. I had a ticket this time and was all ready to go when Dr. Bowman rang me up to say that Admiral Trowbridge, the British Admiral who had been in charge of Danubian shipping, was coming to his office with Mezes, Seymour, and Day to discuss free waterways and especially the Danube, and they needed me to join in, with a refreshed knowledge of Danubian history. So there was nothing to do but swallow my disappointment and forget about the Quai d'Orsay. I had a ripping headache and treaty clauses did not appeal to me, although Dr. Slosson had sat up the night before to prepare Chamberlain's monograph [1] for speedy consumption by Commissioner Henry White, Mezes, Bowman, and myself against the Admiral's coming.

Trowbridge is the man who let the "Breslau" and "Goeben" escape at the opening of the War but was acquitted by the court martial by proving that his actions were controlled by the code instructions he had received purporting to come from the Admiralty, while in reality they came from the German warships. In any case, he had more decorations sewed on his coat than he could get on one side and had started a bright patch of color on the other. A British admiral has yards of gold lace on his sleeves, about twice as much as ours, but he was a quiet-mannered, unassuming talker, set upon presenting his case as the main thing. He is now in command at Belgrade, and after having directed the water-borne transportation of the eastern Mediterranean during the war, is now keen on developing the river systems so as to open up those countries. He has some eighty-three ships at present running cargoes on the Danube, and pointed out that he could put behind one tug ten barges with as much in them as in three hundred train loads. We asked him who owned the ships and he said, "I don't know, I'm running them. This is war-time. When you fellows make peace, then someone will have to find the owners. At present I am running

---

[1] Professor Joseph Chamberlain was the American authority on questions of river transit, especially on the Danube and the Rhine. The reference is to his memorandum covering the legal history of European waterways which was prepared for the Inquiry. This is a good example of the way in which the studies of academic colleagues were put to practical use during negotiations.

the Danube, and for the first time in its history I am sending ships to any port free of embarrassing harbor dues, tariffs or any other of your political devices. There are tons of food up in Hungary and thousands of starving people in Serbia, so I send up ships and get the food to the people who need it; the same with coal. The Bosnian farmers have tons of plum marmalade they can't eat and need to sell. I am going to move that plum marmalade before you fellows make the peace." These are casual indications of the outlook of a man of action.

Then he went on to develop his vision, which was that of free waterways all over Europe by which goods could be shipped from British ports and sent up the Rhine or the Elbe and across canals to the Danube. The Germans have a cross-country canal now. It does not draw much over six feet of water, but somehow boats from the Krupp works came under his guns at Belgrade. He sank two of them and got the German sailors, so he knew what he was talking about. But at present territorial boundaries have to be crossed and tariffs paid. All the great waterways should be free. He said that this vision of free riverways is forced upon a man who sits in Belgrade and sees that wonderful river practically unused. He wants to connect the Morava with the Vardar and so get a waterway to Saloniki. He knows the Serbs well, having served with their army during the war, and hopes they will not be too modernized, as they have a complete farming democracy. Only three men in Serbia own more than a hundred acres. But the Danube must not be their northern frontier, as there are Serbs for sixty miles north of it. When he crossed the river into Neusatz the inhabitants were so Serb that in an hour's time business was going on as usual in spite of changed sovereignty; and when he was at Belgrade, before the Austrians took it, and had heavy guns that could shoot into villages north of the river, the Serbs would not let him shoot because they said, "Those are our brothers and mustn't be disturbed." Anyway a river is a bad boundary line, because you don't know what the other fellow is doing across it. The best line is a row of white stones across an open country where each can see the other and you have no misunderstanding of what they are doing. A row of these white stones now marks the line across Macedonia between Greece and Serbia, and it has been there long enough for the people to get used to it, so it is accepted as permanent. Moreover, the Serbs are not so keen about Macedonia now that they have lived there; it is a barren country with meager possibilities, and all the Serbs were eager to get home to the more smiling landscapes around Uskub and north. They will be satisfied with the arrangements made at Saloniki, where the Greeks are to allow them separate shipping facilities in the harbor. The Serbs and the Greeks refuse to be drawn into a conflict which one of the Allied leaders, whose name I withhold, seemed to want to foment. As for the Bulgarian boundary, it might stand where the Bulgars had it before the war except that the Bulgars should not be allowed to control the railway by having territory so close that they could cross the line to attack a bridge at night. The railway is now running as far as Uskub, but from there on the destruction was carried out thoroughly by the Germans on their retreat. The southern part of the railway is not completely destroyed, the Germans were driven out too quickly; but when they had time they perpetrated a crime not in the laws of war. In the week of the armistice they so wrecked that part of the line, blowing up tunnels, bridges, culverts, embankments and all, that it will take a year to rebuild it. As this had no military value, it simply prevents the country from peaceful rehabilitation.

Asked about the Albanians, whom he knows very well, having been through their country on foot, he said that the central parts should be independent but that the rest was problematic, and so I shall leave it out of my chronicle. He told a good story on Miss Durham, who had formerly greatly admired the Montenegrins, until nursing one hero she incautiously looked in his bag and found sixty human noses, the trophies of his hunt. Then, he said, she transferred her admiration to Albanians.

Evening—Haskins and I dined with Sylvain Lévi, the distinguished French Orientalist. My first glimpse of the real hardships of France during the war in winter-time: ice-cold and pitch-black corridors and a little heat in a grate stove, which they seemed to find very comfortable after the real hardships of the War. Professor Lévi has begun his courses at the Collège de France, but he says that it is impossible to take up the old subjects with anything like the detachment of the scientific mind again. His interest in the archeology of India is only casual compared with his interest in the present.

Our orderly was waiting at the door at 10 P.M., and we were glad to be driven home through the relatively deserted streets, as the Metro strike and the omnibus strike have paralyzed transportation.

[This second meeting of the Conference, which I had missed attending, furnished the framework for so much of what follows that it is necessary to insert a description of what took place at it.[1] It not only launched the League of Nations but was the beginning of the organization of the Conference itself, with the appointment of five commissions charged with the duty of examining the following questions:

1. League of Nations.
2. Responsibility of the authors of the War and enforcement of penalties.
3. Reparation of damage.
4. International Legislation on Labor.
5. International Control of Ports, Waterways, and Railways.

The speeches on the question of the League of Nations were made by Wilson, Lloyd George, Orlando and Léon Bourgeois. At the close of these eloquent appeals, Mr. Hughes of Australia interjected the note of distrust by asking whether it would be possible to discuss the scheme when it was complete. Short statements from Mr. Lou of China and Mr. Dmowski of Poland followed, and then M. Hymans interjected the next note of disharmony by turning from the question of the League to that of procedure. Clemenceau had announced that the commissions were to consist of fifteen members, two appointed by each of the five great Powers and five others to represent all the Powers with special interests. The representatives of the smaller nations then broke loose, Hymans being supported by Sir Robert Borden of Canada, Trumbić of Serbia, Venizelos of Greece, Beneš of Czechoslovakia, Bratianu of Rumania, and others. Clemenceau's reply was, as Beer commented in his Diary, firm to the point of bluntness. In answer to the challenge as to the right of the great Powers to determine by themselves the organization of the Conference, he declared that their credentials lay in the vastness of their sacrifice, in their millions of dead and wounded. Then he turned on his critics who had been raising several different kinds of objections. "I would beg M. Hymans and all those who followed him to let me keep to the point. As soon as

[1] Cf. *Preliminary Peace Conference, Protocol No. 2,* Session of January 25, 1919, printed by the American Delegation to Negotiate Peace.

I indulgently allowed him to wander from it, as soon as the door was opened, everybody rushed in and discussed everything except the subject under discussion. It is my duty to guide the Conference in its work in order to obtain a result. . . . The public is waiting . . . I want to get on. I should very much like you to make up your minds today. . . . You might vote on all the proposals which we put before you today, reserving the right, which all Assemblies have, to insert amendments." Then followed a typical instance of Clemenceau's diplomacy. "Gentlemen, since I began to take part in these discussions I have sacrificed a certain number of personal opinions. I have done this cheerfully, feeling that I was doing something good and useful for the Common Cause. That was what I said to myself just now on hearing the noble words of President Wilson and Mr. Lloyd George. Let all of us, Gentlemen, be animated by the same spirit. The Bureau [1] never wished to hurt anybody at all. On the contrary, it would like to unite you all in one group. Let us, then, start work at once, and in the meantime claims will be presented and your Bureau able to start work." [2]]

Sunday, January 26, 1919

Morning—Spent in my room. First snow of the winter, about half an inch, which melts on the mansards as it falls.

Beer at lunch described his impressions of yesterday's session of the Conference at which he was present. Clemenceau's brutal frankness about the five great Powers and their 12,000,000 men in arms as their title deeds. Belgium's protest taken up by all the lesser Powers, seeking places on commissions. The threat of rebellion was badly handled.

At 2 P.M. I called on Curtis at the Majestic, and while waiting had a few minutes with Sir Malcolm Delevingne and Phelan, attempting to explain the American idea of representation on commissions by men who have a general public reputation at home.

Five o'clock; visit to the apartment of M. Dolléans to meet Francis Delaisi and Ofesty, writers on the labor question from opposite angles. Ofesty a burly, bureaucratic gentleman from the Ministry of Labor; Delaisi more of an economist. Little came of

---

[1] I.e., those in charge of the arrangements.
[2] The result of this application of the steam roller was the nomination of the commissioners on the five commissions to deal with the subjects agreed upon.

the interview, since they were more anxious to learn about America than to describe conditions here.

In the evening dinner in Dr. Mezes' rooms for Mr. and Mrs. Miller, Beer, and myself, which Colonel and Mrs. House joined as we were finishing. Mrs. House was very much interested in her forthcoming visit to Madrid, where she is to be the guest of the American Ambassador and of the Court. The etiquette of the Spanish Court still keeps some flavor of the old régime; only certain kinds of dresses can be worn in the royal presence. The Colonel has been having a pleasant afternoon reading his own obituary, written by Count Bernstorff for the Berlin papers. He has been quite ill for the last ten days, and false news of his demise has given Bernstorff a chance to say some nice things about him. He said that he enjoyed it all and was beginning to feel that he really had been a wise and good man in his lifetime, until someone suggested that it was all propaganda, that Bernstorff knew that he was alive and had merely seized upon the rumor to send in a piece of subtle flattery. When the men-folk went off to smoke in Mezes' room, Colonel House asked of Miller an account of the afternoon's meeting of the Societies for the League of Nations. There has been a convention of leaders of the movement for a league from various countries, and the speech of the afternoon was that of the English labor leader, J. H. Thomas. Mr. Miller had spoken briefly for America.[1] Colonel House was silent most of the evening, which threw the burden of conversation back on the rest of us. At eleven o'clock Beer and I came to my room to find Dr. Slosson had spent a day's religious work typing the plan of the British Labour Section to pass around to our International Law and History Sections. After considering its main provisions until the turning point into Monday morning, I went to bed.

Monday, January 27, 1919

Routine work in my room till lunch. Lunch with Van den Ven of the Belgian Commission and Mr. Maxwell Blake, American Consul General at Tangier. Beer present also. Blake had come to the Conference in the hope of reaching Lansing, or higher still, with his news from Morocco, but was turned over to Beer. A very decent

[1] Cf. Miller Diary, I, 92–3. This was a meeting of the Societies for the League of Nations, at which Mr. Hamilton Holt and Lord Cecil also had spoken. Mr. Miller also recorded, as did Beer, that Colonel House was not pleased with Clemenceau's brusque treatment of the small nations at the plenary session the day before.

fellow who has been eight years in Tangier and knows Morocco thoroughly. He paid a glowing tribute to the way in which the British in Morocco had co-operated with him in securing the open door and had freely shown him all their documentation. Never once in eight years had a British official in any way tried to mislead him, and this at a critical post where national rivalry was keen among Europeans. He left again for Tangier by the afternoon train, while the rest of us found a comfortable nook in Beer's room beside the open fire to discuss the case of Belgium, which has been badly mismanaged in these early sessions of the Conference, giving the Belgians a feeling that the great Powers, and especially America, on whom so many hopes had been placed, were not standing by Belgium in its demands. It was the same situation as Colonel House had been speaking of on Sunday evening.

Beer had to leave at quarter to three for the meeting of the secret session of the great Powers dealing with colonial questions, and returned after five o'clock to call me up to tell the news.[1] We dined together and celebrated the occasion with port wine. Discussed in Beer's room the issues raised till after nine. On the way up to my room I ran into Bowman and five or six colleagues. Joined them in Bowman's office until after eleven discussing our prospects individually and nationally and grouching until the air was blue. Went to sleep on Kipling's *Little Foxes,* which Warrin procured to cheer me up, and a copy of *Professor Knatsche* from Slosson.

Tuesday, January 28, 1919

Morning—Quiet work in my room. Anderson and I at diplomatic history and some dictation.

[1] Beer's Diary on this point is interesting enough to quote in full:
"Council of Ten at Quai d'Orsay continued the discussion of the mandatory principle and the exceptions to it. Japan claimed: (a) Kiao-Chow and railway, (b) German Islands north of Equator. Then Wilson answered these claims to exemption from the mandatory principle, outlining its nature and especially attacking claim of Union of South Africa and Australia. Outlined a very loose form of mandate, and then said if there was a financial deficit League of Nations would make it good to mandatory. Botha and Hughes answered him. All the speeches were rhetorical, inaccurate and not to the point. Hughes, for instance, did not distinguish between the cases of German New Guinea and the Bismarck Archipelago and Solomon Islands. At this point Lloyd George intervened clearly and said that question had been possible exemptions from the mandatory principle, but owing to Mr. Wilson's remarks about League of Nations making good deficits, the question at issue was principle itself, and before accepting it he would have to consult his colonial experts. Until he had done so he requested a postponement of the debate. Wilson expressed his poor opinion of experts who could be expert only in their field and that this was a new subject. Debate to be resumed tomorrow."

Lunch with Philip Kerr, Lloyd George's private secretary and formerly one of the leading members of the Round Table group. He is a nephew of the Duke of Norfolk and belongs to the oldest nobility in England, but that is a mere external. He is idealistic but practical at the same time, and it was an interesting occasion to discuss with him matters which Lloyd George had referred to him and his friends as a result of conferences on colonial questions yesterday and this morning. No one can live through these experiences without realizing how narrow a margin lies between success and failure at this Conference: for instance, in the question of financial responsibility of mandatory Powers to the League of Nations, or rather the responsibility of the League of Nations for the finances of colonial experiments carried out by individual Powers under its authority. This is an absolutely vital question. Would the United States be willing to become responsible for debts incurred in a French colonial experiment nominally under the League of Nations? This was not just the way our discussion ran, but it will indicate its character. In the next place, the fact that the first German colony to be discussed was German Southwest Africa, was absolutely discouraging, for there are few of the German colonies to which the mandatory system could apply so poorly as to this stretch of desert on the edge of the Union of South Africa.

The only cheerful note in the conversation came from the news of Wellington Koo's successful speech, on which Clemenceau warmly congratulated him. This is supposed not to be known, but it has got abroad already.

While the discussion on the colonies was going on, another meeting to deal with the representation of smaller Powers in the commissions of the Conference was held at the same time, under the presidency of Cambon, who succeeded in deftly preventing a small riot by keeping the envoys down to the business before them in the sternest possible way. Meanwhile, our own Colonel got busy to smooth ruffled tempers, and the heads of the Inquiry were engaged in social interviews with their respective small nations. Tonight the temperature is lower in the international atmosphere; and I am free to go out for the first time today, driving to the Majestic for Curtis to take him to Max Lazard's for dinner.

About five minutes before leaving, Beer came to my room, fresh from the Conference, where he had been at the afternoon session, with cheering news as to the possibility of his general plan being carried out by the three great Powers. He had walked home with Massey, Premier of New Zealand, and got him to see the bearing of the mandatory system in the Pacific. The unfortunate thing is that the discussion of the League of Nations should concentrate on South Africa at the first, instead of countries like Armenia. I was to see that Curtis carries the news along to his men, but I found at the Majestic that Smuts had already been in conference with Robert Cecil and that he would be dining with Lloyd George and talking it over at dinner. The English certainly have an efficient way of doing things, and they never leave them half done.

We drove on to Max Lazard's out in Neuilly, a long drive along the great Park of the Bois de Boulogne. As the ground is all covered with snow outside the city itself—not over an inch and a half—it gives one a little feeling of winter in America, but the air is not cold. A few slim sticks of wood in the fireplace furnish the only heat for a large room. It was a family party, with the exception of M. Aftalion, of the Direction des Approvisionnements des Étrangers, a French economist who knew the work of our American economists rather intimately. On arriving at the Crillon at 11:30 I call at Beer's room and discuss things till after midnight.

Experts Become Negotiators

Wednesday, January 29, 1919

A busy morning, including a call from Mr. Lambert, representing the farmers of the Canadian northwest, who will come again tomorrow. He brought a letter from the Hon. Walter Scott, the former Premier of Saskatchewan, and seems like a very worth while representative of western Canada. At luncheon discussed with Bullitt the mission to the Orient which Emir Feisal asked for, and Beer's memorandum on Africa. Dictated for Curtis a statement of the possibility of America's response to the Round Table suggestions of its assuming colonial obligations under the League. Arranged with Anderson for reports for one of the Commissioners. Discussed labor topics with Barry, of the Associated Press, and ran over an article on the African problem for the publicity bureau.

About six Beer drifted in with news of the afternoon's session over the Czechoslovaks. On the way out President Wilson had a very encouraging conversation with Beer and Seymour, the gist of which cannot go down here, but the result of which will be a very general co-operation between British and American specialists in the working out of problems before the Conference.

Miller had me over to dinner to talk over the report of the division chiefs of the Inquiry in which they stated the policies to be recommended for each problem area. The document went to Miller for study in order to see how he might get its points into the treaty, and he is sending it over to me so I can help advise him. He has a habit of hunting me up when he has jobs like this. He has a feeling that specialists studying local problems exclusively tend to present solutions that won't fit the whole. We planned to put on our joint staff Lieutenant Wanger, who is to go to the representatives of different governments and secure for us their documents as they come out.

[The conversation which President Wilson had with Beer and Seymour was destined to mark a distinct step in the history of the

153

Peace Conference. The session which the President had been attending in Pichon's study had been particularly discouraging because the British and Americans had not even the same facts before them. The President, coming out of the Commission, spoke about the slow rate of progress and then, turning to Beer and Seymour, said that they should get together with the British experts to present joint reports to expedite matters. This was what Beer had been specially anxious to bring about, and he came back to the Crillon very much excited over the possibilities which it opened up. It is true that we had been collaborating with the British, and to a lesser degree with the French, experts, but never with full authorization to do so nor in a systematic and organized way.

President Wilson on his part did not let the matter rest with his casual but pointed remark to Beer and Seymour, for he discussed the situation with Colonel House that night, as is evidenced by the entry in Colonel House's diary: "January 30, 1919: I sent for Sir William Tyrrell in accordance with the understanding I had with the President last night regarding the united report which we desire the British and American technical advisers to make concerning boundary questions. I put Tyrrell in touch with Mezes and urged them to facilitate the matter as much as possible." [1] But, as Professor Seymour points out, "Obviously it was unwise to restrict the special work to an informal and self-constituted committee." [2] Accordingly, within the next few days the Supreme Council set up separate Commissions for Rumanian, Polish, Czechoslovak, Greek and Albanian affairs. Other such commissions were set up during the weeks which followed, and the experts on these various organizations were called in from time to time to advise the Commissioners. By the end of the next month this machinery was so important an element in the organization of the Peace Conference that the Supreme Council, on February 27, set up a Central Co-ordinating Commission on Territorial Questions under the presidency of M. Tardieu, with Dr. Mezes as the American representative and Sir Eyre Crowe as the British, and with Professor Moon as the American secretary. This new Commission, however, conflicted in the American Delegation with the existing organization which Dr. Bowman had created, and, as will be noted later, it caused difficulties which were destined ultimately to affect not only the making of the

[1] *The Intimate Papers of Colonel House*, IV, 275.   [2] *Loc. cit.*

Peace Treaty but the relations between President Wilson and Colonel House.[1]

The President could hardly have foreseen this line of development when he made the informal suggestion to Beer and Seymour for a fuller measure of understanding between American and British experts. As a matter of fact, the method was first worked out on the question of mandates, which chiefly concerned the British, because of the fact that the American expert, George Louis Beer, was looked up to by them as an authority whose opinion would carry equal weight with their own.

So far as my own work was concerned, the President's suggestion of joint work among the experts gave a new and unexpected importance to the archive division of the Library, for much of the material communicated to our Delegation had to be kept in confidential files where it could be consulted by those who had a right to have access to it. This led to further developments in the next few days, such as my own visit to the British to get copies of their confidential papers, and the plan to have Lieutenant Wanger go around to the different delegations to secure their documents before they came up for discussion in commissions. It also explains such blind references in my diary as "working all day on reports for current use." It was fortunate, also, that just two days before the President's action I had got the section on Diplomatic History reinstated in the History Division, with the arrival of Professors Anderson and Notestein.

I was able to turn to these activities at the time because my connection with labor legislation had apparently come to an end and I was quite in the dark as to what was planned or under way with regard to it. The Commission on International Labor Legislation called for in the session on the twenty-fifth was constituted on the thirty-first, and at its first meeting, on February first, elected Mr. Gompers president. The other American member was Mr. E. N. Hurley, the Chicago industrialist who served as president of the Shipping Board; for American membership, at least, was based upon the principle of having Capital as well as Labor represented on the Commission. Surprise was expressed in some of the other delegations that there was no official representation of the Department of Labor. Not only was this the case, but no steps were taken

[1] See above, pp. 37 ff., and below, pp. 200 ff.

at the time to bring Mr. Gompers in touch with the technical staff
of the Delegation at the Crillon. Mr. Gompers, who made his headquarters at the Grand Hotel, was accompanied by a number of
his associates in the American Federation of Labor, and naturally
continued to fall back upon these as his advisers. Mr. Hurley was
obliged to leave on February 4, having been called back to America,
and Mr. Henry M. Robinson, the California banker, who had been
Mr. Hurley's colleague on the Shipping Board, and who also took
part in the economic negotiations, acted in his place. As the problems before this Commission were highly technical, difficulties arose
from the start of which we of the Inquiry learned only in a round-
about way, through the members of the British Labor Delegation,
who were naturally concerned to find their plan for a permanent
labor conference blocked chiefly by the objections of the American
members of the Commission. There was nothing, however, that
I could do about it; and it was not until the threatened breakdown
of its negotiations a month later that I was drawn into the work
of the Commission.]

Thursday, January 30, 1919

Lunch with Professor Ferdinand Lot, of the Sorbonne, and
Haskins, of Harvard, both medievalists by profession. Lot has lived
through the whole siege here and looks twenty years older than
when I last saw him. He described giving a history lecture when a
German bomb exploded in the next block while he was in the midst
of the reign of Charlemagne. It was hard to concentrate on medieval history under those conditions. He had only old men and
cripples. Shells burst in his neighbor's yard in the suburb where he
lives. His wife is a Russian; her father died of starvation in Petrograd and she cannot trace her other relatives.

After lunch Professor Marcel Mauss called, a professor of comparative religion at the University of Paris, fresh from the general
headquarters, where he has been interpreter for the Australians.
He was looking better than I have ever seen him and has acquired
a jolly English accent. He has been with the Australians for three
years and as a professor of anthropology has been studying frontier
types. The result has been that he has acquired a fluency in the
colloquialisms of the frontiersman and the soldier without a thought

as to what is and what is not usual in polite, not to say mixed, society. The war has done strange things to professors. He says that his students have nearly all been killed and he has no more interest in his old work; but that is just a mood.

At three I drove up the Champs Elysées to the Astoria Hotel, which the British have transformed into an office building. It is only a step from the Hotel Majestic, both of them lying on the south side of the Etoile, half a block away from the Arc de Triomphe. My task was to arrange with Mr. Harry Henson for handbooks and documents turned out by various branches of the British Government either with an eye to the Peace Conference or for their own use in the direction of foreign policy. By five o'clock the list of their printed documents was sent down to my room in the Crillon.

[As has been noted in the Retrospect, we had had some of these sent over to the Inquiry in New York and more since coming to Paris, but all of these exchanges had been more or less personal; now in conformity with the new plan for inter-Allied co-operation I was to secure access to the material as a whole as a matter of Peace Conference procedure. Most of the studies we had seen were those prepared under Dr. George Prothero's direction by more or less outside experts whose relation to the Foreign Office was somewhat similar to that of the Inquiry with relation to the State Department, but working within rather than without the Foreign Office.]

If the Hôtel Astoria ever had any attraction in peace times, there is singularly little trace of it left in the office building into which the British have transformed it now. It is almost entirely devoid of carpets or any comfortable furniture. The grey French woodwork looks shabby and rather flimsy. In spite of the size of the hotel, the staff seems even more crowded than in our offices at 4 Place de la Concorde. If anyone thinks of a peace conference in terms of magnificence and splendor, he will have his impressions decidedly changed by a glimpse of the working quarters of the two chief Powers that are the guests of the French. The word "guests," by the way, means "paying guests"; for both the British and the American Delegations have already had a good deal of trouble fixing up terms with the French and are likely to have more.

From four to six-thirty discussion and tea in my room with two members of the Belgian Delegation, MM. van den Ven and Mahaim. The latter is the outstanding authority in university circles on the subject of international labor legislation, and is as alert and energetic as he is sincerely devoted to the furtherance of social legislation. He knew very little of what was likely to happen in Berne at the International Labor and Socialist Conference, but was concentrating entirely on the International Labor Bureau.

Mr. Lambert, Secretary of the Canadian Farmers' Association, blew in on us and showed a remarkable grasp of European problems. Professor Young joined us after the Belgians had gone and we discussed Canadian reciprocity.

We are having winter at last, very disagreeable weather, with just enough snow to cover the ground, and damp, cold air. Luckily, we have enough fuel in the Crillon. It must be very bad in the unheated homes of northern Europe. They tell me that England is much worse off than France in these matters. It has suffered more. France has had a great deal of money spent in it by the English and American armies this last year. Someone has estimated it at twenty to thirty million dollars a day. So, although France has suffered from the men killed in the war and the devastation in the invaded territories, it has also profited in other sections from the war.

I have been interrupted twice while writing this, once to know if I have seen Gompers on the labor problems and the other time by Captain Gilchrist, my assistant librarian, to ask if I will back him in his policy toward too aggressive newspaper people! I run the Library mainly from my end of the telephone in my office. It is a new experience.

Dinner with four or five, including George Creel, who is just back from northeastern Europe and gave us a graphic description of conditions there. Vienna gayer than Paris, with lots to eat and amusements in full swing. Budapest and Hungary dead, famine in Slovakia. The neighbors of Hungary keep pushing in the boundary line, as they get a chance to strike it, because Hungary has demobilized its army. The Poles and Czechoslovaks fighting for coal fields. Creel has brought back some beautiful etchings of Simon from Prague.

After dinner Warrin and I worked in my room till after midnight on the critique for Miller. He will have to take it all up with Bowman.

Friday, January 31, 1919

Luncheon with Curtis and E. C. Carter, head of the Y.M.C.A. in France, formerly head of the Y.M.C.A. in India, and one of the best posted men on that country. Curtis said he would propose Carter for Viceroy of India if the choice were to be made on the basis of a sympathetic understanding of India's needs. Discussed Beer's suggestion of a possibility of making India a mandatory of the League of Nations responsible for most of German East Africa, giving India its place among the nations while dealing with the problem of Indian colonization. There is a relatively small negro population, about 3,000,000 for a country much larger than Germany. The settling of the Hindu colonists would be difficult, but there is need for considering the question in view of Indian nationalism, and Beer is bringing it up.

The day's work mostly in my room on reports for current use.[1]

Evening—Dinner with Professor William Rappard of Geneva. He lectured two years in Harvard and speaks English as well as any of us. He was for two years with the International Labor Bureau and is well up on statistics. Beer and I jokingly proposed solving Switzerland's problems by bringing it into the United States of America, a solution which he agreed to if we could get the Senate to pass the bill of annexation! Switzerland has not suffered from lack of a port, owing to the competition of its neighbors for its trade, which is to be kept in mind by those insisting on free ports for land-locked nations. It is not so important as it seems, if there is a possibility of commercial competition. The free navigation of the Rhine, however, must be secured. The improvement of the Rhône would cost too much.

[1] One of these, quoted in the Miller Diary (V, 12), is not without a touch of human interest. It ran as follows:

Prof. Anderson has called my attention to a phrase of Clemenceau's which might, if occasion offered, be recalled in memorandum or in discussion. Referring to a possible settlement of the Alsace-Lorraine problem and the age-long dispute between France and Germany along the Rhine, he looked forward to the coming of a conqueror who would be *"a hero in moderation."*

The phrase occurred in a speech in the French Senate on February 10, 1912, and the extract, freely rendered, ran about as follows:

"There has occurred in the course of centuries as a result of invasions coming from the East, a conflict moving back and forth across the banks of the Rhine, and it would be to the higher interest of civilization that these conflicts cease; that a good settlement—joyfully greeted—should put an end to these alternations of peace and war.

"However, that will be possible only when there shall come a victor who can rise above his victory, and a conqueror who will be a hero in moderation. Napoleon lacked that heroism and Germany is no better."

It has been a wintry day, with wet snow and gloomy skies. My room is on the court, looking out on mansard roofs, and when there is any sunlight it shines in through two great French windows. The courtyard is absolutely quiet; one never hears a sound. Just a few hundred yards away, however, the Conference is again in session. The progress it has been making this week is remarkable. Each day settles something. The British have practically accepted the mandatory principle for all new acquisitions, and even the public knows now that America, too, is likely to become a mandatory.

[In view of subsequent history, this statement that the United States might accept a mandate seems perhaps the farthest from reality of any of the plans then being hammered into shape for the reorganization of the world. But it should be remembered that the idea of mandate was not only of American origin but was the most consistent expression of that generous interpretation of Jeffersonian democracy which Wilson had got the whole world to accept in his Fourteen Points. It could be agreed that for America itself to refuse to accept any of the responsibilities which it was insisting that the other nations should assume would lessen its moral leadership in the world. Wilson himself, however, in the early days of the Peace Conference, had not been ready to accept this extension of American responsibilities, and we did not know exactly how far he had been carried along by the logic of the situation as well as by the arguments advanced by Beer and Curtis. Beer's diary shows how constantly he had this in mind, and as I was with him daily I had been interested in watching developments, while not taking any serious part in a problem which lay outside my field.]

Saturday, February 1, 1919

Lunch with Haskins and Lot of the Sorbonne at a quiet little restaurant near the University, in that part of Paris which seems subdued and aged and symbolizes the old-time France. It used to be a place frequented by professors, and three of them came in while we were there. Two or three soldiers with decorations and medals turned out to be former instructors, now coming back to the University. There was sugarless coffee, cheese, and war bread, and the room was unheated. Lot told of the horrors of war in his little suburban village. He was head of the local "refuge." The war demoralized people, and children were not cared for, so he and his colleagues have been fighting the moral as well as the physical evils.

The University has invited Haskins and me each to deliver a lecture in the amphitheatre of the Sorbonne under the Kahn Foundation. The invitation is phrased with disarming frankness, for the Foundation is described as one *"pour les savants illustres et les professeurs étrangers,"* which is a careful distinction and a chastening one!

Afternoon was spent working in my quarters, with calls from newspaper men and others. Dinner with Mauss at the Crillon.

In the evening I went to Bowman's room for a conference of the heads of divisions called to work out a way for co-operating with the British, under Sir William Tyrrell, who have invited us to study boundary lines together with them. Long discussion over the impossibility of our getting our personal judgments so they would not be distorted by change or comment on the way to the high authorities. Bowman, Young, and I continued the discussion till after two o'clock in the morning, to get a working basis.

Sunday, February 2, 1919

Morning in my room. Lunch with Wellington Koo, Chinese Minister to Washington, whom I had had as a student in history in Columbia in 1909. He has a magnificent apartment in the aristocratic section of the city, rented from some French family, and on the walls are pictures of the time of Louis XIV and Napoleon. Mr. Wei, another old student of mine, sat across from me and helped Koo entertain the Americans. There were Red Cross workers, Miss Root and Miss Bassett Moore, and some young officers of Koo's student days in Columbia. We had a very pleasant time, and when I left the young people were singing Columbia songs around the piano, His Excellency among them. All in all, it was very nice.

In the afternoon I expected to get some work done, but first Beer came in and then Hamilton Holt, publisher and editor of the *Independent,* wishing to talk over the plan of the League of Nations with Beer and myself. This week is the culmination of ten years of Mr. Holt's work. He is anxious to see that the plan adopted embraces a legislature or congress representing the peoples of different countries, and is not simply a group of ambassadors representing the chief executives. Beer and I advised some points of procedure and then Young came in for discussion of the economic side of it.

Warrin came to see me about Belgian indemnities and to shape up his memorandum, and while we were talking Philippe Millet, foreign editor of *Le Temps,* called to interest me in his exposition of the great reform in colonial administration just put through with reference to Algeria. On top of that, Professor Mauss came along to get me out for a walk. Mauss, as a Socialist, lit into Millet with a violent attack on all French colonial administration, but ended by acknowledging that Millet's father, a distinguished colonial administrator, had been one of the few honest French politicians he had known. This enabled me to disentangle the two sufficiently to get Millet away, while I brought Mauss around to unburden himself of a confidential memorandum just prepared for Marshal Foch on how to deal with Germany. Without going into the confidential side of it, it points out the importance of securing from Germany the realization of the wrong done in 1914 and, to that end, the necessity of helping along the consolidation of Socialist institutions in Germany definitely hostile to the old régime. He was afraid French militarists might be blindly playing the game of the German militarists without knowing it.

Dinner with Warrin. We were going to spend the rest of the evening on Belgian boundaries, but Miller set him at work, which prevented it. Miller has been put on the commission to deal with international waterways, etc.

Monday, February 3, 1919

At 9:30 had a call from M. Millet, whom I introduced to Ray Stannard Baker to get American publicity for his articles in *Le Temps*. We arranged for a luncheon on the fourth. Then a call from Mr. Lambert, of the Canadian Farmers' Association, and Mr. Walsh, a friend of Mr. C. J. Doherty, Canadian Minister of Justice, on labor problems and the League of Nations. Am to dine with Mr. Doherty tomorrow evening. Was to have dined tonight with Mark Sullivan of *Collier's,* but C. T. Wang called me up from the Chinese Embassy to ask me if I could dine with him tonight to meet most of the Chinese Delegation.

While dressing for dinner, Colonel Baty of the British Army was announced, and I told him to come on up to my room, if he didn't mind coming while I dressed. He turned out to be a young chap, whom Lord Milner has put in charge of an attempt to collaborate on lectures on Anglo-American history, etc., for the combined armies at the front. I suggested that he put Professor George M. Wrong of Toronto in charge as the best man here. He is now in southern England. I had already spoken to Curtis about him.

The dinner with the Chinese was at the Hôtel Lutetia. The hosts, in addition to Dr. C. T. Wang, were the Chinese Plenipotentiaries, the Minister to Belgium, S. Wei; to Great Britain, Alfred Sze; to Denmark, W. W. Yen; and to the United States, Wellington Koo. They were a very dignified set of young men, none over fifty, and all of them held doctorates from American universities. Dr. Sze, who sat next to me at table, is a Cornell graduate, Dr. Yen is from Virginia, Dr. Wang from Yale, and Dr. Koo from Columbia. The other guests were from the Greek Commission, and their names were as long as the Chinese names were short. Venizelos was to have come, but instead sent an officer with more medals on his coat than I had ever seen before and a civilian whose name I cannot recall. Their secretary, a bright young Greek from Smyrna, had studied in McGill University and was starting for a doctorate at Columbia when the war sent him back to Europe.

In the course of the evening I arranged with Dr. Sze the procedure for handling the question of the opium trade at the Conference and planned with Dr. Wang some propositions on waterways and ports which we are to work out with Mr. Miller. But the most interesting discussion was with Dr. Koo, who was at the meeting of the Commission on the League of Nations this afternoon and described the draft plan which is to be the basis of their work.

There were toasts to the oldest civilization of the Orient and to the oldest of the Occident and then to America, the land in which the ideas of Greece and China can find sympathetic response! I have their signatures on the menu card in modern Greek and Chinese.

Tuesday, February 4, 1919

Morning in room. Call from Dr. Vosnjak, secretary of the Slovenes. Lunch with Philippe Millet and Ray Stannard Baker, Colonel Ayres and Young. Discussed the new French colonial policy in Algeria, where the French have just introduced a reform giving citizenship to the natives if they will give up polygamy. Millet makes the point that French colonial policy must not be judged by English standards, but that it goes back to the Roman idea of extension of a central citizenship to the provincials. Which means that there is a more complete recognition of the provincial when he is recognized, and he becomes more completely French than the natives ever become British under British rule.

After lunch Mark Sullivan, of *Collier's,* with whom I broke an engagement the night before to dine with the Chinese ministers, came to my room to discuss the Peace Conference. He belongs to those who do not believe America will readily shoulder the burden of a mandatory, even for Armenia, and says he cannot vote enthusiastically to put schools in Armenia by American money while the illiteracy exists to such an extent within a few miles of Washington; there is too much to do at home, so he is against going on crusades. He admits that the French and British are making a fine show but doesn't think the people back home are ready to shoulder responsibilities. I spent an hour justifying Wilson.

While Sullivan was talking, Miss Miller, of the Constantinople College for Women, was announced. On going to the reception room, I found her with Colonel Ford, former head of the Red Cross in the Balkans during the Balkan wars, now head of the hospital service at Brest, which was the great point of debarkation, so I brought them up to my room as the only place to talk. Miss Miller left Constantinople on December 6, so she knows the situation there, especially as she knows Turkish. As a former student of mine, she was anxious to give me every item of news she could; among others, told of Ahmed Emin Bey, who took his doctorate in Columbia in 1913 and is now at the head of a newspaper syndicate at Constantinople. I rather expect to see him arrive some day when the enemy delegations come.

Then a conference with David Hunter Miller, who has just been appointed on the Waterways, Ports and Railways Commission. We discussed that and the territorial report of the Inquiry. From that, a taxi to the new press headquarters, 80 Champs Elysées, installed in the Palace Dufayel, built by the head of a huge department store in Paris, the first to introduce instalment buying in France. The house is a huge, ungainly structure, the most ostentatious I have ever seen, a gaudy pile of marble and gilt, with desolate, empty rooms and great galleries. It has been placed at the disposal of the Allied correspondents. I am an honorary member. I met Lambert, secretary of the Canadian Farmers' Association, John Dafoe, the influential editor of the *Winnipeg Free Press,* and Mr. Gorvin, a British official, and discussed Canada's share in the Peace Conference. Mr. Dafoe is the official Canadian press representative, and, although a staunch Liberal, was one of the chief supporters of the Union Government.

In spite of the elegance of the rooms, tea was served in cups as big as porridge bowls. The Press Club has hardly got installed.

Went with Young for dinner at the Majestic. We were the guests of Mr. Doherty, Canadian Minister of Justice, who is fathering a scheme for an international legislature, representative of the people and not of the governments. Hamilton Holt, Frederic Howe and Lincoln Steffens were there, and Mr. Walsh, Mr. P. T. Ahearn and a French Canadian major whose name I did not get. Mr. Doherty is a kindly gentleman, and would make the British Constitution the model for the League of Nations. I argued that it would hardly do to copy the constitution of any country, because the problem of the League is very different from that of national governments. The old divisions—legislative, executive, and judicial—do not apply. The live representative bodies must be the special conferences, held periodically, dealing with the specific problems, such as labor, colonization, communications, etc.

Home by half-past eleven, but got working, and then after that couldn't get to sleep until the wee sma' hours ayont the twal', trying to size up whether this Conference was getting anywhere or not.

Wednesday, February 5, 1919

Working in my room all day. President Coleman of Reed College, Oregon, formerly of Toronto, called with news from the family in New York. He has just started his work at the Y.M.C.A. and is living at Versailles. I kept him for dinner, at which Captain Farabee and Beer joined us. Beer was in session with the French colonial minister. He has been able to affect French colonial policy to some extent, I think. He came in to tell me about it but too many were present.

Thursday, February 6, 1919

In my room all day. Damp and cold wintry weather. Dictated letters all morning and straightened out manuscripts in the afternoon. In the Library met Captain Blankenhorn, formerly of the *New Republic,* in from General Headquarters, who tells me Walter Weyl has sailed for Europe. He agrees with the general verdict here, favorable to the British. Brewster called to take me to call on Mrs. Farrand, wife of Livingston Farrand, President of the University of Colorado,[1] formerly of Columbia. He has had charge of the anti-tuberculosis campaign in France for two years. The Farrands have an apartment on the Champs Elysées, and there is a clause in the lease that when the army returns to march in triumph into Paris down the famous street, the landlord can reserve the windows. He told the Farrands that he had sold them all for 2,400 francs, which I should imagine was about double a month's rent.

Home to have dinner with my two Columbia colleagues, Erskine and Brewster, at the Crillon. Professor John Erskine is President of the new "Khaki University" in France and has a wonderful plan by which all kinds of practical and literary courses are given to the soldiers here, short-term farmers' institutes at embarkation ports, technical courses in the rest camps, etc. He has taken over one dismantled hospital in the hill region of central France, accommodating twelve thousand soldiers, and turned it into a university. He wanted me to lecture there, but that is impossible. They have to draw on the army for the faculty as well. About three thousand soldiers, however, are getting leave to go to English universities. It was twelve when we finished planning for the new educational scheme.

Friday, February 7, 1919

The waiter tells me that there is no milk because of the snowstorm. Just what France would do with a real snowstorm, it is hard to say. There is an inch or two on the mansard roof, and big, sleepy flakes are drifting down to melt at the eaves.

Morning in my room. I have been busy recently with all sorts of questions; one time it will be Constantinople, another the Danube, then African colonies, then the League of Nations, Labor, etc. I have a good staff in the Library, so I seldom bother over it. I

[1] Later of Cornell. Professor Brewster was Provost of Barnard College.

work most of the time in my room, where I have two desks and two telephones. In addition to the regular Paris telephone system, the American Signal Corps has wired the Crillon to give us connection with all American army posts. They have also linked up with the British at the Majestic and the Astoria. The wires are hung from the ceiling along the corridors and give the Crillon perhaps its most distinctive touch of being in army occupation.

Had a visit from Mr. Bernard Flexner and Mr. Jacob De Haas, who brought along a confidential statement of the claims of the Zionists as they will be presented at the Peace Conference. Mr. Flexner is a lawyer from Chicago, and is a brother of Abraham and Simon Flexner. Discussed the legal problem involved in the mandatory system, and am to go at it again Sunday.

Lunch at the Inter-Allied Club, to which I have been elected a member. Baron Rothschild's house has been given over to French, British, and American officers, and the two dining rooms were filled. Colonel Baty and I got a small table where we could discuss the inter-Allied education plan entrusted to him by Lord Milner. He is an attractive young Lieutenant Colonel of the Regular Army and was building a hydro-electric plant in India before the War. He has something still to learn in colonial history. I suggested that instead of trying to feed the boys up on George III and the War of 1812, no matter how revised, it would be well to teach them what a mandatory of the League of Nations would have to do, and then look into the institutions of England and the United States to see what there was to fasten on, especially what there was in common. When I left he was intending to plan his courses over again. The whole job is not very encouraging, and what the boys want is something more practical.

Afternoon—Called at the Astoria to see Commander Eves, head of British Naval Intelligence, to get the handbooks prepared by their specialists. Ran into a quiet, serious officer who, whatever his knowledge of documents, impressed you with his ability to command men. Glad to discover the British had lost track of some of their own manuals, for I have already some of theirs of whose existence they have no record in the Astoria. Any signs of confusion like this give us a fellow feeling.

It has turned quite cold and wintry, and the snow that fell in a slushy soft snowfall is now hard on the trees and covers the ground along the broad Champs Elysées—Elysian Fields crowded with war trophies. I do not get out much to enjoy it for I have to be on my job, such as it is, all the time. Of course there is a great deal of wasted time in such a conference, and some of the most important results come from casual talks with people who haven't their minds quite made up. I sometimes wonder whether we of the Inquiry, or rather, whether I am doing any good at all here; there are so many blocks on the wheels we try to turn. But one can never tell. March will soon be here now and April will open up the bare hillsides, and while all this is going on we must stay in Paris making peace. I doubt if we get it done before the early summer.

Saturday, February 8, 1919

Worked in room all day. In the evening those of us who have not boundaries of states to work over got together at dinner and went to Young's room to discuss the relation of our work with those who have territorial questions to deal with. The problem comes up in a real way, because our Inquiry organization has been considered as mainly directed on territorial problems while history and economics are more general in the very nature of the case. Dr. Mezes does not take up general problems with Colonel House, so sometimes we feel left high and dry. There was an outpouring of criticisms, but we finally decided to go on for the present as before. We all have colds and everyone feels glum.

The possibility of doing real work in the field of labor was emphasized by a visit from Sir Malcolm Delevingne and Mr. Butler, Assistant British Minister of Labour, who came to my room in the morning to ask my help in determining their line of policy in their commission.

[The Labor Commission at its fifth meeting on February 7 had witnessed a very heated set-to between Mr. Gompers and Mr. Barnes, with others joining in. The British proposal for an international labor organization provided that the government of each country should have two votes to balance one each of capital and labor. One can appreciate Mr. Gompers' objections to this double representation of the governments, for according to his way of thinking it meant that labor was left with only one vote against three. He had no such ambition as the leaders of European labor movements to take over the control of government itself. Under his long leadership the American Federation of Labor had always fought shy of what it termed the "socialist" theory of placing the safeguards of labor in the action of governments. His trade union theory had been that the unions could exert a more effective pressure upon politicians if they did not get involved in politics themselves. Mr. Gompers therefore found himself in the paradoxical situation of presiding over a body which was framing a world constitution for Labor, as it was often termed in the oratorical outbursts, in which the accent was placed upon legislation instead of upon the economic organization of the workers. Mr. Gompers' suspicion of "socialist" thinking on the part of his colleagues on the labor body was never concealed from them, and at this meeting he had practically charged Mr. Barnes with betraying Labor into the hands of government officials. Mr. Barnes' reply had drawn an apology from Gompers, but the question was still in the air.

My own judgment was that if governments were to form only one-third of the representation in a body framing labor legislation, there would be little likelihood of it ever meeting, or, if it met, having anything to do. Indeed, I had criticized the British scheme from the start for the extent to which it tried to circumvent government action by proposing to create law in an international body in which the governments formed only a fraction of the membership.

My discussion with Sir Malcolm Delevingne and Mr. Butler, however, was solely with an eye to preventing any such break-up of the Commission as had seemed likely in the heated exchange of personalities the day before. I took no further steps at this moment to straighten the matter out, as the initiative seemed to lie in other hands.]

Sunday, February 9, 1919

Clear and cold. Sunlight pours into the windows and a cheery wood fire is burning. Am ninety per cent better. Worked in the morning as usual. Lunch with Beer and a colonel who is at the head of the supply divisions in France. Learned quite a bit about the army.

Spent the afternoon in my room discussing with Mr. Bernard Flexner the document in which the case of the Zionists will be presented to the Conference. He had drawn up the document in the first place and was interested in my criticisms because I called for

a revision of the statement back to where he had had it before other
members of the committee changed it. He stated that it had already
passed the British authorities and Emir Feisal. With Arabia and
the British satisfied, there seems little for the Peace Conference to
do but to register the decree. We talked as lawyers, and he jokingly
invited me to Jerusalem as my legal fee. That's better than Feisal's
invitation to come within a few miles of Mecca!

In the evening at dinner had as guests Drs. Zolgar and Vosnjak,
two Slovene representatives. Mr. Miller and I were to discuss with
them communications from the Danube to the Adriatic. At the last
moment Miller called me up from Colonel House's room, saying
that he could not come as he was on a rush job. Trumbić, the
Croatian leader in the Serbian Delegation, had also to beg off at the
last moment. So Young, Beer and Anderson joined us and then we
adjourned to my room after dinner and got along famously till midnight. Zolgar speaks French only haltingly, and as it was evident
he was translating it from German, Beer ventured a few German
words in the dining room until we called him off for fear someone
would draw a wrong conclusion. Most of the discussion of international railways and free ports is conjuring up imaginary schemes,
where simple business arrangements of shipping bonded goods
through international railway agreements will meet the situation.
Why an American should hesitate over this, with our experience of
the New York Central and Lehigh running through southern Canada, or the Grand Trunk through Maine, it is hard to see.

Monday, February 10, 1919

Morning—Worked in my room as usual. Beer and I had a luncheon engagement with Philip Kerr, Lloyd George's private secretary,
at the Premier's house in the Rue Nitot. It turned out to be overlooking the quiet square of the Place des Etats-Unis. We were met
at the door by Kerr and taken into a sumptuous apartment. In the
reception room there was a gorgeous full-sized figure painting by
Hoppner. Along the walls of the drawing room were Gainsboroughs, Lawrences, and other old English masters, along with rich
tapestries—exquisite pieces. Kerr explained that it was the Paris
flat of Lady Mitchelham and was loaned by her to the British Prime
Minister for the Peace Conference. Lloyd George had been called
back to London to open Parliament, and Lord Milner had come to

take his place. We were shortly joined by Sir Maurice Hankey, a slightly built, quick-motioned, clerical-looking soldier, who has been secretary of the Imperial War Cabinet since the creation of that body, about 1907. It was known first as the Committee of Imperial Defence, an obscure antecedent of the supreme body now in command of the entire resources of the British Empire. He has been present at every Imperial and Inter-Allied Conference since, and I learn from others that no one else knows so much of what has taken place. He has kept a diary.

Soon we were joined by Lord Milner, and after chatting a few moments before the fire sat down to lunch in the adjoining room. Everyone recognizes that Milner is the ablest brain in the Imperial service dealing with genuinely Imperial problems. He reminds one of Elihu Root, both in manner and to some extent in appearance, though with a fuller forehead and less irregular features; quiet, but forceful, not reticent in comment but carefully choosing his words when giving an opinion, much like a philosophical lawyer. Naturally we discussed the League of Nations as it is taking shape in Paris now. There was some doubt expressed as to the exact function of mandatory States under varying circumstances, and the advisability of bringing under one general system of political philosophy the government of the whole world. One thing I can quote, as it does not apply to the realm of diplomacy. Milner said that Britain had succeeded well where it had really tried hard in handling primitive peoples, but that was an entirely different job in colonial administration from the co-operation in government necessary where the people governed were of about the same grade of intelligence as their governors. He indicated that in his mind this second task was so different from the first as to be hardly in the same category of colonization, and said that it was so difficult a job that he wondered if the British or any other nation could ever succeed at it.

The question which required the greatest wisdom in statecraft was to determine at what stage, and how far, a people of capacity but immaturity should have their rights of self-government admitted. He said that the dividing line seemed to be reached when the governed people began to express themselves in abstract terms, that is, in the demand for constitutions and institutional bodies, instead of in terms of personalities. Colonial administration could be highly successful so long as it was a question of personal confidence in the administrator and personal rule by him. For this type of government what is needed is not so much technical knowledge as dependable character and good common sense. This is what the British public school system has developed in the young men who go out to savage tribes with training only in mathematics and the humanities, especially the classics. The strange paradox of their success in colonial administration is not so inexplicable after all, for both by position and by racial prejudice they naturally take a position of aloofness and have an innate sense of their own superiority which primitive peoples readily recognize as a sign of leadership. But Milner said that this stage of the colonial problem was rapidly narrowing down with the growth of education and he did not look for a long continuance of the old British colonial system. I asked him if he would be a little more definite about the second stage to which he referred—that in which the natives were thinking in general or abstract terms. He said that there was no exact way to define it, but that as nearly as one could state it, it was about when a people began to demand written or formal safeguards for their rights. He said that the turning point sometimes came before the native people were really ready for the reform for which they were asking, but that even if they were not ready or able to take on constitutional government, they were likely to cause the old personal type of government to fail as soon as they ceased to look to the personal qualifications of those governing them as the essential basis of relationship.[1]

Naturally, the luncheon passed rapidly, but although Kerr told us Milner had an engagement or two, it was two-thirty before we left the table, so I imagine that we did not bore him overmuch, for he is not of the tolerant type of social diplomat.

After leaving, we drove to the British headquarters at the Astoria for a conference with Lord Percy and straightened out some African matters Beer had on his hands.

[1] This was of course before Milner's famous report on Egypt, but it is a clear indication of the fact that he had already come to the conclusions which became the basis of that report. The visit to Milner made a great impression on me, for it completely changed my impression of him. I had always thought of him as the outstanding exponent of British imperialism, which shows that I was not even at that time fully aware of the statesmanlike outlook of the man. For it was Milner who more than any other left his impress on the group of young men, most of them his former assistants, who through the Round Table did so much to transform the British Empire into a Commonwealth of Nations.

Tuesday, February 11, 1919

Lunch with Carter, head of the Y.M.C.A. Call from Coleman, for whom I tried to get some material concerning work done by French women in munitions, telephoning Madame Lazard. She invited us both to dinner, and I accepted when she told me that Lazard himself is now working with the French Ministry of Labor on plans for international labor legislation by the Peace Conference.

Dinner was a pleasant, quiet family affair, very enjoyable and profitable. The car did not come to bring us home and it is about two miles to the nearest subway, so we walked along under the winter moon, beside the Bois de Boulogne, a perfect winter night with the snow on the ground and ice underfoot.

Wednesday, February 12, 1919

In the morning a conference on Spitzbergen with the British Foreign Office specialist, named Carr, a businesslike gentleman without much detailed knowledge of the task before him; but all Russia is his field as well. Lunch with Curtis, Rappard, Shepardson and Beer on the eternal question of the League of Nations, having mainly in mind the Swiss difficulties.

After lunch Warrin and I ran over his memorandum on the claims of Belgium, the statement of which was somewhat modified as a result.

At 4:30 Miss Miller, of Constantinople, came to have tea with me. She described Constantinople during the war as a back-water; it was difficult to find out what happened, and people were indifferent. Upon the whole it was a poor place to be. From her description of Saloniki I should like to see it. The British have done wonders there. They had to build roads in every direction and have great highways now on which unbroken streams of motor lorries are always going. There are miles of hospitals, which tell the story of malarial fever. At one time the army had over thirty thousand malarial cases. It is a dismal country, but Saloniki itself is a wonderful seaport, with snow-capped mountains in the distance visible around the town. The city itself has been burned down.

Dinner with Beer and Haskins, discussing Belgian claims. Chat with Mark Sullivan, sailing for America tomorrow. With Miller till 1:30 on the proof of the draft of the central text of the whole Conference, the Covenant of the League.

[This was the famous Miller-Hurst draft, the first complete product of the League of Nations Commission. It was turned over to Mr. Miller to have it printed that night so as to be ready for the morning session. This meant rapid and concentrated work, and while I stopped at one-thirty, Mr. Miller went on till after five, receiving and correcting the proofs. The number of relatively small technicalities which might be of great importance in a document like this called for the most careful scrutiny.

The one incident of this night's work that I recall clearly was the way we listed the British Dominions as members of the League. The accepted method of listing sovereign states in diplomatic documents is strictly alphabetical. It was clear that although the Dominions were to be full members of the League, they were not sovereign states and could not be listed other than under the British Empire. But as their membership was equal to that of the independent states it would not do to have them listed apart as though they were of an inferior status in the League. Our first step toward solving this question was to decide not to number the states in the list. Then it occurred to me to treat the British Dominions as I had often done in syllabi in history courses in Columbia, that is, to use a simple indention, which would indicate a different category without changing the list as a whole. So we sent the list of members to the printer with this device, grouping the Dominions under the "British Empire" and slightly indenting the margin. That is the way the list has always been printed ever since, and the issue has already been raised as to its significance in terms of sovereignty itself.[1]]

Thursday, February 13, 1919

Spent the morning at work in my room. At eleven o'clock went to Society of Visitors to deposit my old overcoat for refugees. Walked across the bridges and back through garden of the Tuileries —my first walk out on my own affairs in about a month. I had the impression, coming through the quiet garden of the Tuileries, of almost an escape from prison. A beautiful park, especially in winter, when the long regular lines of trees stand out against the snowy

---

[1] On the problems which this was to create in subsequent British history, see Appendix V.

background, but I always pity a nude statue in winter. Wandered on over to the boulevards and got a few more collars, for the most efficient implement of the industrial revolution in France is the laundry mangle. Home by luncheon time to meet Philip Kerr, and he, Beer, and I discussed the fate of the world to some advantage.

At quarter to three I was getting into a car with Westermann to go to the meeting of the Big Ten, which was discussing the fate of Syria. The little Army Dodge car slipped through the sentries at the gate of the French Foreign Office without a challenge, and we drove up to the steps at the west side where the porters were in wait for us. Again unchallenged, because Westermann had been there before, we passed the flunkies and went on up the stairway to the first floor, deposited our hats and coats, and passed on through a row of magnificent rooms, all furnished in red and with huge candelabra. Over against the huge fireplace of the antechamber to the conference room Lord Milner was already talking with his associates, and shortly after Balfour came in, while Arnold Toynbee and Mr. Ormsby Gore came up to Westermann and myself for a little chat. Then a group of Syrians, seven or eight, came in and effusively greeted Westermann, who did not hesitate to show that he was not carried away. In a minute or so President Wilson and Mr. Lansing appeared and two short, thick-set Frenchmen came out of a side door and shook hands with them; they were Clemenceau and Pichon. I had a better look at them in the conference room later. The door at the south end of the room opened and there was a general movement towards it. The State Department official told us to take our places at the south side of the room, behind President Wilson. The conference room is about forty by sixty, I should think, with a very high ceiling. The lower part of the wall is carved oak panels and the woodwork over the door, extending in panels up to the ceiling, richly carved. There are three huge windows with long silken curtains on the south side of the room. A massive bronze electrolier hangs by a heavy chain in the center of the room, but the main decoration is a series of gorgeous panels of Gobelin tapestry set in the upper half of the walls representing the domestic life of Henry IV, in so far as it might fittingly be represented in tapestry. Marie de Medici's silken gowns almost rustled on the walls. A set of high-backed, upholstered chairs ran around the room, with little tables in front of them and a row of less important chairs behind. The plenipotentiaries were to have their secretaries at their elbows, and Westermann and I were to be the two experts upon whom Mr. Wilson and Mr. Lansing were to rely when questions came up concerning which we might conceivably be able to offer some information. Westermann did succeed in offering some very helpfully at a critical point in the discussion, but I simply watched the operations.

Clemenceau had his desk in front of the fireplace, with his back to the chimney. There was a table at his left hand for the witnesses who were called in. Professor Mantoux, the translator, sat at his right hand, a little to the rear, and Pichon close to Mantoux. I sat next along the wall behind the President, close enough to engage in whispered conversation, if need be. Next to the American group came the British, with Balfour, Milner and the Maharajah of Bikaner in the high-backed seats, and behind them Sir Maurice Hankey, Mr. Arnold Toynbee and Major Ormsby Gore. Then came two Japanese, Baron Makino and another, and at the corner of the room, Sonnino and Orlando, with the Italian secretaries behind them. There were some American and English secretaries at the right-hand corner, then a row of chairs for delegates from Syria, facing the plenipotentiaries, while at the back right-hand corner, opposite where we sat, was a group of French secretaries.

I was looking at the back of President Wilson's head all the time, but over his shoulder I could see Lansing occupied at the thing he spends his time on at every session, sketching with his left hand, on a pad on his knee, the faces of the other men present. He is really a first-class sketcher and the postures in which he caught Clemenceau were well worth preserving. Pichon's drooping moustache and irregular, low brow and unexpressive face caught his eye as well; he has a dour, sullen look. But the most interesting figure was Clemenceau. In the conference room he is by no means the rugged, venerable figure pictured to us during the war, the *Père Victoire* of the trenches, much less "*le tigre*" of the Chamber of Deputies, but a comfortable looking, well dressed bourgeois, with what seems like a touch of foppishness in wearing all the time fawn-colored gloves.[1] Settled back, half-sunk in his armchair, with his eyes on the ceiling, he gave the impression of not listening more than half

---

[1] I never found out the reason for this. Albert Thomas said jokingly that it was to conceal his tiger-claws!

the time, but if there was any point worth noting he was always on deck. This apparent, but deceptive, listlessness may be a self-protective mannerism acquired in Parliament; in any case it is more than shared by Balfour. Two things about Clemenceau particularly strike one, his eyes and his voice. The eyes are large and dark and kindly but inscrutable; they seem to be trustworthy and yet to suggest that perhaps there is something concealed, not dishonestly, but simply going beyond the thought expressed, so that one hardly knows at what stage of agreement one has arrived—puzzling, deep-set eyes. The other thing most noticeable is the timbre of his voice. I had expected a shrill, metallic voice, but Clemenceau has a rich, sad note in his voice, hard to characterize, musical but not resonant, suggesting somewhat the broken voice of an old man but sufficiently rich to carry perhaps further than any other in the room. He is a man without frills. He had hardly sat down before he declared the session open, and, after some formal business, stated that President Bliss of Beirut College would address the representatives of the Powers on Syria. Then he rose from his chair to greet Bliss in person and escort him to his chair. President Bliss, a distinguished looking college president of the long, thin Yankee type, gave his evidence with a quiet but forceful and convincing manner, calling for a commission to visit Syria. Balfour at first seemed rather bored with the whole proceeding, much as he must have acted in Parliament through debates. At times he was apparently asleep, yet when something was said affecting the interests or honor of England, he was suddenly on the job, showing that he must have been listening all the time. His intervention was at first phrased in a suave, almost apologetic tone, but when he did not get the answer he was after, this quality disappeared as he persisted, and finally, when the incident—rather a trivial one at first—seemed to him of sufficient importance, a distinctly different note rang in his voice. He was no longer the complacent, thoughtful auditor, but there was a touch of iron which was quite a contrast with his usual casual way of talking and showed for the first time the element of command. Milner then added something very similar to what Balfour had said, in much the same tone, but one would imagine that it was more in the line of Milner's habitual manner of getting his way.[1]

[1] The incident here described had to do with Dr. Bliss's effort to discount the evidence concerning Syria which would be given in Paris by those whom he regarded as being in reality agents of the French. To make his point he said that as Syria

After President Bliss, a Syrian commission appeared, and the leader, Chekri Ghanem, an Arab-looking gentleman with a long, forked, grey beard, read through his horn glasses a long account and plea which took two hours and a half to deliver and translate. Just as he was starting, Westermann slipped a note to Wilson to tell him that Chekri Ghanem had not been in Syria for the last thirty-five years, having spent all his time in France. This hint was enough to destroy Wilson's interest in the long, ineffective outpouring of pathetic eloquence which followed. Before long he got up from his chair, wandered over to the other side of the room, and stared out of the windows, with his hands in his coat-tails, clearly disconcerting the French. Clemenceau spoke over his shoulder to Pichon in a stage whisper, which carried to me as I was directly in line behind, asking savagely, "What did you get the fellow here for, anyway?" Pichon, spreading out his hands in impotent protest, said, "Well, I didn't know he was going to carry on this way." It was a complete give-away.

Even at best it was a long waste of time, for when the Syrian was half through and suggested apologetically that perhaps he was taking too long, Clemenceau interrupted the hearing to discuss with the members of the Commission whether they should listen to the whole report or not. While the discussion was going on, the old Syrian, looking anxiously at the faces around the room, let the pages he had just been reading slip back nervously through his fingers on to the pile of manuscript below. Finally, when Clemenceau courteously informed him that he had better finish it, he gathered them up again and began about three pages back and read them all over again, apparently without knowing the difference. As it had been a particularly gross section, in which he stated that the

was under martial law it was impossible to get an accurate statement of the Syrian point of view except by an examination on the spot by commissioners authorized by the Peace Conference. This mention of martial law was what stirred Mr. Balfour to protest, as General Allenby was in control in Syria. He wanted Dr. Bliss to explain what he meant. Dr. Bliss refused to, because he said they should find out the situation on the spot and not take his word for it; but then Balfour retorted that the honor of the British Government was at stake in this because it implied that British martial law was preventing the Conference from getting accurate information. Dr. Bliss tried to head off the attack by saying that he wasn't talking about British martial law in any country, but Balfour wouldn't let it drop and finally asked Dr. Bliss point-blank if the British were using martial law to prevent the Conference from getting anti-British evidence. By this time Dr. Bliss had had enough and blurted out, "Quite the contrary." This was all that Balfour wanted and he sank back satisfied. Clemenceau took no part in this dialogue. After all, the proponents of French claims in Syria were the clericals.

Syrians would rather be delivered back to the Turks than live under British rule, it was a test of the patience of the Commission.

The reason they allowed him to go on was, obviously, the need of conciliating that particular group of Syrians by giving it the satisfaction of having talked to the Commission. When you think how many such groups there are in Paris now, you can see how difficult it is for the main business to get done; yet in these last ten days the Commission on the League has succeeded in turning out the most important document in the international history of Europe or of the world, and in such a way as to win almost universal approval.

After the Syrian hearing was over, Clemenceau was about to close the session when President Wilson rose and in a somewhat tentative way said that he would like to bring something to the attention of the Commission; he hardly knew whether they would think he was justified in doing so, but he had promised a delegation of women that he would ask the Peace Conference if they would make provision for a consideration of problems of especial interest to women. There was a moment's silence and then Clemenceau said, "But we have provided for such questions in the Commission for International Labor." Wilson said that this was not just what he had in mind. Clemenceau interrupted with a sharp little exclamation, "Ah, it's the suffrage?" Wilson admitted that that was one of the problems proposed, and then Clemenceau explained how deeply interested he was in woman suffrage but that this was not the place for it, that it belonged to domestic legislation. Wilson said that he would not urge the point, but he felt in duty bound to bring it to their attention. Then a funny thing happened. Each of the members of the Commission seemed to feel it was his duty to say something. Balfour began by telling how long he had fought for woman suffrage, and of course his sister, Mrs. Fawcett, had been one of the chief pioneers in the British woman suffrage movement;[1] but both he and Milner emphatically endorsed Clemenceau's point of view. Orlando hadn't much to say, but Sonnino protested that he had stood out for woman suffrage in Italy under the most difficult political conditions; but of course the matter was purely domestic and should not form a part of the Treaty. When every one else has spoken it was evident that the Japanese, seated away toward the end of the row, felt called upon to say something too, and

[1] This was a mistake. Mrs. Fawcett was not Lord Balfour's sister.

Makino made a little speech in English, expressing his appreciation of the part played by women in civilization; but he, too, agreed that this was not the place to recognize their political rights. Clemenceau understands English but not Japanese English, and as there was a little buzz of conversation at the close of the incident he turned to Pichon and said in an aside, *"Qu'est-ce qu'il dit, le petit?"* (What's the little chap saying?) in a tone like that in which one would inquire what a young child was saying at the end of a table, when it didn't much matter what he said so long as he hadn't made a break. But Clemenceau's voice is very penetrating and I'm quite sure Makino heard it.

When they took up the question of presenting the report of the League of Nations at the next meeting of the plenary session someone asked whether it was really before the whole session or not, and Balfour informed Clemenceau that it was "the whole caboodle!" which needed an explanation from the translator before Clemenceau got it. A little phrase like that will show how informal some of the discussion was; although, of course, when the Commission is really at work it is quite impressive. Clemenceau is not a dignified figure but a very energetic one and keeps things moving as rapidly as possible. He has no ceremony about him at the opening or closing of a session.

On the way out Lansing, who has all along quite ignored the group of specialists except when thrown in personal contact, showed some surprise when Lord Milner reached across to shake hands with me and chat about the session.

I walked home. The moon had risen, though it was only half-past six, and misty reflections of lights on the wet pavement of the Place de la Concorde recalled the tones of Edwin Scott's pictures of twilight in Paris. There is little traffic on the Seine now, but at the moment of crossing the bridge a tug was pulling up against the current a row of barges, with their long tillers manned by two or three bargemen to swing them clear of the bridge abutments, and a few Seine fishers still remained on the bank patiently waiting. They are always there, and I have never seen them catch a fish.

I had to call off a very interesting meeting during the afternoon. Rappard, with Delevingne and Butler, the British Labor men, were to have had tea with me and to have straightened out some problems on the Swiss labor program. Rappard is a very keen and sympathetic scholar.

Had dinner with Beer and a Congressman from Ohio who had just been over to London and back on an airplane. I think I shall have to take that trip some day. He said that at the height of six thousand feet the Scottish aviator turned to him and explained that he was going to sail pretty high up because he wasn't sure of his engine and the higher up he went the farther he could slide down and pick his landing place. The Congressman said he began to think of his five children at home and asked how much of the distance over the British Channel there was that they couldn't reach by sliding to either shore. He was told that there was a stretch of about six miles in the air which would land them in the water, but they soon made the six miles and then were sure of landing in Britain no matter what happened. The main trouble with the trip to London now is that it costs eighty dollars.

In Beer's room later, I told the story of the afternoon to Bowman and Mezes, which brought the clock around to about eleven. Then Bowman remembered that the memorandum on Spitzbergen was due at breakfast time in the morning, so I ended the day and began the next by disposing of the fate of Spitzbergen in my room and typing the recommendation myself before going to bed.[1] A fairly good day's work.

---

[1] The text of this memorandum is short enough for quotation:

Spitzbergen

It is recommended:

1. That the government of Spitzbergen be entrusted to Norway as mandatory of the League of Nations.

2. That the terms of the mandate shall safeguard rights of other nationals, and that to this end an opportunity be offered to those interested in the present development of Spitzbergen to state their claims and views before a commission of the Peace Conference.

3. That the terms of the mandate shall further include provisions for the protection of wild life upon the islands.

Discussion

Spitzbergen is "No man's land" (terra nullius), its status having been definitely so recognized prior to the war by the interested European powers. Its disposition therefore is a matter for the Peace Conference. It should not, however, be considered in the light of a colony; it is rather a great mineral deposit than a land capable of settlement.

Its future depends upon engineers; therefore they should be consulted before exact conditions can be determined for its development. Any attempt to settle the problem without the advice of competent experts might be disastrous for the future.

British business interests are by far the most important, but the relative proximity of Norway gives its claims priority.

Friday, February 14, 1919

Mostly routine work. Call from Dr. Pitamić, expert in international law for the Yugoslavs, with whom I made arrangements to use our books. Mauss brought Professor Simiand, one of the most brilliant professors of the Sorbonne, an economist and sociologist, and took us out to a pleasant little oyster and chop house back of the Madeleine. We had a pleasant talk on fundamental things. Simiand is quiet, unobtrusive, scholarly.

Afternoon in my room. This was the afternoon of the great session of the Conference on the League of Nations, but so great was the demand for admission that none of the Inquiry staff except Bowman got in, and he only by good luck at the last moment, so the staff missed seeing the final show.

At about five o'clock Dr. A. Rihbany, a Syrian by birth but now pastor of the Unitarian Church in Boston, came to see me in the interest of Syria and he had a remarkably good story to tell. He wants America to commit itself to something in the Near East. I invited him to dinner with Beer and Westermann and we arranged before the evening was over to get him in touch with the British and with Dr. Bliss. After he left, Beer and I discussed the League of Nations and I learned from Bowman the story of the afternoon's session.

From twelve to one I forgot all about diplomacy and had one of the best of all my hours in Paris reading *Adventures in Contentment* by David Grayson (Ray Stannard Baker).

[This was the session of the Peace Conference at which Wilson finally launched the Covenant of the League of Nations, perhaps the crowning day of his whole life. As my diary shows I was working at other things. Immediately after the session, the President sailed for America on the "George Washington," remaining away from Paris exactly one month, from February 14 to March 14.]

Saturday, February 15, 1919

Went with Beer to British headquarters at the Astoria to help with a plan for a conference with Mr. Hugessen, the British expert on Liberia. A call on the labor men (who were out).

Dinner in the evening as the guest of the Cercle Artistique et Littéraire to meet Professor Lichtenberger, of the Sorbonne, who had wanted to discuss with me the plan of the French Committee for the History of the War. A national committee had been formed in connection with the Musée de la Guerre to preserve and study the history of the War in all its phases, and they are anxious to work in touch with a similar organization in America. It naturally interests me very much and we made good progress toward an understanding of how to get together. The dinner was in honor of Mr. Hoover, who spoke, though rather poorly. Clémentel, Minister of Commerce, presided, and conferred on General Dawes, head of the American Supply Service, the decoration of the Commander of the Legion of Honor. After hanging the ribbon around his neck with the big decoration at his throat, Clémentel leaned over and kissed the General on both cheeks in the usual French way, to the obvious embarrassment of the General. Then they pinned a lesser decoration on the coat of Frank Simonds, whose articles in the *Tribune* and in the London *Times* recently have drawn the attention of Frenchmen. Both made short speeches, but the General said the only significant things in telling how entirely dependent he was at a critical stage of the war on French help.

Sunday, February 16, 1919

Rainy, but March-like weather. Took a little stroll in the Tuileries Gardens. Dismal and deserted. At a little after two went to the Trocadero, the largest hall in Paris, to see the French Society of Veterans of Paris celebrate the anniversary of the defense of Verdun. There was a row of generals on the stage. The Bishop of Verdun and one other orator gave the only speeches of the occasion. The rest of the program was music, mostly classical, with some songs from Shakespeare; it was much more impressive than the patriotic eloquence one rather expected. The music of a French military band is quite different from ours. It has more wood instruments and the music is richer and sweeter. I found it very moving, especially in such an audience, which was mostly either in uniform or in black. But the most wonderful thing was four harpists playing together side by side, the best harpists in France. They played in such perfect time that it was like one great harp; and when they struck up Hasselman's "Patrouille," you could hear the march of military bands and the soft hum of singing soldiers—at least that is what I heard.

Monday, February 17, 1919

Routine work in the morning. The Syrian problem at luncheon. Dr. Rihbany was invited to meet Colonel Lawrence and Mr. Curtis so as to learn from them in an authoritative way the plans of both the Arabs and the English. Beer had the luncheon and Curtis brought an American monologist, Miss Ruth Draper, who was to give a performance at the Hôtel Majestic in the evening, to which all were invited. I did not go but instead had dinner with Mr. Miller at the Hôtel Meurice, where we talked over the history of the past two weeks, and I learned the intimate story of the drawing up of the Constitution of the League of Nations. Miller and I were alone and opened up on all sorts of propositions until after eleven. He has made good as an international law specialist and has led the most strenuous life I have ever heard of, seldom getting through his day's work until near dawn and starting next day with the rest of the office force. Day by day he has had the minutes and the document which is up for discussion printed and distributed by nine o'clock, whatever hour the Conference stopped the night before.

It has been dismally cold and rainy. There is ice and snow in southern Europe, more than they have had in recent years.

Tuesday, February 18, 1919

Routine work in the room all day, writing letters home in the afternoon. In the evening walked up to the Press Club, at the Dufayel palace, for dinner with Walter Weyl, Fred Howe, former Immigration Commissioner for the Port of New York, and Professor Marshall Brown, of Princeton. Brown has been in Palestine and has just come from Constantinople, where he had the chance to tell the Sultan some plain truths. He is now going to Budapest to report on conditions in Hungary. He and I, and even Howe, spent the evening arguing with Weyl against his extreme fear that we may injure the Germans too much if we ask them to pay what they ought to, since the private German citizens, of course, were not to blame for the war. Howe had gone as far as Brindisi, on the road to Syria, as American Commissioner, and then decided that he might easily be made the tool of a certain interested government and came back in disobedience of orders. We walked home down the Champs Elysées, with the moon just showing through moving banks of clouds over the tree tops. Scores of American soldiers were sauntering home to get into barracks by ten forty-five, when the gates are shut. A little more letter writing, then a gentle tap at the door from Bowman, and a discussion till twelve-thirty of what we were to do from now on, mixed with comments on the world in general.

Wednesday, February 19, 1919

Morning in Library. Lunch with Dr. Putnam, Librarian of Congress, who had invited, in addition to Dean Haskins, Headlam-Morley, the historian of the Foreign Office, an authority on Germany; H. W. C. Davis, former specialist on the thirteenth century and a leading Oxford don, now an economist largely responsible for the program of the Ministry of Blockade; and Mr. Cecil Hurst of the Foreign Office, the specialist in drafting treaties and, in a sense, secretary of the British International Law Section. Davis told me of the plan of the British Government for publishing histories of the work of each of the Government departments during the war. His Ministry of Blockade has put its history in his hands, and he said that in his opinion the Carnegie plan would fit into these Government publications if we thought it out together, which I hope we can do. It will lessen the amount of work to be done on the Carnegie history in any case.

With Headlam-Morley I brought up the question of a publication of all documents on British foreign policy from 1904. He has been working at these and is the only man alive who has been through all British diplomatic material from the beginning of the Entente. He wants to publish it in a Report to Parliament, but he has no objection to an American scholar working with him, and I am going to try and have Professor Dunning or Professor Monroe Smith in on this job.[1] If they won't do it, I myself will at least have an editorial hand in it. It will be the most important set of documents yet published. It will reveal British history during these years more than anything else. We are to get together soon and make our plans.

After lunch I conducted the party through the American establishment, and they were much impressed with its extent and with the mechanism for research. The afternoon was spent in the Library. Dr. Prothero sent down the confidential handbooks of the British specialists for distribution.

[1] Both of Columbia University.

At four-thirty Sir Malcolm Delevingne, Mr. Phelan and Beer came in for tea and we discussed labor problems.

[The Labor Commission was on the rocks again. At the ninth meeting, on February 17, the British proposal (as amended by M. Vandervelde) allowing the Governments to have two delegates in the Labor Conferences, had gone through in spite of Gompers' vigorous opposition. Then they came to grips on the next point of vital interest to the Americans: how could labor legislation be made by treaties in the case of a federal state, the central government of which did not have a constitutional right to control labor legislation. This was to be the stumbling block before the Commission for days to come and was the point on which I was finally drawn into actual participation in the work of the Commission.]

While we were at tea General Currie's aide-de-camp called, with orders to bring me along in his car to the Hotel Ritz. I couldn't go then, having guests, but went as soon as possible. However, my visit to Currie has been told in a letter, so I leave that out.[1]

Dinner with the Yugoslavs as guest of Dr. Zolgar, Minister Plenipotentiary. I sat on his right and Dr. Scott on his left. Mr. Beer was the only other American, as Young and Bowman had a hurried call for memoranda on indemnities to be ready before midnight. On my right was Dr. Schvegl, which being interpreted is "Schwegel," Austrian consul in St. Louis, Winnipeg and other American cities. He spoke English very well. He was in command of a band of 400 Albanian brigands on the Austrian side and then, when the Armistice was signed, suddenly found that he was a Slovene and spelled his name differently. There is something grotesque about this nationality business. I did not feel well and got dizzier and dizzier as the meal went on and was unable to eat anything. A hacking cough warned me that it was likely the influenza and so, to take no risks, I left the table, the Slovenes procuring for me the car of the Portuguese to bring me home, as they seemed to be having an

---

[1] This letter is missing. General Sir Arthur W. Currie, Commander-in-Chief of the Canadian forces in the war, and I both came from Strathroy, Ontario, and as boys we had gone to school together. I had lost track of him for over twenty-five years, as he had gone to British Columbia and I to New York. He had come to Paris for a few days and was staying at the Ritz Hotel, and hearing that I was at the Crillon sent over to find me. Memories of far-off days came back to both of us, though he had a better memory than I for details; it was the present that seemed unreal. There was no talk of politics or peace terms; I sensed that Currie, as a military man, was meticulously careful not to express any opinions or let the conversation drift over on to the subject of the Peace Conference, which was the province of the Prime Minister, Sir Robert Borden, and his civil advisers.

entente cordiale in the hotel. In any case the Portuguese Minister had a luxurious sedan. I got home and saw the doctor. Grippe. [It was the height of the epidemic.]

Thursday, February 20 to Tuesday, February 25, 1919

In my room fighting the grippe, having called off the luncheon with Currie and all other engagements until Sunday by way of prevention. Read everything in sight and got caught up with the news and after the first two days had a pretty good rest of it, although the grippe makes one very weak. The doctor says that I had a very lucky escape.

On the twenty-second and twenty-third I was to have been the guest of the French Government on a trip to Rheims, Soissons, etc., but gave my seat in the car to Anderson.[1] Beer invited me for lunch Sunday with an interesting group including Millet, but I decided not to risk it and stayed at home. By Sunday I had read all the current diplomatic history available and was ready for a change, which Slosson supplied, by copies of *Punch,* the *Independent* and other papers.

By Monday I was taking meals in the dining room again but did not go out until Tuesday evening, February 25.

Beer and I went to dine with Lord Milner on Tuesday evening. We had a good closed car and, although it was raining miserably, I was none the worse for the adventure. For one reason Milner, as an old man, had a nice, warm wood fire in the grate, and the apartment was nicely heated.

We were rather astonished to have Milner meet us with an apology that he had asked us alone to have a talk with him and he hoped we didn't mind! We three had a quiet little dinner and evening's talk.

In the course of that evening there were few of the more pressing problems which we did not thresh out, and that very honestly and openly. Beer had been all afternoon at the meeting of the Commission on Morocco and had certain criticisms to make of the

---

[1] Miller's Diary, February 22 (I, 131–2) shows that while confined to my room I was busy at the labor problem. "Doctor Shotwell telephoned me about the constitutional questions arising in connection with the labor Convention project [Document 410], and upon inquiry from Mr. Auchincloss I found that Mr. Robinson of the Shipping Board, one of the American Delegates on this Commission of Labor, had referred to Dr. Scott, and I accordingly telephoned Doctor Shotwell that the matter was in Doctor Scott's charge and that I saw no reason why he should not refer the British Delegate to Doctor Scott."

speeches he had listened to. Milner has that diffident, quiet way that the cultured Englishman has of depreciating his knowledge while showing all the time that he has a grasp on fundamentals. We dealt with some problems of interest to the Dominions and one or two other topics. The apartment we were in was the one I described earlier, which was made over for the British Prime Minister in Paris.

I shall not soon forget the quiet evening spent in that luxurious apartment, with a soft glow of candelabra and firelight reaching rather dimly back to the tapestried wall, hung with Gainsboroughs, Lawrences, Romneys, etc., and the old man opposite planning, as we talked, the policies of the British Empire.

Wednesday, February 26, 1919

Was out today for the first time and took a walk across the Place de la Concorde. There is still a wet touch in the wind and the streets are not yet dry. But the air is fresher and brushes away the clouds of March, light masses with rainy fringes, so that blue sky is showing over the chimney pots. The only flag above the square filled with the German cannon is the Stars and Stripes. For the Crillon is American territory so long as we are there. We have "diplomatic immunity."

Afternoon at the Library. The London *Times* has loaned the Library from its London office a complete file from 1887 to the present, and I have to arrange space for it.

Yesterday and the day before the British Labor delegates were around to see me again to secure a wording for their proposed labor conference which would not run contrary to the United States Constitution. It becomes more and more evident as the Conference goes on that the United States is at a great disadvantage in the making of treaties, owing to its federal structure and to its congressional control of foreign policy.

I forgot to mention a long talk with Lieutenant (former professor) Dorsey, of Chicago University, a famous anthropologist who has traveled all over the world and written his travels for the *Chicago Tribune*. He has just come from Spain and was particularly interesting as presenting the Spanish viewpoint on Morocco.

I have also been seeing something of Mr. Franklin Hoyt, head of the Education Division of Houghton Mifflin, who has come in from field work with the Y.M.C.A. We were planning the publication of the studies which we of the Inquiry made for the Peace Conference. Young and I would edit them. Permission would have to be got first, but that ought not to be difficult.

[Professor Young and I had been for a number of years the economic and historical advisers to the Houghton Mifflin Company in the Education Division.]

Thursday, February 27, 1919

Lunch as a guest of the Polish Delegation. Bowman, Young and I, and two younger men, Morison and Fuller, engaged on Polish research, were guests of the Polish Delegation at the apartment of a wealthy Pole, M. Pulaski, descendant of the Pulaski of the American Revolution. His apartment, in the Rue La Perouse, right beside the Etoile, is the headquarters of the Paris Committee of the Poles, and we had a formal luncheon with an equal number of Poles. At the end of lunch—full menu and champagne—M. Pulaski rose in a dignified manner and spoke of the historic occasion which brought us together; but none of us was quite sure just what the occasion was. We were being treated as plenipotentiaries. There was some mistake, or else it was a rather touching demonstration of the depth of feeling behind the Polish national movement. His speech, delivered in French, was translated by a similar stately gentleman who sat beside me, a Polish novelist who had lived many years in London, knew George Moore and other interesting English literary lights. Bowman tried to bring matters down from the clouds by replying jokingly without getting up. On adjourning to the drawing room, however, we found a formal gathering of some twenty Polish leaders, who stiffly shook hands with each other and with us. M. Pulaski took charge of the ceremonies and introduced one after another, asking them to present the different phases of the Polish claims: their demands for Danzig, Posen, Lemberg and the north and east. Unfortunately, it was overdone. Historians treated us to disquisitions on the superlative quality of Polish toleration (the one nation in all history that had consistently never persecuted anyone!). Representatives of outlying territories on the borders of Poland pleaded for Poland irredenta. Maps and statistics were at hand. It was half-past five when the session was over. At the close Bowman replied for us in a very happy speech, but it was only by executing a flank movement on the stairs that we succeeded in breaking through the serried ranks of geographers and economists who were prepared to exact conversion at the price of another five-hour talk. However, we postponed that for a couple of days and made for the car. Young and I are still unconvinced that the Danzig Corridor is wise, or is even in Poland's own interest.

The thing that interested me was to look at the variety of racial types calling themselves Poles. There was a minister of the gospel with a white tie and grey whiskers and a look of constant denunciation of sin in his rather mirthless face; he was a Lutheran superintendent from Polish Prussia. There was another type of Lutheran minister from another section who tried to make for godliness by unctuous hand-rubbing and lack of self-confidence. The one had a square, hard head and the other a round head and a melted-butter countenance. Both these gentlemen were much pained when Bowman ventured to challenge their figures as they pleaded the cause of "the vast majority of the Poles in those regions." Then there was a blond, blue-eyed, round-faced Saxon with a Polish name, but unmistakably Germanic in type. He had been in business in New York. The man beside him came from the Czech frontier, bewhiskered, vivacious, and irrepressible. Romer, the great geographer from Lemberg, has aquiline features, prominent eyebrows, a thin mouth, and carries out further the accentuation of an artistic temperament by leonine hair and bristling goatee. The financial expert, a tall man with a quiet, businesslike manner, might have come from Carolina, or wherever the drawl develops in the voice. Pulaski himself has a high forehead and high cheekbones, with penetrating dark eyes. Some others present were of obviously pure Russian blood and some again with a touch of Tartar. Yet all were fairly vibrant with Polish nationalism. History is more important than anthropology. When one thinks that these men are representative of the conservative groups and that they are faced with a decided opposition from socialists, so that the racial and religious differences are cut across by a growing class consciousness in Poland, and that the country has not yet got its boundaries, one can see that there are difficulties enough ahead of the new Republic of Poland.

Evening 7:30—Dinner with Monod, who was *chef-de-cabinet* of the French High Commission to the United States. I put up to him the problem of a better handling of French Foreign Office publications, on which I have made a little headway, and hope to get some results. He is also going to interest himself in securing an interview for some of our specialists with prominent French statesmen. Young, Manley Hudson and I then discussed until midnight the way things are going, in rather pessimistic mood, having in mind the day's experiences.

Friday, February 28, 1919

Morning—Routine work. Lunch with Headlam-Morley, after a short visit with Dr. G. W. Prothero, editor of the *Quarterly*, and head of the History Research of the "Inquiry" of the British Foreign Office. Headlam-Morley and I had a long and very successful interview over the plan for handling the *Blue Books* of war and pre-war history, and he will push along with the British Government the proposition to have an American historian co-operate with him in the preparation of the documentary statement of pre-war history. Noticed casually at lunch a young lad in civilian clothes, gaily twirling his hat as he came into the room and acting very much like a young boy. A second look showed that it was Colonel Lawrence. He is the most amazing youth the British Isles ever turned out; he doesn't look over seventeen.

Coming out, I ran into the British Labor Delegation and had five minutes' talk with Mr. Barnes. They are up against the American Constitution, with all of its difficulties in treaty making, and were just starting off to another session of their commission. I refused their invitation to ride down with them, for I hadn't had a walk for a fortnight, and strolled down the Champs Elysées, watching the motor traffic of all nationalities, mainly British and American, with their insignia on their cars. The British cars are painted a light green and are decidedly more chic than the mud-colored, khaki American cars. Children were crowding around the *guignol,* and in the flower beds of the Rond Point the little daisies suggesting that March is due next morning.

Saturday, March 1, 1919

Started work on Chinese questions and the settlement of Manchuria with Mr. Miller, a sudden jump from international labor. Lunch with Beer and a quiet day's work. Dinner at the Crillon in the evening with President Bliss, of Beirut College. Dr. Bliss had read or heard of my little book on the "Religious Revolution of Today" and had many memories of Amherst College, but his most interesting anecdotes were about the War. He said that before the War he knew an Oxford boy who came out to Syria to study the fortifications of the crusaders, as he was writing a history of the crusades. He was a shy, quiet fellow but eccentric and daredevil and would go out on night expeditions by himself where he was sure to be held up by bandits, but always got off safely. His name was Lawrence. During the War the British airplanes dropped propaganda pamphlets on the campus of the college which the students picked up, with the result that the Turks made trouble for them. Once when Dr. Bliss got over to Athens, he ran into this same young Lawrence, who came up with a smile and asked him if he had got his literature, and he told Lawrence for heaven's sake to stop it! But even then it never occurred to him that this Oxford student was Colonel Lawrence, practically master of Arabia. Dr. Bliss is one of the most attractive men I have ever met, and he extends an invitation to visit him at Beirut, which I should like immensely to do.

Worked till late on a memorandum on Manchuria.

Sunday, March 2, 1919

I had been kept up late by the Chinese problem after I left Bliss, and when breakfast was brought this morning I thought that the waiter had made a mistake by an hour and it was only quarter past seven. It needed the verification of the telephone girl to find out that the clock had been set forward an hour, which I had been too sleepy to remember.

Lunch with Beer, Young, and Haskins. Things in general under consideration. A long talk with Warrin in my room, explaining to a lawyer the philosophy of socialism. More convinced than ever that the way to understand modern economics is the historical approach through the Industrial Revolution. A short walk with Beer in the afternoon along the Champs Elysées, which has become reminiscent of the old-time Paris. Heaps of little children at their games and the crowded little audiences at the Punch and Judy shows shouting with the same appreciative laughter I used to listen to seven years ago. Only two shrill young voices were missing.

Evening—Dinner with Arthur Currie and Lady Currie at the Ritz, in their drawing room. Stories of the four years at the front. I find him entirely unaffected, sincere and straightforward. We pick up the thread of life where we left it a quarter of a century ago. I suppose, in a sense, no one grows old. He has invited me to go up to his headquarters and stay a week with him going over the battlefields, but of course I cannot get away that long and can only hope for a few days' leave. He said he would send the car to Paris for me, or we might start from Abbeville.

He told me the story of the Canadians in the closing months of the War. From August 8, 1918 to the Armistice the four Canadian divisions alone fought and defeated one-quarter of all the German armies on the western front. They had against them 47 of the 180 German divisions, of which 99 were on the line against the British from the sea to the south of Amiens. And during all of this fighting they never lost a gun, but took over 30,000 prisoners.

Monday, March 3, 1919

Found it hard to get up on time on the new schedule and was only half dressed at nine when Royal Meeker of the American Department of Labor was announced, an old fellow student in Columbia twenty years ago. He has been in England looking into the labor situation and is convinced that there will be a gigantic social transformation without revolution. I got him in touch with Max Lazard so that he could analyze the work of the International Labor Commission here. The Lazards have had the influenza; six in bed at the same time.

Luncheon was quite a function. I had the Curries at the Crillon to meet Beer, Dr. and Mrs. Mezes, Young, and Captain Blankenhorn, whom I had previously invited to lunch at that time. Blankenhorn came over with Lippmann to carry on propaganda with the Germans last year. He is now in the military intelligence work. Had met him at Bruère's.

Currie makes the impression on everyone of a big man in every sense of the word. He has an uncanny grasp of facts. He remembers what took place every day, so far as I can find out, since the War began: how many yards of front they took on October 10, 1916, how many men and what divisions were engaged, etc. Blankenhorn says that he has met the British, American and French General Staffs, or most of them, and he has never seen such a commanding personality combined with such absolute mastery of detail. Most generals, he said, need to refer to their memoranda for what happened two days before, whereas Currie has it all in his head.

I hope to get up to the front before the end of the month and keep special track of the story of the War as he tells it.

In the afternoon I took a walk in the Tuileries gardens and after a dinner with Beer and Anderson and some further consideration of China, another stroll across the bridges and then a good night's rest.

Tuesday, March 4, 1919

Morning—Routine work in my room and in the Library, taking up questions of the Far East in connection with the problem of Manchuria and the Japanese-Chinese settlement.

A beautiful, warm, spring-like day. Dean Haskins and I walked to the Majestic to lunch with Dr. Prothero. Toynbee, who has been writing on questions of Turkey and the Near East, a very brilliant young Oxford don, joined us and we discussed things in general. The dining room is not quite the interesting place it was earlier in the Conference, but the Canadian table had Sir Robert Borden and his colleagues. New Zealand had Mr. Massey and Sir Joseph Ward. Apparently Mr. Massey has brought his family along, as each time I have been there he has been surrounded by a group of young girls and gives the impression of presiding at a family table.

I learn from Phelan that Delevingne has the grippe, and consequently is not able to go back to London to lay the British plan before the Government, although Barnes and Butler have gone.

[The Labor Commission had adjourned on the last day of February to permit the members to consult their governments about the way the proposal for the International Labor Organization was shaping up and also to consult the legal experts on constitutional questions. Gompers, however, instead of consulting the American experts, had used the interval for a trip to Italy, where he was royally received. Phelan found himself the only member of the British Delegation able to remain on active duty in Paris and came around to see me to interest me once more in the situation. I held back, however, having no authority to proceed and no very clear idea as to whether any proposals on my part might not be taken amiss by Mr. Gompers and Mr. Robinson, neither of whom I had met in

Paris. Phelan, however, had had the cause too much at heart to accept this refusal and came back the next day to discuss the problem again. Royal Meeker, of the American Department of Labor, sat in with us.]

We walked back again down the Champs Elysées. Paris for the first time was out in something like spring dress. The little children were throwing confetti, as it was Mardi Gras. Across the street, walking down parallel with us, were two huge Greeks in their national costume, one with bright blue trousers tucked into big military boots and a gay little fez on his head, the other in pure white with short skirts of pleated linen and something that looked like a combination suit underneath. Bright red tassels on the curving prow of each shoe and a rakish little cap above one ear, completed the costume of this member of the Greek Delegation to this League of Nations.

Afternoon—Routine work. In the evening, after dinner together, Beer and I took a stroll through the streets up as far as the Opera and back to see if Paris was gay enough to meet the old spirit of the Mardi Gras. Except for American boys and a few English, the streets were pretty sadly quiet. There was no confetti throwing on the boulevards, the Government having forbidden it. The more one sees of Paris, the stronger grows the impression of a very sad city, especially if one can remember it in the days before the War. Blue sky and a crescent moon above the Eiffel Tower, as we look over the Place de la Concorde coming home.

Wednesday, March 5, 1919

Discussed with Miller the Manchurian problem and came to practical agreement. Am turning over details to Anderson.

[The reference is to a suggestion of mine for a territorial adjustment between Japan and China. It was that that section of southeastern Manchuria which lies between Port Arthur and Korea should be ceded to Japan. The cession of this territory in absolute sovereignty would then cancel all of Japan's other claims upon China. In that way the "Twenty-one Demands" would be got rid of, and Japanese-Chinese relations start on a new basis. The proposal was founded upon the fact, already evident to any student of international administration, that if the anomalous situation in Manchuria were not cleared up the result would almost inevitably be further conflict. The arrangement I suggested not only would have left Japan access to its ports of Dairen and Port Arthur but would have saved for it the battlefields of the Russo-Japanese War which have such sacred associations for the Japanese people. Whether the boundary line would have been drawn so as to include the mines which Japan regards as an essential part of its Manchurian holdings would be a question of detailed negotiation, but the proposed ceded territory would include little of the rich agricultural plain of Manchuria proper. China would be left with the central and northern regions of Manchuria, that is to say, the bulk of it, with access to it both by the Chinese Eastern Railway system, running from Peking to Mukden, and the Liao River with the harbor of Newchang.

The Chinese Delegation at the Peace Conference was, however, advised to put its faith in the full support of President Wilson against yielding in any such manner as this to the demands of Japan, and my suggestion received so slight a hearing that it is not mentioned again in my diary.[1]]

Lunch with Beer, Max Lazard and Anderson. Labor problems to the fore. Then China for a while, and at four-thirty Phelan of the British Labour Ministry came to take tea with me, bringing as a personal souvenir one of the few typewritten copies of the British official proposal for international labor legislation. Meeker was also present.

At half-past seven, with Beer, Hornbeck, Day, and Captain Yale, who had been American attaché with General Allenby in Palestine, went by special invitation to dine with Emir Feisal and his staff. They have a house on the Avenue du Bois de Boulogne, a very pretentious and very ugly house with semi-oriental furnishings. Feisal disliked the bad taste and spoke of it. Unfortunately, the Arabs have come to the conclusion that unless they dress like Europeans their cause will suffer, for people have been talking as if they were

[1] Mr. Miller has the following reference to it in his Diary (I, 151):
"In the morning Doctor Shotwell came in and discussed with me the papers left by Dr. Wang of the Chinese Delegation a few days ago. He returned the typewritten paper but retained the printed paper regarding the 21 demands. I told him that there was necessity for a broad solution of the Eastern question; that the Japanese had to get something, and I told him of the President's conversation with me, and of the conversation between Colonel House and Mr. Balfour, at which I was present. Shotwell's idea was of having a cession of some territory to Japan with the protection of the rights of China in all the rest, respectively east and west of the river system running down through Manchuria. I suggested that this be gotten up with an appropriate map, for further consideration, to which he agreed."

half-civilized, so the Emir had a Prince Albert coat cut like a clergyman's around the neck and a stiff white collar. He looks dignified in anything and his gracious manner was able to counteract the atrociousness of his attire.

He had with him his Chief of Staff, who wore a uniform like that of the British. He is a young fellow who was with the Germans and Turks in the early part of the war. There he quietly gathered together all their information, and then slipped away from Damascus over the desert on a furious ride to join Feisal and guided the Arab troops against the Turks. He was a pleasant, young fellow who might be about one year out of college. His brother, a doctor trained in the French medical school in Syria, was quite pale-skinned and anything but Oriental, while the Colonel (I suppose he was a colonel) had the dark complexion of a man burned by the sun. I sat between the two brothers at table and we talked in French—in fact, they speak only Arabic and French. Colonel Lawrence was there in civilian clothes, very boyish looking except when the note of command came into his voice as he told the irrepressible young Arabs to refrain from talking politics as they had promised him they would. He is settling their diplomatic problems and doesn't intend to have things boggled up by any young doctor or Arab colonel. The Colonel told me that the Emir has sent back to Arabia for some Arabian horses and camels to come to Paris in the early summer when there are to be some national sports held here, of which I had not heard. He said that camels differ among themselves as horses do. There are race camels and draught camels, and a race camel can beat a horse, even on a short race. Lawrence said that he once rode on one camel a hundred and thirty miles in a day, and any decent camel can do fifty or sixty miles. They are planning to go to America after they take Paris by storm. I might add that the Feisal dinner was a Parisian affair and I noticed that half the Arabs had no objection to champagne.

Arriving home, we took a little walk, Beer, Hornbeck and I. Hornbeck talked over Chinese problems. Most of us, however, are more concerned about Europe. The situation in Germany is very ominous, and if it blows up there, as it may do any day, heaven only knows where to live quietly and safely in this old world. The British here with whom I have talked are very blue. There is not much likelihood of revolution in England, yet there is a constant menace, and in any case a great social revolution is under way. Everyone agrees on that. As for France, I think it is the strongest bulwark of society, of the rights of property and the sacred old order of things. If Bolshevism should start here it would run up against the strongest opposition anywhere in Europe. The consequences would not be pleasant. No one, or at least very few, of the bourgeoisie expects revolution here. But—

Negotiating the Labor Clauses

Thursday, March 6, 1919

Began the day on China with Hornbeck.

At eleven Phelan called, and I went with him to the Meurice to see Professor Felix Frankfurter, of the Harvard Law School, who during the war was in that section of the United States Department of Labor which had to settle strikes. He agreed substantially with the points I had taken right through with reference to British labor proposals, and I am going once more to take up the labor problem to get it a little farther on.

[While the leaders of the Labor Commission were consulting their experts as noted above,[1] Mr. Phelan kept busy his own way and laid the whole matter before Professor Frankfurter, both as a lawyer and an expert on American labor conditions. Frankfurter was ill at the time with grippe. He told Phelan that in his opinion it would be nothing short of an international scandal if, after having promised labor legislation with such a magnificent gesture at the first meeting of the Peace Conference, there should be a complete breakdown on a technical question. He also insisted that under the circumstances I ought to get back on the job and try to solve the problem of American participation in co-operation with the British or any others who could help prevent so disastrous a fiasco. When I called on Frankfurter with Phelan, I yielded to their joint arguments that I take the matter up, although with a very distinct feeling that coming at it this way, without authorization, I could not do anything more than make some informal suggestions for the commissioners to accept or reject as they saw fit.

It was easier, however, to deplore a breakdown than to avert it. The British plan would have set up an international parliament of labor with power to make international laws in the form of treaties. It was the kind of proposal that one would never expect the British, of all governments, to support. It was in contradiction with Mr.

[1] See above, p. 194.

199

Gompers' philosophy that Labor should abstain from taking direct part in the making of legislation, but should use the existing political parties to that end. The contrast which the British plan presented to this point of view was heightened by a long series of provisions for the international punishment of any State not living up to its agreement under the Treaty. Mr. Miller's comment on the first form of the Draft Convention was that it was "a joke" and that it could not be made over into anything else.

All in all, it was not unnatural that Mr. Robinson and Mr. Gompers should have become discouraged over the possibility of adjusting such a plan to American thinking. This hesitation, however, was interpreted in the Commission as mere obstruction, and the Europeans had come to the conclusion that Mr. Robinson, from the standpoint of American capital, was no more anxious for the Commission to succeed than Mr. Gompers from the standpoint of that unionist philosophy which he had impressed upon the American Federation of Labor. The situation was a serious one, however, for European labor was in a very restive and critical state of mind, with Bolshevism threatening on the East and revolution flaming up in Central Europe. A downright failure of the Labor Commission was therefore no trivial matter, however indifferent the Americans might seem to be. It was these considerations which led me to take the risk and go ahead with the effort to find the missing formula which would permit us to erect an international organization for labor that would be non-revolutionary and work through governments themselves to build up the safeguards of labor the world over.]

Lunch with Mezes and Beer. Discussion all afternoon on the questions of Constantinople, Asia Minor and the Adriatic. An important discussion, since Mezes is now on the Central Co-ordinating Committee on Territorial Questions. Then a walk with Beer along the boulevards, back home, and this narrative of the day.

[This incident had far-reaching consequences. It led in the first instance to a rift in the American Delegation itself and ultimately, I am convinced, to the series of events which, more than any other, caused the alienation between President Wilson and Colonel House. On February 27 Dr. Mezes had been appointed the American representative on a new body called the Central Co-ordinating Committee on Territorial Questions. The tentative origins of the committee dated from the twenty-ninth of January, when President Wilson had taken the decisive step of calling for the co-ordination of the reports of the American and British experts on the various territorial questions.[1] But in the meantime, as I have noted above, the whole series of commissions had been established during the month of February to deal separately with each major territorial question, and Dr. Bowman saw the danger of confusion rather than co-ordination in view of the fact that this Central Commission could not be in full possession of all the intricate facts which lay behind the long discussions and decisions of the commissions already established. It might be urged, on the other hand, that the specialist was not always fully aware of the wider political questions involved in a purely local settlement. The historian of the Peace Conference will find in the issue which was thus joined a problem of fundamental interest, and one which ultimately bears upon the final judgment concerning the justice, or rather the wisdom, of the decisions taken.

It happened that both Beer and I had had assigned to us fields that overlapped the more closely delimited problems. The discussion of mandates covered Turkey and the Eastern Mediterranean as much as Africa and the Pacific, for at that time Constantinople and Asia Minor were considered as possible mandates, while from the Italian point of view the question of Italian colonies in Africa threw back the discussion on to Italy's other claims in the Adriatic. As for the province of the Division of History, I had been called into all kinds of problems, from Manchuria to Spitzbergen, and the very first work that had been asked of me was concerning the Dalmatian Coast.

Nevertheless, from the standpoint of the organization of our work it was unfortunate that Dr. Mezes should have asked us for our opinion—which we had no right to withhold from him in view of his recent appointment—without consulting our other colleagues. Just what steps he proposed taking in this regard we neither knew at the time nor expected to be told, as he had never made it a practice to confide his plan of action to us in matters of this kind. That he did not call in the specialists on the local problem was doubly wrong, because they held to a different opinion from that shared by Beer and myself. For both of us felt—Beer much more

[1] See above, pp. 153 ff.

than I—that the Italians were not getting a proper hearing from us at the Peace Conference because of American disapproval of the Treaty of London, for which the other signatories were surely also responsible, and that their foolish concentration upon Fiume put them still further in the wrong. The political consequences for the future had to be kept in mind, as much as any purely local question, in any lasting peace settlement.[1] In my talk with Dr. Mezes, therefore, I emphasized the need of a more generous attitude toward Italy either in Africa or in Asia Minor, where the French were apparently carrying things before them, in order to distract Italian attention from Fiume.

Mr. Miller records that Dr. Mezes called him up the next day and seems to have received somewhat the same general advice from him as I had given. My own part in the incident went no further than some later conversations with Beer. I was too much taken up with the labor problem in the succeeding days to give more than casual attention to the problem in which Beer continued to be involved because of his negotiations with the Italian colonial expert, Signor Piacentini.

The results, however, were disastrous later, when Dr. Mezes presented a set of recommendations, which Dr. Bowman and his associates in the Adriatic questions disowned, in a personal letter to President Wilson after he returned from the United States on March 14.]

Friday, March 7, 1919

Work in morning on routine lines. In the afternoon I conducted the Curries over historic Paris. I had prepared by getting a letter from the French High Commission for Franco-American affairs which opened doors otherwise closed, since the museums are not yet open, and we saw the prison of the Revolution (the Conciergerie), the Musée de Cluny, and the Panthéon, which is now entirely closed but which Currie wanted especially to see. Then we saw the Musée Carnavalet. I had had the French Government authorities telephone our coming in advance, and one of the directors was there to take us through the rooms by ourselves. It was after six when we finished sight-seeing, and even that was fast time because we drove in Currie's car. Then they came to dinner with me at the Crillon, and

[1] Cf. *Intimate Papers of Colonel House*, IV, 438–9.

it was nearly midnight when he finished telling the story of the war to a group of us, including Bowman and Mrs. Bowman. He invited me to choose my own time to visit the Canadian front.

While I was away sight-seeing, they put me on the commission to deal with the economic questions in the Treaty, as secretary to the American Delegation on a joint body attempting to get permanent and just business arrangements in the final settlement. I protested that I was the last person to attempt to straighten out an international bank account, but Mr. Thomas Lamont, who is the chief financial specialist, insists to the contrary, and so I shall have to give it a trial.

Saturday, March 8, 1919

Decided not to accept the secretaryship after examining the situation and lunching with Mr. Walter Carter, the British secretary, at the Majestic. Meanwhile I had been appointed, and the French secretary-general began to call for information as to the American personnel and program, by messenger as well as over the telephone, but Mr. Lamont's organization had apparently gone off to play golf. In any case, there was no one around to take the matter up with, and I dropped it.

Dined with Beer and Warrin, and Warrin insisted on my going to the theatre. We arrived in the midst of the first act of a modern adaptation of Aristophanes' *Lysistrata,* in which the women strike against Athens fighting longer in the war with Thebes. The modern adaptation has a Parisian flavor, which I found disagreeable.

Sunday, March 9, 1919

In the morning I definitely shelved the secretaryship.

Diplomacy, like war, goes on without respect to days, but by noon I decided to have a real rest and took Beer in a car out to Versailles. We lunched at the Hôtel des Réservoirs. It was filled up with Y.M.C.A. delegates, who were holding a convention in Versailles. We then drove through the park hurriedly and back home. It was a cold, dreary drive, with a wet, cutting March wind. It got the cobwebs out of our brains but was not enjoyable as a drive.

A note was waiting in my room to say that Colonel House would see me at five o'clock on international labor legislation, in answer to my request for an interview. When I spoke to him I found that he had been led to share fully the view of the American delegates on the Labor Commission that nothing could be done with the British proposal because it looked too much like a super-state. I argued that this was not the way to view the situation, that if there was anything in the idea of international labor legislation at all, then the United States ought to have a point of view of its own and not merely come forward as a negative critic of European plans. It seemed to me that Wilson's championship of democracy would make a sorry showing at the Peace Conference if his Delegation were to blame for failing to set up a common-sense plan which might be put through as a compromise between American ideas and those of Europe. I told him that I was sure it was possible to secure such a compromise and in addition we might even have a special concession for the United States, in view of its Constitutional limitations. The Colonel placed the matter in my hands, telling me to get in touch with Major Berry, head of the Pressmen's Union of America, who has been the Colonel's liaison with the American labor leaders while in Paris.

I got busy at once. Instead of going to Max Lazard's for tea, as I had intended, I sent for Royal Meeker and we worked on the labor problem until dinner time. Then we went up to see the British at the Majestic. We dined with them and worked on a revised text until eleven, when Meeker and I walked home. The rain clears off nightly at Paris, and no matter what kind of a day, you can walk under stars after any evening session.

[Although Colonel House placed the solution of the labor negotiations in my hands, the position in which I found myself remained irregular and at times embarrassing. His instructions were entirely informal and I had no written authorization from him, still less from Mr. Lansing or the President, to undertake the task. Fortunately, the purpose of my intervention was so well understood that it was never questioned by the other delegations. So far as the American Delegation was concerned, all that happened was that Colonel House informed the American labor leaders of his wishes; this was quite evident two days later when I met Mr. Gompers for the first time, for I found him fully informed about the situation, and he at once cordially accepted my position as technical adviser. The anomalous situation was never entirely corrected, and when I found myself seated on the Labor Commission I had no other credentials than the invitation of Mr. Gompers in the first instance and of Mr. Robinson later. In reality, however, my task was that of technical adviser to the whole Commission rather than to the American Labor Delegation, for unless I could secure acceptance of the British to a modification of their plan, there was still no hope of agreement. This situation was recognized when the Commission appointed a sub-committee on March 17 to study the text of a possible compromise, and explains my appointment to that committee not as a delegate but as technical adviser to the committee as a whole.

My first day's work was therefore with the British, in an effort to get them to accept a modification of their plan for a labor parliament which would not give the appearance of a super-state making labor laws for all the world. This was the impression which their first plan had made upon those of my colleagues with whom I had spoken. There was no use going to Mr. Gompers until I could secure a new formula as a basis for negotiation. The formula, however, had to be one which would fully recognize the fact that the United States could not undertake any obligation to accept labor legislation in the form of treaties, because, as had been so forcibly pointed out by both Mr. Gompers and Mr. Robinson, the Constitution of the United States placed labor legislation under the states and not under the Federal Government. A tentative proposal that the states themselves should be represented in the international conference and thus negotiate directly with foreign governments was equally unconstitutional; and on the surface of things the impasse seemed insurmountable. For the Europeans on their part would have regarded the plan as a failure if the powers of the international parliament were to go no further than the expression of "pious opinions," as Mr. Barnes called them. This would have been a complete disillussionment to the European labor world, however much such meetings might resemble the annual conferences of the American Federation of Labor! I at once set to work, therefore, and got the British to accept a dual procedure, starting from the point that if the International Labor Conferences would vote recommendations for labor legislation so carefully drafted both in form and content as to be capable of enactment into law, an enactment could follow immediately in the case of those States that had no such technical difficulties as the United States, and the same text would furnish a program of legislation for federal governments. Ultimately these two alternatives were openly recognized in the Treaty, and the United

States secured in that way exceptional treatment by having it understood that any convention adopted by a labor conference would be treated as a recommendation for labor legislation by the United States instead of as a treaty obligation. The pages which follow show how difficult it was to secure this concession to the American Constitution in terms which would not lessen the effectiveness of the organization for the Europeans. A detailed study of this whole incident shows how an apparently impossible situation can ultimately be solved if there is sufficient good will and patience on both sides, combined with a real desire to see the result attained. Negotiation of this text was the most important work on the agenda of the Labor Commission down to the time Mr. Gompers left Paris on March 27; for the issue at stake was the existence of the International Labor Organization itself.]

Monday, March 10, 1919

Worked all day on the labor program, with Frankfurter and James Brown Scott, and the British, and got an amendment which seemed to satisfy.

At four-thirty, Dr. Zolgar, of the Yugoslavs, came with a demand for a consideration of the revision of the Austro-Yugoslav boundary.

Then Dr. Glazebrook, American Consul General in Jerusalem, a fine old patriarchal gentleman, called. As the representative of the Allies in Palestine he had charge of relief during the war, and described how the high dignitaries of the different churches there, Catholic, Orthodox Greek, Armenian, Coptic, etc., and the heads of the different Jewish sects deposited their pride at his front door and came to beg help, and as he saved out some money for the Mohammedans, the Grand Mufti of the Mosque of Omar came to tell him that on a Friday they prayed for him in the Mosque and he was the only Christian who had ever been prayed for in the Mosque of Omar. He reminded the Mufti that there was one other Christian who had had that distinction, the Kaiser, but the Mufti said that the Kaiser had made out that he was the Messiah, promised in the Koran, so they did not reckon him a Christian. Dr. Glazebrook said the reason the Turkish effort to make the War a Holy War failed was because the Arab mind is very logical and they said that if they were to wage war on the unbelieving English, they would have to put the Germans in the same boat.

I had Max Lazard for dinner, as he is working with the French Ministry of Labor, and took him up to the British headquarters again, where I began an evening session once more with Mr. Barnes and the whole British Labor Delegation returned from London. Another night tramp down the Champs Elysées. I am commencing to know the different captured guns when I see them.

Tuesday, March 11, 1919

By nine o'clock was in conference with the American Labor Delegation and at ten went over with Gompers to the session of the Commission, where I was brought in as the American specialist. I had meanwhile got both Gompers and Barnes to delay the main discussion on the proposed British draft one more day, and so they killed time beautifully for two hours discussing minor points. The delegations of the different nations had adjourned for ten days to go home to their governments and people and learn the public attitude toward the proposed legislation, and each delegation in turn laid these results before the Commission, which made an interesting session. After lunch I worked all afternoon at the revision, calling in legal advisers, especially Frankfurter. At half-past five I took the results to Gompers' office, but was unable to make my points in a discussion lasting till after seven.

Dressed for a dinner given by the French Government to part of the American Delegation at the club house set aside for the Allied press, the Maison Dufayel. On arriving I found it was a most distinguished gathering.

At the head of the stairway, where I was standing for a moment, General Pershing came up—my first glimpse of him. I was introduced to him by Westermann, who knew his people in America, and I had a nice little chat with him. He has a very pleasant way of talking, is not at all stand-offish, nor has he any superior airs. He doesn't talk down to you and there is a merry twinkle in his eye which the moving pictures fail to get. As I was standing talking to him, I noticed a French officer beside me sketching a profile farther down the hall which I at once recognized as that of Marshal Foch, and as Pershing turned away to meet someone, I concentrated attention on the new lion. The sketch of Foch by that officer was the cleverest drawing I have ever seen. In very few lines he caught the features, not as a cartoonist, but with expression as well. Incidentally, he had all the honors on his coat that France could give, but I don't know who he was. Foch strikes you at first as a meditative type of man, with eyes that seem half dreamy at times, gray eyes something like those of Sir Douglas Haig—in fact both look like Scotchmen. Later when he spoke there was fire in his voice; but it was not the ringing voice of a young vigorous man but rather the tired voice of an old man. His drooping mustache is another resemblance to Haig, and I have an idea that that and the bushy eyebrows in both cases help to make them look less energetic than they are. General Bliss was there as well; he and Mr. Lamont sat together. He looks something like a Chinese mandarin, owing to the shape of his mustache, the contraction of his eyes and his wizened skin. Jusserand, Tardieu, Lansing and a whole group of others were there, and Ambassador Sharp read a little essay as his contribution—the least impressive figure I have seen in public life that I can recall. Then Foch made a stirring speech on what America had contributed to win the War, and Lansing made his best speech, indicating the need of dealing sternly but justly with Germany and doing it at once. I had a few words with Wickham Steed, now the editor of the London *Times,* and he said that he had been looking for me so that we could get together at dinner again, and we arranged to do so next week.

Coming home I walked down the Champs Elysées and by appointment met Phelan and Butler coming back from a dinner at the Ministry of Labor. We arranged to have the British hold off any step toward a break until the day after.

Wednesday, March 12, 1919

The Labor Commission met in the offices of the Ministry of Labor, 80 Rue de Varennes, a modern building of pretentious architecture. The session was held in a conference room with huge paintings of agricultural and industrial scenes on the walls, above the very ordinary oak panels. A huge chimney-piece in seventeenth century style was behind the chairman, with marble statues set in niches and alternate black and white marble slabs which fairly shrieked at the other decorations of the room.

[The session was a trying one. Mr. Robinson made a long speech pointing out the Constitutional difficulties in the way of American acceptance of any plan for national, let alone international, labor legislation. It was only a more formal and detailed statement of what the Commission had heard before, whenever Mr. Gompers or Mr. Robinson spoke. But the European members apparently kept thinking that the mysteries of the American Constitution would yet be solved in a way to permit them to go on with the negotiations. Otherwise, why had they ever been called together? Mr. Robinson's speech, far from solving anything, merely seemed to imply that nothing like the proposals they were working at would ever be accepted. Mr. Barnes replied, speaking with obvious self-restraint, insisting that unless the International Labor Organization could really draw up draft conventions for legislation by the signatory states it would be merely passing pious resolutions. Finally, as the impasse seemed complete, it was decided to agree to the American request to adjourn until next week and finish other business first. When the session was over, on the drive back to the Crillon with Mr. Robinson, he turned this job on the Labor Commission over to me. It must have seemed as though there was little job left.]

Lunch, still discussing labor. In the afternoon I had a visit from the most picturesque character in labor, Andrew Furuseth, head of the Seamen's Union of America, who came to my room to get a line on the work of the Commission. He has done more than any other one man for seamen and is responsible for the La Follette law, but, as Slosson said, is a psychological curiosity. He began with a little lecture on the history of the French Revolution and the relation of capitalism to the War, and in spite of some inaccuracies of detail in history, it was another instance of how the historical approach helps to clarify the larger issues of the social question, for he was drawing the main lessons from this war very intelligently. He is an old man and a blunt one, but honest and attractive.

The talk with Mr. Furuseth was interrupted by a call from John Kingsbury from Red Cross headquarters, and Dr. Butterfield, head of the Massachusetts Agricultural College. Butterfield is anxious to have Agriculture represented in the League of Nations and wanted advice to get his memorandum before the attention of the proper authorities. We went for a walk along the Seine and discussed the proposition. I suggested that a start be made by interesting Italy, where the International Agricultural Institute at Rome could be made the nucleus of the new organization, and decided to leave it to Beer, who is to see a representative of the Italian Government next day to put it up to him.

The spring has come. The horse-chestnut trees are in bud, rhododendrons are in flower in the Champs Elysées. April skies and clouds.

In the evening Headlam-Morley of the British Delegation, historian of the Foreign Office, dined as my guest, and I had Beer as well. We spent the evening in my room. This was an old engagement, and I had to knock off. from Labor to talk on boundary questions in Europe. Later I brought up again the plan I had been pushing for the publication by the British Foreign Office of all its documents since the formation of the Entente. Headlam-Morley is a quiet, scholarly man of good common sense and a kindly sense of humor. I am looking forward to keeping in touch with him in London later. After he left I was in telephonic touch with the British on plans for the next day, almost begun.

Thursday, March 13, 1919

Went over to the conference with Preston Slosson without waiting for Gompers to arrive, and so did not see him before the meeting. The meeting place has been shifted back once more to the former palace of the Archbishop of Paris, now taken over for industrial and social government departments; we met in what was formerly a chapel. When the session began, Mr. Gompers called me from the lower corner of the room, where I was hoping to remain in obscurity, and introduced me to the Commission as the substitute for Mr. Robinson. This was against my wish, as I did not want to be involved in votes for which I had no responsibility, but there was no way out.

At noon I met Beer, who was just coming back from his appointment with the Italians, where he had been very successful.

At three, back again in the Commission. The session lasted until after six. Then Gompers and his associates and I took a drive up the Champs Elysées. Back again to the Crillon to dinner.

Dinner with Beer, Hornbeck and Colonel Mason. After dinner, worked all evening in my room on the text of the labor agreement, with Beer, Frankfurter and Shepardson. A brilliant suggestion from Beer solved the first main difficulty and we came to agreement on a second point and Frankfurter did the drafting, so that I had little share in the actual manipulation of the text, but it would never have been done if I had not started the compromise. A good evening's work, ending at an early hour.

[This was the work of finding a formula which would be satisfactory to both American and European Governments. The record of these sessions and of the next four days throws little light on what was actually done in securing agreement between the European and the American points of view, and thus reaching a compromise that enabled the Commission to proceed with the draft convention creating the International Labor Organization. One reason for this was because the story dealt with actual negotiations, and the diary and letters home avoided giving a clue to those which were regarded as confidential at the time. Another was the speed with which we had to work at this time.

The diary does not mention the fact that at the afternoon session of the Commission I was appointed on a sub-committee to draft the Labor Charter. This was the statement of the ideals of economic and social justice which it was proposed to insert in the Treaty of Peace. While the formal proposition was made by the Italian Delegation, it was ardently supported by Mr. Gompers and Mr. Vandervelde of Belgium. To Mr. Gompers the Labor Charter was of deep personal interest because it was the statement of those general principles for which he and the American Federation of Labor had fought. The clauses which bore directly upon this experience of his caused him to urge them time and again upon the attention of the Labor Commission, which, while it was in sympathy with the general idea of a Labor Charter, found it hard to understand the emphasis upon certain points which had been of prime importance in American Labor history. Mr. Gompers' eagerness to secure acceptance of his text tended partly, however, to spoil his case, for from time to time he would interject these questions of the rights of labor into the discussion of an entirely different subject—the creation of an international body to deal with them. There was an added difficulty in the fact that the articles were not carefully phrased. After much redrafting they were reduced from nineteen to nine, and those who had worked at it were anxious both on their own and on Mr. Gompers' account that the text should be incorporated in the Treaty with no further modification. But, as appeared later, the drafting was too hastily done. Mr. Gompers was obliged to leave the scene, and the Labor Charter came in for such heavy criticism that it seemed for a while as though it might prevent the acceptance by the Peace Conference of most of the other work done by the Labor Commission.[1]]

Friday, March 14, 1919

A call from Mr. William Buckler, of the American Embassy in London, assuring us of the advantage of coming into touch with the British on the labor draft.

Without waiting for Mr. Gompers, Slosson and I drove over to the archbishop's palace, and from ten till one were in session with the Commission. Dealt mainly with agenda for meeting of the first world Labor Conference in Washington next autumn. After the session, came back to the Crillon for lunch with Beer, Mezes, Major Thomas, our Italian specialist, and Signor Piacentini of the Italian Delegation, formerly in Italian colonies in Africa and during the war in Albania. With him we took up in detail the revision of the statement of Italy's claims on the Adriatic and in Africa.[2] By three o'clock I was back at the labor conference on the sub-committee to draft the Labor Charter. We worked at it until quarter to seven, when I drove back with Lazard, and later in the evening we returned to the dining room of the old archbishop's palace and dictated material till after ten. Then I returned to the Crillon and met Phelan of the British Delegation and we talked till a very late hour.

Saturday, March 15, 1919

Began bright and early and by nine was on my way in the car to call on Gompers at the Grand Hotel to talk over the results of the drafting commission and post him on how to proceed in today's session. They sent me right up to his room and when I knocked on the door a very sleepy voice gave warning that its owner was not yet visible. Ten minutes later I was back at the Crillon, arguing with Andrew Furuseth of the Seamen's Union to show him that inter-

---

[1] Work on the Labor Charter continued, off and on, until April 27. The record of the effort to construct a satisfactory text is inadequate. Some light is thrown upon it by the narrative and texts in *The Origins of the International Labor Organization*, referred to above, and *Législation Internationale du Travail* (Les Éditions Internationale, Paris, 1932), the volume in the documentary history of the Peace Conference, "La Paix de Versailles," the editor of which is the distinguished French international lawyer, Professor de Lapradelle.

[2] Cf. March 6.

national labor legislation did not necessarily imply a loss of anything he had gained in his long struggle for the betterment of the lot of American seamen. I left him unconvinced.

At the session they were drawing up plans for the first International Labor Conference, and I succeeded in getting them to take up at it as a separate item in the program, the question of the treatment of children. It now stands on the agenda along with the eight-hour day and the provisions with reference to women in industry. I have now carried as far as it can be carried by this Conference the first plan I drafted, and it has received the endorsement of the labor delegations of all the countries represented.

I had luncheon with Professor Rappard, Major Pumpelly and Sir William Beveridge, of the British Board of Trade, and we had a very pleasant talk, mostly about the economic consequences of the War.

In the afternoon, after getting the texts a little farther on, as it was a beautiful spring day, Dr. Mezes and I took a stroll in the garden of the Tuileries where he had discovered four very beautiful little statues of children running. They are as dainty bits of statuary as I have ever seen. Then we wandered around the neighborhood in the hunt for historical spots; found the church of St. Roche, still chipped by the cannonade of Napoleon when he first crushed the Paris mob. Not a word about the Conference; we talked history and art.

Dinner with Mr. and Mrs. Thomas W. Lamont of the Morgan firm at the Meurice. Mr. John Maynard Keynes, of the British Treasury, and M. Monet, the most energetic member of the French financial group, were of the party. They had just returned from Brussels, where Keynes presided at the conference with the Germans at which they were obliged to surrender their fleet. The description of the meeting was very interesting. In this world of incredible happenings no one seemed to think it queer that the German navy should make its final surrender to an official of the Treasury! But the blockade is an economic weapon, and not the least terrible, as the tales of starvation in Germany prove. Mr. Keynes was in high good humor.

Sunday, March 16, 1919

Spent the morning with Robinson, Furuseth and Flynn (of the Seamen's Union). They approved my recommendation in its draft form after a good deal of discussion. After lunch with Beer and Young, I took the draft out to Max Lazard's house in Neuilly, and he pointed out the difficulty which the French would still have in accepting the proposal. The crocuses are up in his garden and the daisies shining in his lawn. The rose bushes are commencing to show red on the stems and fruit trees are almost out. Sitting at his desk one looks out across the lawn on a quiet country scene through the long French windows and even an hour of change from the Crillon is a great mental rest.

In order to make headway with the compromise labor text, I cut short the afternoon at Neuilly and drove back to the hotel. Worked steadily at an alternative text, in the effort to satisfy the French. Our copies came through the mimeograph just after one o'clock.

Monday, March 17, 1919

Perhaps the busiest day of my life. Began early and by a quarter to nine was riding over to the Quai d'Orsay with Dr. James Brown Scott. Put up to him, as an international lawyer, the issue confronting us and the proposed solution for his approval. Succeeded. Between then and ten o'clock had to present all alternatives to Mr. Robinson and help him to choose one which combined several points in the different ones I had in hand and to understand the problems so that he could present them. At the session he introduced them in general form and then, stating that the propositions were really mine, surrendered his chair to me and left me to make the fight for them.[1] The first effect was rather encouraging, for Mr. Barnes admitted that I had convinced him that we had the nucleus of a better scheme than had formerly been brought up if the differences still in evidence could be composed.

Lunch was a rather hurried affair, as we had to prepare, for the three o'clock meeting of the Commission, new mimeographs, in

[1] The stenographic record of the proceedings of the Commission contains the only copy of what I said. Unfortunately the American secretary took only fragmentary notes of the debates and the shorthand text of the English secretary has been destroyed. The French text, printed in *La Législation Internationale du Travail,* is very faulty in the case of English speeches, having followed the summaries of the translator, but the translation of it in *The Origins of the International Labor Organization* (II, 261 ff.) gives a fair idea of the closing passages of the debate on this occasion. According to it, Mr. Robinson left to me only the defense of the new sanction clauses; but my speech bore almost entirely on the question of recommendations.

French and English, of the proposals at the stage in which they were left by the morning's session. In order to make headway, a sub-committee was appointed, consisting of Sir Malcolm Delevingne, Professor Mahaim, and Mr. Robinson, with myself as technical adviser.

What I wanted to do most of all at the Peace Conference has now come true—to negotiate that part of the general treaty which has to do with improving the conditions of the working people of the world. Tonight I feel that success is at last assured.

Dinner with Young, Beer, Ray Stannard Baker and Sweetser. After dinner worked with Anderson on the text. Walter Weyl dropped in after nine and spent the rest of the evening talking Dalmatia. The trip to Italy did him a lot of good.

[It is hard to reconstruct the story of this effort at drafting the vital clause (Article 19 in the Report of our Commission, 405 of the Treaty) in Part XIII of the Treaty. I proposed that the proposals of the International Labor Organization should not take the form of draft treaties, which was what the Europeans held out for, but that they should be drawn up as recommendations for legislation. The Conference might, however, by a two-thirds vote, embody a recommendation in a Draft Convention, which if passed by the same majority would be transmitted by the Secretary of the League to the governments concerned. Then the governments could adhere, singly or together, as they saw fit. The problem was to make the recommendation more than the "pious wish," which Mr. Barnes and M. Fontaine regarded as utterly ineffective. In my speech before the Commission I made the point that far from lessening the scope of the International Labor Organization this would enlarge its sphere of action, because it could deal with more questions than those which were absolutely ripe for legislation and, by the increased pressure of public opinion, could act as a stimulant to the enactment of reform. I recalled the fact that the actual amount of international labor legislation in the past had been almost infinitesimal, limited as it had been to prohibition of night work for women and the use of white phosphorus in matches. I tried to paint a different picture of the future place of the body which we were bringing into existence than that narrowly legal conception which had governed their discussion hitherto.]

Tuesday, March 18, 1919

Morning—Meeting in Mr. Robinson's room in the Crillon of the sub-committee to draft the joint agreement. Came the nearest to a break of any time since I began my work on it. I had taken my overcoat and was ready to leave the room when the obstructing member gave way. The result was a partial arrangement by which the differences were whittled down to one main point. Tonight, hopeful of tomorrow's session in the Commission, after a struggle for ten days as hard as I have ever had at anything, I am happy in the hope that the situation is saved.

By eleven o'clock I had gained the issue sufficiently to be able to go over to the Commission. The session, which had already begun, was the one at which a delegation of the leaders of national and international organizations of women presented their proposals.[1]

Lunch with Beer and Frank Simonds, who is one of the most brilliant conversationalists I have met. He had some caustic remarks to make as to the use of specialists by the American Peace Commission which, of course, we enjoyed. Afternoon was spent in a final effort to secure harmony in the sub-committee, and finally, at about four-thirty, we reached it. The total result is recognized as a great improvement on the original plan, and while the credit belongs to every person in the whole negotiation, I was happy to receive the congratulations of the French and British Delegations over the telephone just before dinner, when they learned the news. The text is now ready in French and English for tomorrow's full session.

Dinner with Mr. Hoyt of Houghton Mifflin's, with whom I planned some more volumes on the history of the Peace Conference and of the problems it is to bring to America. We dined at a quiet little restaurant opposite the Tuileries.

[This was the central point in the negotiation of the constitution of the International Labor Organization. As the negotiations took

[1] The Conference of Allied Woman Suffragists was represented by Mrs. Borden Harriman and Mrs. George Rublee for the United States, and Mrs. Corbett Ashby for Great Britain. There were also French, Belgian, and Italian representatives of this and other organizations. While their program was mainly concerned with the condition of women in industry, it covered as well most of the points in the Labor program and even extended beyond it. As Mr. Barnes pointed out after the delegation had gone, the proposals would have been more effective if they had been better organized so that the Commission could readily see which of them were intended to be inscribed in the Treaty of Peace and which were to be discussed in the Labor Conference in Washington.

place in a conference of which no record was kept, I can set down here only what I can now recall.

I had been asked in as adviser to the Committee as a whole and was therefore technically not representing the American Delegation. Mr. Robinson, however, was called out part of the time, and I found myself in a double position, with an international and a national mandate at the same time. This was all the more embarrassing as M. Mahaim did not attend, leaving the matter between the British and ourselves. The session of the Committee was extremely lively, with frank exchanges of opinion on more than the subject matter.

Mr. Gompers and Mr. Robinson had pointed out in the Commission that a federal government like that of the United States would have to be accorded special treatment in view of the fact that the limitation on its powers made impossible the acceptance of a draft convention on labor from the International Labor Organization. This, however, seemed to imply special privileges to such a government, while holding the other signatories to more rigid terms. So long as the issue was stated in these terms, which seemed to bring up the question of the equality of sovereign states, no progress was made. But when the starting point of discussion was shifted from draft treaties to recommendations, it was possible to build up two alternative procedures, as is now provided in Article 405; and it was only an added step from that to securing permission for a federal state to use the one of these regularly, which its constitution called for.

The clause that went into the Treaty reads as follows: "In the case of a federal State, the power of which to enter into conventions on labor matters is subject to limitations, it shall be in the discretion of that Government to treat a draft convention to which such limitations apply as a recommendation only, and the provisions of this Article with respect to recommendations shall apply in such case."

But there was more to this incident than the rephrasing of a single clause. I had never liked the elaborate provisions for foreign inspection of labor conditions in a country and for applying penalties against a violator of the treaty. The British and French Delegations had emphasized the need for such measures, because in their past experience they had found that some of even the European Governments would sign obligations of this sort and not carry them through, and they did not wish to assume the obligations of the draft conventions on their own part unless there were adequate assurance that they would be observed by all the signatories. The result of this way of thinking had been the insertion of a whole series of clauses calling for inspection and creating an international sanction for international labor legislation.[1] In spite of the logic behind this reasoning, the result was unpalatable to an American, because it bore a specious resemblance to a super-state. Therefore, I proposed that all of the sanction clauses should be boiled down to a general statement, placing the responsibility for final action upon the Council of the League of Nations. If, however, my proposal for the treatment of draft conventions as recommendations in the case of nations like our own were accepted, then I was willing to waive my objection to the sanction clauses, because they would only apply after the enactment of labor legislation by States in which there would be full provision for enforcement. To this extent it seemed to me, therefore, that my objection to the sanction clause was very largely met by the treatment of draft conventions as resolutions in our case. I therefore yielded on that point, on condition that the British yield on the other. Mr. Robinson, however, was unwilling to do so. As I look back at the incident I am inclined to think that Mr. Robinson was right, and that the constitution of the International Labor Organization would not in reality have lost anything, but in consequence would have gained in coherence and simplicity, if all of the complicated provisions for enforcement were boiled down to a provision for inspection and reference to the World Court for any charge of violation of the Treaty. But at the time it was quite impossible to secure this concession from a Commission the leading members of which had had years of experience in dealing with evasions of the law and who wished to make sure that this labor legislation would be a reality. In particular, Sir Malcolm Delevingne, as an official of the Home Office, had spent much of his life dealing with such questions, and his interest in labor legislation was too genuine to permit him to accept anything short of a well-rounded system of enforcement. So strongly did the British feel about the situation and so completely had they given up hopes of reaching agreement with the American delegates, that they had their trunks packed to leave for London, and were ready to go immediately in the event of the failure of our conference. The concessions which both Sir Malcolm Delevingne and

[1] Reference is to what later became Articles 409 to 420 of the Treaty of Versailles.

I made, Mr. Robinson agreed to, rather than see the whole effort fail.]

Wednesday, March 19, 1919

A date in history. Just how much a date, I don't know yet, but we passed the labor program through the Commission.

I began the day by running into Mr. Furuseth and found him deeply suspicious of what was being done, for fear reactionary England might some day bind the American Senate to relax the laws protecting seamen. Spent the intervals during the debate of the morning considering means to safeguard them in the coming organization. With a suggestion from the French, this may be done. Furnished Mr. Robinson with some points for the debate and took Anderson over to it. Sir Malcolm presented the joint report of the sub-committee and as I had distributed copies of both French and English texts to each delegate, the debate ran rapidly to a vote, in about two hours. At twelve, by my watch, the Commission accepted the report, so that the work of the last ten days was finally ended by a complete success.

At the afternoon session the whole Draft Convention came up for adoption. Some recommendations for changes by the women's delegation were considered and slight changes in wording made. At five-thirty the vote was taken: eleven for, and one against (not on the points I had worked on), one absent and two abstentions, which made a two-thirds majority and a final acceptance. In view of the importance of the vote, it was taken by roll-call. Then followed some discussion as to whether the terms of the Labor Charter, the next business before us, should be inserted in the Treaty of Peace or connected with the League of Nations, and I foresee I shall have to handle this problem also.

This may be the place to describe more fully the building we meet in. The former chapel of the archbishop, in which the sessions are held, was once a banquet room, but I didn't know till yesterday what gay banquets had been held there in the old régime. It now appears that before the building was taken over by the archbishop, its noble owner was no less than Madame de Pompadour: [1] so here you have the vicissitudes of France, from Pompadour to archbishop, from archbishop to Ministry of Labor. The room itself is about fifty feet

[1] It later turned out that this was not so. See below, p. 318.

long, of elegant proportions and with gay little bas-reliefs about the doors. The wood carving on the walls is mostly cornucopias of fruits and other indications of plenty, none too appropriate in a Ministry of Labor in contemporary France. After the session I saw some of the other rooms and have seldom seen finer. The official residence of the Minister is here, and his private office is the main drawing room, with beautiful tapestries and fine old furniture; as good a room as those of Fontainebleau. Through the windows one looks into a quiet garden flanked with old stone walls; against the green mound at the farther end a group of statuary stands out in contrast. There is a little fountain in the foreground just bubbling up through a group of shells. The leaves are not yet out on the trees and so you can see the apartment houses beyond, but in summer it must be very restful and beautiful.

Evening—Out to Max Lazard's for dinner with Mr. Barnes, taking Beer along to the Majestic, where I had to refuse an invitation to dine with Miss Gertrude Bell, the Arabian explorer, whom Colonel Lawrence had invited me to meet with Beer. A quiet family party at Lazard's which we left early to come home to a reception in the Crillon by Colonel House to which all the big dignitaries were invited, but as it was pretty late before I got to the hotel, we passed in one swinging door while Lloyd George passed out the other, and upstairs Balfour was getting into his coat. Instead of going in, I spent the rest of the evening with Beer in his room.

Thursday, March 20, 1919

Two sessions, morning and afternoon, on the Labor Charter, and a particularly heavy bit of lobbying on account of the American seamen in between. A very trying day's work, which began early and ended late. The whole work so far seems likely to be compromised by the opposition of organized labor in America, unless further changes are made, owing to their suspicion of European diplomats.

[Mr. Gompers was really in a very difficult position at Paris. He was accompanied by a fairly large group of the heads of various unions in the American Federation of Labor.[1] This body of his intimate and long-tried associates formed something like a small American labor cabinet in their headquarters at the Grand Hotel,

---

[1] The group consisted of James Duncan, John R. Alpine, Frank Duffy, and William Green.

and, as Mr. Gompers put it to me, he had the double task of first assuring himself that all was right in the day's work at the Commission and then assuring his colleagues, some of whom were afraid that he might be carried away by the novel situation in which he found himself. This was a doubt which he shared sufficiently to make it all the more difficult to secure their backing for American participation in a device which had been labelled socialistic and in which governments and capital combined would have a majority. This doubt was never fully met in their minds by my argument that the remedy lay in securing the right kind of governments so that the double representation of the governments would throw the majority with labor instead of with capital; and I had to confess that there was a strong and genuine basis for their hesitancy. It was clear that our task was not yet complete so long as this situation was not absolutely cleared up.

Mr. Gompers sought to carry his associates along with him by bringing them to listen to the debates of the Commission, and this led him to seize the occasion to make a long and stirring speech on the rights of labor which was necessary for maintaining his own leadership in America but was more suited for a public convention than for a commission appointed for the technical task of drafting a legal document. The result of this manœuvre was, upon the whole, unfortunate, for the keenest critic of the labor clauses, Mr. Furuseth, had left the session before Mr. Gompers made the most eloquent speech which he delivered for the Commission, a fact which led to a repetition of the scene the following day. I particularly recall an expression in Mr. Gompers' speech which I have often referred to later as one of the finest examples of pure Anglo-Saxon eloquence: "Men do not know how safe a thing freedom is."]

Friday, March 21, 1919

A repetition of the previous days. I have been acting as commissioner again. Continuation of discussion on the Labor Charter. Luncheon at the Maison Dufayel arranged by the French Government for some of our Delegation, with Professor Bergson as the chief lion to meet. He recalled me when M. Monod, who had arranged the luncheon, jogged his memory, but I think his recollection was rather in the nature of an official duty than as an illustration of the "reality of duration," of which his philosophy makes so much. It was quite a luncheon. There were some twenty or more there, including Beer, Haskins and Bowman, with Judge Mack, who had just arrived, Frankfurter, Melville Stone, head of the Associated Press, etc.

The afternoon session was held in the regular Ministry of Labor building in the Rue de Varennes. We came to another serious difference between the American and the European points of view in the problem interesting Mr. Furuseth. The debate lasted till six o'clock and we separated wondering how we were ever going to straighten it out.

[Mr. Gompers, seeing that Mr. Furuseth was present, repeated some of the speech of the preceding day, to the obvious annoyance of Mr. Barnes and others present, who did not understand the situation and were anxious to get on with the drafting of the clauses. I saw that Mr. Furuseth was giving more attention to the reception of the speech than the speech itself and left my place at the head of the table to sit beside him to try to draw him back to what Mr. Gompers was saying, but he told me that he needed no further proof that the British Delegation was creating this organization for the sole purpose of crushing out the liberties which labor had already won on the high seas through the La Follette Seamen's Act, which, as is well known, was Furuseth's own creation. I told him in this whispered conversation that he was entirely misjudging Mr. Barnes, but could not at that moment, out of loyalty to Mr. Gompers, reveal the fact that the annoyance visible around the table was due to Mr. Gompers' having repeated the speech for Mr. Furuseth's own benefit. Instead I asked him if he would be satisfied that he had misjudged the situation if I could secure for the next day's session the insertion of a clause stating that no action of the International Labor Organization was ever to lessen the existing safeguards of labor. He said that this would meet all his objections but that it would be utterly impossible for me to secure any such statement from a body of men whose real purpose was to thwart the Seamen's Act.

This is the clue to my negotiations of that afternoon and the following morning. I drafted the amendment, which Mr. Furuseth said would enable him to accept the Labor organization, in the simplest and most straightforward language:

In no case shall any Member be asked or required, as a result of the adoption of any recommendation or draft convention by the Conference, to lessen the protection afforded by its existing legislation to the workers concerned.

I had some difficulty getting the British and French to agree to inserting this clause, as they said it implied a distrust of the labor organization which none of them felt was justified. They were still suffering under a misapprehension of Mr. Gompers' action which I could not dispel. However, by dint of strong insistence I got their consent and was ready to move it at the opening of the morning session, where, to Mr. Furuseth's surprise, it passed without opposition. I should perhaps add, however, that it turned out subsequently that Mr. Furuseth's suspicions were not allayed and he became the chief opponent of the labor sections at the meeting of the American Federation of Labor.[1]]

In the evening Beer had Philip Kerr for a quiet dinner which we held in Young's room with just the four of us. Kerr's view of Europe at present is pessimistic; but I was struck with the fact that in spite of his pessimistic outlook, he retains a personal optimism which seems in direct contradiction to his views. After he had gone, Beer explained that the basis of his personal confidence in the ultimate solution is his religion.

Saturday, March 22, 1919

With a consciousness that this was the decisive session of the Commission, I gathered together my various suggestions for the pro-

---

[1] As a caution to the historian in dealing with records of this kind, I quote a somewhat contradictory account of the same matter in Mr. Gompers' autobiography, *Seventy Years of Life and Labor*, II, 493. "The second big fight I made was for the principle that the International Labor Office or its annual assembly shall not propose to any country a law, convention, or treaty which contains lower standards than obtain in that country. After the acceptance of the American proposals safeguarding the rights of federated governments (such as ours) this proposal was the crux upon which our commission was about to split. I announced that unless that proposal was adopted by the commission Mr. Robinson and I would be forced to refrain from signing the report and we would submit a minority report to the Plenary Council. We proceeded to argue this question for days and in addition to conferring with my associate, Mr. Robinson, and with my A. F. of L. associates, I also had a conference with Andrew Furuseth who aided us in framing this safeguard. He assured me that if our proposal was made part of the plan, he regarded the document as perfectly safe, sound, and of great benefit to labor of all countries, particularly of those countries which were more backward, while it would safeguard the working people of the United States from any attempt to lower the American standards of life and work. After the die had been cast by my statement to the commission, they adopted the principle by practically a unanimous vote, the Japanese delegation again refraining from voting." The Minutes of the Labor Commission show that the clause which I had drafted had not come up for discussion at any previous session, and that Mr. Robinson had been absent during this whole discussion on the American Seamen's Act.

posed American amendment and drove along with Gompers, Anderson, and Slosson to the session. The representatives of the other Powers had realized the seriousness of our attitude and met it by proposing to insert practically what we had been demanding. After a couple of hours, in the attempt to get the wording exactly to our liking, the text was amended to meet the American request and Mr. Gompers and I exchanged congratulations quietly to each other, for it was the most important clause in all the document for us.[1] Some more items were disposed of and the session prolonged till half-past one and then we broke up, having completed the whole program of the Commission. We meet again on Monday to hear the report of the Secretary giving the history of the whole work of the Commission and on Tuesday it is to be presented to the Council of Ten.

The result is this: Two weeks ago they were on the point of breaking up in complete disagreement. In the first week we succeeded in getting the British to meet our Constitutional difficulties, and in the second week the Commission to realize and comply with the demands of American organized labor. Now everyone is happy and the work is done. I am ready to turn to diplomatic history again. I met Furuseth in the corridor of the hotel after lunch and although two days ago he expressed in the plainest American idiom his distrust of everything I was doing, he told me this afternoon that so far as he was concerned, he would be glad to have me elected as an honorary member of the Seamen's Union.

In the afternoon Beer, Young and I took one of the Crillon cars for a spin in the country. We went south on the road to Orléans for about five miles—a cobbled road, none too good—and then struck into a wonderful country road lined with high trees all the way, and drove for miles between pleasant fields in a country with long, sloping hills and through almost untouched woods.

We struck back by another road, a little farther to the west, and came along a crest of the hill to Chatillon, the fort on the hilltop where the garrison of Paris tried to break the German line of siege of 1871. From the hill you look down over southwestern Paris and the valley of the Seine, a beautiful, far-reaching basin with the hills of St. Cloud beyond. Then, through the slums across the river, back to the city.

[1] An exaggeration which shows how important the immediate task seems when one has concentrated intently upon it.

Sunday, March 23, 1919

A beautiful March morning. After breakfast I wandered over to the Library, which I had not visited for a week, and found no need for going again in a hurry as everything was in order. Then a walk up the Champs Elysées with Felix Frankfurter, who is much pleased with the results of the Labor Commission. Dr. Prothero came to luncheon. He is the editor of the *Quarterly Review,* one of the most influential magazines of opinion in the world. Afterwards, Beer and I drove up to the Majestic and on to the Bois de Boulogne where we wandered up and down the different alley-ways of the park, which is just beginning to show signs of Spring. Both of us, however, were feeling rather depressed with the news we had just learned of the outbreak of troubles in Hungary, which, if they spread, may make waste paper of our conventions for a while to come. In short we felt almost as depressed as if our own work were not going well.

Back to the Majestic for a tea with Colonel Lawrence, who was very entertaining with his irrepressible fund of humor applied to the most serious proposals for the settlement of the Near East. Hogarth was there too, and it struck one as incongruous to see a distinguished archeologist dressed in the uniform of the British navy. After dinner, which was a quiet family party in Bowman's rooms, we had an evening with Oswald Villard of the New York *Nation* who had just come back from a month in Germany and brought the most vivid accounts imaginable of the sufferings of the poor Germans. If one-tenth of what he says is true they have had a heavy penalty dealt out to them. He is sure that German militarism is over and that the good German people will be peaceful from now on if the French can only be induced to treat them kindly so as not to rouse their more evil natures. He was in Munich and present at the Parliament when Eisner was shot, and gave a graphic description.

Monday, March 24, 1919

Rainy morning, with the sun breaking through towards noon. The day ended again in rain, but the weather is warmer and the buds are starting on the trees. At ten we began our last session of the Labor Commission to listen to the report of the Secretary, Mr. Butler of the British Delegation. The whole thing was passed finally and then the Commission broke up, with mutual votes of thanks and some eloquence on the historic character of the Commission in the movement for social welfare. They paid a tribute to the work of the sub-committee that saved the day, and everyone was too intent on self-congratulation to remember past difficulties. We shook hands all round and separated, until no one knows when. Our Report has still to be presented to the Conference.

Lunch with Mr. Leland Harrison of the State Department. Enlisted his support in securing a plenary session instead of a simple committee meeting for the final ceremony. Spent the afternoon at the Ministry of Labor, in final redaction of the text of the Report and am putting it through the Government printing office here tonight. Mr. Barnes was to have dined with me, but had an invitation to the opera and will not come till Thursday.

The one thing that stands out most in what ought to be a historic day was that while my secretary was typing at the Ministry of Labor, I got a few minutes' quiet on the balcony looking into the garden with the fresh green of the lawn and the buds on the trees to suggest springtime. Pigeons nested in the upper branches and flew to the tip of the cross above the dome of the Invalides. The Peace Conference seemed a long way off. As I write this and look up to the roof-line of the Crillon, an American sentry is pacing back and forth on the flat roof with a gun on his shoulder.

Tuesday, March 25, 1919

The news from Hungary of the new Soviet Government makes the Peace Conference here sit up and get to work, and the first thing it does towards clearing up the situation is to stop the meetings of the Supreme Council (the Ten) and have Lloyd George, Orlando, Clemenceau and Wilson take the whole matter in their own hands. There are some who dimly recall a slogan for public diplomacy but the memory is rather faint. As a matter of fact, every person is glad to have the big chiefs get together and do something, although *Le Temps* is afraid that France may be out-voted, for it calls for more light on the scope and powers assumed by the four Premiers. The tone of pessimism prevails in our Delegation, I think somewhat unduly, for there is a distinct advantage in having the Magyar question get us back to realities, if one has the ultimate settlement in mind rather than having a treaty signed in the next few weeks.

Spent the morning at the Astoria going over the proof of the Report of the Labor Commission with Butler and Phelan. Gave the copy to the printer and had a quiet lunch with Professor Mahaim at the Hôtel Lotti, Belgian headquarters, a nice little hotel near the Continental. He is going back to Liége, where he is Professor of Economics and Jurisprudence. He hopes to come to America to the first meeting of the International Labor Conference in October and expects to give some university lectures. He is a serious man of pleasant manner, one of the earliest pioneers of the movement for labor legislation.[1]

I read proof in the afternoon and took it easy. Signor Cabrini, one of the Italian delegates on the Commission, was to have dined with me but sent word that he was too ill to come. Frank Warrin has celebrated my part in the labor negotiations by a poem in French. At dinner Colonel Ayres, Major Thomas, Beer, Walter Weyl and I continued the discussion of the night before. It was late when we broke up, but I strolled over to Walter Weyl's hotel with him and we walked back and forth along the Boulevard. After all, I have met few men who can match Walter Weyl in fair-mindedness and breadth of view.

Wednesday, March 26, 1919

Grey skies continue and the spring comes slowly. At nine, Major George L. Berry came to my room to say good-bye and to invite me to his home in Tennessee. He is going back with Gompers and the rest of the labor leaders. The printing press supplied the rest of our necessary copies of the Commission's documents by nine-fifteen, and I ran over to the Ministry of Labor to get M. Fontaine to accept a modification and then exchanged with the British our copies of the Report for their copies of the proposed Covenant. Said good-bye to Mr. Gompers and his crowd, who left at noon.

One chapter of the Peace Conference is definitely closed. Now I hope to turn to diplomatic history; but this week-end Beer and I are going out to Château Thierry and Soissons.

Revolutions are in the air. The revolution in Hungary is just the beginning, most people here think.

Thursday, March 27, 1919

That closed chapter is opened again. The Report has to be put through the Peace Conference and that means getting the dignitaries

---

[1] Professor Mahaim continued his career with marked distinction after the Peace Conference, becoming president of the Labor Conference and of the Governing Body.

interested and making some important corrections before it sees the light. I had M. Fontaine for lunch, a quiet Frenchman beyond middle life, who had spent many years as head of the staff of the Labor Office here.

[Looking back at this record across the intervening years I am struck with the fact that it was not until the labor negotiations seemed to me practically over that I mentioned any contact with M. Fontaine. By the time the Peace Conference was over, and in the years which followed, I learned to look to him for even more than the sanity of judgment and mastery of his subject which one expects to find in the highest places of French government service. In addition to these qualities he represented the best traditions of French liberalism, holding in check a natural tendency toward the doctrine of *laissez faire* by a vivid sense of the need for social legislation. Indeed, as I came to know, not from him but from others, he had been the instigator and the drafter of practically the entire program of the social legislation of the Third Republic after it became republican and democratic. It was a fitting reward for such services that he should later be the President of the Governing Body of the International Labor Office. During the meetings of the Commission he had retained the self-effacing manner of a government official yielding his place to the political spokesmen in debate and seldom intervening except on some technical point. But his hand was on the helm of the French Delegation throughout the whole of the negotiations. This single-hearted devotion to a humanitarian cause was all the more striking when one came to know his wide cultural interests and his family connections which lay in the more conservative elements of the wealthy bourgeoisie. In his home the masterpieces of French art looked down upon a salon of the most outstanding figures in the literary life of the day. It was there that one came to realize how little after all of contemporary France was represented by Foch or even Clemenceau. But these were to be discoveries of the days to come.]

After lunch I went to see Dr. Mezes about work in diplomatic history on Constantinople and the Straits, but came to the conclusion that although it might be pleasant to me, it would not be quite as real work as I had been doing. So I wandered over to Mr. Miller's office to see what he was busy at. I found him revising the text of the Covenant, which everyone admits needs revision. He at once offered me a job and I worked away for the afternoon, suggesting some departures from the existing text.

[This had reference to the constitution of the Council. There were two different problems to be solved: the representation of the lesser Powers and the representation of Germany. The wording of the draft text was not satisfactory in either respect. I suggested a formula which would have made the election of any further permanent members of the Council not a coöption of the Council, with the Assembly approving—substantially as it stands in the Covenant —but would have placed the choice in the hands of the Assembly.[1]]

I worked on the text until dinner time, but had to hurry away to receive Mr. Barnes, whom I had invited to dine with me in order to have an all-round discussion on the labor problem with some of my associates present.

We dined with Professors Taussig and Haskins and Whitney Shepardson in Young's room. Mr. Barnes brought his secretary, Mr. Hodgson, who had once worked on the *Encyclopædia Britannica* in the days when I was editing it. The chief subject of discussion was the Labor Charter rather than the Labor Organization; for the constitutional clauses have been more carefully drafted and have undergone the fire of debate far more than the clauses of the Labor Charter.

[We all felt that the text of this so-called charter of liberties for the working classes had been hurried through and was not in proper form. Some way had to be found for straightening it out, and the suggestion that I made was accepted, that, before it was presented in plenary session, it should be viséd by the Council of Ten, as this would give us a chance to have it referred back for redrafting. Mr. Barnes was anxious to have the text retain its strong appeal and not be too emasculated by either legalistic or diplomatic hands.]

Friday, March 28, 1919

I was up at the Majestic as soon as there was a chance of seeing Sir Malcolm and Mr. Barnes and spent the morning discussing Sir Malcolm's revision of the Labor Charter, made the night before while Barnes and I were talking. I got my suggestions for the way to hitch up the Labor Conference to the League of Nations through

[1] Cf. the Miller Diary (VII, 247), Document 622.

to Lord Robert Cecil by way of Mr. Baker, who is attached to Cecil's staff for labor problems. Walked back home with Barnes and Hodgson down the Champs Elysées. Struck by the number of American soldiers on the Champs.

After lunch went over to the French Ministry of Labor to arrange the revision with Fontaine. Found him working in the wonderful old boudoir which had become his office, with windows overlooking the garden. Max Lazard was there, and after we got it fixed up I drove him over to the house he once lived in, on the Rue Babylon. He has now turned it over to the French Association against Unemployment, which he largely supports out of his fortune. He took me upstairs to show me the view from the windows. It was once a lodge at the gate of a mansion of the Orléans family. The Austrian Embassy then acquired the property. There are about four acres of woods, lawn and garden, beautifully laid out, right in the heart of the most fashionable part of Paris. One wonders what American millionaire will be the next owner. Across the street were the gardens of a nunnery, fully as large, although laid out in vegetables. The white bonneted, blue skirted nuns were out busy gardening, along with a number of workmen. I suppose there is no other house in Paris with quite the country-like setting of this of Max Lazard's.

Dinner with Lincoln Steffens, Young and Taussig. Steffens is straight back from Russia, where he was sent with Bullitt to talk to Lenin. Of all evenings in Paris, this was as interesting as any I have spent. As between extreme nationalists as they paint themselves and Bolshevists as Steffens paints them, give me Bolshevists.

[The reference to the problem of connecting the Labor Conference with the League of Nations raises an issue which covers a much wider field than that of Labor. The theory of the League which I held in the early days of the Peace Conference and which had often been discussed between Beer, members of the British Round Table group and myself, was that at the center of the structure provision should be made for periodically recurring conferences dealing with different problems of government, such as colonies, economic relations, labor, and the like. As the Peace Conference went on and rumors from Washington grew more pronounced week by week of the threat of America's refusal to join the League, the chief anxiety of the Labor Commission was to make sure that whatever happened to the League, Labor would still have its parliament. On the other hand, apart from this question of expediency, there was every reason for linking the Labor Organization with the League; and the problem was how to do this effectively and still leave the Labor Organization a chance to continue with the United States as a member even if the Covenant failed of adoption by the United States. I therefore proposed that the Covenant should contain an article providing specifically for periodic conferences so that the Labor Conference would have a place made for it in the normal functioning of the League yet would be sufficiently autonomous to have a membership of its own. This, as a matter of fact, was the way in which the International Labor Organization was ultimately related to the League, but the principle itself received no clear recognition in the Covenant.

The memorandum which I drafted to suggest a revision in the Covenant that would deal with this situation is of particular interest in view of the proposals which have been made looking to fuller participation of the United States in the League. At the time it was submitted to Colonel House and other members of the American Delegation, however, it seemed so completely foreign to the outlook of the Commission on the Covenant that little attention was given to it. The memorandum follows.

SUGGESTION FOR AN AMENDMENT OF THE COVENANT MAKING PROVISION FOR ASSOCIATION WITH THE LEAGUE

Article 1 should be amended as follows:
Existing Article 1 becomes Section A.
Section B:—
(b) States not Members may become Associates of the League through membership of the periodic conferences held under the auspices of the League. Such Associates assume no further responsibilities than arise from the action of the conferences in which they participate.

Proposed amendment of Article 2.
Add to the existing Article the words "and also of periodical recurring Conferences dealing with specific matters of international interest."

Proposed amendment to Article 23.
Add (g) "to give effect to these and similar objects of the League there shall be called periodically Conferences which may include all States which associate themselves for these specific purposes."

The bearing of this proposal upon the subsequent history of the League and its relation to the United States surely needs no elaboration.[1] Written as it was, after the opposition in the Senate had begun to assume formidable proportions, it shaped a reservation for the United States, without mentioning it, which could have made the United States, as an Associate of the League, a full member of the most important functioning bodies, those specifically directed to the solution of the major problems of international relations. The argument that I used to support the claim that the League would work out substantially along these lines was that the Assembly would prove to be a relatively weak body, instead of the strong organization which seemed indicated by its size and its prestige. It would accentuate the greatest element of weakness in all legislative bodies, namely, heterogeneity. Legislative bodies suffer from the fact that all kinds and conditions of men represent in them all kinds and conditions of interests. In a world assembly the confusion which reigns in so many parliaments would be multiplied by the number of nations present. Therefore it would follow that the Council, instead of being a mere executive for the Assembly, would inevitably become the real center of League action. That is why I tried to get a different set-up for the Council. Had the Assembly, however, been supplemented by a series of periodic conferences called for specific purposes, there would have been better media for League activities than bureaus subordinate to the Council and Assembly, incapable of initiative on their own account, but merely carrying out the limited terms of reference assigned to them by the group of statesmen who would probably more and more represent Foreign Offices if the League succeeded.

It was urged against my proposal that it opened the door to too indiscriminate an extension of the sphere of activities of the League. Lord Cecil especially was strongly opposed to any such development; and, in those days of tentative thinking, it must be admitted that the case against a formal recognition of special conferences was a strong one. Liberal criticism of the Covenant, at that time, chiefly concentrated upon the fact that the League of Nations was, after all, a league of governments rather than of peoples, and there was a widespread demand for something like popular representation in the

---

[1] It is discussed in my volume, *On the Rim of the Abyss* (Macmillan, 1936). See also below, p. 253.

new world parliament. This would never have worked, and it was above all necessary to avoid opening the door to any such mistaken parallels with national legislative bodies.

My proposal, however, has in reality no such vague outlines as this, and was, as a matter of fact, diametrically opposed to it. It was an effort to secure more instead of less definite functioning, by the creation of bodies to deal with the major issues in and for themselves, with limited agenda, operating strictly within defined terms of reference.

Once again, in 1924, the issue was squarely raised as to the possibility of applying this kind of structure for disarmament procedure. In the so-called "American plan," which General Bliss, Mr. Miller and I took to Geneva at the Assembly of that year, we proposed that the question of disarmament should be dealt with as a continuing problem, never wholly solved, raising major issues from year to year for which the ordinary machinery of the League was entirely inadequate. The proposal for a regular series of periodically recurring conferences on disarmament, with its special secretariat as a recognized branch of the League's organization, was not even then accepted for fear of the growth of a quasi-autonomous body at the expense of the rest of the constitution of the League. The proposal, brought forward again at the Assembly of 1925, finally became a central recommendation of the League's program of disarmament.]

Saturday, March 29, 1919

Called on Dragoni, head of the International Institute of Agriculture of Rome, to propose its inclusion among the bureaus of the League of Nations. Dragoni is a distinguished looking Italian with a fair command of English. I asked him for dinner on Monday evening to meet Butterfield of the Massachusetts Institute of Agriculture. Butterfield is now head of the new army college of agriculture at Baume, in central France, and so I called on Kingsbury to telegraph him to come to the Monday conference.

After lunch I had a telephone call from Lieutenant Orville Peets of Woodstock, and drove over at once to see him. I found with him Captain Jenkinson of Woodstock. The Captain has been with the Y.M.C.A. through the Argonne fighting and has been up in the front line for the whole of it. He said he had been in the trenches when the guns were so hot you could boil coffee on them. However, he came off without a scratch. Mr. Peets left the Y.M.C.A. for the army and is a member of the Intelligence Staff. I shall try to get him into the army educational commission to teach art.

At three I was at the Ministry of Labor with the editorial committee working on the final text of the report. After the session I took a stroll in the quiet corner of Paris beyond the tomb of Napoleon, up to the statue of Pasteur. You get a striking contrast looking over the shoulder of the very impressive monument to Pasteur down the long avenue of trees to the tomb of Napoleon. Coming into the hotel, I ran into Colonel Lawrence and brought him up to tea in my room, discussing the relation of education to the problems of the Near East. Beer joined us shortly and invited Lawrence to dinner with us and Mr. and Mrs. Bullitt, and Professor Rappard. Bullitt is keen on Russia, and having a journalist's eye for the dramatic and ear for the news, he gave us a lively picture. If Bolshevism is willing to make the compromise which Bullitt is sure it will, the situation is not so desperate as people have been describing it.

Sunday, March 30, 1919

My first day at the front. By half past six I was getting breakfast in the soldiers' mess at 4 Place de la Concorde. They have the kitchen of a well-known restaurant and tables in the covered courtyard and serve about 600 men a day. I had coffee, well-cooked pancakes and porridge with condensed milk, all in tin dishes.

The day was very cold, in fact one of the most wintry days we have had, with a real snowstorm and a cold north wind. The wind kept up all day and the snow by fits and starts. But all the same our Cadillac made 250 miles before we got back, and a good part of that over roads filled with holes, some worn by war traffic, some shell holes just roughly filled in. The driver, however, had driven trucks by night without lights along the front and had taken other parties out before, and so when he let it out to fifty miles an hour, I said nothing. The one thing I wasn't used to was going down hill at toboggan speed. He seemed to feel that if it kept its nose pointed up the road the car wouldn't swerve; anyway we came through safely. So much for the road.

It was eight o'clock when we left the gate of Paris and started down the long road towards Meaux, the same military road that runs to Rheims and Verdun. In an hour from the time we left the Crillon we were looking across the beet fields to the little hamlet of Monthyon, two or three kilometers away, from which the first cannon of the Battle of the Marne was fired by the Germans at noon on September 5, 1914. They were the beet fields across which the Moroccan brigade had charged in the open; long and wide, without so much cover as weeds, and almost as level as a floor. Beyond them, on the horizon to the northeast, the trees around two villages marked the position of von Kluck's army, as it had halted on its way to the Marne in order to repulse this unexpected flank attack. The German line was well concealed as it ran through broken, wooded country; but the French forced them from it on the first day of the battle. We followed a little country lane across the center of the battlefield. In front of us was Neufmontiers, behind a little stream where the Germans had had their machine guns, and up the hill beyond it were the village and woods of Penchard, commanding the whole countryside. The fields are being plowed again, but they are marked with graves, each with its little wooden cross and tag, and with a branch of palm stuck in at the head by the Society for the Memory of Fallen Soldiers. These palms were bent over in the wind and half covered with snow, and added to the dreary suggestion of the battlefield more than anything else. Except for the graves, however, the country here has recovered much of its normal character and many of the barns are roofed again and the farmers are at work, for the first Battle of the Marne left relatively few permanent traces. We went on to Chambry, which changed hands from French to Germans several times on the sixth and seventh of September. There must have been desperate fighting at the high stone walls around the farm buildings. At Varreddes, we suddently found ourselves on the edge of the great valley of the Marne. Then for the first time we realized how high we were above the valley. The northern plain is like a plateau, with the Marne cut through it almost as deep as the upper Hudson valley, only with less precipitous hills. Here and there along the higher reaches are woodlands. Looking down from the hill above Varreddes we could see the Marne with the bridges and villages. The bridge at Varreddes was blown up on the retreat, and we went over the temporary iron span to Trilport on the south of the river to strike the main road to Château Thierry. We were soon winding along beside the Marne in as picturesque a road as you could imagine.

At La Ferté-sous-Jouarre, where, if I remember rightly, the British crossed the Marne, we came back again to the northern bank. Then, about ten miles on, while going up a long slope into a wood, we suddenly came upon a little row of graves by the roadside, with the American flag above them. We had reached the American line in the Second Battle of the Marne, where, in June 1918, the Germans were held back again from what looked like an easy march to Paris. In the woods beside the road were little dugouts, and, over the brow of the hill, the big trees along the road were all cut down. There had been heavy fighting here, for the American army took about a month to get as far as we went in the next half-hour. Even from the hilltop one could see the havoc caused by our artillery. The village of Vaux, lying in the next transverse valley, was a mass of splintered ruins and rubble. There were only a few walls standing, yet in three of the battered houses we found families returned to what had been their homes, living in utterly miserable conditions.

From Vaux we turned up a little side road through woods and fields to Bouresches. On the western slope facing Bouresches there is now an American cemetery, a beautiful spot with a commemorative chapel. Just ahead of us was the famous Belleau Wood, the Bois de Belleau, which crowns a rocky hill about three miles long and a mile across. Shell holes and tangles of barbed wire in the fields and shrapnel in the road are reminders of the fight. The trees are splintered or shot away, and the brush is thick over the trenches and dugouts where the remains of battle are still lying. The Wilderness which Grant's men fought over around Richmond was nothing to this. Some shallow graves had been blown open by shells and left untouched ever since. These had been German graves; the French and American graves down by the roadside were kept in better order. I wandered on into the woods alone and felt the uncanny silence of the place. But the birds are beginning to come back, hunting nests for spring. From Belleau we went to Château Thierry, passing the dugouts of the Germans on the western hill slope. From this high vantage point one looks down on the picturesque city and the long panorama of the Marne valley. There is a fine old ruined castle above the town which we had time to see while the driver mended a tire. Then we took the road straight north about ten miles more through undulating country crowned with woods, to the village of Brécy, where we turned under the railroad track back up a simple country road to find a little spur running off from the single-track line into the woods. This was the site of one of the long-distance guns that shelled Paris. The switch ran into the woods not more than a couple of hundred feet, and in the track, between ties, little boxes had been sunk at irregular intervals, the meaning of which became clear when we saw a small tree set in one. The Germans had planted little trees along the line of the track by day and removed them by night to hide the gun emplacement from aviators. The emplacement is about twenty feet in diameter and the table supporting the gun runs on ball bearings. There were pneumatic valves and the whole apparatus was a highly delicate piece of mechanism. I gathered up some nuts and bolts and on the edge of the wood a shell case which may have been used by an anti-aircraft gun. There was a big dump of ammunition and supplies still by the railroad track but otherwise no sign of war, and the fields are already plowed and the country looks prosperous.

It was now nearly three o'clock and we went on to Fère-en-Tardenois, a half-ruined town of some size. We followed the country road to the east to the American cemetery, lying on the hillside in the midst of great wide-stretching fields. There are about 500 graves, among which one of the party went vainly hunting for a name in order to write home to parents who had had no word of their son who had fought in this sector. We found that of Joyce Kilmer, however, the poet, a former Columbia University man. From there we decided that although it was late in the afternoon, we might have daylight for a glimpse of Rheims, and drove as fast as was safe to do through a series of ruined towns along the picturesque road through Romigny, Ville-en-Tardenois, Bligny and Pargny, arriving at Rheims about half past five.

The ruins of Rheims are appalling; but we had seen ruins before and it was simply as though the little village of Vaux were multiplied many times. When we drove in front of the cathedral, however, all previous impressions were wiped out. No description will ever be adequate to depict the impressive majesty of that ruin. It looms up much magnified by the destruction of the houses around and the bare stone walls without roof and shattered by explosions on every face of it; in a sense more magnificent than before. In the old days it was so perfect a harmony and so rich in detail that one failed to take in the variety and extent of the creations of sculpture and architecture which combined in it. Now that it is mutilated, the eye is arrested by every detail of what is left and so the height strikes one all the more. Even on the statuaries at the portal there are more mutilations than I had expected. Quite a number of the large figures at the doorway are smashed, the damage having been done before they were able to protect the rest by sandbags. Strangely enough, the slender stone pillars of the colonnades around the top of the walls connecting the flying buttresses are surprisingly intact. The towers also are not destroyed. There are gaping holes in the vault of the nave and the base of the whole church is surrounded by piles of stone rubbish fallen from the walls. A rough fence keeps out sightseers. The statue of Jeanne d'Arc was safely taken away from in front of the cathedral and has not been replaced. Close in front of its base is a gaping hole where a huge shell had exploded. We had only a half hour in Rheims, for with only one good extra tire left it was well not to have too long a run by night.

We picked our way through the streets, where the car had just room to run between piles of rubbish, and found a little restaurant with temporary roofing over ruined walls. We had a good supper on sauerkraut and sausages with some Rheims wine, for six francs apiece. The proprietor was a Pole, the first to come into Rheims to profit from the tourists.

Coming back from Rheims, we had a better view than going in, for it had been snowing as we approached the city. The road runs for a couple of miles at least along through the real No Man's Land, across the trenches which defended Rheims on the west in the last German offensive. The barbed wire is still standing and stretches away over the open country in an irregular line. The section we saw was about fifteen to twenty feet wide. The fields were pockmarked with shell craters, mostly small ones. Turning with the road up a hill lying due west of the city, which I suppose is the one called the Mountain of Rheims in the accounts of the battle, we had a glimpse back over the fields. The ghost of a city is still dominated by the cathedral towers, and looking back over the desolation that lay between, it left one with a last impression as vivid as the first.

From Dormans we followed the valley of the Marne all the way to Meaux, along the main trunk road which fed the army of defense. It is wonderfully well kept up, considering the traffic, and has few of the pit holes we had to knock over on the northern roads. The towns here showed less of the effects of war, but they were all depressingly desolate, with most houses closed and few people in sight, although it was Sunday evening. To be sure, it was a bleak March day and the chill in the air got into one's bones and added to the general feeling of discomfort. We followed the river along its southern bank for some fifty miles, catching now and then a gleam of reflected light from its surface. It was dark before we reached Meaux, which is a city of considerable size. However, the narrow main street runs close enough to the cathedral for us to see that it is a fine, impressive building. Then we turned on the searchlights and struck the long, straight road for Paris.

It is a distinct experience to drive by night with searchlights along these roads with the columns of trees on either side absolutely regular for miles on end. The light strikes the tree trunks and leaves a sort of wall of darkness on the outside, giving one the impression of riding through a covered gallery—at fifty miles an hour. We had our third blow-out on the bleak top of a hill on the southern edge of Ourcq battlefield, beside a deserted ruin of a beet factory. We still had a good distance to make and were just fitting in our last spare tube when a car drew up behind us and the khaki driver jumped out and came up to us and was greeted by our own with a request for an extra tube. This was instantly supplied. The little incident gave one a feeling of the omnipresence of the American army in France.

By ten o'clock I was lugging the souvenirs into my office and wiping the mud off my overcoat.

Monday, March 31, 1919

Morning—I was waited on by a small delegation of American labor women, Miss Mary Anderson of the Trade Union League and Miss Rose Schneidermann, who arrived from America too late to influence the first draft, at least, of the Labor Convention. We had a good long talk, and I was glad to have their approval of what had been done. They had only a few minor suggestions.

Was to have had Dragoni of the Rome Agricultural Institute for dinner, but as Butterfield could not come up from Baume for a week, we postponed this.

Was busy most of the day trying to make sure that the Labor Report would receive the attention of the whole conference and would be accepted in a general session. Found little interest in it, as everyone was busy on his own particular job. The Commissioners are worn out trying to keep up with the mass of routine that comes in from so many different quarters.

In the evening I went up to the Majestic to report the result of the day's lobbying in the American Delegation and found my British colleagues in about my own state of mind, which was irritation and uncertainty as to whether our work was really going to be given its place or snowed under by the interest in political and territorial settlement.

Tuesday, April 1, 1919

After a good deal of pushing, we succeeded in getting the question of whether the Labor Report was to have a full-dress hearing or not on the agenda for the meeting of the Foreign Ministers this afternoon. In the morning I had a session with Mr. Lansing for a few minutes in his office on the elegant first floor of the Crillon. He has almost as fine a room as Pichon and showed about as much understanding of the labor problem as Pichon might. However, we got it before the Foreign Ministers, and at three o'clock I drove over with Mr. Harrison of the State Department to the Quai d'Orsay, where shortly Mr. Robinson and then Mr. Barnes joined us, and we went into the session.

The Ten has dissolved, and the four Prime Ministers, Wilson, Lloyd George, Orlando and Clemenceau, meet by themselves in Wilson's house to try to hurry the terms of peace. This leaves the Foreign Ministers, five of them, to meet by themselves, and it is that meeting which we attended. Pichon presided and had Tardieu with him, and there were Lansing, Balfour, Sonnino, and Makino, the Japanese.

The discussion at this meeting was most discouraging. Mr. Barnes pleaded for a full session of the Peace Conference in order to lay the results of the Labor Commission before the world in a meeting of all governments. If he could not get that, he wanted a full publication of our report distributed to the whole Conference.

The chief objector was Mr. Lansing, who showed anything but enthusiasm for the work that had been done. It was, as he strongly argued, a departure from diplomatic practice which might make further adjustment necessary in years to come and would be bothersome for foreign offices to carry out. Baron Sonnino was almost as strong in opposition; Mr. Balfour, strangely enough, was less conservative than most of his colleagues and showed that he appreciated the importance of the political bearing of Labor in the Peace Conference more than the other ministers did. The result of the afternoon's work, however, was about as discouraging as anything that has happened in the whole course of our work, for the rigid mind of the foreign office official is about the last in the world to decide whether or not something should be done for Labor in this Peace Conference.

I brought Barnes and Delevingne to my room for afternoon tea, of which they both declared themselves sadly in need, in view of the failure of the Foreign Ministers to grant the degree of attention to the Commission which Mr. Barnes asked. As a matter of fact, he was about as hot a Briton as I have seen in Paris, and Sir Malcolm said that if I hadn't asked him home to tea he would have gone up to his room to have an old-fashioned cry, as he used to have in boyhood days. However, I do not think that a better plan could be followed than to get the criticisms on this scheme before it is made public in a spectacular way, for the labor clauses were hurriedly thrown in at the close of the session and are by no means well done; besides there are some points to be changed with reference to the representation of women on the Governing Body which ought to be put into shape before the document is formally accepted by the Peace Conference.

In the evening I was busy getting copies of the document for publication and ran up once more to the Majestic for the necessary copies, which Ray Stannard Baker will be sending over to the American weeklies.

Wednesday, April 2, 1919

Captain Osterhout for breakfast. He was a student of mine in Columbia and has been in the courier service of the Delegation, going back and forth across Central Europe all through the winter. His story of the conditions there makes one as anxious for the speedy signing of the Treaty as the journalists have become, and that's saying all that could be said! He secured an army trunk for me from the commissariat (which I paid for properly enough) and I am hoping to send home all the articles which I gathered on the battlefields, from machine gun ratchets to flattened bullets from the streets of Ypres, and, of course, helmets and brass cartridges. I suppose every one of the two millions of the A. E. F. is carrying home about the same kind of things that I am sending.

I worked on some of the labor problems in the morning. Barnes has not given up his fight to get a plenary conference for the Labor Report. He has written an exceedingly strong letter to Lloyd George criticizing the action, or rather the inaction, of the Council of Ten but pointing out that the final decision to put the matter up to the President and Prime Ministers is, after all, a good solution, for the Council of the Four will have a better sense of the value of our work than the foreign office people. Thus a three days' delay can be expected now, but Lloyd George can hardly let Labor down completely after having left to Barnes the task of meeting the activities of Henderson and his friends by action at the Peace Conference itself.

Lunch with Piacentini of the Italian Delegation and Akers-Douglas of the British, discussing with Beer the Morocco negotiations. In the afternoon a long talk with Johann Castberg, president of the Norwegian Odelsting, ex-Minister of Justice and of Social Reform, who is in Paris looking after the interests of Norway at the Peace Conference and is particularly interested in labor; a pleasant but powerful type of man. He seemed well pleased with what we had done and said that he considered it was the most important thing that had taken place in Paris. He also is interested in the Seamen's Act, and I learned that Furuseth has gone to Norway.

Beer and I took a walk in the afternoon to the Louvre and spent an hour in the museum. The Luxembourg gallery of painting, recent acquisitions, and the sculpture rooms were open; but nothing of the old masters. We sauntered home through the Luxembourg Gardens and when I got to my room had a call from William Fullerton, author of the book, *Problems of Power*. He is considering doing a life of Clemenceau for Houghton Mifflin, in the series I planned with Mr. Hoyt.

Thursday, April 3, 1919

Morning—At lunch we had as guest R. H. Brand of the British Commission, member of the financial section. The drift of the discussion was rather sad upon the whole, although the English seem to have put their house in order sufficiently to weather the storm through a very courageous policy of heavy taxation of income and capital. Brand said that at one time the bankers in England memorialized the Government, asking that a higher rate of taxation be placed on capital, although it was then bearing far more than other countries had risked. The contrast with some other of our Allies is pretty strong, but the effect of its foresight is that now England is partly able to meet its obligations, while bankruptcy faces the others.

I spent a part of the day writing letters and at tea had a talk on Japanese problems with Pat Gallagher, who came to Beer's room. This irrepressible Irish correspondent of the *Herald* has been one of the joys of tired amateur diplomats in the Crillon. He was in the Far East for some years. He knows most of the gossip before we do and so we always like to see him come around. In the evening I had Walter Weyl to dinner and took him to a show that the soldiers are putting on in the Theatre of the Y.M.C.A. It was entitled a "Buck on Leave"—"buck" being the name now used for soldier, instead of "doughboy." It was a sort of vaudeville, with most of the hits against the officers. One joke will give an idea of the type of humor. While the audience was assembling a Military Policeman came down the aisle and hauled a private out of his seat. The private objected that the seat was his but the policeman ordered him to get out, and in the altercation that followed told him it was reserved for an officer. The soldier then gave in, with a protest to the audience that this was the first time he had ever known an officer to take the place of a soldier at the front! Another joke was along this line. The chief spokesman pretended to see a sad looking man, whom he promptly identified as an officer, and asked him why he was so sad. The answer was that he was about to lose the best job he ever had. Then someone dressed like General Pershing came on the stage, and Buck went up to him, shook hands, and called him "Jack." It was all very simple humor and a commonplace show, but I think it is one of the most significant things I have seen in Paris, for no other army in war-time could have ventured such freedom with their officers, many of whom, of course, were present. We came away very much impressed with the quality of the resiliency in an army that can stand such give and take.

[While I was taking the night off, Barnes was busy fighting to get the British Empire Delegation behind him in support of our demand for a general session on the Labor Clauses. Lloyd George responded to Mr. Barnes' appeal with unreserved acceptance of the labor demands, and it was the Prime Minister who forced on a reluctant delegation the proposal that a plenary session should be held. The Dominions were the chief objectors, and Lloyd George had to remind them several times that their conservative attitude might help the spread of Bolshevism throughout Europe if they refused to co-operate in putting this draft convention into the Peace Treaty. Mr. Barnes told me next day that M. Clemenceau also supported the plan to have the Convention adopted by the plenary session.]

Friday, April 4, 1919

Spent the morning taking the two American women labor delegates, Rose Schneidermann and Mary Anderson, to see Mr. Barnes and the British Delegation at the Majestic. They wanted to have a modification made, but we decided to leave the established text since there was a definite recognition of women workers in it.

Lunch with Professor Augustin Bernard, a French authority on colonial history and Morocco, whom Beer brought, a very keen and open-minded man.

Saturday, April 5, 1919

At nine-thirty we had our pictures taken with Colonel House in his office.

Lunched with Fontaine at his apartment, meeting Seignobos, the historian. Fontaine grows on one; he is a man of wide culture. His walls are filled with pictures, among others two magnificent portraits by Carrière of Fontaine and his daughter, with all of Carrière's delicate handling of color and shadow and at the same time a marvelous interpretation of character in the faces. Seignobos is a little old man, talking fast and furiously, very well satisfied with our labor business, which he seems to hold in higher regard than we do. A Pole was there from our Labor Commission, M. Patek of the Supreme Court of Poland, a very able advocate, who found much sympathy in his French auditors. Fontaine has three boys in the twenties in uniform and one daughter, who has studied medicine.

I walked home, as it was a beautiful spring day, and did not get much work under way in the afternoon, but at five-thirty drove over to the Ritz Hotel, where one of the women suffrage delegates, the wife of a banker, had asked me to meet with her and the two American labor women. I found them there, but the hostess out, and we escaped from a pink tea with High Society in the Ritz tea garden. Instead, I took them to the little English tea room of Smith & Son around the corner and then for a stroll in the Tuileries gardens. They are going back to America prepared to fight hard to make our labor program a success.

A quiet dinner (with Ray Stannard Baker all depressed), and after it Colonel Ayres and I went over the maps of the battle fronts in my room to plan for tomorrow's trip.

The Battlefields of the Aisne

Sunday, April 6, 1919

The morning was chill as we left Paris, with a white mist lying low over the city and country. We followed the same route over the battlefield of the Ourcq, but in the haze we could hardly make out the distant villages—Monthyon and Penchard—along the great plain on the north. The objects in the landscape were not so clearly cut as in the snow of the week before. From Chambry, instead of going south to the Marne Valley at Varreddes, as on the previous visit, we turned north to Etrépilly, down the hillside which a little brook has cut through the plain. Practically every little stream here has worn a valley more or less like the Marne. On the crest of the hill above were clusters of little crosses in the grain fields marking the point where the attacking French had been mown down on the last days of the battle of the Marne. Then on, over the same kind of open fields, to another valley where the Ourcq Canal and Stream, both about the same size, were crossed at Lizy. This ended the Ourcq battlefield, and we struck across country to Château-Thierry, and on to Rheims.

Going in the other direction along the Marne valley from the return trip of last Sunday I was more impressed with the signs of war. The opposite hill slope has few fields that are not marked with the chalk pile of a shell burst. Every village across the stream showed gaping shell holes in the walls. At Dormans we passed through a long, wide village street, on both sides of which were long rows of French army trucks. The houses were badly smashed and those by the bridge all in ruins; but people were coming back to the town. It was a picturesque sign of war to see so many French soldiers there, apparently returning from the frontier. I forgot to mention that earlier on the trip several times we met marching companies of French poilus coming out of the mist along the roadside, and at a couple of places German prisoners driving wagons.

Rheims was reached at about eleven o'clock. We visited the ruins at the same time with the Queen of Rumania and her little suite.

Rheims is as dead a city as Pompeii, and the ruins remind one somewhat of those of antiquity. In fact, from Rheims on, as far as Soissons, we all had the impression, I think, of having passed out of the modern world back into a vanished civilization. Last Sunday I said that Rheims was much more terrible than the Marne front. This Sunday we went on from Rheims into the wilderness of the war, and now, as I look back at it, it is simply the symbol of the whole vast desolation. From Rheims we took the road along the Aisne front to Laon, a straight turnpike across what was once as prosperous a farming country as those cultivated fields along the Ourcq, but now for about fifteen or twenty miles an uninhabited desert. Through it ran continuous lines of trenches with white chalky parapets, stretching over the fields as far as the eye could see, unendingly, with barbed wire entanglements in all directions. Not a soul in sight. Absolute silence. We stopped for lunch by a trench side and the only sign of life was the song of a meadow lark.

Before we finished, however, a group of refugees came up the road from Rheims, two women and three men in middle life with three children. They were carrying baskets of food on their heads and shoulders and a bundle of household truck. As they trudged on, over a slight rise in the roadway, they started laughing and singing. They were apparently nearing "home." Other nations have called these people "volatile"! A little later, we came to a stream crossing the road and on the temporary bridge I asked an old woman how much farther it was to Berry-au-Bac. She gave a wave of her hand at the pulverized stone piles near and said, in a tone that struck us all, *"Berry-au-Bac, c'est ici."* There are no walls left high enough to have a roof, none over six or seven feet. The old woman was the only person in sight. The stream was the Aisne. We crossed it, verging toward the hilly country which the Germans held so long.

Just beyond Berry-au-Bac, we turned west to a gaunt hillside, which had been visible from away across the plain, the famous heights of Craonne, at the east end of the Chemin des Dames. Imagine a hill about four or five hundred feet high of chalky rock, so pulverized that it was simply a great pile of chalk powder slightly discolored with ground-up rubbish which had been blown into it, not an inch of it that had not been smashed by heavy shells, and not a blade of grass nor even a sign of any ruin; nothing but a vast pile of powdered refuse. That was the height of Craonne. The road had been repaired up the hillside so the car could take it, and on the edge of the slope we halted by some extra high piles of dust and stone, suddenly realizing we were in what had been the town of Craonne. It was as much worse than Berry-au-Bac as Berry-au-Bac was worse than Rheims. Nothing was left above ground, though here and there one could make out cellars, especially where they had been used for dugouts. I walked up what was once the village street and entered a hillside dugout, walking straight in for about a hundred feet. It was well-timbered, with a very narrow passage and would not hold many men. Just under the brow of the hill were corrugated iron sheds with bunks in them. In one there was a kitchen with a range, in others I noticed the installation of electric lights and little stoves to make the quarters cozy; but they were as poor sheds as one would care to pass a night in, let alone live in through a winter on the desolate hillside. German helmets and other spoils of war were lying about.

From Craonne we swung up the hill to the flat top of the long ridge that runs east and west about two or three miles from the Aisne and parallel with it. It is this which constitutes the great natural bastion known as "Chemin des Dames"—the Ladies' Roadway. When we got to the hilltop we had hoped to follow the roadway of the Chemin des Dames itself along the whole hillcrest. But our car got only a few car-lengths on that road, the most famous in France, for all trace of it has disappeared, at least at the eastern end, in a wilderness of shell craters. Even if one could trace it for a distance, there would be danger of getting lost, because there is no sign of direction, and one shell crater is like another. We could not look across the top of the hill to the valley of the Ailette on the north and so did not see the northern German position, but south of us lay the Valley of the Aisne and the trench-guarded plain toward Rheims as far as the eye could carry; and from the height of four hundred feet or so, with a level country below, one can see for many miles.

On through the ruins of Oulches, Jumigny, and Paissy, skirting the brow of the hilltop along the street of the strangest village I have yet seen. Behind each house is a cave dug by the quarry workers in the hillside. These were alternately strongholds of French or German armies when each was in occupation. The street is a narrow one and runs along the edge of a precipice, so that you look straight down a hundred feet or so below you from the car. We kept along this southern slope for a little distance, and then struck down to the Aisne itself, which we followed to Bourg with the height along the north at regular distance all the way.

We were now down in the river valley beside the stream. There were trenches along the roadside, for at one time in the war the Aisne itself was the front. The valley is much less attractive than the Marne. It is marshy much of the way, the hills are more abrupt, and I rather imagine that even before the war the country was not quite so well cultivated as the Marne Valley, where every foot of ground is worked down to the water's edge. At Vailly, formerly a town of over three thousand inhabitants, a well-dressed leading citizen told us that only a hundred and fifty had come back to their houses, which were not in very bad repair—by comparison. At Bucy-le-long there were Annamite troops lounging along the street front. They are used to rebuild the roads and drive camions.

We were at Soissons between five and six. The town is much less battered than Rheims but the cathedral has suffered more. A great slender shaft of stone is all that remains of the great southern tower, perched perilously at the corner of the façade and looking as though it were likely to fall at any time. The roof of the nave is completely knocked in. Some of the apse is still intact but the church as a whole was so badly destroyed as to be beyond repair.

From Soissons we took the road to Villers-Cotterets up the southern hill from which there was a good view of Soissons nestling at the foot of the slopes in the Aisne Valley. We were going south-west to Paris. There is a little stream entering the Aisne here from the south. Through a wide, deep valley, and on both hillsides, the Germans had held strongly fortified positions along the salient which they had pushed into the French lines in their last drive, the one our troops checked at Château-Thierry. Along the roadside, as in so many miles of the day's trip, there were rifle pits and machine gun nests. As we came to the top of the hill, however, and came out on that same wide-spreading plain which is characteristic of the whole country from here to the Marne, we ran into signs of harder fighting, and soon came upon half a dozen tanks close by the roadside where they had been blown into a wreck by artillery. They were French tanks belonging to those troops whom Foch flung on the German flank on the eighteenth of August, last, which brought the final victory. One came with surprise upon them, however, standing in the middle of ordinary farm fields, for south of Soissons the country is beginning to resume its ordinary appearance. Farmers have begun plowing. Our road ran through the forest of Villers-Cotterets where Mangin hid the army with which he attacked the German flank. It is certainly a forest to hide in. We drove through it for some ten miles on a road marked on the map "not good for autos," but it had been rebuilt and was good enough for 55 miles an hour. We told the chauffeur that we were not in any hurry and the next time we examined the speedometer it had been put out of business, but we kept whizzing past things at the same rate.

The country from Villers-Cotterets to Paris is a great plain of cultivated fields with little hamlets set rather far apart and here and there a town with a long street and more or less rickety houses. We came through Crépy to Senlis along a road absolutely straight for twenty miles or so, with long avenues of trees on both sides, most of the way to Paris. Senlis was the last town the Germans got to in August, 1914, and they had burned down one street and shot the mayor because of some shooting in the town, but the cathedral is untouched. Twilight was falling as we stopped beside it. Inside a service was being held, the confirmation of a group of young girls dressed in white with white veils, and the altar was brightly lighted in front of them. The congregation, however, of old and middle-aged women, was almost entirely in mourning.

From Senlis we struck across the forest of Chantilly on the long road home through many miles of elm-like avenues, passing the airdromes of Le Bourget, arriving at the Crillon at about half past seven. We had gone nearly three hundred miles, two hundred of which were over battlefields.

Monday, April 7, 1919

Sunday night, on arriving at the hotel, Storck, Bowman's secretary, told me of the sudden death of Frary, one of my assistants in the Library. He caught cold last Sunday on a trip to the front. As late as Wednesday he had gone to the Economic Commission to act as secretary. It was a case of quick and virulent pneumonia. It was a hard blow to most of us, for he had won friends in the whole delegation by his ability and his generous, sunny nature. We arranged for funeral services in the American Church.

Today another of the Library staff was reported seriously ill, Miss Florence Wilson, formerly of Columbia University Library, then of the Inquiry. The doctor diagnosed it as measles and ordered her removal to the military hospital. Inquiry showed that the hospital was dreaded by everyone and that no arrangements were possible for separate care of women. So, as she was partly under the auspices of the Y.M.C.A., Lieutenant Berle and I spent the afternoon rushing from Red Cross headquarters to their attending physician in Passy and finally back to Miss Wilson's apartment, where the doctor confirmed the diagnosis, and I drove him to the Institut Pasteur. On the way over I asked him about sanitary conditions in France and the report was not reassuring. He got the last vacant bed in the institution and so Miss Wilson had to be carried down the steep, winding stairs of the quaint old boarding house near the Luxembourg in which she had been living, put on a stretcher and taken in the ambulance to the hospital.

Tuesday, April 8, 1919

In my room during the morning, making arrangements with reference to the funeral, dictating letters, etc. The funeral was at two o'clock, a simple but impressive ceremony. About a hundred members of the staff were present.

As we came out, Bowman, Major Patterson and I walked along the Seine to get away for a moment from all thought of the Peace Conference. There is no escape, however, from the reminders of the war, even in those park-like avenues where the children are playing. The sky was clear blue and away high over us a daredevil aeronaut was playing in the sky, not only looping backwards and forwards, but falling like a leaf in the wind and then catching himself, shooting up and back again in nose dive and tail dive. We were glad to get indoors and shake off the nervous tension.

At four o'clock I was at Fontaine's office at a meeting of the delegates to consider plans for the general session of the Peace Conference to be held on Friday, at which the labor document is to be presented. The Japanese have received orders from home to sign upon securing a slight modification, and so the British Empire, with reluctant India, is also obliged to get in line and we expect unanimous consent.

[The difficulties of Japan in accepting the labor clauses of the Treaty were much more real than those of the United States; for the actual conditions of labor, although above the average of Asiatic countries, were still considerably below those of the other Powers represented on the Commission. Special consideration was given to the Asiatic countries by a provision which recognized different degrees of industrial development, climatic conditions or other circumstances which might make the application of uniform standards for labor impossible. It was clear, however, that the Japanese negotiators were frequently embarrassed in the discussion by the fact that they had to admit a lower level of living in Japan at the very time when, in the League of Nations Commission, they were insisting upon racial equality. The embarrassment took the form of reticence rather than of any strong word of protest about being placed in a false position, and the Japanese negotiators won the respect of every one by their obviously sincere effort to find a way to co-operate. They were evidently acting under strict orders from home, however, and on more than one occasion when asked their opinion they avoided replying by pleading a breakdown in the cable communications with Tokyo, until this diplomatic device became too obvious and the Japanese themselves saw the humor of it. The only one of the Japanese Delegation whom I got to know at all intimately was Dr. Oka, and a more competent, straight-thinking and liberal-minded economist it would be hard to find. As a matter of fact, of all the signatories of the Labor Section of the Treaty of Versailles, it was Japan which took it most seriously in the period immediately following. Its delegation to the Washington Labor Conference was the largest of any, and its government at once began to take measures to bring the labor legislation of the country more into accord with American and European standards.[1]]

I had dinner with Miller and spent the evening with him discussing plans for the future. There has been a great wave of despondency over the Conference recently which is due to several things, but among them I believe the main thing is that we do not

---

[1] I called attention to this fact in a letter to the London *Times* of November 21, 1919.

know what is being done. The talk with Miller, who knows more than the rest, gave me the feeling that much of the criticism is not justified. He showed me the new text of the League of Nations and I was happy to find that they had followed the order I had suggested with reference to the opening clauses, but the recognition of periodic conferences as an integral part of the League which I tried to secure is only partially met.

[In the first report of the Commission which drafted the Covenant, the articles on the membership of the League of Nations followed the description of the Assembly and Council. I had pointed this out to Mr. Miller previously, and the result was, as the diary states, that Article 2 of the first draft became, in a revised form, Article I of the Covenant.[1]

The other proposal, for recognition of periodic conferences, seemed to me at the time to have been partly met by the second sentence in Article 24 of the Covenant: "All such international bureaux and all commissions for the regulation of matters of international interest hereafter constituted shall be placed under the direction of the League."[2] The subsequent history of the League has more than once made it clear that this vague phraseology, while it permits the League to use conferences and other semi-external instruments from time to time, does not point the path of synthetic development in this direction. The compromise text therefore did not, in reality, achieve what I was aiming at, which was to put an emphasis upon the conference method in international affairs so that public opinion would not concentrate its judgment of the League upon its failure or success in the purely police activities of preserving peace or averting war.]

Wednesday, April 9, 1919

In my room this morning, with no work pressing. Lunch with Walter Weyl and Philippe Millet. We discussed the peace with Germany in rather a somber mood. In the afternoon sent Colonel House some suggestions for the discussion on the labor document when it comes up in the plenary session. Then a drive up to the British headquarters, but failed to find my man. A quiet dinner talking about Italy of the Renaissance with Major Thomas. Read a while and so enjoyed a real day's rest.

[1] Miller, *Drafting of the Covenant,* II, 648, 668.   [2] *Ibid.,* I, 341; II, 356.

Morning spent in routine work, partly in connection with the British changes in the text for tomorrow. Recast my memorandum suggesting the course to be pursued by ourselves at the plenary session.

In the afternoon I went over to the Panthéon, to a ceremony in honor of the dead writers of France, killed in the war. A wreath was laid upon a catafalque draped with the tricolor and on a dais under the dome. Behind it was arranged a band of the Garde Républicaine with their full dress helmets of gold and long *crinières* (mane or crest of horsehair). A choir from the Schola Cantorum also took part. I have seldom heard anything more affecting than "taps," sounding through the vacant spaces of the Panthéon and the voices of the choir in Palestrina's old music of four hundred years ago. General Malleterre read the names of 450 French writers who had been killed in the war and there were poems written by poets in the war. But again the audience was as significant as the ceremony. Whenever a thing like this happens, you realize how deeply France has been stricken.

After the ceremony I went over to the Sorbonne for Professor Haskins' lecture in the series in which I have to figure later. It was a good lecture, and there was an audience of some two hundred, fairly sprinkled with gray-bearded professors, although the afternoon-tea lady was also in evidence. If I have half as many I shall be surprised.

Spent the evening quietly at the Crillon with Sir Malcolm Delevingne, who had dinner with me, and together we fixed up the last bit of planning for the great day of the Labor Charter. There was some doubt about Lord Sinha's attitude with reference to the application of the Convention to India. The thing he took most exception to was the clause with reference to children, as a child is supposed to be grown up in India by the age of fourteen. I pointed out how serious it would be if Sinha took a purely negative attitude, and got Sir Malcolm to work through Barnes on Sinha to change his speech. Sir Malcolm fell in with this and took my suggestion to Barnes, who strongly supported it and got Lord Sinha to adjust his speech accordingly. Sir Malcolm and I also rigged up some other plans and then he went back to the Majestic to put them through. As the League of Nations Commission was in session at the Crillon in Colonel House's office, I couldn't reach anyone else.

Friday, April 11, 1919

A beautiful warm April day, although I didn't step into the sunshine until I left in the afternoon for the séance at the Quai d'Orsay. In the morning I was at the telephone talking with Sir Malcolm and learned that things were going well at his end. I saw Robinson and got him to move in on Lansing. Then I prepared a further memorandum for the President through Colonel House.

In the course of the morning a typical incident happened. The French secretariat sent over an Italian text of the Report of the Commission, and a separate French text, stating that the previous one with English and French in parallel columns was withdrawn because the Italians had refused to come to the plenary session at the last moment if the English and French texts were used in this way as the official languages of the Conference. Also ran into the timidity of our authorized secretaries in a vain effort to get tickets of admission for my colleagues.

At luncheon Oulahan, of the *New York Times,* and Sweetser, of the Press Bureau, discussed the Treaty with Anderson and me. The journalists are much depressed. In a treaty of this size it is hard to see the woods for the trees. If the terms are decent enough for the nations to get along with each other for the time being, then the good work that is being done in other lines may make this Conference one to be proud of after all. But it has managed to put itself in the worst light with the public, the newspapers are down on it and nobody knows what is going on, so that all the dismal gossip circulates in Paris in a blue and sulphurous haze. At the last moment before going to the Conference I dictated directly to the machine an additional suggestion for the President.

[This was simply an *aide memoire* for the President's speech. In addition to a suggestion that he refer to the invitation to hold the first meeting of the International Labor Conference at Washington, I suggested that the nine points of the Labor Charter should be accepted, in view of the Japanese-British amendment to Article 19 which would permit each country to apply these principles in its own way and under its own special conditions. The principle, therefore, could be accepted although the wording was to be readjusted. As for the participation of the United States, I fell back upon the argument, which I had advanced time and again, that the position taken by the United States would enlarge rather than lessen the scope of future conferences by making provision for recommendations for legislation instead of only draft conventions. The procedure which America proposed would have more chance of developing common ideals of social justice than the alternative procedure by way of treaties.]

At 2:45 I was in the car with Beer (to whom Frank Simonds surrendered his newspaper pass) en route across the bridge to the Foreign Office for the Fourth Plenary Session of the Peace Conference. Driving up to the steps of the Foreign Office, we arrived just as the official British moving picture man was taking a picture of Barnes and his colleagues standing chatting on the doorstep. They hailed my arrival and dragged me forward into the picture, and so the incident is preserved in the records of the British history of the Peace Conference. There were other pictures taken in the course of the session, but the light was poor and the crowd too great. There were also several artists sketching, among them a Japanese.

Meanwhile, the audience began to filter in. The Labor Commission was assigned a row of chairs close beside the horseshoe table toward the head, so I had a very fine point of vantage. It happened strangely enough that the man behind whom I was seated was Sir Robert Borden, who got very busy with the other Dominion Premiers in the course of the debate, trying to make sure that the Dominions were not being dragged into obligations in the labor field unless they were represented in the League of Nations. Balfour sat a few feet away and this time was anything but asleep. In the course of the session he worked away on the document, intent upon killing the "nine points" of the Labor Charter. Bonar Law beside him looks like a rather ordinary business man, with none of Balfour's intellectual power and none of Lloyd George's quick comprehension, at least none written on his face. The three men at the center of the table, Lloyd George, Clemenceau, and Wilson, are fundamentally alike in their ability to apply a principle immediately to any given situation. All three certainly came to the room without fully knowing what was ahead of them, and yet they did what I imagine was exactly the right thing to do—that is, if they follow up the situation where they left it. After Wilson got seated and the room was filling up, House came in, leaned over the President's chair and handed him my second memorandum. The President studied it carefully; but either the opportunity did not offer itself to him (I think that it did), or else he, perhaps, felt that it was not wise for America to speak too definitely at this juncture, for he used only the first point of the memorandum, a point on which he scarcely needed one. Perhaps the private discussions carried on from Balfour's end of the table drove all else out of his mind when he rose to speak. I should explain that all of this discussion around the head table, which brought the veins out on Balfour's flushed face and the twinkle into Clemenceau's eyes, was carried on while speeches were being made. As Walter Weyl said later, the chief use of speeches is to enable the leading statesmen to discuss matters among themselves while the audience is being entertained.

First of all about the room. The previous sessions had been held in the Room of the Clock (Salle de l'Horloge), so called from a marble clock on the mantelpiece, a room large enough for the Conference but very poorly provided with room for the journalists. The session of the Ten which I attended before was in a still smaller room, which is the official office of the French Foreign Minister. This time we passed through a suite of elegant antechambers to the banquet hall of the French Foreign Office. There are three windows on each side, with mirrors interspersed in the usual French way. The ceiling has Renaissance frescoes (of the late nineteenth century), and there are some eight enormous electroliers which when lighted gave a real touch of magnificence to the otherwise business-like assembly. A huge table covered with green baize was fitted like a horseshoe around the southern half of the room at which the ministers plenipotentiary were seated. At the north end, chairs for the journalists were arranged in regular rows with room for those behind to stand up if they should get interested, which they mostly did.

At three o'clock Clemenceau rose and in very rapid French said: "Gentlemen, the session is open. The first thing on the program is to pass the minutes of the last plenary session. The minutes are passed. Then the Report of International Labor Legislation Commission. Mr. Barnes has the floor." Say that as rapidly as you can in French and you can see how quickly we got into action. Mr. Barnes then made his speech. It was a very fine presentation. The only trouble with speech-making at a diplomatic conference is that the translation makes one listen twice over to everything said so that the fine effect of the original is sure to be pretty well lost. Colliard, the French Minister of Labor, followed with a little written speech which I have reason to believe had been prepared by Max Lazard, perhaps in conjunction with M. Fontaine. But the finest speech of the day was Vandervelde's, who was speaking both as a Socialist and as Minister of State in Belgium.[1] He hailed the document as one of the most notable steps in history ever taken by organized governments. His speech was extemporaneous. He told me afterwards that he has no copy but that the Socialist paper will print a full text and he will send me one. The English translation was not very happy. Then followed desultory speeches, a series of little addresses by each of the Latin-American States registering their reservations to Article 37 "which was contrary to their constitutions." While the talk was going on, I had a good look at Paderewski, who sat across the table from me. He has a very strong face, more powerful, however, than delicate, but with great distinction. I met him at the end of the session and had a little chat with him. I was talking to Patek, our Polish member of the Labor Commission, and when Paderewski came up to us he took me for a Pole! When he heard my French, however, he addressed me in good American.

The speech-making went on. Lord Sinha, for India, said almost exactly what I had suggested to Delevingne. The Maharajah of Bikaner spoke for the princes of India in a choice little speech in which he pointed out that his fellow princes would be the "competent authorities" in their states to whom the matter should be referred. The thing I regretted most was that Japan did not speak, for, as a matter of fact, it was Japanese acquiescence in the plan as a whole, when modified by the amendment that the proposed labor treaties should be drawn up in conformity with varying civilizations, which enabled India to come along. In a word, the Japanese have

[1] This speech of Vandervelde's was especially remarkable since he came into the session after it had begun, having just arrived by airplane from Brussels. He had been unable to leave Brussels until the night before, and then had found the train connections broken and no Belgian airplane available; so he had been forced to stay over night at a little town between Brussels and Paris and was picked up there by a British army airplane in order to reach Paris in time to speak at the session.

enabled the convention to become a world treaty and they are not getting the credit they deserve.

After the South Americans had finished, the chairman rose and said, "Gentlemen, you have heard the Report and the British amendment. [He had previously put an amendment by Sir Robert Borden.] The Report is now to be adopted." There was an instant's pause and then he quickly added, "It is adopted unanimously. The session is over." Everyone rose and there was a general hubbub. We were congratulated on all sides; but in the midst of our success we felt that something had been put over on us. The quick adjournment after the passage prevented us from bringing up that part of our Report upon which Mr. Gompers set much weight—the Labor Charter. We knew that Mr. Balfour would do his best to prevent its passage, at least in its present form, but while we are ready to agree that the statement of the case is by no means perfect, we are equally sure that the labor world will not rest satisfied with the erection of an organization in which the government vote is double that of either labor or capital if it gets to know that a statement of the program of Labor has been rejected by the Peace Conference. The Labor Charter must now be taken up as seriously as the constitution of the International Labor Organization. Instead of being at the end of our task we are only half way through. Mr. Balfour will be the chief obstacle. As the discussion was going on he was working on the text with a blue lead pencil. At the close of the session Sir Malcolm asked him what had happened to the "Nine Points." His face was still flushed from his heavy work at the end table, and he blurted out that the points both disquieted him and seemed foolish. Clemenceau's comment was in its way equally characteristic. When he came along to where Barnes, Sir Malcolm and I were discussing the situation, Barnes asked him where the Nine Points were. Clemenceau was coughing as he paused to talk to us. He has an irritation from his wound,[1] and the bullet still lodges in the back of the lung, but he was in excellent spirits and laughing through his coughing fit, tapped his chest with his forefinger and said in good English, "Points! I have one of them in here." Obviously the treaty makers have to take up that matter by itself later.

We came out into the anteroom where the diplomats were gathered in groups to talk it over and had tea at a sort of bar at the

---

[1] He had been shot on February 19.

far end of the room. I had a passing word with the two dignitaries of India and ran into Hughes of Australia, who had been feared by the British Delegation as an *enfant terrible* who might have broken loose but whose worst disturbance was insisting that all his neighbors round the table sign his autograph book. For the fun of the thing, I sent him over to the delegate from Panama to add his signature to the rest.

The DAY was over. At dinner Walter Weyl and I decided to spend the evening celebrating by going to the opera for the first time.

It seems like an incongruous ending of an historic day to describe the opera in Paris at Peace Conference time, but in itself it was distinctive and notable. The house was full from cellar to garret and we took the last two seats in the orchestra to hear Berlioz' *Faust*. Many uniforms, and especially American, gave a distinctive note to the audience, but France is beginning to throw off the pall of the war and Frenchmen were there in full dress, a thing they did not do when we first came to Paris. Marguerite was sung by Chenal, the most famous of French prima donnas, and the staging far surpassed anything I ever saw at the Metropolitan. The Labor Charter was a long way off, and yet perhaps the work we have just finished at the Quai d'Orsay may help to bring these creations of art into the lives of more of the workers of the world, when it is recognized that the rebuilding of civilization depends fundamentally upon Labor.

Saturday, April 12, 1919

Spent morning in room catching up with the diary. Saw Steed of the London *Times* and got him to give credit to Japan for its readiness to co-operate on the labor program. He sent an intelligent Paris correspondent around to us to get the story in detail.

I called to see Mezes and found that he was intending to return to America shortly. In fact, the specialists will be clearing out before very long. Their reports are mostly in already and their work largely done. I am in doubt whether to remain much after the early part of May or not. Miller wants me to work with him and I could have plenty of other things to do, but I should be glad to settle down to my history of the War. However, there is a little more to do on the labor problem yet: the Charter must not be allowed to disappear. I had a brief telephone conversation with

Vandervelde about it, and he invited me to lunch on Monday. He is anxious to push on the program.

It has been a rainy and dismal day, but in the afternoon I took a stroll over toward the Palais Royal and eventually found a little cobbler who would repair old shoes and a portfolio for ten francs. There was a nice little confectionery shop on the same back street, not fashionable but clean. Two chocolate éclairs were one franc fifty, or fifteen cents apiece. That gives an idea of prices in Paris. Someone here unwarily ate an apple in a restaurant and they charged him five francs for it.

In the evening I finished up some routine work and then went with Beer and Captain Crandall to the theatre to see Guitry, the Irving of France, in a play representing the life of Pasteur. It is a remarkable and daring thing. The first act represents him as a teacher in the Ecole Normale with a little group of students. It is the day of the proclamation of war with Prussia in 1870, and as the boys go off to fight the Germans, Pasteur stays at his laboratory to fight microbes, the greatest enemy of mankind. It then goes on to take up the big pages of his life, his dispute with the doctors of the old school in the academy of medicine, the first child upon whom he risked vaccination for hydrophobia, and finally the honors paid to him at the close of his life.

Sunday, April 13, 1919

In my room all morning. Another rainy day, clearing up about noon to a beautiful spring sky with just a little nip in the air. Luncheon with Beer and Weyl and then Slosson and I wandered over across the river to the Panthéon of the War. It is a huge panorama such as they used to have at Gettysburg, etc. There are portraits in the foreground of all the statesmen and leading generals. Most of the portraits are very good. Behind them stretch vast landscapes of northern France. There is the illusion of distance, but the most impressive thing is the way in which the figures in the foreground stand out lifelike against a sort of parapet which stretches around the whole panorama. After leaving it, we came back across the river into the Sunday afternoon crowds that sauntered up and down the Champs Elysées. The trees are slowly coming out in leaf and the magnolias are in bloom. Home to my room to rest and bring the record up to the present minute.

Had an invitation to tea but did not go. I don't mind talking to diplomats in broken French, but for me to talk to afternoon-tea ladies in any language is an unnecessary affliction for
us both.

Monday, April 14, 1919

Began today the second stage of the labor negotiations. It is
terribly important to put this through because Mr. Gompers is no
longer present to defend that part of the work of the Labor Commission which he has most at heart, embodying as it does, for the
acceptance of all the world, the principles for which he has fought
so long and not always successfully in the United States.

By luncheon I had the text ready to take along to discuss with
Vandervelde. He seemed quite satisfied with it. Madame Vandervelde was there, and in addition to Professor Mahaim, who had
come down from Belgium for the first meeting of the committee to
organize the Labor Conference, there was Mr. Bernhard Berensen,
the art critic.

In the afternoon there was a meeting at the Ministry of Labor
of the committee which had been appointed in fulfilment of the
decision at the Plenary Session to prepare the first Labor Conference. I stayed at home, however, working still on the labor clauses
to meet the objections raised by the British to Gompers' theory of
economics.

Tuesday, April 15, 1919

Worked at the labor clauses during the whole morning with
Delevingne and Robinson. Lunched with Philippe Millet of *Le
Temps* at the Press Club. I want to have him do French colonial
policy for the Carnegie history; he is one of the most open-minded
Frenchmen I have met. I went on up to the Majestic with my version of the labor clauses to get Barnes' approval, and he drove me
down to the Crillon, where I joined Robinson on further study and
changes.[1]

Wednesday, April 16, 1919

The whole day spent on labor clauses. At ten o'clock Dr. Oka,
Sir Malcolm Delevingne and I met in Young's room and worked till

[1] Mr. Miller's Diary shows that he was also consulted and kept Colonel House
informed.

noon trying to meet the Japanese difficulties. We had lunch with Mr. Frederick Whyte, editor of the *New Europe,* an exceedingly good type of Briton. Had two pictures of myself taken for preservation in some musty archive of the history of the Conference, one in the Library with Captain Gilchrist [1] and the other at my desk in my room with Slosson. At three-thirty, on a call from Fontaine, I went to the Ministry of Labor and got the French reaction to my re-editing, and then from five to half-past seven worked with the Japanese experts, Delevingne, and Young and finally got a possible text, which Delevingne took at once to Balfour.

[The problem had been to find a formula to cover the field of the rights of alien labor—having in mind California—which would avoid the question of equality of status and yet substantially safeguard the immigrant. The text of the eighth point of the Charter which I proposed, read as follows: "The standards set by the laws of any country with respect to the conditions of labor should be applied to foreign workers lawfully resident therein." [2]]

After dinner I drove up to the Majestic to learn the state of negotiations and found that so far they had gone well. Barnes drove me back to the Crillon on his way to the Japanese headquarters to come to a final conclusion with them.

In the hall of the hotel I ran into William Allen White, who had been wanting an interview with me on the labor business for his Kansas papers, and Miss Ida Tarbell, whose invitation to lunch has been on my desk for the last two days, snowed under by the labor papers. I expect to see her tomorrow morning.

Thursday, April 17, 1919

Morning—I took a stroll to a cobbler where I left a pair of shoes and enjoyed the quiet of the early morning streets, a rare experience for a prisoner of the Crillon. Coming back, I wandered over to the Hôtel Veuillemont to call on Miss Ida Tarbell, and had a talk of an hour or so with her. I found her much more optimistic than most of the correspondents and ready to help along the labor program when she gets a chance. I am to see her when she comes back from a trip. She has nothing of the airs of a distinguished writer.

Spent the rest of the day working on the labor program. In the afternoon had a call from Professor Pupin of Columbia, who took

[1] Now Librarian of Rochester University.   [2] See below, pp. 267 ff.

tea in my room. He is here to look after the interests of the South
Slavs as against the Italians and if all South Slavs were as reasonable and as genial as he, their case would be farther on.

I hurried up to the Majestic then for a glance at the redraft of
our labor clauses which Mr. Balfour had indulged in and of which
Mr. Barnes sent me word. I found Barnes very despondent, with
the fight mostly gone out of him, for he considered that the redraft
was very different from the original and would be unsatisfactory
to labor. Then I hurried down to the Hôtel Petrograd for dinner
with Rose Schneidermann and Mary Anderson, the two women delegates. Professor Frankfurter was there and we continued our labor
discussion across the table. I left rather early, getting back to the
hotel in time to spend the rest of the evening with Slosson on the
draft of the Labor Charter, redrafting Balfour's redraft, which
proved to be possible. Intent on leaving no stone unturned, I got
in touch with Miller, but he was editing the last sections of the
League of Nations text and it was half-past twelve before he was
able to send for me, and it was two before the night's work was
done. Miller preferred my original draft, and there we left it.

If any man at this conference has earned a place in history it is
David Hunter Miller, and he is the last man to claim it. Since we
came to Paris, he has taken no rest; the night before he stopped
work at four o'clock and his average day runs from nine or nine-
thirty in the morning to anywhere from one to four the next morning, and yet he retains a sure and swift judgment and an unruffled
temper, although he has capacity for anger in a fine, healthy way
at any time. I shall look forward to working with him rather more
intimately from now on.

[Mr. Barnes's loyalty to Mr. Gompers under this difficult situation, which threw him in opposition to most of the leaders of the
British Delegation, was one of the finest things that happened at
the Peace Conference. Most of the clauses which meant most to
Mr. Gompers, such as a declaration in favor of trial by jury, seemed
even to European labor leaders on the Commission, and still more
to other members of the Peace Conference, to be quite out of place
in a purely labor statement, yet they had a real meaning in the
history of the American struggle for a recognition of the right of
labor to organize under the law.

The most important of these principles in Mr. Gompers' eyes

was the one which was most puzzling to the Europeans. It was that "in law and in practice it should be held that the labor of a human being is not a commodity or article of commerce." Few of those in Paris knew that in Mr. Gompers' long fight for the right of collective bargaining and the legality of the Labor Union movement in the United States, this clause had become "Labor's Magna Charta." [1] It had been the justification for excepting labor from the operation of the Clayton Anti-Trust Law of 1914. Mr. Gompers sincerely and earnestly held that this declaration marked the last stage of the liberation of labor from slavery. In Lincoln's day man himself had been made free; in the Clayton bill his labor as well was declared to be a part of himself and not the property of other men, to be bought and sold in a "labor market" as the slave himself had been bought and sold in the slave market fifty years before. The practical result of the declaration was equally important in Mr. Gompers' mind, for if labor were a commodity, then a labor union would be a trust in restraint of trade and would be illegal in the new anti-trust legislation. But it was equally inevitable that the moment the phrase reached the eye of an economist unfamiliar with the history of American labor, it would strike him as unsound. There had been a number of such economists in the Labor Commission, and as I was on the drafting committee it fell to me to secure Mr. Gompers' consent to a phrase which would not open a theoretical debate but would recognize the practice based upon Mr. Gompers' philosophy. The phrase agreed upon, therefore, was that "in right and in fact the labor of a human being should not be *treated* as merchandise or an article of commerce." [2] It seemed to me at the time that this would avoid difficulties with conservative statesmen; but when Mr. Balfour's eye caught the phrase in the Plenary Session of April 11, he made himself the center of an un-

[1] That is the title which he gives it in the chapter dealing with it in his autobiography.

[2] This was substantially the expression used in President Wilson's speech at the opening of the American Federation of Labor Building in Washington in 1916, which Mr. Gompers himself quotes in his autobiography (*op. cit.*, II, 299) as "a statement to which my mind often recurs with gratification." The statement was: "Mr. Gompers was referring just now to the sixth section of the Clayton Anti-Trust Law, the section in which the obvious is stated—namely, that a man's labor is not a commodity but a part of his life, and that, therefore, the courts must not treat it as if it were a commodity, but must treat it as if it were a part of his life. I am sorry that there were any judges in the United States who had to be told that. It is so obvious that it seems to me that that section of the Clayton Act were a return to the primer of human liberty but if the judges have to have the primer opened before them, I am willing to open it."

yielding opposition and carried the British Delegation with him, to force a modification in the final text which was bound to make it unacceptable to Mr. Gompers. This incident was doubly unfortunate because Mr. Gompers, then back in the United States, found himself in the extremely embarrassing position of having to face the American Federation of Labor with a text containing a formula which in his eyes was as meaningless as his own text had been to Mr. Balfour. Mr. Balfour's comment was that the clause must surely be intended to mean that labor should not be treated merely as merchandise. He added, "It is nonsense as it stands." The final text was still further weakened to read that labor should not be regarded merely as merchandise, a text which was thought to be ambiguous enough to meet both points of view but in reality failed to give satisfaction to Mr. Gompers. In the days which followed I spent much futile effort in trying to eliminate that word "merely" from the text of the labor charter or to find a substitute phrase which would not do violence to Mr. Gompers' convictions. Looking back at it now, this seems like a strange and almost trivial preoccupation, but so much depended upon the support which Mr. Gompers could bring not only to the labor section of the Treaty but to the Treaty as a whole, that he had a right to expect that his colleagues would do their best to keep as closely as possible to the text which had been agreed upon while he was there. I was still working on this formula, when finally, on April 27, Mr. Robinson, without letting me know of his intentions, went to a conference with the British, the Japanese and the Belgians and accepted the formula, "that labor should not be *regarded merely* as a commodity or article of commerce." The printer was then waiting for the text, which was passed in that form at the Plenary Session the next day.

This much of explanation seems necessary for what follows. Even with it the references are sometimes none too clear, but the full story can be told only by the documents themselves.[1]]

Friday, April 18, 1919

Began the day in good time, getting the various drafts into proper shape and putting a memorandum through to those highest up. Had lunch with Pupin and Beer and tea at the Continental

---

[1] The student of the subject will find a fuller documented account in *The Origins of the International Labor Organization*, I, 212–219.

with Mr. Edward Filene of Boston, who is here on account of the American Chamber of Commerce to help trade relations with France. Phelan called just before dinner and we walked over to Frankfurter's hotel to get him to work with Christie, Sir Robert Borden's secretary, whom Frankfurter knew at Harvard; for I had found out from a conversation with Christie that morning at the Majestic that the opposition of the Dominions to our labor program was the chief reason of Balfour's activities. I had made little progress with Christie in my interview; in fact, he impressed me as being personally hostile to the whole labor program. The Oriental labor question is of course extremely difficult for the Dominions, but the Japanese have met us half way, and I am anxious to meet them half way in return.

At dinner with Pupin again. After dinner Walter Weyl and Sweetser and I walked over to the Seine, as it was the first warm night of the Spring. We sat on the parapet by the river and discussed the history of the Conference to our heart's *dis*content; for some of the phases of this history certainly do not run to our liking. Yet, all in all, I would rather take an optimistic view than the deadly pessimism of a man like Frank Simonds with whose judgment on things I continually disagree.

Saturday, April 19, 1919

Dictated in the morning. Drove over to the Gare du Nord to get tickets for tomorrow's trip to Currie's headquarters on the Canadian front. The station was crowded with people going back north and it was extremely difficult to get anything done, owing to the typical French disorder in crowds.

In the afternoon I learned that the British Delegation had accepted Balfour's draft of the labor clauses, and had a despondent talk with Barnes over the telephone. As a result, I got busy with a message to our Chief to salvage at least my modifications before it is finally adopted.

Had a quiet little stroll along the Seine in the late afternoon and came back for a dinner by myself, but dined instead with Dr. Putnam, Librarian of Congress.

In the evening I had a call from Miss Wilson, who is back again from the hospital, none the worse for her two weeks' holiday with the measles, and enthusiastic over the treatment there. Am to leave at quarter to seven in the morning for the long-expected trip to the Canadian front. Bowman, Young and Beer are going with me.

[The text of the memorandum which I submitted to Colonel House offers a clearer picture of the evolution of the Labor Clauses or Labor Charter than any description of the negotiations. It is therefore quoted below, although it has been published in *The Origins of the International Labor Organization.*[1]]

LABOR CLAUSES FOR INSERTION IN THE TREATY OF PEACE

Proposed Draft:

With a view to bringing about at the earliest possible date a general improvement in the conditions of labor, the High Contracting Parties declare their acceptance of the following principles, subject to such modifications in the case of particular countries as are necessary in view of substantial differences in the industrial conditions resulting from an imperfect development of industrial organization, climatic conditions or other special circumstances. They engage, after consideration of the recommendations to be made by the International Labor Conference as to their practical application, to take all possible steps to secure the realization of these principles or of what are, in the case of countries where the special circumstances aforesaid obtain, approximately equivalent principles.

1. The labor of a worker should not be treated merely as a commodity or article of commerce.

2. Every worker should be secured a living wage, that is, a wage adequate to maintain a reasonable standard of life.

3. The right of association, for all lawful purposes, of both workers and employers, should be recognized.

4. The hours of work in industry should be based on eight hours a day or forty-eight hours a week.

5. Every worker should be secured a weekly rest, which should include Sunday wherever possible.

6. In order to safeguard their education and physical development:
   (a) the employment of children under the age of fourteen years in industrial and commercial occupations should be prohibited.
   (b) the employment of young persons between the ages of fourteen and eighteen in such occupations should be allowed only on condition that their education (technical or general) be continued and that the work itself be not prejudicial to their physical development.

7. Equal pay should be given to women and to men for work of equal value in quantity and quality.

[1] Vol. II, pp. 410, 411.

8. The standards set by the laws of any country with respect to the conditions of labor should be applied to foreign workers lawfully resident therein.

9. Each State should make provision for a system of inspection, in which women should take part, in order to ensure the enforcement of the laws and regulations for the protection of the workers.

The Canadian Front

Sunday, April 20, 1919 [1]

It was Easter Sunday. When we reached the Gare du Nord in the early morning, the station was already filled by an animated French crowd pushing past inefficient guards with much gesticulation and little good humor. We found a compartment by ourselves and settled down for the journey to Lille, where we were due at about two o'clock but which we did not reach until about four. The train was on time as far as the station next south of Amiens; but from there on it stopped every little while, running very slowly through the war area, so that we had a good chance to see a section of the Somme battlefield from the railroad. Before reaching Amiens the railroad lies just along the rear of the position which the French troops held when the Germans broke through toward Amiens in March, 1918. We could see these positions from the train. In this old farming country the fields had been plowed along the slopes in terrace formation, leaving strips of sod, which run like belts through the fields, to prevent the hills from washing away. Along the western slopes of these hills the French soldiers had dug into the face of these sodded embankments and built their field shelters; the whole countryside was scarred with these shallow excavations. The subsoil is chalky rock and the surface is only a few inches thick, so that every time the soldiers dug they threw out a great white landmark. This is true of the whole country from Vimy south to Verdun. Every trench lies like an open scar across the fields, and one wonders how it ever could have been a defense, since it seems to invite the attention of the enemy. The real defense must lie in the fact that there were so many of them.

I have never read any description of this use of the terraces along the plowed lands for defense; but here we were looking in at the back of the French line, and it was as though the whole system of defense were there before us. So far there were no serious signs of

---

[1] Dictated immediately after returning to Paris.

destruction, just a house here and there unroofed along the suburbs
of Amiens; but when, in a few minutes, we turned to go up the
Somme at the Amiens junction of Longueau we were right in the
midst of the desolation of the war. The Somme itself is an insignificant stream, not half as large as the Aisne or a quarter as large
as the Marne, but its valley is filled with swamps and stretches
from rather steep bluffs on either side anywhere from a quarter to
half a mile across. The hills are rather formidable and bare of trees,
while the swampy valley has the rather natural desolation of over-
grown underbrush or flooded marsh.

The villages now began to show the signs of bombardment, and
by the time we reached the Ancre valley at Corbie there was
nothing but ruins in sight. The train ran along the Ancre, past
Albert, towards Bapaume through the very heart of the battlefield,
but, being in the depression, although a relatively slight one, we did
not get the full impression of the desolate country which we got
later while riding over the country roads. From Albert the train
went through Arras to Douai and Lille; the first sign of real houses,
habitable and inhabited, was at Douai. Later we found that Arras
was not so badly shot up as other towns.

General Currie was to meet us at Lille, but there was no sign
of him at the station although I had telegraphed our coming through
Sir Robert Borden's secretary. So we walked over to the Hôtel
Bellevue, on the main square, where I left the party to try to get
trace of him. Inquiry at the French army post led to my going to
the American army post, which I found in the hands of the navy!
A kind young officer drove me in his car through some two miles
of streets (Lille is a city of about 200,000) to the headquarters of
the Fifth British Army. There they put me in telephone communication with Canadian headquarters near Brussels. That telephone
talk was interesting, for I had first to call up British headquarters
near Boulogne and then, it happened by mistake, was given
Cologne! Currie was at Antwerp and had not received our tele-
grams; so I called up again at nine in the evening. He sent word
that he would be at Lille in the early morning. We went over to a
fine old hotel with rooms on a quiet courtyard and spent the night.
It was the Hôtel de l'Europe, where the Kaiser was quartered during his visit to Lille, and on the door of our bedroom was penciled
the name of a German captain who was quartered there.

Monday, April 21, 1919

We had the morning to wander around the city, for Currie did not arrive till about eleven o'clock. It is a busy town, but the busiest scenes are where the great lines of British army trucks line up in the main square or go rumbling through the narrow streets. There are British soldiers everywhere, many more than French. Lille was heavily bombarded in October, 1915 by the Allies, but the ruins are all in one relatively small part of the city, almost as though a fire had swept along a certain section and left the rest untouched. It did not suffer anything in the German retreat. We were struck with the general appearance of well-being; I rather doubt the extreme stories of suffering in Lille at present, except among the very poor. The British army has been spending thousands daily and the shops are busy. We had a good dinner at the hotel, and in the morning a plate of pastry and good chocolate in a confectionery. To be sure, the little cakes were twenty cents apiece, but people were buying them all the same. I left the confectionery to go back to the hotel and found one of Currie's cars in front of it, with Major O'Connor, his A.D.C., in charge. He told me the General was having his cup of coffee in the Bellevue Café, which is a huge affair on the main square where I had seen all Lille at coffee the previous evening (one franc a cup). Here I found the General, and we drove back to the hotel to get ready for the journey. I went with Beer in Currie's car, and Young and Bowman went in O'Connor's. He comes from Ottawa, and is a charming companion.

Practically all the Canadian troops had already left the Continent, and Currie had been making his final arrangements before following them to England. He had worked till three o'clock that night and about three the night before to straighten up all the details, and had then taken the road between six and seven in the morning to get to us so we could have a good day's run on Monday. It was more than I had counted on, that he should spend his last two days on the Continent going over the battlefields with me. He is coming back after a visit to England, but only for a partial trip.

We turned out of Lille by the Menin gate on the north side and took the long road to Menin. It is a perfectly flat country and across fields to the east we could see Roubaix and Tourcoing, but practically all the way to Menin there was little sign of war. We were well behind the old German lines, and when the British broke

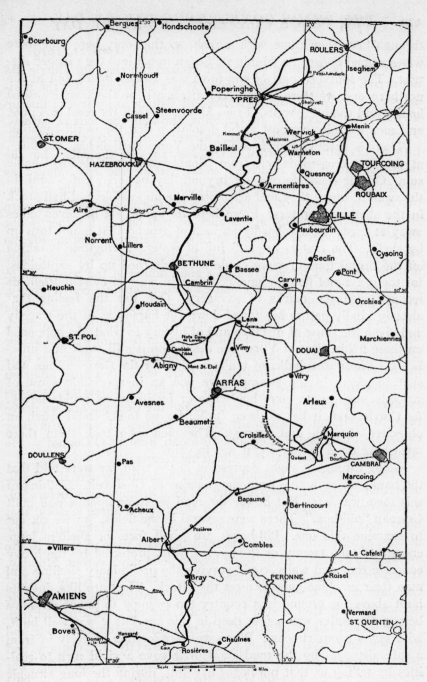

MAP OF CANADIAN FRONT

Line of the trip ———

through here they came with a rush, so that only here and there was a ruined house. At Menin we began to get into the ravaged district. The southern part of the town was almost intact, but at the northern end we were in the real aftermath of the war, smashed houses and tumbling walls. From Menin we took the road to Ypres, and soon were in the most awful desolation that the world contains.

There is nothing anywhere like the Ypres battlefields. Gheluwe, at the first crossroads out from Menin, was an indistinguishable ruin. On the roadside, not far beyond, lay battered tanks sunk in the swamp, where they had attempted the impossible and had stuck in the shell-hole craters. From here to Ypres, six or seven miles away at least, there is hardly an inch of ground that is not torn up by shells. The craters are still full of water. Springtime is taking off the brutal tone of mere crude earth churned up by explosions, for the grass and flowers have come again, and on most battlefields has softened the marks of savagery. One has the feeling that already kindly nature has toned down the harshness of the tragedy and given the sense of distance and of history to what has happened on those fields. But at Ypres the desolation is still stark and unrelieved. Those torn hulks of tanks headed for the German lines and shot to pieces in the swamps give one an inexpressible sense of struggle, such as no mere landscape or fortifications could convey. As Currie said, it has all been futile, for no tanks could reach an objective through that morass. The men who took them there must have done so knowing it was in vain.

Going through a slight depression in the road, we were told that the banks on each side were the remains of Gheluvelt. Nothing of this town was left. But beside the road we came upon a well built German "pill-box." There were several in the fields, but we got out to examine this one. Pill-boxes are small forts or shelters large enough to take twenty or thirty men, who, protected by the heavy concrete roof and walls, could survive the preliminary shelling and man their machine guns to meet the attack. They are like dugouts built above the ground in a country too swampy to put them down below; the water was a foot deep in this one but it was well built, with seven compartments. When we were looking gingerly in from a safe, dry spot by the roadside, Currie gave a vivid turn to realities by telling us that pill-boxes like this, during the long struggle for Passchendaele, had at least that much water in them; and men slept there, and wounded men came to such shelters with a sense of utter relief when there were dead and dying all around.

We passed through Hooge without my knowing it, there being nothing to indicate the spot, and then drove into what used to be Ypres. The town itself has no house left, not one. The strongly built jail buildings to the west and the walls of the famous Cloth Hall and a few churches are still partially standing, but no one lives among these ruins of a famous city. What surprised me most was a point of which I do not remember ever having read—the strength of the old medieval walls of Ypres. They rise from the moat some thirty feet or more and the ramparts behind are fifty feet or more across, with trees growing on the sodded top. These enormous ramparts of the old city furnished real shelter and protection. Underneath, in comfortable and safe quarters, were rooms used by the British like dugouts.

General Currie took us past one of the rooms to a sally port through the wall to show where they went across the marshes to the front lines. Then we clambered up and looked across the swamps to the crest of the nearby hills where the German line ran by Zillebeke and Voormzeele along the south and southeast. It reminded me of the view across the desolate Campagna from the walls of Rome, and yet only five years ago every inch of that ground was under intensive cultivation. Now even the trees are dead and their bare trunks stand like sinister symbols of the war. We walked along the street to the Cloth Hall, and Currie showed us where he had bought a pair of gloves when he first came to Ypres, in a good shop in the public square. There is nothing there now but some thistles growing from the rubbish on a heap of stones, none of it more than breast-high. The massive old walls of the Cloth Hall have been partially shored up to prevent them from falling; but it is too much of a ruin to recall any more distant past than the war of 1915.

As we turned down the street toward the northern canal on the way to St. Julien, Currie pointed out the street corner where he was shelled when coming in from his first great fight after the gas attack at the second battle of Ypres. He had had no sleep for five days, and as he came through the shell fire, he said that his senses were so dulled that it hardly seemed worth while to go out of his way to avoid the shelling.

From what was once the northern gate of Ypres, we crossed the Canal along the road to St. Jean, St. Julien and Poelcappelle. This is the road which marked the Canadian left boundary on the twenty-second of April, 1915, when the Germans first used gas to break the Allied line. Over to the west lay Bixschoote and Langemarck and beyond that the naked woods of Houthulst. The Germans drove in upon the African French troops at five o'clock on that afternoon, following up their gas attack until they were within less than two miles of Ypres. From that Thursday afternoon for ten days the British line stretched across that open country with no defense works other than shallow trenches hastily dug, facing gas and holding the weight of the German army back from Calais. In this battle Currie won his first laurels; and, looking over that desolate world, one realized what superhuman strength the Canadians had shown in the desperate defense. Of course, it is all much worse now, for nothing whatever is left of these places to mark where they stood. A broken tank mired beside the road gave evidence of the later fighting; but it is only when you look across these short distances of the open fields around Ypres that you realize that it was by pure heroism that the Allied cause was saved at such a crisis.

From Poelcappelle we swung around southeast by Westroosebeke to Passchendaele. The ridge is visible from Ypres and in fact it is hardly more than a rim of the cup in which Ypres lies, or, rather the saucer, for the grade is very slight. At Passchendaele we got out from the cars and walked up a mound of débris at the crossroads, which was all that was left of the Passchendaele church. When Currie first came to Ypres it was a shining landmark dominating the whole countryside. Now there is not a wall or a sign of a wall, just a mass of churned up débris, piled ten or twelve feet high beside the road. From the top of it we could see the whole battlefield. Across the ruins of Ypres to the west the church spire of Poperinghe, behind the British lines, was clearly visible and to the southwest the series of heights dominated by Mont Kemmel (which had already come into view as far back as Menin and indeed soon after we left Lille). It was here, at Passchendaele, that the Canadians pushed the Germans farthest back across the Flanders marshes. They were brought up from the line they had won down by Arras to win the crest of the ridge, in the hope that the Germans might be pushed far enough east to relieve Ypres.

Looking back over the field they won, we could see the Graven-stafel and Zonnebeke line; and in that short distance of about 2400 yards Currie told us that his army had lost 16,000 men. "It is no wonder," he remarked, looking over that waste of country, "that this is sacred ground for Canada." It took the stretcher bearers six hours, stumbling through the mire in the night, to carry a wounded man back to a dressing station. Through all these miles of country around Ypres, the shell craters touch and overlap and every inch has been ploughed up again and again. Across this sea of Flanders mud the only roads were those the Canadians taught the Europeans how to build, plank roads laid down section after section as rapidly as the trucks could haul them up. It was an application to war engineering of the homely expedient of pioneering days, when the swamps were bridged by "corduroy" roads of logs. The British engineers, with experience in India, had started out by trying to metal the roads by night, a process which yielded only a few yards of almost impassable road from a truck load, if that much. They had been slow to admit that the colonials could improve on their work; but the Canadian sawmills supplied the planks, and the movement of artillery became possible.

Leaving Passchendaele by the Zonnebeke road—a plank road still—we came back to Ypres again. Passing through it to the Lille gate, by which we had first entered it, we turned southwest towards Mont Kemmel, which dominates the whole countryside, with Messines Ridge to the east. We did not climb either, but skirted the eastern base of the hill and then the western base of the ridge to the open country south. Here the road was unrepaired, and while the cars went back for a detour, we walked across country alongside the Canadian trenches, which were still intact, with their dugouts. Down in the hollow was the farm house, "La Plus Douce Ferme," not altogether in ruins (which means that its walls were standing and a corner of the roof), in which Bairnsfather drew his first sketches of the British Tommies. There were long trenches through the swampy basin of the Douve, reaching up the sloping cross-ridges north and south, which run into Messines Ridge at right angles. Currie and I wandered through the rows of willow trunks that line the fences along which these trenches clung, hunting for landmarks familiar to him in the long time the Canadians held that sector. He knew the trees and fields along through here as a farmer would know his farm; but already the earth was filling in sections of the line so as to make it a little difficult to trace.

Meanwhile the cars had gone from Wulverghem to Neuve Eglise, joining us on the hill slope, and we went on around the edge of Hill 65 into the next swampy woods, famous as Ploegsteert (Plug Street!). A short run southeast to Romarin and we were over the Belgian frontier into France; but no one could know the difference for there are no signs to indicate the frontier. Then across the road to Nieppe through level fields which are being reclaimed, for from Ploegsteert south we passed from wilderness to agricultural country again. The houses are mostly gone, however, and people are living in improvised shacks, for in their last advance the Germans over-ran the country. Nieppe is only a short distance west of Armentières on the main road, but although we could see that town, we turned aside from it and followed the road that runs along the Lys River southwest to Estaires, where we crossed the Lys River and canal. Here the damage had been mainly done during the last German drive and the houses showed only such ruin as single shells would cause, which of course was enough. Most of the population seemed to be back in Estaires and in the towns to the south.

We took the good straight road through Locon to Béthune, a fair-sized city only partially destroyed, which means that some sections are almost intact. There were children playing in the streets and people going about their affairs, although the La Bassée Canal, which cuts across the town, is not in use and the normal business of the city has hardly begun. It had the worn and dirty look of all those towns behind the lines, which one becomes familiar with on the whole front from the Marne north. Some of the hardest fighting took place just west of La Bassée. We followed the long, winding street to Noeux Les Mines and found ourselves in the single coal region within the French lines, where for the first time we saw smoke from a tall chimney. The coal region of northern France is a small, narrow tract stretching to Lens, which is only a few miles to the southeast. The Germans were able to drop heavy shells on to the pitheads, and so terrorized the miners that even the mines left inside the French lines were not much worked as long as the Germans held the salient. This is a beautiful, softly rolling plain, the southern edge of which is bounded by a steep bluff, the Ridge of Notre Dame. It runs in from the sea to just southeast of Lens and its eastern end is the crest of Notre Dame de Lorette. In the spring of 1915 the French flung the weight of their whole attack against the labyrinth on the western slope of Vimy Ridge, and down the Souchez Valley, and against the eastern spur of Notre Dame de Lorette from which they finally dislodged the enemy. Many French dead witnessed to the value of that hill for France, in protecting the few coal mines left to the country.

We swung to the west through Bouvigny and Servins up the steep ridge and found ourselves behind it in a pleasant valley, untouched by the scars of war. Just at twilight we pulled into a little hamlet, Camblain l'Abbé, which was our objective for the night. In a château here, under the shelter of a wooded hill and untouched by bombing or artillery, Currie had his headquarters for some months. The hut of the Canadian Officers Club was a pleasant and cheery shed with fireplace and stoves and easy chairs. Beside it was another sleeping hut with little canvas partitions and real cots. On the village green they had made a tennis court and a football ground, and as the meadow slopes up gradually to the west, it offers a good grandstand. Here Currie said that he once reviewed in a massed band all the Highland pipers in the Canadian army. It had been an unforgetable experience, for he has a very keen sense of the part played by his pipers in his battles.

Tuesday, April 22, 1919

It was a cold night, and in the morning the hoarfrost was shining on the roofs and over the fields. The countryside was apparently untouched by the war, but the population of France has suffered where the country itself shows no signs of it. I attended Mass for a few minutes in the little village church and found the congregation made up entirely of women in black, with heavy crêpe veils, and a few scared-looking children. On the ridge just behind there was a French military cemetery; and the pathetic wreaths with their inscriptions from parents, wives and children brought home in a personal way the tragedy of the labyrinth just over the hill.

By nine o'clock the frost had gone, and under a warm spring sky we swung down towards Arras, stopping just under the edge of Mont St. Eloi. This is a single, dominating mound, which played somewhat the rôle in this part of the country that Kemmel does south of Ypres and Monchy east of Arras. There is a ruined monastery on the top, and from it and a massive farm building close by one had a clear view of the German line along the eastern hillsides. For it is on the hill next west of Vimy, or, if we count the Neuville–St. Vaast position, the second west of Vimy. This was very familiar ground to Currie, who pointed out where his headquarters were as they fought the battle of Vimy Ridge. There were dugouts everywhere along the roadsides. The ground stretches away in long billows, although these are more like real hills than to the east, where the main German defenses lay. From the ruins of Neuville, where we climbed another heap of rubbish that was once a church, we drove down a valley road through Souchez, with Ablain St. Nazaire on our left. This is the part of the French front along the southern slopes of Notre Dame de Lorette which cost such heavy fighting early in the war. Everything was in ruins here, but when we turned along the little Souchez stream northeast through Angres to Liévin, we became conscious of more recent devastation. The houses were battered up so short a time ago that grass is not yet growing on the ruins, and we came in through a mile or so of freshly destroyed city, into the heart of what was once Lens.

It was a new sensation to come into a town even more destroyed than Rheims, so soon after the destruction had taken place. As we climbed up the mound which had been the cathedral of Lens and looked over the city, of which no house remains intact, the impression of confusion was appalling. There had been no time to pull away the beams and rafters of the houses, and they were sticking up, splintered and twisted, at all angles out of the mass of bricks and stone. Most of the woodwork has disappeared from Rheims, having been used for firewood or something else. Rheims, as I said before, reminds one of Pompeii and has something of the note of distance and of history; but Lens is simply a modern, commonplace mining town reduced to ruins and showing all its ugliness. Perhaps the red brick marks out the crudities of the disaster more than the grey stone of Champagne.

From the point of vantage offered by the ruins of the church we looked back to the southwest. Immediately in the foreground on the south was a big pile of refuse from the coal mines which the British fought up to, but which the Germans held against them; while on the more distant southwestern horizon one could plainly see the long line of Vimy Ridge, looking much more formidable

At Passchendaele, the farthest point of the Canadian advance. Our party is standing on the ruins of the Church, and General Currie, pointing southwest toward Sanctuary Wood, has just explained that between there and this spot he lost 18,000 men.

The ruins of Lens looking toward Vimy Ridge

and steep when viewed from the valley than from the western side. Along the north a similar line of hills with villages of miners, St. Pierre and others, framed the valley in which Lens lay, and anyone could see why the British did not descend from these hills into that basin until they were good and ready to take it, especially when it was filled with gas.[1] We had our pictures taken here, as also at Passchendaele and Ypres, but no picture can give any real impression of what we saw.

From the church at Lens we could see the road to Arras, cutting straight away over Vimy Ridge. It reminded one somewhat, from Lens, of the straight line of the Appian Road across the Campagna to the Alban Hills. Going up it, we looked back to Lens from across the railroad to the British side of the slag heap banked up to the little Souchez stream. The intensity of the struggle here was evident in the close lines of the front trenches across the valley and up the hills, and the disorder in the very ruins themselves. As we rode along the approaches to Vimy Ridge and finally mounted it, we looked down as into a cup, with Lens in the middle, for the ridge is quite steep and the hill a real one.

The field of Vimy Ridge! The road to Arras runs along the middle of the crest for some distance, and from it we now looked westward down the long slope up which the Canadians charged, long and terrible fields, pocked with weeks of artillery fire and honeycombed with machine-gun nests. There is no such suggestion of the horror of war in the landscape here as at Passchendaele, for one looks across the fields rather than into them. Yet that is what made it so perfect a defense for the German machine-gunners. The capture of the ground on which we stood was one of the greatest exploits of the war, and has made the name of Vimy forever famous above those of so many other obscure places in northern France and Flanders which were the scenes of battles, great in any other war but already passing from memory. It was not enough to take

[1] The height behind was Hill 70, the capture of which on August 15, 1917 was the first battle planned by Currie himself. It was not even suggested by any higher command. *Cf.* Lt.-Col. Wilfred Bovey in *Canadian Defence Quarterly*, July 1926, p. 146: "He recognized the strategic importance of a point which, as was proved nine months later, ensured the safety of the last coal reserves of France, and he saw at the same time that the only way to capture Lens without great loss of life, was to pinch it out by seizing first on a point to the north. He demonstrated that common sense, combined with experience and thought, could be as good a guide to the tactician as all the maxims and the manuals of the colleges, and the Battle of Hill 70 was probably, for the number of troops engaged and the results obtained, the most costly fight for the Germans in which we ever took part."

the Ridge, however. It had to be held against the German attack of March, 1918, when it seemed as though the whole northern front might crumble in. It was north of Vimy that the Portuguese broke and so allowed the Germans to push in that dangerous salient south of Ypres. Currie had to extend his line against the German advance and made use of every available man in his command to strengthen the defenses of the Ridge. There were four Canadian Divisions against thirteen German. In order not to show their weakness the Canadians kept up local offensives, and through all those critical days the Vimy line stood fast, one of the few sections of the whole battle front from Ypres to Verdun on which the German advance made no impression.

At a crossroads here an impressive stone cross had been erected to the memory of the Canadian artillerymen who fell in that vicinity. A little distance up the road we turned to the east, to Thélus, once a hamlet, now indistinguishable, and through the fields to the south of it, walked the short distance to the monument erected to Currie's own division which had broken far through that part of the German line. It bears this inscription: "In proud memory of the soldiers of the First Canadian Division who fell in the investment, assault and defence of Vimy Ridge, March 4, April 9, and July 23, A.D. 1917. This mark is set by their comrades in arms. Gloria in excelsis Deo, Christmas 1917." From this spot on the ridge, here a broad plateau, we could see, midway on the southern horizon, the ruined profile of Arras cathedral, rising from its half-hidden position behind the hillside and over the roofs of the town. It was some five miles or more away. To the west the bluff of Mont St. Eloi, with its ruined towers and lookout, was plainly visible; while farther north the slopes of Notre Dame de Lorette flanked the depression at the base of Vimy, through which ran the road we had taken to Lens. Turning to the east, there were row after row of billowy hills, and beyond them a faint gray blur on the landscape was recognized as Bourlon Wood—far behind the Hindenburg lines.

I began now to understand what became more evident an hour or so later, when we struck the Hindenburg line itself, that the strongest defenses in this war were these long, level slopes across which machine gun fire could sweep even with the ground and farther than could be overcome in any rapid charge. By Ypres the swamps were a protection against advance from either side, but in this central part of the British line the country lies in long, gentle swells whose even crests run almost uniformly north and south. There are wave after wave of these, so when one ridge is taken there is another just behind; except, of course, where a stream cuts through, as the Souchez does at Lens, or the Scarpe at Arras, or the Ancre at Albert.

Along the road near here we came upon a burial party of British soldiers, busy that very morning carrying in the dead on stretchers. They had just been digging long trenches in the British cemetery for the nameless soldiers whose remains still lie scattered around that battlefield. They were wearing masks saturated in chemicals across their faces. Out over the fields we saw two or three other groups bringing in their loads on the stretchers. It is strange how little one is affected by these scenes. The incident was almost as casual as any other on the journey. Soon we left Vimy behind us and were on the paved road running through the lines of trees to Arras.

We went rapidly through the city, past the ruins of the cathedral —a heavy building of the seventeenth century whose massive walls are still standing, though in ruins. In some of the streets there were shops almost untouched, with glass replaced in the windows and business going on. I should say that about five-sixths of Arras had been destroyed; it is vastly different from Lens and will soon be rebuilt. Even the railway station, which stood very heavy bombardment, was left with enough walls standing to be restored, although the bridge over which we crossed the track was one where General Currie himself had been heavily shelled as he tried to cross it once on a more earnest mission.

From Arras we took the long straight road that leads to Cambrai. Across this road the Hindenburg line extended between those long wave-like slopes whose full meaning now became so clear. It was down this road on August 26 last that Currie's men started in to break the Hindenburg line, and did it. So that here we were once more on a famous Canadian battlefield.[1]

In their drive of 1918, the Germans had reached a line running straight across the road a short distance out of Arras, almost in its

[1] The breaking of the Hindenburg line took place after the battle of Amiens, described later on. The exploit is all the more remarkable in view of the fact that the interval between the two battles was only eighteen days, hardly time for more than moving the Canadian Corps from one battlefield to the other.

suburbs. The Hindenburg line was only one of their defenses. Every rolling hillcrest and slope for miles ahead of us had its rows of barbed wire, its trenches, machine gun nests; while the artillery could hide behind the succeeding slopes. Just a little off the road toward the north, the mound and ruined village of Monchy le Preux, the most notable German stronghold in the field, was in plain evidence. The British had captured it with heavy loss on the day after the Canadians took Vimy Ridge, and had held it until March, 1918. It was carried in the first Canadian assault on August 26, but the country behind it was sufficiently difficult to hold up the British troops who attacked along Currie's left when he smashed through the main lines down the broad road ahead of us. There was less sign of destruction here, however, than in the northern battlefields; for in the last great offensive they used a shell with an instantaneous fuse which burst upon the surface of the ground and tore the barbed wire to pieces without making huge pits in the earth. The farmers, German prisoners and soldiers already are pulling up the barbed wire and filling in the trenches preparatory to the Spring plowing. The scene of the most glorious exploits of the British and Canadian troops is rapidly losing the character of a battlefield. Only the little graveyards here and there along the roadways and the absence of houses tell the story.

We passed on down the long hill to the little Sensée stream and up the slopes beyond to La Brioche. Here we turned sharply to the south along a winding country road through the two villages of Villers and Cagnicourt, following the sweep of Currie's men as they had turned toward the southeast through woods and slopes and hamlets just behind the Hindenburg line. At a point in the road north of Quéant, which lay in the valley below us, we got out from our cars to inspect the most interesting, strategic spot of the whole journey; for we were just behind Croisilles and Bullecourt, at that strong point where the Quéant-Drocourt switch joined the Hindenburg line. This switch line was a double defense west of Cambrai, and as the Canadians had got in behind it without having to shell the wire out of the ground, the whole mass of wire defenses was still intact. By breaking through the Hindenburg line farther north and running down parallel to it on the eastern side, they had cleared the Germans out of their nests and dugouts here by taking them on their flank and the rear. So just across the fields to the south the patches of barbed wire stood out like vineyards, and, viewed from a little distance, impressed one chiefly by the mathematical regularity of the long lines of short posts with their wire attached. There were belts of these entanglements, about a plowland wide, stretching at regular intervals across the fields to the southeastern slopes.

Quéant is a little village half a mile or so to the west. The walls of its houses still stand. Apart from the strategic interest of the spot, the trenches here were, like the barbed wire itself, the most perfect creation of German military science on the whole front, and it gave one an added thrill of pride in the work of the Canadian army to realize that this had been taken by strategy as well as valor. The trenches were so deep that the soldiers manning the walls of them had to mount three rows of steps to get high enough to peep over the edges. Along the bottoms lay the duck-board walks, and wickerwork held up the terraces wherever necessary. However, as the trenches ran through the dry hillsides, the chalky, soft rock formation needed little support.

A short walk from the road brought us to a German dugout running straight in from the trench wall, and we went down a stairway of forty steps to the chambers of the dugout in which Currie had his headquarters after the break through of his Corps had allowed the Royal Naval Division to take in reverse this young Gibraltar. Everything was lined with good, fresh planking, and the stairway although at a very steep angle was as good as any carpenter could build. The total depth underground must have been at least forty-five feet. Just a little distance away we visited a similar dugout where the Prince of Wales stayed as Currie's guest for some time, while he was planning and pushing on the battle of Cambrai.

We turned back to the first crossroads and then continued east down into the valley through Inchy to the famous Canal du Nord. This was not completed when the war began and at this point was dry, although the sustaining walls of earth formed two enormous embankments along the valley. Here we were on the stage of the next Canadian manœuvre and an exceedingly brilliant one. The whole Canadian army was here thrust across the canal on a twenty-six hundred yard front. Then, in addition to advancing straight on up the slopes in front of them, which are crowned by the famous stronghold of Bourlon Wood, they swung back north again toward and across the Cambrai road, broadening their front and "fanning out," to use Currie's expression, so as to widen their front several times over.[1] The Germans behind that part of the canal had the protection of woods, so they had to be smothered with smoke shells to prevent their machine gunners sighting the Canadians on the open fields. To keep the barrage rolling ahead of the men and at the same time prevent the Germans, who were being outflanked, from enfilading the ranks of the charging columns, the Canadian artillery had to be "frog-leaped"; that is, while one battery was firing, its neighbor was galloped rapidly farther to the front into a new position, sighted, and set to work so accurately as to reach just over their own front line and so steadily as to break down the resistance of the German infantry.

The victory was absolute and complete. I have lost my note of the exact number taken on the first day's advance here, but as I recall it, over two hundred guns were taken from the Germans. In general plan the battle was just the counterpart of the one before, breaking through a single section of the German defense (this time the Canal du Nord) and then sweeping them up from the flank. The Cambrai road was reached at exactly the hour planned for, late in the afternoon. By nightfall the front line was four miles beyond the canal; the commanding heights of Bourlon and the ridge to the north, overlooking the Sensée valley, were securely in Canadian hands. Only an army in perfect morale, under a leadership in which it had confidence, could achieve a victory like this, fought with mathematical precision.

We drove along the roadway beside the canal following the advance until we struck the Cambrai road again close to Marquion and then went on up the long slope toward Cambrai as far as Raillencourt, about two miles and a half from Cambrai, whose church towers and buildings were well in sight. Ahead of us was the scene of the last, and in some ways the most tragic, fighting in which the Canadian Corps was engaged, when the Germans flung against it a heavy concentration of troops and artillery, to hold it in check. But we had no time to go on to Valenciennes and Mons, where the Canadian advance ended on Armistice day—the city at which the British had entered the war in 1914.

[1] It fanned out to a width of over nine miles.

Instead of going into Cambrai, we turned to the south along a back country road to Fontaine, to see what lay behind the German defenses. We were now east of Bourlon Wood, a ragged and frightful place, where the British tanks had finally come to grief in the great surprise attack of General Byng the year before.

From the wall of a barn on the roadside at Raillencourt we tore down a large German sign which was of enough interest for General Currie to take along with him to preserve in the Ottawa museum. It read as follows:

Soldaten! Das Geld liegt auf der Strasse, im Gelände und in Schützen-graben! Sammelt!
(Soldiers! Money lies in the street, in the fields and in rifle pits! Gather it up!)

The road runs through a cutting in the fields, and the roadsides are honeycombed with dugouts. Little, narrow-gauge railways run through the depressions of the fields here as in so many other parts of the front. In many cases they run along the sides of the road as well, and where the British army is in occupation they are still used by the salvage corps. The engines use gasoline and haul good heavy trucks. Currie used them, in the face of British criticism, for heavy field artillery up to nine-inch guns. His men got to a point where they could mount a nine-inch gun on one of these trucks in three minutes, whereas the officer who came to inspect had allowed him two hours and even then thought it couldn't be done in that time.

This road ran through the ruins of Fontaine-Notre-Dame, of which the walls are still more or less intact. From there the long straight road from Cambrai to Bapaume took us back through the slopes and ridges of the Hindenburg system. Bapaume was ruined long enough ago to have lost the disorder and crudity so evident in Lens. In about half the town the walls of the houses are standing, although the church is a heap of ruins. People were coming back to fix up shelters against the back walls of shops and houses. When we left Bapaume, however, for Albert, on the road which ran west across the main front of the Somme battlefield, there was not a single evidence of a wall of a house higher than a foot or two from the ground, except for one ruined mill. Again we met those long sinister slopes. At Warlencourt the road mounts a hill overlooking the basin of the stream that later becomes the Ancre. This slope had been the bulwark of the Germans before Bapaume. A little to the left, over in a field, was one of those strange mounds to be found all the way from Notre Dame de Lorette, at Monchy, and elsewhere along the front, which engineering had transformed into miniature forts. It was the famous Butte de Warlencourt, but looked like a mere nubbin in the field. Its sides are pounded to dust heaps, and crosses to the fallen French are on the summit.

At Courcelette is the Canadian burial post for this region. We turned off the main road to the little village. Nothing is left of it, but in its place there are long sheet-iron sheds of the Canadian company. The lieutenant in charge invited us in for afternoon tea and was much honored when Currie consented to accept. While tea was brewing, I wandered up the cutting to the east—for the roads cut through by some quarries here—and found, just a few yards to the east of the main sunken road, the British and German front line trenches running parallel, with only one thin parapet between.[1] Courcelette had seen heavy Canadian fighting in the Somme battle, and the sunken road we were on had been the objective of a hard charge. The burial corps had already gathered in from the battlefields over 3900 bodies, of which more than a third could be identified by marks or trinkets. A pleasant Scotch chaplain joined us here and the lieutenant in charge of the post gave us some shell cases which we carried away as souvenirs.

The next place on the road to Albert was once the town of Pozières, but the only way we knew its location was that another desolate road turned into ours at that point. There was absolutely no sign that any house had ever been there and the grass was already growing over the powdered ruins so as to obliterate even their trace. We were now on the main battle line of the first stabilized defense and swung rapidly through to Albert.

The Virgin had disappeared from the great brick church where she hung so many months, and Albert is almost in the state of ruin of Bapaume, but the damage is much more recent, as the chief destruction came from the British artillery last summer. As we turned into the main square of the town, Currie pointed out the spot where he was knighted. But the square must have looked quite

[1] This was apparently a mistake. There was always a no man's land in this area.

different when the houses were standing and it was lined with British troops; for it was now a mass of disorder from the piles of brick shot into it.

From Albert we turned quickly south instead of going on straight to Amiens, in order to visit the battlefield just east of Amiens and south of the Somme where the Germans were driven back last August from their menace to the town of Villers-Bretonneux. The road from Albert to Bray went over the crest of the bluff east of the Ancre and then down a long hill to the Somme, which we crossed on an improvised bridge. The valley is about a mile wide, and filled with marshes. The hills rise very steeply on either side, chalk hills along the base of which the road runs south of the Somme to Mericourt, then up over the flat farming country to Rosières, where we turned at right angles west to Caix. We were well behind the farthest German lines, about eight miles behind them at Caix (Cakes, the English call it). The Canadians had pushed the Germans back those eight miles in one day, August 8, 1918; so our road from Caix to Amiens reached the battlefield the wrong way on, and it may make a clearer story to tell it as though we had come at it from the British side, instead of as we actually did, from that of the Germans.

The road from Amiens to Roye and Noyon strikes off in a southeasterly direction straight across the fields, as the one from Amiens to Albert, Bapaume and Cambrai strikes northeast. It crosses the Somme at Amiens itself, and the railroad junction is down about two miles east of the city along the banks of the stream where the southern tributaries join. From this point (Longueau) and from Boves, a little farther south, the British and Canadian troops marched east to the village of Domart, where the road sinks down to the valley of the little creek called the Luce. The stream itself is insignificant, not more than five or six feet wide in the main bed, but, like the Somme and all these streams in this chalky country, it has worn a deep valley with blufflike banks rising to the level uplands. The flats of the streamlet are from a quarter to a third of a mile in width and roads run along both sides with bridges crossing the swamp at the intersections of cross ravines that cut the banks and are used by cross country roads for little hamlets up on the plateau. It is a very difficult country, for the stream twists and turns and there are woods on the heights at intervals; yet this was the scene of the farthest advance ever made in a single day by the Allied troops. On the eighth of August last they drove the Germans from their trenches and pushed them back 14,000 yards without stopping. The point where they "kicked off" (that seems to be the Canadian expression for beginning an attack) was Domart, a little farming village lying on the main road from Amiens at the point where it crosses the valley of the Luce.

After their exploits at Vimy it was but natural that Canadian troops should be chosen to deliver this blow against the German line by Amiens and that Currie should be the one to lead them. The success of the plan, however, depended upon keeping it absolutely secret, and even those high up were not told. To set rumor moving the wrong way, some Canadian companies were openly and ostentatiously sent to the neighborhood of Ypres, and so well was the strategic secret kept that a number of Currie's fellow generals protested against this move, which seemed to indicate reopening hostilities in Flanders. Moving down by night marches, the main body of the Canadian troops were meanwhile sent around Amiens to the very southern tip of the British front. It was from there that they turned east to take their places in the British line at Domart and along the Luce towards Hangard, the next village north. There they hid in ambush to await the signal to attack.

There is a single bridge across the Luce at Domart, where the road crosses the stream and swamp, and by some lucky chance the Germans had not destroyed that bridge. Currie's plan was to get a brigade of infantrymen across the stream the night before the attack and hide them in the marshes towards the base of the opposite hills along which the German front-line trenches ran, just under a rough wood on the hillcrest. Meanwhile, although the artillery had been got in position, not a single gun had registered on its German target before it opened up on the signal for battle.

The attack was timed for 4:20 A.M. Ten minutes before the zero hour Currie launched a squadron of a dozen tanks across the bridge and along the swamp road. They had been concealed among the houses of the village. In order to drown the noise of the tanks and keep the Germans off their guard a squadron of heavy bombing planes flew low over the German positions, using the noise of their engines as effectively as their bombs. He had done this three nights hand-running, so that when the real attack came the Germans were taken unawares, and exactly on the minute the tanks were leading the charge up the hill and through the German positions.

North of Domart, at the next village, Hangard, Currie pointed out a single tree in the field just west of the little roadway leading up towards Villers-Bretonneux as being on the Canadian line. There they pushed straight east over the fields. He also pointed out the spot in a little ravine on the southern hillside opposite, where he established himself after the first push through, made his head-quarters and had lunch on the field of victory. It is a long eight miles to Caix, and to rout the Germans from their trenches and push them back that far in one day, through such a difficult country, is an incredible achievement. Currie said with a smile that the one sad incident of that day happened down by Domart when he saw his heavy howitzers with their throats turned up to the farthest possible angle and all utterly useless because the enemy had been driven back so far that the artillery could not reach them.

At Caix, Currie pointed south across the fields to the church spire of Le Quesnel, from which he said he saw the most moving pageant he had seen in the whole war, the day after his victory. The Germans had had to give in to the south as well as towards Roye, and on the Canadian right the French came in to push them farther back. Then, for the only time in all the war, he saw its pageantry. Over the broad fields, where one can see for miles, columns of infantry were marching out in the open, cavalry dashing along the roads, field artillery galloping into position, and the advance furnished all the spectacle that one associates with great manœuvres. Prisoners also were filing back, for Currie's men had taken 7,000 on the day of the attack and about two hundred guns.[1]

Here I end the journey of over 300 miles along the most historic spots of the modern world. A cold wind was blowing in on us as we swung rapidly along the road to Amiens and the sun was just setting over the roofs of the city, whose cathedral with its slender central spire stood out against the western horizon visible from as far back in the fields as Villers-Bretonneux. It was only when one looked ahead to the prize that the Germans failed to win that one realized

---

[1] During the whole operation at the battle of Amiens, the Canadians advanced 14 miles, fought against 15 German divisions, of which 10 were directly engaged and thoroughly defeated, captured 190 guns and 9,311 prisoners. (Cf. *Report of the Ministry—Overseas Military Forces of Canada 1918*, p. 141.) Yet, as has been noted above, the Canadian Corps was allowed no time to rest on its laurels. It was immediately transferred to the Arras front and thrown against the Hindenburg line.

the meaning for civilization of the achievement of those men along the swamps of the Luce on August 8, 1918.

The lights were lighted in the streets of Amiens by the time we got there, and when we turned in at the Hôtel du Rhin we found the other car with Major O'Connor, Bowman and Young already there. They had taken the straight road from Cambrai to Amiens and already had time to see the cathedral. We joined them at dinner. Then Currie and O'Connor left once more for the long night run back to Camblain l'Abbé, where they would arrive about midnight; for Currie had to take the morning boat from Boulogne. He had spent his last days in France with us, travelling some three hundred miles. We turned in for the night with the feeling that we had passed two of the most historic days that we have lived through in our trip to Europe.

Wednesday, April 23, 1919

In the morning the train we were to take to Paris left from Longueau junction at about eleven, so we had plenty of time to visit the cathedral. It is almost untouched. There is one broken flying buttress and a small hole in the roof, visible from the outside only, and the rear windows are badly shattered, but the glass in the great rose windows is unbroken and the cathedral inside shows little sign of war except for the piles of sandbags on great iron supports which protect the choir stalls and sculpture.

German prisoners were clearing away the sandbags that had protected the portal of the southern transept on the outside and had already cleared them off the scaffolding that protected the sculptures of the front portals, so that through the scaffolding one could see the statues untouched and uninjured. The Germans have left the cathedral of Amiens practically intact. In the town itself there are numerous ruins but they are of individual houses and stores scattered here and there and are clearly the work of aviators rather than of bombardment. Except for these, Amiens had recovered its normal appearance, and we had an early lunch of chocolate and cakes in as dainty a confectioner's as in Lille.

By half past ten we were tucked away in a one-horse cab, with our piles of junk, helmets and cartridge cases and the like, stacked in at our feet, and jolted down the cobbled road to the railroad station—four tired and rather sleepy passengers for whom there were no seats on the train. We sat on our valises in the aisle, and reached Paris in time for a late lunch.

Paris seemed almost like home after the desolate world we had been through. The warm sunlight of the afternoon was also grateful after the chilly winds up north.

While I was unpacking, Slosson came in at three and handed me the mimeographed statement of the President on Fiume. We appreciated at once the gravity of the new crisis. The general effect of the President's message, however, has been to cheer us up, with the exception of Beer, who was for giving Fiume to the Italians, accepting the Treaty of London line as a substantial and practical thing. I went only part way with him in this. The Italians have been their own worst enemies from the time Italy entered the war, for instead of talking of high ideals, they have been openly practicing practical politics—*sacro egoismo*—so that now they have no great fund of public sympathy to fall back on anywhere. Germany will be sure to make the most of this and use the incident to smash the League of Nations. Some compromise must be found.

The Launching of the International
Labor Organization

Thursday, April 24, 1919

Called on M. Fontaine at the Ministry of Labor. Pushed on the Labor Charter a little farther. Miss Ida Tarbell came to lunch with me. She is going to lecture for Chautauquas this summer, and I gave her a full supply of literature on the international labor program, Anglo-American relations and other useful information.

A quiet day.

[Throughout February and most of March the various commissions of the Peace Conference had been busily at work, drafting their sections of the Peace Treaty. In April these reports were drawn together and the Treaty as a whole began to take shape. The description given here of the completion of the work of the Labor Clauses can be paralleled in most of the other sections of the Treaty. So close was our concentration on the task in hand that it was not until then that most of us—at least in the American Delegation—became aware of the character of the Treaty as a whole. This has been touched upon in the "Retrospect."]

Friday, April 25, 1919

In my room all morning working on labor clauses. Lunch with Frank Altschul, who brought letters from home. Spent the afternoon writing letters and the evening in discussion of the Italian situation. Neither summer nor a peace treaty seems ready to appear.

Saturday, April 26, 1919

The Italians are all leaving, but that news creates hardly a ripple at the Hôtel de Crillon, although most of us recognize the seriousness of the situation. Worked all day on the labor clauses of the Treaty of Peace, trying to get an agreement to prevent the Balfour draft from passing without change. About half past nine met Colonel and Mrs. House just leaving for a night train to visit Amiens and the front. I had a chance to have a word with him on the labor clauses and found him in agreement with me. He made some comments on the Italian situation which showed that he was unperturbed, because of his faith in the ultimate principles involved. His comment on Orlando was to the effect that he should eliminate himself in view of the situation. I read myself to sleep late that night with David Grayson's *Friendly Road,* which was a restful tonic.

Sunday, April 27, 1919

An early morning telephone call from Mr. Robinson. After breakfast was busy redrafting the clauses again, not knowing that Mr. Robinson was already in conference with Sir Robert Borden, the Japanese and the Belgians. As they reached an agreement, my morning's work was not needed, and the clauses were sent to the printer at eleven o'clock for the plenary session next day.

Had lunch with Beer and Slosson. After it, wandered over to the river bank where they were having a boat race from the different armies, French, American, New Zealand and some other teams. I saw one heat, but it was not half so exciting as the feat of an aviator who swooped down almost to touch the water between the bridges and then shot up a few hundred feet and rolled over and over in the air. He may have been having a good time, but about a quarter of a million Parisians held their breath while he did it. There are little shacks in the Tuileries Gardens along the banks of the Seine west of the Place de la Concorde and quite a village of them on the esplanade of the Invalides, where some of the buildings of the World's Fair used to be. They have held these small fairs yearly for the past three years here in Paris and in Lyons. It was an idea of the mayor of Lyons to stimulate trade and to outrival the German fairs, such as Leipzig. Paris is rapidly changing its aspect. The streets are much fuller of traffic and it is regaining a good deal of its pre-war appearance. The trees in the Champs Elysées are all out in leaf but a cold wind and frequent rains retard the spring. There was a beautiful sunset which I saw later by the river; these misty north-European skies are very beautiful.

The day began with a snowstorm, the snow falling in heavy flakes blown by a cold east wind. It turned to rain in the afternoon, and was a chilly birthday for the League of Nations. I spent part of the morning going from the Ministry of Labor to various head-quarters, Japanese, etc., helping M. Fontaine make sure that the French text of the clauses would be in shape.

The plenary session of the Peace Conference was called for three o'clock to receive the final reports of the Commissions on the League of Nations and the Labor Charter. I drove over with Frank Warrin at half past two to be sure of a seat and found myself assigned a place at the side of the room by the end of the head table, only a few feet away from the British Delegation. It was so close that I caught all the by-play of the Prime Ministers as they talked among themselves while the speeches were being made. If, as some one said the other time, the chief reason for the speech-making at a plenary session was to give the men at the head table a chance to discuss the propositions before they were voted, they used the opportunity to the full. This was so much the case that, when Borden was introducing the labor clauses, reading in a monotonous voice from the paper before them, the lack of attention was such that he became annoyed at the ill manners of his confrères, and called them to order himself—"them" being particularly Lloyd George. Clemenceau, for all his duties as presiding officer, was almost as irrepressible. Wilson, I am glad to say, acted in a more befitting manner.

There is not much new to add to the description of the earlier plenary sessions. It was held in the same hall as the previous one and there was the same crowd of journalists standing on their chairs at the back of the hall, which was, if anything, more crowded than on the earlier occasion, since the League of Nations Commission as well as the Labor Commission was present. Lord Robert Cecil sat just back of Balfour's place and sometimes consulted with him. He and Balfour as cousins understand each other perfectly and there is an evident tie of affection.

The preparatory diplomacy had apparently been thoroughly successful, and those who went expecting a scrap—which included most of the journalists—were disappointed. Baron Makino for Japan made a very eloquent and dignified appeal for equality of race treatment, but recognizing that this was not the time to push his case withdrew all opposition to the Covenant in its present form, thus gaining much more for Japan than if he had attempted to stand out. It was a very statesmanlike attitude, although a Chinese delegate told me it was decided upon only twenty-four hours before. Hymans for Belgium also made a good speech, expressing the disappointment of the Belgians that Geneva had been selected for the capital instead of Brussels, but in view of the fact that Belgium is one of the smaller Powers chosen for the directing committee, it withdrew its opposition. Léon Bourgeois for France made a long speech which he read poorly, and yet when he demanded greater guarantees for peace by way of disarmament in the name of the 1,700,000 dead of France, as well as those of her Allies, even his ineffective delivery gained a certain solemnity. However, France withheld amendment. Then followed a long speech in broken French by the delegate from Panama on the principles of international law, which no one listened to, and another long one, in Spanish, on the Monroe Doctrine by the delegate of Honduras. Neither of these was translated, and in the midst of the Honduras speech, which sorely tried the patience of the delegates, Lloyd George got up and as he passed my corner turned to his secretary, Kerr, beside me and said, "I'm not going to sit and listen to this any longer," and asked him jokingly if he didn't want to go out and have a cup of tea with him in the next room (they were serving tea and other things at a little counter at the far end of the anteroom outside). Wilson made almost no speech and the whole session was oratorically a disappointment, but Clemenceau made up for its prosaic quality by his handling of it at the close.[1] After the speeches he rose and said rapidly and almost in one long breath: "Has anyone else got anything more to say? No person wants to speak. The report is before you. Any amendments?" There was just the slightest pause and silence, then he added at once: "The report is adopted."

[1] My diary fails to record one little incident which showed Clemenceau's slight regard for his Foreign Minister, Pichon. Just after the speeches Pichon rose at the side of the table and proposed Monte Carlo for membership in the League of Nations. It was clear that the subject had never been discussed and that Pichon, for some reason personal to himself, thought that he could slip the nomination through in the general session without anyone venturing to oppose. Clemenceau straightened up, angry and alert and in a rasping voice asked Pichon what was the meaning of it. Pichon replied nervously and haltingly that he didn't know any reason why Monte Carlo should not be made a member of the League. Clemenceau called back, "Well, I know one anyway," and, without paying any more attention to Pichon who sat down confused and utterly discomfited, Clemenceau turned back to the meeting and went ahead without paying any more attention to the side of the room where his delegation was sitting.

Instantly a great buzz of conversation swept over the hall, showing the suppressed excitement, particularly on the part of the journalists, a fair number of whom rushed for the doors to send their cables home. The project of the League of Nations had passed its first stage in becoming world law, so far as the Peace Conference as a whole was concerned. At the earlier session it was simply laid before the Conference for its consideration, and no vote had been taken.

Then came the Labor Charter. Mr. Barnes explained that the form in which the clauses were presented by the Labor Commission had been the result of hasty drafting, that they had been partly redrafted through the efforts of Sir Robert Borden (enlisted by Mr. Balfour), and that he was willing to accept the new draft and understood that it met with the approval of those members of the Labor Commission who were available. Borden then started in to read his new draft but had to call the table to order to secure attention. He has a dominating personality. Then they called on Vandervelde to support the new draft, which he did, changing a word or two in the French text, the significance of which I had to explain to Balfour, who seemed a little nervous at any changes. After all, in spite of his age and readiness to drop asleep once in a while, Balfour strikes me as the most alert gentleman on the English front bench. He seems to be always on deck at the critical moments. The change was from "salariés industriels" to "travailleurs salariés," which brought in agricultural laborers.[1] I had a word with Lord Sinha after the session and he assured me that in India they would keep to the English text, which limits the scope of these clauses to "industrial wage-earners." There being no dissent, the labor clauses were declared carried and the session was over, having lasted about two hours and a half.

It is hard now to know whether we were assisting at an epoch-making event in the social history of the world or simply registering

[1] This is a good example of the importance of a single word in a treaty. The change from "industrial wage-earners" to "wage-earning workers" proved to be so important a matter in the history of the International Labor Organization that it was taken to the World Court for an advisory opinion. The Italians wanted to include farm laborers and the French to exclude them from the operation of the clause. In order to prove the Italian claim, the Italian Government published the Procès-Verbal of the debates of the Commission. This resulted in the first publication of the text in the *Official Bulletin* of the International Labor Office, Volume I (covering April, 1919–August, 1920), Geneva, 1923.

ineffective good intentions. The results of this session are going to depend very largely on what is done at the other sessions when the Treaty of Peace is actually signed, for the new era which the legislation of this plenary session formally inaugurated will have to make good in every phase of the agreement. If the Treaty of Peace is just, however harsh it may be, the League of Nations will be a reality, and if the Governments carry out, honestly and in good faith, the lines of the policies in regard to labor laid down in the Peace Treaty, we shall have gone a great step forward. As it is, we have simply prepared the way.

Miller, Warrin and I rode home, and I found waiting for me a letter from Sir Percy Wyndham, British High Commissioner to Warsaw, who is on his way there now, enclosing one from Alison Phillips.[1] I called up the Majestic and then went to see Wyndham, brought him back to dinner with Beer and Warrin and we had a pleasant evening, joined later by Jordan Stabler, head of the Latin American section of the State Department. Wyndham, who is a cousin of George Wyndham, the author of the Irish land bill, and belongs to an old English family, looks very much like the late King Edward the Seventh and has the quiet and restrained good manners of the English aristocrat. He had been for four years Minister to Colombia and showed in talking with Stabler a complete knowledge of the details of South American politics. He says he knows nothing whatever about the Poles, however, and claims to be properly scared about his new job. He leaves on Friday.

I spent the last part of the evening reading more chapters of *The Friendly Road*. Ray Stannard Baker has been my one diversion in Paris. Incidentally, and for no reason that either Baker or I can understand, he and I are constantly taken for each other by even such presumably close observers as the secret service men at the doors of the Crillon, not to mention the elevator boys. There is really very little resemblance.

---

[1] Professor Alison Phillips of Trinity College, Dublin, an old colleague and friend from my days on the *Encyclopædia Britannica*, 1904, the author of *The Continental System,* the outstanding study of the history of the Holy Alliance and the effect upon Europe of the Congress of Vienna. Professor Phillips was profoundly skeptical of the whole Wilsonian philosophy, and as a close student of German history and literature (he had translated into English verse from Middle High German the epic of Walter von der Vogelweide) he was much disturbed over the apparent failure to measure properly the place of Germany in European history.

Tuesday, April 29, 1919

Cold, rainy morning with hail storms between showers. The Labor work being over, I sorted out some of the papers and have given orders to the Library to start packing books. Most of the day, however, was spent trying to make sure of clauses in the treaty of peace by which Germany must both return to their owners all documents and archives it has taken from other countries and open up its own archives for historical investigation. Mr. Miller, who had me to lunch at the Meurice, is backing me in this and the proposition has gone up to headquarters. It will mean a great deal for history if it is adopted. The item about the seized documents will be put in in any case, and if I get both through I can call it a good day's work.

[There were many complaints from the occupied area, and especially from Belgium, of the loss of their archives. There was nothing new in this, as Napoleon had planned to make the newly founded national archives of France a central archive for all Europe and to enrich it, the way he had the Louvre, by treating documents as though they were the spoils of war. The other clause, which did not get into the Treaty, read as follows: "All existing official papers and documents of Germany or of any State of Germany shall for five years be accessible to persons duly authorized by the Council of the League of Nations to examine the same, under the direction of the Secretary General of the League. Publication of the text of any such papers shall be made under the direction of the Council of the League of Nations." I had hoped by this text to establish a procedure for the League of Nations which would not be limited to Germany alone. It was in line with the effort which I made to have British documents opened to American scholars who would be personally satisfactory to the British Government.[1] Subsequently Germany published its documents of its own accord, and the British and French Foreign Offices have done the same with reference to the diplomacy that had to do with the years preceding the War. I may add, as a strange sequel to this unsuccessful effort to force open the German archives in the Treaty of Peace, that a few years later I was taken into the document room of the German Foreign Office and offered absolute freedom to consult any document I wished. It was the German Government, which, acting on its own initiative,

[1] See above, p. 185; also Document 893 of the Miller Diary, IX, 216.

led the others in the publication of diplomatic records. Now the whole movement is under way, resulting in a vast addition to our knowledge of the history of the years preceding the World War.]

Wednesday, April 30, 1919

A cold, dreary day with a chilly rain falling. I pushed as far as I could with the British and French the clause for the Treaty which would open German archives to historical investigation. Then I called with Warrin upon Colonel Réquin of the General Staff, who was Foch's adjutant at the Marne, to get him to go with us on a projected trip over that battlefield. As the Germans are to be given the Treaty at Versailles Friday and Saturday, he may not be free to go with us. He has never been back to that battlefield since the battle itself and is anxious to go. In any case, he is preparing maps for us and an itinerary, calling upon the resources of the General Staff to help. Réquin is a good caricaturist and has preserved many comical sketches of the Supreme War Council and the generals. His picture of kindly old Joffre will some day be in a gallery.

Coming back I took a walk with Mezes in the rain, and we discussed the Italian crisis, being for once pretty well in agreement, although I do not go as far as Mezes. Lunch with Shepardson and Beer discussing holiday times in England. Shepardson is off to the golf links next week and most of the specialists are packing up. I am getting the books in the Library ready for shipment in the next two weeks, but am making no plans about myself as yet.

In the afternoon I stayed in my room and had a call from William Allen White, who is writing articles for *Harper's Magazine* and for his Kansas papers on the work of our Labor Commission. White has not lost his head here in the whirl of conflicting emotions and sees possibilities for the future in the work already done.

The connection between the Labor Conference and the League of Nations needs to be brought out. In the second paragraph of Article XXIV of the Covenant, vague but very broad powers are given to the Secretariat to gather and distribute all relevant information in matters of international interest and the further statement is made that it shall "render any other assistance which may be necessary or desirable." That is the clause inserted to meet my demand for a recognition, officially in the Covenant, of the periodic conferences which will be held to deal with such matters as Labor and which will ultimately, if the League prospers, form a series of specific parliaments. The demand for a representative body like a world parliament, which Norman Angell urged and the League of Free Nations sent me cables about, is met here in a way which will escape attention until it begins to show by real activities what is meant. I called Mr. White's attention to this and found, as I expected, that he had no idea of the real situation. Even the farmers' bureau (International Institute of Agriculture at Rome) may add its periodic conferences and secure their official recognition by the League. In short, as Mr. White put it when he got the idea, "There can be a group of soviets, a bankers' soviet, a labor soviet, a shippers' soviet, etc., and all of them can be articulated with the national governments." If we can develop this scheme, it may furnish an outlet for the practical needs of international politics in such a way as to lessen the strong nationalism which is the aftermath of the war.

I have spent a little time on my Sorbonne lecture today, but have just reached that stage where I am sorry I consented to give it, and particularly sorry that I agreed to try it in French.

[This attempt to interpret the Covenant as having indirectly made provision for periodically recurring conferences in special fields bears witness rather to my own continued interest in that plan than to any recognition of it on the part of the framers of the Covenant. My conviction that this was the right line to follow in the constitution of the League was so strong as to lead me to read into the Covenant more than was justified by the text.]

Thursday, May 1, 1919

Labor's day in Europe. It began as usual with a cold, drizzling rain, which lasted on till just after three o'clock in the afternoon, the hour set for the workingmen's demonstration in the Place de la Concorde in front of the hotel. Evidently Providence was on the side of the capitalists.

I spent a quiet morning mostly in my room and over at the Library. Lunch with Mr. Charles Strachey of the British Foreign Office, a most interesting, unofficial looking man of middle life. He is a cousin of the Strachey of the *Spectator*, and his father was a high British official in India, at one time substituting for viceroy. The conversation, about Victorian England and literary and historical topics, was broken into by the waiters crowding to the windows to see the demonstration. There were not more than a few hundred people in front of the hotel, working people of Paris with cloth caps, wearing little rosettes of red ribbon in their buttonholes. They were being hustled along by the police and just as they reached the corner in front of the Crillon a company of cavalry rode into them waving their hands and although pushing their horses into the crowd, still apparently acting with a good deal of good humor. Some demonstrators seized the bridles of horses and gesticulated at the riders, but the crowd was much too weak to stand up against the horsemen and was forced up a side street west of the hotel. They say that at the next street corner a man was trampled to death by a horse, but it was hard to run the rumor down.

Stepping out of the hotel I saw a man with a bad cut down the back of his head and across his neck. He was having his hand bandaged as well, having had two fingers cut off, and was soon in a Red Cross ambulance that was stationed on the opposite side of the street. Then I went down towards the east end of the square to the real scene of battle, for this cutting had been done not by the soldiers but by the police, who are skilled in breaking up crowds but who individually strike one as cowardly and provocative. They lose their nerve and kick men when they are down and in general act as though they were afraid of the crowd. On the other hand, they are skillfully manœuvred to push different sections of the crowd different ways and so break it up.

From the balcony of our office building we had a grandstand view of the Rue Royale down which the mob had come. It had pushed through from the grand boulevards past cavalry companies stationed across the street, who did not seem to oppose its advance, and it had come on with red banners to defy the police and hold the demonstration. The police were massed in between the companies of cavalry and any fighting there was—mainly with sticks, fists and kicking—was with the police. The crowd we saw from the Crillon windows was the vanguard that had pushed through to the Place de la Concorde, but the spectacle in the Rue Royale was more menacing. The street in front was empty, but at the far end, where the boulevards empty into it, there were heavy, swaying masses. The cordon of cavalry stretched right across the street below, and opened up to let infantry march through them from the square behind, and these troops, moving up toward the crowd, with their rifles ready for use, gave us a tense moment. Fortunately, when face to face with the crowd they halted, grounded arms, and merely stood on guard. Along the garden of the Tuileries there was a whole regiment of cavalry and another along the banks of the Seine; but nothing really happened after this first skirmish, and half an hour later I walked across to the river through a practically empty square over to the Pont Alexandre III. There was an army kitchen serving out coffee to the troops there, and one of the soldiers with whom I had a little chat told me that they had been ordered out from Versailles at two in the morning. He didn't mind it for himself, but his horse had had nothing to eat all day. He told me that the cavalry was drawn from central France. He was from Lyons and it didn't take much questioning to see that he had little sympathy with the police.

I walked around among the horses for quite a distance and had the growing feeling of depression to see so much preparation for civil war. Between sixty and a hundred thousand troops were concentrated on Paris. It gave an unexpected turn to the historic suggestions of captured German cannon along the Champs Elysées to see French troops quartered amongst them in anticipation of a renewal of the commune. They were seated on the park chairs and making themselves comfortable in that complete abandon which the French soldier is capable of. Some had thrown a tarpaulin over the barrels of the large German guns and made a roof that way to shelter them from the rain. Practically all were smoking and looked bored but still good-natured.

In the evening Dr. Isaiah Bowman and his wife gave a farewell dinner to the President of the Council of Poland, Paderewski, and the Foreign Minister, Dmowski. It was an elaborate if quiet affair, given in one of the private rooms of the Crillon. The large round table was scattered with red roses and red and white decorations, since Poland's flag is red and white. The favors were lilies of the valley, in honor of May Day. The other members of the Inquiry present were Dr. Lord, who has been American Commissioner in Poland, and Professors Seymour and Day.

Madame Paderewski was very gracious and so was he. He says that he has forever given up music now, and even that he cares for it no longer. The only music he has written recently is a Polish national hymn, and Madame Paderewski said that at a meeting in Warsaw not long ago which had this hymn on the program he quite forgot to call for it. I asked her if he gives the same amount of nervous energy to his speeches that he used to put into the preparation for a concert, but she says that politics doesn't call for an artistic temperament and that her husband now can lead a perfectly normal life. As for Dmowski, he told me that music is mere noise to him and that he never was at any of Paderewski's concerts until almost the very last, when Paderewski took him along to one at Brighton, in England.

After dinner the waiters gave an exhibition of their skill in removing the signs of the banquet by taking the table apart and moving it from the room and substituting for it a small drawing-room table with a bouquet of flowers on it—all done in less than two minutes—and we sat around the fireplace. But the Polish statesmen, with Lord, Bowman and Colonel Embick, went away to the office for an hour's discussion of the Armistice.

Toward midnight I looked out over the roof of the Crillon and saw against the sky the dark figure of the sentry posted there, walking up and down with his gun on his shoulder, and it gave a queer sense of a beleaguered city, in the midst of the unsettled social forces of Europe today.

[The restoration of Poland by the Paris Peace Conference owes much—if not, indeed, most—to the American Delegation; and its frontiers were largely determined by Dr. Bowman, who traced them with scrupulous care on the basis of exhaustive demographic surveys. Professor Lord, as a partisan of Poland, sought to gain all for the Poles that sympathy for their tragic history could demand. The British, however, were uneasy at the extent to which this preoccupation with the restoration was cutting into the map of Europe. The Foreign Office, and especially Mr. Headlam-Morley, were afraid that the seeds of a future war would be sown in a corridor stretching across Germany in order to give Poland "free and secure access to the sea," even if this corridor were guaranteed by an "international covenant" as in the thirteenth of Wilson's Fourteen Points. I took no part in these negotiations, but in the private discussions of the Inquiry group I joined with Young and Beer in questioning the wisdom of the exact terms arrived at. We all recognized the extreme difficulty of the problem—that a nation of thirty million could not be restored to its national home without displacing others. But at bottom the German-Polish question is not merely one of territory. It will not be settled until the attitude of each nation toward the other is changed; for arrogance on Germany's part breeds resentment on the part of the Poles, and now the Poles can strike back.]

Friday, May 2, 1919

Mr. Robinson has asked me definitely to go to London for the meeting of the Organizing Committee of the Labor Conference next Tuesday, and if duly appointed, I shall have to go. Meanwhile, Mr. Miller has telephoned over that the trip to Verdun is cancelled. The Treaty has to be got into shape for the Germans and he cannot be spared. It is planned to present it on Monday, and if there should be any chance of my having a look in at that historic session I should be sorry to miss it for any trip to London, however interesting. However, I hardly think there is any chance of my being present; that would be almost too much good luck.

More or less killed time today and in the afternoon went to the exhibition of Yugoslav, Spanish and Venetian art in the Petit Palais. It is a loan exhibition for the benefit of war refugees. The Spanish section has some fine Goyas and Zuloagas but the Yugoslav sculpture as well as painting belongs to that decadent school which is conceited enough to call itself futurist. Most of the things were more or less revolting. It is a positive relief to turn from this straining for effect to the calm masterpieces of the Spanish painters, or the delicate jewel-like Venetian scenes of Guardi. Beer and I came home and had tea together and were joined by Philippe Millet of *Le Temps*.

In the interval between tea and dinner I was called in to see Dr. Mezes. He evidently had some good news to communicate. First of all he set me the job of finding the Latin equivalent for the "League of Nations" which I said might be "Societas Gentium" or "Societas Civitatum." The request comes from high up. In the next place he invited me to go with him to the Comédie Française that evening. But the third thing explained the other two. He had just had an afternoon's walk and talk with his brother-in-law and passed on to me some very cordial comments on my work in the labor matter. I hurried through dinner with Millet and Beer and then went off to the theatre. It was "L'Amoureuse," the story of a too-loving wife who annoys her husband by sitting on his knee when he wants to write scientific treatises. But all ends happily, though with a certain Gallic interlude, which lends just enough interest to the play to get it across with the aid of some magnificent acting. The play is worthless, but as the concierge in the hotel informed me, it is *trés recherché,* and we had to take a whole box in order to get a seat.

Saturday, May 3, 1919

Read some in my room and tried to get around to working on the Sorbonne lecture, which is beginning to loom up uncomfortably near. After lunch I drove over to the Bibliothèque Nationale, intending to work there, but found it closed. Then about four o'clock, after futile efforts to get anything down on paper, I strolled in the Scotch mist up the Champs Elysées to the Grand Palais where the Salon has just been opened; the first exhibition of French art in five years. It is an enormous affair with about three thousand entries, but is so well hung that one hasn't the sense of crowding. The sculpture is on the main floor, which is arranged with little flower beds and gravel walks. The war does not stand out as a theme as I had expected. To be sure, there are few rooms without one or more war scenes, but the percentage is hardly more than one in seven or one in ten. There are a number, however, with crêpe tied to the edge of the frame, or in the case of sculpture fastened to the pedestal, when the artist has been killed in the war. Another point of interest is the very slight influence which the cubists and futurists, etc., have had on the general trend of French art. There is one row of rooms in which the grotesque predominates, but on the whole the exhibition is along the normal lines of the history of art. There were no painters I knew on the line and I saw nothing in the whole exhibition as good as a little street arab on the canvas that hangs in my own front room in New York. Next year I hope to see some more of that kind on the line in the Grand Palais.

I stayed only a couple of hours. At dinner I sat where I could see a birthday party which Lieutenant Berle was giving to the little daughter of Herbert Adams Gibbons. She is about eleven years old and he had arranged a table for her with a cake and candles on it. From where I could see her, the child's face in the Crillon gave me a full realization of how dull and dried up a lot of old fogies we have been sitting around here without a chance to have so much as a look into a child's face.

After dinner I stole away upstairs and got my overcoat and took a little walk around the Place de la Concorde. It was a wonderful nocturne with just enough light in the sky to show the Eiffel Tower in the distance across the dark square. It reminded me of evenings in Washington the first year of the War when we used to watch the searchlights pick out the shaft of the Washington monument against the night sky. The light lasts longer here and seems almost absorbed by the clouds along with the moisture. Of course, compared with Paris, the air of Washington those summer nights was clear and dry, although I remember it as soft and moist. One could never paint a Whistler nocturne in Washington, and Paris this Spring is suggestive of nocturne in more ways than one.

I went to bed early and read away in the autobiography of Rihbany, the Syrian who has been calling on me from time to time and who is trying to get the United States to interest itself in Syria. It is entitled *A Far Journey* and is a well-told, graphic narrative.

Sunday, May 4, 1919

Mr. Miller called me over to work for him on some treaty clauses dealing with the protection of minorities in Poland and in eastern Europe generally. It is sometimes a little alarming to find that your mere opinion is really going to be taken as the basis for an international agreement and that the wording which comes to you somewhat casually may be written into a charter of liberties for millions of people. In the short time I spent in Miller's office we recast the statement of the conditions of citizenship for the peoples of eastern Europe, and he wrote my name at the top of the sheet containing the draft. However, I hope it will be much modified before it is finally adopted.

I had to run off to lunch at Max Lazard's with Beer. Max Lazard and Madame have just returned from a motor trip along the English coast hunting for summer residences, and have found a place in north Devon. We had a nice quiet luncheon and afterwards sat out on their lawn, which is sprinkled with daisies and forget-me-nots. Then we walked through the Bois de Boulogne back to Paris to take tea with Philippe Millet, foreign editor of *Le Temps*. They have a nice, old-fashioned house surrounded by trees, although apartment houses have been built up on either side. I met Jean Herbette, the principal editor of *Le Temps,* and had an interesting conversation with him and Wickham Steed. There was quite a little company of writers. Millet has in mind a weekly review of international politics, and wanted me to contribute.

The appointment to the Organizing Committee for the Washington Labor Conference means going over to London at once. Shepardson came in, after I had gone to bed, to say that if I would go he would join me. As I was undecided whether to take the Committee appointment or stay and work with Miller on treaty revision, I settled the matter by tossing a penny, which came heads up for London.

Monday, May 5, 1919

The credentials for the Organizing Committee of the Labor Conference, signed by Secretary Lansing, reached me at twenty minutes past ten and the only train which would get me there in time left at eleven, so I telephoned the British and got Barnes' secretary to telephone to London that I would be late for the meeting. He offered to arrange to send me over in a British airplane, but as there is no insurance covering air risks, I declined the temptation. The air journey to London is only about two hours. Rappard, of Geneva, insists on our going together on the five o'clock train and Beer and Shepardson are going along to make a party. We go to Havre and take the night boat for Southampton.

It was an interesting comment on government efficiency that the only way to get our tickets all arranged for was to give up inquiring around the Crillon or the executive offices of the American mission and turn the matter over to the hotel clerk in the Meurice, where Rappard is staying.

I called up Miller to say that I was going and was hoping that would settle the minorities question so far as I was concerned, but instead he said that some of it would keep till I came back.

A Glimpse of London and Oxford

First Meeting of the Labor Conference Organizing Committee

We left by the five o'clock train for Havre, and with the memory of the former trips through battle wildernesses, this journey down the valley of the Seine seemed almost like a trip through fairyland. The orchards were in bloom and the poplar trees along the roadways were flushed with the first reddish tinge from the opening leaves. It was a lyric landscape all the way. The farmers plow in long strips down the gently rolling hillsides and these were far enough away so that it seemed almost as though strips of tapestry of different colors had been unrolled down the long rim of the valley. It was the first warm day of the year and almost the first cloudless sky.

The only signs of war along the valley of the Seine are those of prosperity. Large sheds at various sidings, particularly towards Rouen, and great numbers of freight cars taken from Germany standing on the sidings marked "Danzig," "Essen" and "Hamburg." There were a few German prisoners but not many, and relatively few soldiers.

We reached Havre after twilight and drove through the dark streets to the wharves past many taverns filled with the soldiers of all the Allied armies. In the harbor were those same little fishing smacks I used to watch steal out of Harfleur in the twilight seven years ago. On the wharf we realized the advantages of having a diplomatic passport, for while the crowd thronged the waiting room in a long tiresome wait for the passport visé and the customs, we were taken straight through and were on deck first.

We found, of course, that the boat was full, and the steward offered us of his charity to make arrangements with the engineers to give up their berths and rooms for 30 shillings each, or 42 francs. As it was a choice between this and sitting up on deck all night, we accepted the charity, but we decided that the engineers will soon be retiring from business if the ship is as crowded every night.

We had a calm sea all the way across and I kept the porthole open and spent part of the night looking out across the water in the bright moonlight. Coal freighters moved in, in black shadowy masses, across the line of the moonlight on the water and the Channel lights were flashing from the headlands again. The Channel, like the Seine valley, had obliterated all the traces of war. I was up early to see the morning break over England, but instead of the gay sunshine of Normandy there was a grey mist over the Isle of Wight, and Portsmouth was completely lost in haze. We passed black troop-ships anchored in the Solent with their decks swarming with khaki clad troops on the way back to South Africa. The only signs of war on land were the seaplane sheds at the point of the Isle of Wight, and two great seaplanes anchored out from shore.

At Southampton we received the same diplomatic courtesy but it was not of much value, for the train stayed in the dockyards until the last Italian immigrant had been examined and his luggage stowed away in the train. I was surprised to see the number of Italians in our boatload. There must have been thirty or forty, some in the Italian uniform. I asked a longshoreman boss what the Italians worked at and his reply was, "Aw, nothin'."

After a three-hour wait, the train pulled out through the slum district of Southampton on the road to London. The English landscape, like the French, shows the effect of war mainly in added freight sheds, but the most notable change was the great increase in small gardens. Every vacant field has been divided up into little garden plots where the working classes can grow their vegetables. The plan was a development from the Allotment Act of some eight or nine years ago by which vacant land near towns and uncultivated meadows on great estates could be appropriated by action of the district councils for use of the working people of the district. The thrift which this encouraged in pre-war days was a necessary basis on which to build when the submarine blockade threatened to starve England into defeat. But even more interesting than the use of the allotments during the war is their use after the war, for they are being continued this year the same as last and entirely by the private enterprise of the working people, who seem to be getting more than vegetables from their work in the open air at the close of their day in the factory. In any case, this increased use of waste spaces as garden plots is the most notable outward change that the war has brought to the English countryside. There are no ugly fields of refuse with ashes and tin cans such as one sees along the fringes of American cities. Although economists here have assured me that the allotment way of working in small driblets of hand labor is a poor and unprofitable method of production, my guess is that it is the very reverse.

The London and Southwestern Railway runs from Southampton to Winchester along the valley of the little willow-fringed stream where Izaak Walton used to fish, and then up over the high chalk plain of the North Downs through Basingstoke to London. It is interesting, in view of what the war has taught us of geography, to see that these chalky uplands of Hampshire and Surrey are just the continuation of the long ridges over which the English army fought from Vimy to the Somme. There is only a thin skim of earth on top, so thin that they plow a shallow furrow, and the fields stretch away in long, even slopes just as they do in France except that the English fields are cut with hedgerows and there are more woods along the broken hillsides.

London was the busiest city I have ever stepped into. We had been directed by Sir Eric Drummond, the newly appointed Secretary-General of the League of Nations, to the Metropole Hotel and had telegraphed ahead, but when our taxi drew up in front of it we discovered it hadn't been turned back by the Government from its war service in the Ministry of Munitions. Then we started on a taxicab Odyssey from hotel to hotel. It soon became apparent that the only sure place to sleep in London was on the Embankment or in Trafalgar Square; so after we had been refused at the Russell Square Hotel and had lunched there, Rappard and I went to the Labor Conference, Shepardson to Oxford, and Beer took the taxi man—whom we had kept waiting all the while, because if we had let him go there would have been little chance of getting another—and started on the hunt all afternoon. He tried over thirty hotels and then lost count. About five o'clock he came to tell me that there was no hope in London. So we telephoned to Oxford and luckily found rooms there.

The train left at seven-thirty and got in about nine. The lady at the Randolph showed us two empty double rooms at one-tenth the price of a room in the Ritz, so we took both just to have an empty bed to look at after having faced the alternative of cold stones on a London Square. We left our luggage in Oxford to come back the next night so as to make sure of a place to sleep; but when we got down to London there was a telegram to Beer from Mezes calling him back to Paris. So he bought a new valise and some things for the night and I went back to Oxford alone.

[Thrust into my diary at this point is a crumpled page of notes recalling a walk by moonlight through the streets of Oxford, up Broad Street, New Lane, Queen's Lane, High Street, and then down a little rose lane to the cottage where we once lived right under Magdalen tower. There from the bridge one could see the deer park where Colonel Lawrence used to ramble nights like this. The turrets of Magdalen against a cloudless sky with the stars between the trees; students in their gowns coming from the quadrangle; old Oxford, quiet, untouched by time except to make it more beautiful. It was impossible to believe that there had been a war, and above all that Oxford had been part of it, yet almost next door to Magdalen a sign in the window read, "Used hospital chairs for sale. Broken ones may be used for wheelbarrows." Yet this was *der Tag!* The very same day that Germany received at Versailles the terms of the Treaty it must sign.

The evening was spent at Balliol in Urquhart's rooms, Shepardson, as an old Rhodes scholar, taking me along with him. A group of young dons, back from the trenches, all eager to forget, reviving Oxford memories across the chasm of the four years. The talk was mostly about Greek philosophy, with keen humor and ready attack upon any careless slip. I did not know till the evening was over that the man in holy orders beside me had gone out to No Man's Land to bring back his brother's body in the face of German fire, that next to him was a D.S.O., and that the quiet chap at the corner of the table had won his colonelship from the ranks. Any mention of the war in that company, however, would have been regarded as utterly unforgivable.]

The object of the London trip, as mentioned before, was to organize a program for the Labor Conference. I went as representative of the United States on the Organizing Committee but found myself in a strange position at the last moment, for although the President has invited the Labor Conference to meet in Washington, our constitutional lawyers have discovered that he has no authority to do so, as all such invitations must come from Congress. My own appointment therefore was limited by these conditions. But I assured the committee that there would be no question but that Congress would ratify our action, which took no small amount of assurance! In any case, we went ahead and got out a long series of questions on labor legislation to be sent to the different countries so as to have the material ready for a conference in October.

As the time is limited, we cabled the questions to all the distant Governments such as America, Bolivia, Brazil, the Dominions and India, China, Cuba, Ecuador, Guatemala, Honduras, Japan, Nicaragua, Panama, Peru, Siam and Uruguay and half a dozen others. Each cable is two or three thousand words long, and the British Foreign Office will have quite a bill to collect from the League of Nations, which will have to pay for the Labor budget.

As a matter of fact, the work of our committee in London was, so far as I know, the first positive international act under the auspices of the League of Nations.

The Organizing Committee has been given fine offices at 53 Parliament Street, fronting on the street just around the corner from the Parliament buildings; and a small staff has been set aside for the correspondence and the handling of material. The Minister of Labour, Sir Robert Horne, had us over for a rather formal interview in his own office and the British were apparently intending to push the thing through in their usual efficient way right up to the October Conference; but I insisted that the seat of the Committee be changed to Washington on September first, foreseeing trouble if a separate committee in Washington should plan one set of activities while a European committee was planning another. I also had to prevent the Committee from planning a kind of conference which would, I think, have been a failure. Fontaine and Delevingne, being government functionaries, are mainly interested in getting their work done in a workmanlike way and have little patience with the wastefulness of parliamentary procedure, so they were planning to have the procedure of the conference arranged by separate commissions, with the Conference meeting only to ratify. They were rather appalled at the idea of an international conference debating these questions in all the languages of the globe and so were inclined to minimize the work of the general sessions. I succeeded in heading off a motion which would have made the commissions very formal and would have subordinated the general sessions to them; for if I know anything about American labor it is that it is tired of commissions, either of investigation or executive action, and the only hope for the International Labor Conference is to give it the publicity of a parliament. Labor men cannot let themselves be drawn into a position where they can be charged with secret diplomacy. The alternative may be wasteful but it is the only way to succeed.

Phelan heartily agreed with me and will spend some time between now and July 15, when we meet next, getting the English to agree. Meanwhile I am left to handle the situation from Paris, as I have been appointed with M. Fontaine to draft the rules of procedure for the Washington Conference.

Before leaving London, I telephoned to the Canadian headquarters and had Currie on the wire. He told me to come along at once to his office at Oxford Circus. His whole family had just dropped in on him. His daughter is fifteen and his son nine. They are coming to France next week and are to be brought on to Paris for a day or so after a trip over the front. I had to rush off for the train and took a little Canadian orderly to carry back from the station the souvenirs we had brought.

We had an uneventful return trip to Paris where we arrived Friday noon.

Instead of Negotiations . . .

Coming into Paris again after London, one is struck with the relative quiet of this city as compared with the crowded streets of London. I never saw anything so busy as the London streets. One has to push one's way through the crowds as at a fair. Paris is a much more gracious town and has a sort of feminine beauty, while the chief characteristic of London is strength and vigor. The Crillon was like home again, and I spent the afternoon getting oriented on the Peace Conference news. Mezes had no more data as to when I was to plan to leave, but Bowman and Young are leaving for America next week. A visit from Barnes took up the evening, and we discussed the labor situation in my room till late at night. He is to take up with some of the nations represented here, and I with others, the collaboration of their Governments on the program of the Washington Conference.

[Had there been a negotiated peace, the Peace Conference would have begun with the completion of the draft treaty and its presentation to the Germans. Negotiations should have followed on the basis of that program, and the Germans should have been offered a full and free opportunity to make their case in the give and take of discussion. The members of the Labor Commission felt that they had no reason to be doubtful of the outcome in any such procedure. As it was, however, in the notes exchanged there is a complete documentary history of the substitute for negotiations.[1]]

Saturday, May 10, 1919

Marked time. We are waiting for the Germans to reply. Went over to the Bibliothèque Nationale to find it still closed, and so worked in my room part of the time on the Sorbonne lecture but not making much progress. In the afternoon took a stroll with Beer through the

[1] These are given in *The Origins of the International Labor Organization*, I, 234-254.

Champs Elysées; watched the crowds from a rented chair. Spent the evening writing letters. Colonel House has not been able to see the President yet about his plans for setting up the offices of the League of Nations.

Sunday, May 11, 1919

Routine work in the room all day. The weather is perfect; warm spring sunshine, tempting one to a walk in the suburbs. Instead, I strolled along the boulevards in the late afternoon. Seats in front of the cafés were at a premium. Coming back from London the distaste for this kind of stupidity, sitting vacantly watching the crowds pass on the sidewalk, was keener than ever.

Monday, May 12, 1919

Took a stroll along the river bank in the morning; lunched with Beer and Piacentini, who told us the story of the Fiume question from the Italian side. Beer later saw Curtis and got the full English version, which we talked over at tea time.

At Colonel House's request, conveyed through his secretary, Mr. Gordon Auchincloss, I am to work out the needs of the Labor Section of the League so as to help in calculating the housing problem.

In the evening the heads of divisions of the Inquiry gave Bowman a dinner, as it was his last night in Paris. We made it an intimate affair, almost like a family party. There was no speech-making, but a frank exchange of confidences. Strangely enough, the most appreciative person here with reference to the work of the Inquiry seems now to be no other than Lansing, who was anything but cordial in the earlier stages. Bowman and Young leave by the seven o'clock train for Brest.

Tuesday, May 13, 1919

A lovely, warm Spring day. Wasted most of the morning having my picture taken for a "Golden Book" of the Conference. There were a number of others similarly unemployed.

In the afternoon I received a hurried call from the Secretariat telling me that I was to act on the Committee of Five [1] that had been appointed to consider the answer to be made to the German reply to our Labor sections in the Treaty.

[1] As alternate for Mr. Robinson.

We met at three o'clock. Mr. Barnes represented Great Britain; M. Fontaine, France; M. Tosti, Italy; and finally Otchiai came for Japan.

The British as usual had got ahead of the rest, having received their German text in time for a carefully drafted reply, so there was little for us to do but edit it. I made very few suggestions. The German criticism is based on the theory that we have not given Labor a real international parliament after all. Their proposal recalls the Socialist International, with its revolutionary concepts of Labor making its own laws for itself in an international body which is above parliaments. We suspect very strongly that this is not an honest statement of Germany's real feeling about Labor and is an effort to stir up revolutionary discontent against the Allied Governments in their own countries. The Germans who have just put down radical socialism in a civil war in the streets of Berlin cannot expect us to take this seriously. They utterly misjudge the temper of the British and the French. This is inexcusable after the fiasco of May first, unless the Germans are so cut off from the outside world as not to know what has been going on there.

Our meeting was singularly informal. The large French windows of the old banqueting hall were thrown open on the garden and when the session was over we walked right out into the shade of the chestnut trees, which are in bloom. I must correct here a statement of an earlier date that the house belonged to Madame Pompadour. Fontaine says that is not the case and that it has no particular historical associations of the old régime. In any case, it is a quiet, restful spot with a little fountain playing amidst the lawn.

The answer to the Germans having been drafted, Barnes drove home in my car and I took him to the Majestic to get, if possible, a proof of the document we prepared in London. I went in with him for tea with Mrs. Barnes and his two daughters and son, who had just arrived in Paris for a short visit. She is a quiet, motherly woman with a good Scotch face. The son is a captain in the British army.

Wednesday, May 14, 1919

In these warm Spring days the temptation to escape from the Crillon grows on me. Nothing especial to record all day.

In the evening Barnes sent word that the Four (Wilson, Lloyd George, Clemenceau and Orlando) were asking our Labor Committee to reassemble, to consider whether the Germans might be admitted into the Labor Organization before they were let into the League of Nations. It is a question of a good deal of importance because the Germans will likely use any privileges granted them as an entering wedge to open up the League. On the other hand, it is important to get industrial Germany to tie herself as soon as possible to the same labor restrictions as we take on.

Beer is busy at the Fiume problem and the Belgians in Africa. It looks as though he might have some success at both. Lord Milner sent for him, to ask his advice.

Thursday, May 15, 1919

A busy day. An early morning visit to Miller's office to point out the importance to the League of Nations Committee of any possible action by the Labor Committee. The way things are done here, the League of Nations might find itself compromised by the action of the Four in dealing with Labor. As there was no possibility of delaying action, which Miller also wanted, I secured a recommendation in our report that the question should not be settled without reference to the League of Nations Committee, which is just the same as if we had asked for a delay.

At ten o'clock I was at the Bibliothèque Nationale, going with Haskins to a meeting of a committee representing the different learned academies of the Allied countries, under the presidency of the President of the Institut. The plan is to form an academic union of these societies, and it was decided to have the permanent seat in Brussels.[1] It was a very distinguished little gathering. Italy sent the historians Lanciani and DeSanctis. Belgium sent the historian Pirenne. There were about twelve of us. We met again in the afternoon and have a final session Saturday morning. It brings as well an invitation to a reception at the Institut and dinner by the president of the Institut on Sunday. I am there as representative of the American Historical Association. It was really a great experience to get out of this diplomatic and political atmosphere and be seated around a table in the quiet office of the librarian of the national library.

---

[1] This was the origin of the International Union of Academies (*Union Académique Internationale*), which has played an important part in the post-war history of the European academies and is responsible for the creation of the American Council of Learned Societies.

The contrast of my present work with this quiet academic atmosphere was made all the more striking by what happened when I left the morning session. I had kept my car outside so as to drive rapidly to the meeting of the Labor Committee. Mr. Barnes, as usual, was ahead of the game, since the British secretary, Sir Maurice Hankey, sees to it that he gets the documents on time, while mine drift in to me after the event is over. However, his reply suited me except the final paragraph, which I recast. Then I drove over to the President's house by invitation to deliver the document and discuss the question. Mr. Barnes was to meet me there, and both go in to the Four together. My driver was intent on beating the British Empire and broke all the speed laws getting over to the President's house. But the British driver knew his old Europe better than we did and slipped up a side street while we went around by the Champs Elysées. It was a symbol of more than a morning's drive.

This was my first visit to the present residence of the President. It is on the Place des Etats-Unis and is a large mansion, in fact was popularly called a palace even before he took it. It, like the flat of the British Prime Minister (which is relatively unpretentious compared with our magnificence) belongs to the wealthy Jewish banking and merchant class. There are policemen from the end of the square all the way up to the house. Two sentry boxes stand on each side of the driveway and are occupied by French soldiers in spick-and-span new uniforms, standing with fixed bayonets. As we got out of cars and started for the doorway, both of these stately Frenchmen presented arms. Just inside the doorway were two American army officers, apparently captain and lieutenant of the guard. They also saluted as we passed. Then on the first step of the stairway, just in front of the glass door, two of the finest looking young American soldiers you ever saw were standing rigidly at attention. As we passed them, they clicked heels and presented arms with a precision that would have brought joy to the heart of Frederick Wilhelm I.

Inside there was a butler to take our hats and a secret service man to look us over quietly from the corner of the stair and two secretaries in the hall above, where I found Philip Kerr, Lloyd George's secretary, sitting cooling his heels by the window of the antechamber. Sir Maurice Hankey soon joined us and told us that another matter was under discussion by the Four and that they had got so deeply into it that they couldn't take up the labor matter after all!

The hall and drawing room are much more ornate than the Lloyd George apartment, and while there is a profusion of art objects there is too much magnificence. As we were going away, Mr. Barnes commented that our President lived in more state than the King of England so far as actual contact with the outside world was concerned. He said that anyone who has any business to see the King can get to him without any trouble, and that only one red-coated butler stands in the way as you present your card in Buckingham Palace. I was a little surprised at this, and it was not until Beer recalled to my mind the fact that the Right Honorable George N. Barnes is a Privy Councilor and so has a right to have access to His Majesty that I realized why Barnes should find King George so easy of approach. However, I doubt if anything in England can outdo the impression of the presence chamber which one gets at the Bischoffsheim Palace.

The soldiers all saluted once more as we came down and out on to the street. I drove back to the Crillon for a hurried lunch to get back in the afternoon to the adjourned meeting of the savants in the Bibliothèque Nationale.

Just after lunch Mezes got the whole group of the Inquiry together, for the first time since they came to Paris, and told us that the Conference was practically over and that we might go home when it suited us. He told me privately, however, that he wanted to see me personally before I made my own plans. This means that the United States is not going to interest itself in the settlement of Turkey or the Near East and there is great dissatisfaction in certain quarters. The League of Nations is starting with a pretty serious handicap in a world that is by no means settled.

In the evening I had Fontaine's secretary, Mr. Pone, over in my room working on the French translation of as much of my lecture as is done.

Friday, May 16, 1919

A conference with Mezes on the closing up of the Library. The books are being packed. Thanks to the Library staff, and chiefly to Captain Gilchrist, I have not had to worry over it at all during the Peace Conference. He has arranged all the business papers and bought and housed the books without my giving them more than a casual oversight.

Lunched with Frankfurter, Beer and Shepardson. Frankfurter was much worked up over a letter from Warsaw giving an account of the terrible pogroms which the Poles are guilty of. I told him I thought that there were only two courses for Zionism: either it must keep out of the larger political game and limit itself to something like the old Rothschild benevolent associations, or else, if it goes into politics, it will have to go in strong. Any half measures arousing illusory hopes in the Polish Jewish population will simply invite pogroms. Upon the whole, I am inclined to be anti-Zionist for the Jews' own sake.

Dined with Beer and Gallagher, the correspondent of the *Herald,* who has traveled all over Asia and is much worked up with fear of an American-Japanese war. However, we both discount his views. After dinner Beer told me how he had been struggling with the Fiume question. He and Miller have taken the Italian case in hand, while Douglas Johnson stands for the Yugoslavs. Colonel House tries to reach a compromise between the two. It is almost incredible, but this world-incident has narrowed down to an internal dispute in the Inquiry. The Premier of Italy turns to Beer and Miller for support, while Trumbić relies on Johnson. The Italians have made very great concessions, so great as to cause Orlando's political fall when the news comes out. He said to Beer that he was looking forward to retiring from public life a discredited man, but had some satisfaction in thinking he might become a professor again. Meanwhile Johnson upholds the honor of the exact sciences by refusing to budge the Yugoslav frontiers one inch from where he traced his own suggested frontier on the map. So, as Beer put it, the world is really waiting for a solution until Johnson can be brought to make some compromise between geography and politics.

Saturday, May 17, 1919

At nine o'clock our committee forming the International Union of Academies met at the Bibliothèque Nationale for its final session and we drew up the proposed constitution of this central body of the learned Academies in the Philological, Historical and Social Sciences. Our committee meets again in October to hear reports from the different countries. There was a long discussion on the exact title of the academic union. The French use the word "Moral" Sciences where we use "Social"; and most of the men on our committee were seventy-five years old, or thereabout, and didn't like any new-fangled "Social" Sciences. The only really live European on the Committee was Pirenne, the Belgian historian. I should add that the Japanese, Professor Anesaki, who walked home with me, also struck me as keenly alert.

When I got to the Crillon I found that Robinson had returned from London, and we had a long conference on the situation in the Labor world.

At five o'clock I had Mauss and Hubert here and they took me out to tea at Laurent's restaurant on the Champs Elysées. It was only when I sat down close to an orchestra playing American ragtime that I realized how quiet our life at the Crillon had been.

Tried to work at my Sorbonne lecture in the evening but with few ideas.

Sunday, May 18, 1919

Beautiful Spring day which I spent most of in my room, working on my lecture.

In the afternoon Slosson and I took a walk over to the boulevards to see the procession in honor of Joan of Arc. The cult in her honor has been systematically fostered by the Nationalist parties as against the Socialists and Radicals so that poor little Joan has been made more or less of a party leader in the Third Republic. Sunday's procession was therefore a mixture of a Christian Endeavor and a Tammany Hall. There were little bands of Sunday school and parish school children, with their cassocked priests, and Boy Scout bands trying vainly to keep their little feet in time, but it was the most ragged bit of marching I have ever seen. The grown-ups, men and women, flowed down the street like a congregation moving down an aisle or a Sunday school picnic moving over to the pumpkin pie. They were carrying wreaths to lay in tribute at the statue of Joan down by the Tuileries. The most interesting phase of the celebration was the almost complete absence of police. These good little people were not going to smash windows.

We wandered around through the Tuileries Gardens, which were crowded for once, and I never noticed before the real magnificence of those gardens when *en fête*. The fountains there and at the Place de la Concorde were playing to the full, and they are magnificent both in the size of the jets of water and the setting against the trees of the gardens.

In the evening I had dinner at the house of M. Emile Senart, who has presided over our Union of Academies. It was the most impressive private French house I have been in. There were at least six men-servants waiting on us at the banquet table, and even the group of dried-up old savants that we were became more or less mellow after a dinner of many courses and a little of the finest French wine. However, I should not care to repeat this kind of social ceremony very often.

Monday, May 19, 1919

A beautiful Spring day again with nothing special to record.

At seven-thirty I had dinner at the Palais d'Orsay across the Seine as the guest of the president of the Academy of Inscriptions and Belles-Lettres, Professor Paul Girard. This sounds more royal than it was, for the Palais d'Orsay is the hotel attached to the railway station and not the Ministry of Foreign Affairs. The French call a hotel a palace and a city hall an Hôtel de Ville. It was the same group of scholars that has now met together seven or eight times and we are getting well acquainted, and although I hardly expected it, we had a really good time. Girard made a very elegant little speech in good classic form on the importance of the work we had in hand, and Pirenne, the Belgian historian, replied in an equally touching toast to the learned French societies who had so honored us by this invitation to co-operate with them. I was glad of the chance to brush up my French in preparation for tomorrow at the Sorbonne, for I have few chances in Paris. As I was coming away, I saw a huge banquet in an adjoining room which turned out to be an aëronautic club celebrating the (false) news of Hawker's arrival in Ireland. An enthusiastic aviator came out and walked home with me across the Place de la Concorde. He imparted to me a vision of future flights to America.

Tuesday, May 20, 1919

The whole day was given up to my Sorbonne lecture. I spent the morning going over the French of it with M. Pone of the Ministry of Labor whose French I used in place of my own, as I was afraid to use my own translation for fear of making breaks. As a matter of fact, I only finished the text in French at about four and lectured at five.

The lecture itself went all right to the extent at least that only one old gentleman left before I was through. I had a very slight audience. As it was so late in the season and was the most glorious weather outside, there were relatively few present of those who pass the dreary winter afternoons taking lectures for amusement. I should say that of the seventy-five or a hundred people present, at least ninety per cent were in the neighborhood of sixty years of age, and I had the satisfaction of knowing a dozen or so professors of the University of Paris sat through the function. At the close the economist Professor Charles Gide and two or three others spoke to me. I shall carry away the memories of that lecture more than any other I have ever given simply because of the honor attached to talking in the old Sorbonne.

I walked home through the Luxembourg Gardens, where the shells from the German long-range gun fell into the basin of the fountain. The gardens were much more beautiful than I had remembered them. The trees were full of blossoms and very green and I had quite forgotten the extent of the grove. The walk down through the Latin Quarter home brought up a good many memories of student days and over by the Medici fountain I caught myself for a moment subconsciously hunting for two little girls I used to know, among the wee kiddies playing there.

Wednesday, May 21, 1919

This morning I had a call from Mr. Widdemer of the Y.M.C.A., asking me if I could undertake the writing of the history of the Y.M.C.A. during the war. The job has great historical possibilities both in the actual story of events and in the interpretation of that semi-religious, semi-sport organization under circumstances here in France which rather tested the religiosity and certainly developed the sport. Later, when I was down in Colonel House's office, I ran into Mr. Miller who had just learned that he must return on Tuesday, so he pulled me over to lunch and he planned some other important things, with reference to his Washington trip. He also planned to take the next day off on a trip to the front, and Warrin and I worked on the plan in the afternoon. I also put through some further labor legislation with Mr. Robinson. I worked on a cable to head off anti-Canadian feeling in the American labor leaders.[1]

In the evening Slosson and I were Warrin's guests at a performance of "Louise" at the Opéra Comique. We found the last act very powerful, particularly the scene where the father recalls the childhood lullabies to win the daughter back home.

[1] Mr. Gompers was in trouble over the fact that the British Dominions were to be in the International Labor Organization on their own footing, thus giving the British Empire an apparent predominance in it. This resulted from the amendment which was moved by Sir Robert Borden at the plenary session when the Constitution of the Labor Organization was passed, that provisions for membership in it should conform to those of the Covenant. The text of the cable to Gompers read: "The President has decided that it is wise to accede to the request of Canada that it, and the other British Dominions, shall be treated as separate members of the International Labor Conference instead of being held to representation of a purely English delegation.

"The wisdom of this decision is clear for the following reasons:

"What seems, at first glance, like giving an unduly large representation to the British Empire is bound to work to the advantage of the United States, because in questions arising in international labor the Dominions will be found to side with the United States instead of with the mother country. There is not a question before the Conference at present upon which Canada, for instance, will not probably be found to vote according to established American policies. The problems of immigration and conditions of labor in the Dominions are more like those in the United States than anywhere else in the world, and by recognizing the Dominions as separate States the Government of the United States will be able to secure a degree of support which may be very much needed in view of contrasting conditions in Europe.

"Quite apart from policy, it is only just to give Canada the only piece of recognition that it has asked at the Peace Conference, namely, in this field. It alone, along with the United States, fought the war for no advantage to itself and gained nothing from it. It called 600,000 men under arms and Canadian troops were in the forefront in every battlefield from Amiens to Belgium. They pushed the Germans farthest back in 1917; they held Vimy Ridge when all the rest of the British line was crumbling, a year ago this May, and so saved Europe. They broke the German line at Amiens, pushing them back 14,000 yards in a single day—the largest gain of any single day's fighting in the war and, finally, it was Canadian troops that broke the Hindenburg line and so smashed through the German defenses to Cambrai and at the armistice they were at Mons in the farthest forefront of the Allied forces.

"President Wilson is justified in recognizing in them Allies in peace as in war, and this act of neighborliness should be welcomed by the leaders of American labor as a first step toward the recognition of our common interests in the great reforms for which we have now erected a new but well constructed machinery of the International Labor Conference."

Verdun, the Argonne, and the Marshes of St. Gond

Thursday, May 22, 1919

The morning was spent largely in getting maps for the trip and straightening out the incidental routine. By two o'clock in the afternoon we were speeding along the great highway to the Marne Valley. From the time we left Paris until we drew up in the entrance of the Hôtel de la Haute-Mère-Dieu at Châlons we had a ride through a hundred and ninety-seven kilometers of the most glorious country of France in the most glorious June weather (for May) that the Marne valley ever saw. As far as Epernay there are vineyards and the hilly country is dotted with little, picturesque villages with red tiled roofs. New roofs are appearing on shored-up walls, and there is work in fields. From Epernay on across the long rolling plain of Châlons the main crop seems to be wheat.

We had hardly got into the hotel at Châlons before the hotel proprietress herself came rather flustered up to our rooms to announce that General Duport, the commanding general of Châlons, had sent his aide-de-camp to say that he had received word from Paris that we were coming and he was waiting down below. We went down to find a dapper young officer, with a gold and white silk brassard to mark out that he was a special envoy from headquarters, and new kid gloves, who stood rigidly at salute when we came down the stairs and then announced that his general had sent his regrets that it was impossible for him to be there in person, but was there anything he might do to contribute to our happiness? Without pausing to find out, he went on to say that the general had detailed him to accompany us and would place an extra car at our disposal for the rest of the journey.

At dinner I learned that the champagne served in the champagne country is non-sparkling, but retains a soft, delicious, grapy taste mixed with sunshine. The waiter whom we consulted expressed a firm but mild surprise that anyone should want to drink a champagne with bubbles in it in its own country. That is the kind they ship abroad.

Professor Haskins was to join us by the midnight train, so we took a midnight walk through the dark square in the dimly lighted street of this army-ridden town to the station. A train had just drawn in for Alsace-Lorraine, but the German sleeping-cars, appropriated by the French, were not as suggestive of the conquest as the campanies of French soldiers cluttered up with all kinds of bags and parcels clambering onto a dark fourth- or fifth-class passenger train on a sidetrack marked Verdun. To see these sleepy little fellows starting off that way in the night gave one a pretty clear impression of what the Châlons station must have been throughout the war.

We slept in a fine old-world sort of bedroom and can recommend the Haute-Mère-Dieu.

Friday, May 23, 1919

By eight o'clock the French army car was at our door with two soldiers on the front seat and another young officer inside who was to accompany us. He turned out to be a student of theology at the Protestant faculty in training for pastor, who had been wounded at Verdun, and was a delightful, good natured young fellow indeed.

Our two cars took the road for Verdun at a good fast pace through a richly cultivated farming country. The long, gently rolling Châlons plains end rather abruptly in rugged hills about Ste. Menehould and from there to Clermont we passed through the southern end of the Argonne Forest. At least half the distance along the main road was taken up with apple orchards still in bloom. So far there had been almost no sign of war. But one little village at a crossroads had been wiped out, I think it was Gizaucourt. And yet this road ran along back of the French line and fed Verdun as well as furnishing the main back-line connection along the Champagne front. Ste. Menehould had had some houses destroyed, but nothing to mention in comparison with the real damage of the war. At Clermont, however, at least half the town was destroyed; but that had been done in 1914. There the road suddenly looks out from the wooded hills over the valley of a little stream, and we followed that through Dombasle where we took a hill road across the heights west of the Meuse to Verdun. The little stretch of road by Dombasle had been occupied by a heavy French battery and there wasn't much left of the town. We hadn't gone far up the hill road till we found ourselves looking out over the whole region west of Verdun. On the hilltop we pulled up by the fortress of Sartelles and looked across the rows of long, high hills of the greatest battlefield in history and had them pointed out one by one, Mort Homme, Froide Terre, Douaumont. I think the first impression was one of surprise to find them all within the compass of such a relatively short horizon. Afterwards, going over the hills, one realizes that they were farther away than they seemed, but the whole basin of the defense can hardly have been more than three to seven miles out from the city. We went down the long hill into the valley and Verdun itself came in sight. It lies very closely hidden in the valley at the edge of a promontory that juts out into the river flats. The center of this promontory is the citadel and our officer took us there to pay our respects to the commandant.

When we arrived it was nearly noon and we found the commandant of the citadel waiting for us. He was a fine type of old soldier from southern France, wore a monocle and a good many decorations, and he took us in to show us our quarters, for we were to be his guests at Verdun. As the Germans had shelled the town, the only places left intact for visitors were the tunnels or galleries which the French had built through the solid rock of the citadel. They have built seven and a half kilometers of these galleries from fifteen to twenty feet wide and about as high. We were shown rooms in one of these tunnels, or rather compartments, with wooden partitions part way to the ceiling and all the comforts of officer life at Verdun—a little cot bed and a looking glass.

We lunched in the commandant's private dining room off the officers' messhall, a brightly lighted little room (the citadel has its own electric light plant) hung with flags and decorated with coats of arms. The commandant had set aside another officer, this time one who had commanded at some of the hardest fighting near the fortress of Vaux, to show us the battlefields. So after lunch we drove up the long hill to Vaux.

No description of the battlefield of Verdun is possible. I cannot conceive of anything more awful than the great bare hills around

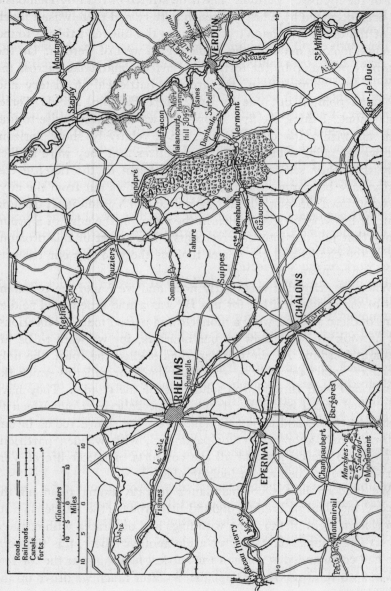

MAP OF VERDUN, THE ARGONNE, AND THE MARSHES OF ST. GOND

Douaumont. Ypres is of another quality. Both of them symbolize the utmost that has ever been suffered and endured by men from the beginning of the world.

The earth on all those hilltops has been churned up not only once but many times over, and during the hardest part of the fighting the landmarks were indistinguishable at the close of each day. Yet men stayed in those shell holes, most of which were daily reduced again to powder. I asked the commandant for an estimate of the number who had died there. He placed the French losses at about three hundred thousand, and the German at as many, and he said that most of the bodies of those dead have been literally blown into the soil. Even along the little footpath we took to Douaumont, we passed shell craters with the bones of skeletons showing openly. Hardly any effort has been made, apparently, to gather together the relics of the dead, but then the whole vast battlefield is so covered with these indistinguishable shell craters that it seems like a hopeless task to set to work on any one section.[1]

The most outstanding single incident at Verdun was not the visit to the forts themselves but to a spot on the crest of the hill west of Douaumont where one company of the 137th French infantry had received orders to stand against the German attack no matter what happened. There is a stretch of crater tops along what was once their trench, and protruding from the earth stands the line of the end of their rifles about six inches or so above the top of the ground. The line is nearly straight, though here and there a rifle was bent backward by the force of the explosions; and buried beside their guns are those Breton soldiers. Until a few days ago the bayonets were still on the muzzles of their rifles but vandals have carried some of them off. The officer who showed us this spot with its perfectly incredible witness of the heroism of those men was himself a Breton. He was furious at the vandalism and then and there gave orders to another officer in charge of the erection of a cross not far away to erect a fence around "the trench of the bayonets."[2] I think the

---

[1] Anyone who has visited Verdun recently may think that this forecast has been belied by the erection of the great Mortuary on the height at Douaumont. But the national cemetery in front contains only a fraction of those who perished in the surrounding fields.

[2] The first monument to be set up on the battlefield of Verdun was the one erected over this "trench of the bayonets" from funds given by an American. The trench is now roofed with concrete masonry resting on heavy columns, but neither the incongruity of the monument nor the crowds which now swarm from sight-seeing buses can lessen the poignant appeal of those few feet of earth.

story of those Breton soldiers will go down in history along with Thermopylae.

The forts of Vaux and Douaumont were never really destroyed, which shows what strength they must have had as compared with those of Belgium. The moats were filled up with debris, although forty feet deep or so and as wide, and the outlines of the forts from the outside are almost indistinguishable where the piles of debris have been flung against them by explosions. But inside the forts the galleries, such as those we were in at the citadel of Verdun, were practically intact, although they showed the marks of machine gun batteries where the French and Germans fought in the dark in those narrow tunnels for three whole days without water, and, for the French, almost without hope.

Douaumont is much larger than Vaux, and the caretaker is living there with his wife and young son about seven or eight years old. It was Miller's opinion that not the least significant thing we saw at Verdun was the little chap seated at a rough table in a gallery of the fort with his schoolbooks spread out in front of him working away at his lessons and so busy at them that he hardly looked up to see us when we came into the room.

We went back to Verdun in the late afternoon, going down the Ravine de la Dame where there once was a forest but where now there is not a tree trunk more than a foot or so above the ground; nothing but pounded earth. On many other parts of the field, however, weeds were beginning to grow and large expanses of buttercups were shining gaily in the sunlight. From the end of the ravine we came back down the valley of the Meuse for dinner in Verdun citadel. On the way we had just time to visit the cathedral, which has some fine old Romanesque chapels and although rather a mixture of styles and spoiled by the seventeenth century is not without a touch of the grandiose. I am not sure but that the cathedrals which have been injured by German artillery have gained a certain dignity from their very destruction. This is true even of Rheims.

Dinner in the citadel. The colonel repeated his apologies that the commanding general of the east was absent from Verdun. However, the commandant himself made up for the general's absence. We toasted France and its allies and associates in arms and then we wrote our names in the Golden Book of Verdun (Livre d'Or) which is kept in the strong box of the citadel. We all felt more or less as

MENU AT THE CITADEL OF VERDUN

though we had been signing the roll of the Knights of the Garter or any other most distinguished order. There were the names of Albert of Belgium and Jellicoe and many European statesmen. I should add as well that there were quite a number of other American signatures.

Then the commandant took us through the tunnels and galleries of the citadel. He is very proud of these, having dug two kilometers himself. There was a chapel with some beautiful statuary and carved woodwork rescued from the cathedral; but the hall which he had fitted up for an amateur theatre was the most interesting place. Its walls were hung with banners and it was there that the ceremony took place in which the city of Verdun itself was accorded military honors. But the commandant gave a humorous touch to the incident by remarking that the flags were in the way of the cinema so he had got rid of most of them to have a good movie show once a week. There was also a huge bakery with apparatus for mixing bread for thousands of men and even a mill in one of the galleries, and little railway tracks ran through them all. After a couple of miles or so of tramping through these galleries, we came out to the southern parapet and sat in the twilight close by where some French and Russian soldiers were talking in a mixture of languages.

Saturday, May 24, 1919

There was no sunlight in the windows of our bedroom because there were no windows. When we came out from the tunnels to the open air even the privilege of sleeping in the citadel of Verdun seemed relatively slight compared with that of being out in the open. Mr. Miller and I took a little stroll between six and seven along the road between the city wall and the citadel and saw some three or four hundred German prisoners marching out to the day's work with picks and shovels on their backs. They were a husky looking lot, as were all the hundreds of prisoners we saw on the trip, thousands I suppose, who were not taking life too seriously, although the little poilu guards with the long, glittering bayonets on their rifles gave a serious touch to the situation.

Our cars were ready after breakfast and we started off for a whole day's trip up through the west side of the Verdun defenses over toward the Argonne. The roadway carried us back again to the

hilltop from which we had first seen Verdun. From it we struck
north across the intervening valleys and hills through the little
ruined village of Esnes to Hill 304. It lies just west of Mort
Homme, the crest of which the Germans just failed to take in the
great offensive of March 1916. These hills on the west of the Meuse
tell the same story as those on the east but do not stand out so
prominently on the landscape, as there is ridge after ridge of them.
On the crest of 304 we were able to locate approximately the farthest
advance of the German line. There was one French dugout there
opening in from one of the trenches which ran down thirty or forty
steps almost perpendicularly; and yet, looking across the field of
shell craters in which this trench ran, one would never guess that
there was anything like it there. We went down the hillside toward
Malancourt and were soon on the spot where the American army
joined with the French in the great battle of last September. From
Malancourt to Montfaucon there is a long hill and in it we noted not
only shell holes but also peculiar oblong shaped holes dug straight
into the hillside with the earth thrown towards the north. There were
many of these along through the fields; and we suddenly realized we
had come upon the American advance, for these were the hastily dug
rifle and machine gun pits which marked the American attack. They
were scattered at more or less irregular intervals on every hillside
from here to Grand Pré, a stretch of thirty or forty miles.

Montfaucon, which the Americans almost reached on the first day
of their attack, is a village on a hilltop that dominates the whole
country for many miles. The Germans were here for four years. It
is only when you climb that very steep hill and look back down the
long meadows and orchards to the south that you realize what the
American army accomplished when it drove the Germans out. It
was heroism to match anything that the War revealed, for it was a
long open hillside, the worst of all places to attack, and our boys had
no time to dig their way up from field to field. Cool courage and an
unflinching purpose were pitted against German experience and
won. It is a spot to quicken the pulse of any American. There is
almost nothing left of the town, which is a wilderness at present.
From there we turned across country, to follow the valley of the
little stream on the east of the Argonne forest to Grand Pré. It was
a good motor road and we reached Grand Pré about noon, a town

badly battered but not entirely destroyed, where the American connection was made for troops coming up through the Argonne on the west and southwest.

We now turned west along the northern edge of the Argonne forest, following a road which ran behind the German lines. There we found a regular little German village, deserted, of course, that had once been the residence of a part of the German High Command. There were rustic houses in the woods, and villas with pleasant little rustic walks neatly railed and paved. Some of the houses had three or four rooms, and fireplaces, and were as pleasant as any country chalet. There was a fountain in the center of the courtyard and there were heavy concrete dugouts for hospitals. None of it apparently had ever been hit by an Allied airplane or gun. The invaders seemed to have made themselves only too comfortable in those pleasant quarters during all these years. We had a picnic lunch by the roadside, made somewhat uncomfortable by too many poisonous looking flies and mosquitoes. A little farther on we found a camp of German prisoners along the same roadside.

Leaving the Argonne region, we swung out along the truck road behind the German road towards Rheims. Our road was to the Germans much what the road of yesterday was to the French. There were still signs up, "Kolonenweg," which must have meant that it was a roadway for columns of troops to march along. But there was no comparison between the other road and this in the amount of war preparations visible. The French rear looked like the work of amateurs beside these massed evidences of technical calculations. To be sure, we may have been nearer the front, although we were at least two or three miles north of it and our road ran for long distances along a little stream with medium-sized hills. Yet for all those miles there was hardly a place that had not been fortified, made into gun emplacements or where the hills were not honeycombed with dugouts. It would be hard to find anywhere a more impressive reminder of the might of German military preparations; and all this, in turn, was protected from the American advance by a wilderness. The fastnesses of the Argonne matched the swamps of Ypres and the hills of Verdun.

A railroad ran in behind to feed this back line, and although there were marks here and there of explosions of French shells, it was not until we reached Somme-Py down towards the front on the southwest that the roadbed was much destroyed. There it ceased to be a railroad at all.

It was a long run through this Champagne country, and from time to time all the way along we got glimpses along the battered hilltops of the front line to the south. We did not turn aside to Tahure, although we could see it clearly a couple of miles away, but kept along the country road, where the farmers are starting to work again, to reach Rheims from the northeast. It was an experience to come upon it from behind the barbed wire of the German lines after seven solid hours of motoring in what was German territory for four years. Going into Rheims I counted seven successive lines of entrenchment and barbed wire before we reached No Man's Land, which was a little stretch of swampy meadows less than a quarter of a mile wide, and not more than half a mile north of the city itself.

At Rheims we had the experience of a lifetime. I had been there twice before but this time we were guests of the French Government, and when our young officer went to get the permit to show us the cathedral, he was told that the Cardinal Archbishop of Rheims was waiting to receive us. We went over at once to the cathedral square and found the old Cardinal standing by the doorway of the cathedral yard, waiting for us. He received us very graciously, dressed in his cassock of black silk, his cardinal stockings and gold buckled shoes, with his hat encircled by a twisted black and red hatband. He was a pleasant, little man about seventy-five years old with very kindly face and ready smile, but every inch a dignitary. First of all, he came out in the square of the cathedral with us and pointing upwards told how the Germans had used inflammable shells on the scaffolding that surrounded the northwest corner of the tower. This fire injured the cathedral more than anything else. Even the subsequent shell fire was hardly as disastrous, although it crumpled and smashed the statuary on that corner and some of those figures were among the most famous of medieval sculpture. They are nearly all completely ruined. A little group naturally gathered to listen to his description and a couple of little girls drew up rather timidly to kiss his ring. An officer of the French army with the ribbon of the Legion of Honor asked if he might join us on the visit to the cathedral itself. The Cardinal had to refuse, saying that he had orders to show us the cathedral and no one else, so we went in the eastern gateway and found ourselves in the cathedral itself, alone except for a few German prisoners who were wheeling away the rubbish that had fallen from the ceiling. There is an enormous hole just in the center of the church vaulting above the old high altar, which was covered with a mound of rubbish ten or fifteen feet high. Just as we came up to it the German prisoners' shovels had uncovered the corner of the marble altar itself, which was the first glimpse the archbishop had had of it since the destruction. We wandered all around the cathedral with the archbishop describing the bombardment; but it is best not to try to repeat his story. Two or three things only stand out. That old man stayed in Rheims the whole four years and watched the shells exploding day and night from only half a block away. He convinced us all that the French army never used the cathedral for a point of observation and that it was even scrupulously careful to avoid the appearance of it. This is a point I am glad to have clear in my mind. He described the shells hitting the turrets above the flying buttresses and said that it was particularly impressive at night to look out at the great somber mass of the cathedral with the sudden illumination of the exploding shell, followed by the crash of the falling masonry. Then he took us over to his palace, to show us the former banqueting hall where the kings of France banqueted after the ceremony of anointment and coronation. Jeanne d'Arc had toasted her king there and all the long line of Capetian kings had banqueted in the room. Its crypt goes back to Merovingian times. Only the walls are left standing now. There are traces still of the delicate ornaments of the medieval fireplace, but the building itself is almost beyond repair. Behind it is the little chapel of the archbishops themselves, a Gothic gem of which only the walls are standing.

The archbishop showed us these and then invited us over to his palace for afternoon tea; but we felt that we had already imposed too much on his kindness, and besides were due at Châlons in an hour or so. So we said good-bye and followed him out to the square.

We took the road southeast to Châlons, getting out at Pompelle, about two miles east of the city, to visit the powdered fragments of the fortress which the Germans took from the French at the last offensive there; then along the great straight avenue to Châlons, slowly receding from the signs of war. We passed through the same plains as on the south and east of Châlons and came to the city through a big military camp.

We found at the hotel the card of General Duport with an invitation to dinner at headquarters. The general sent his dapper young aide over to bring us to dinner and we found ourselves in an old French château with quite a group of officers and some American Red Cross nurses, who confided to us that they suspected that they had been asked over to serve as interpreters in case we couldn't talk French. There were fifteen of us at dinner.

After dinner we had the Star Spangled Banner from an orchestra in the next room and some very lovely music.

Châlons is far enough behind the lines that only a few shells reached it and the damage from aviators is slight; but there was a hole in the mirror of the salon of the hotel where we stayed, made by a broken fragment of shell that had fallen in the garden outside.

We slept well in the Hôtel de la Haute-Mère-Dieu and in the morning started on the last day's journey. A telegram had come to General Duport telling that Colonel Réquin would meet us at Champaubert to show us the battlefield of Foch's army in the first battle of the Marne. Réquin was the staff officer of Foch who carried the order to the famous Forty-second Division for its march across the battlefront on September 8 and 9, 1914, the manœuvre that drove the German center back across the Marne. It was Réquin who had arranged our trip from Paris and we were glad to meet him and spend the rest of the journey under his personal guidance.

Sunday, May 25, 1919

Leaving Châlons in the early morning, we had an uneventful ride down the long straight road southwest from Châlons that leads towards the marshes of St. Gond. There were very few signs of war here. Once in a while there was the side of a barn blown out or there were loopholes in the walls, but there was little to suggest the memory of those first days of September 1914, when the vanguard of the German army marched down this road. It runs in a general westerly direction parallel with the Marne but a few miles south.

At ten o'clock we reached Champaubert, which is hardly more than a crossroads, but on the corner stands a monument to Napoleon the First, recalling how this country was once before the scene of a last defense of Paris when Napoleon faced the Allies here in 1814. We found the American army car with Captain George, Colonel Réquin, Madame Réquin and Mrs. Miller. He had had his adjutant draw some maps for us to explain the battlefield and we looked these over and then started down the crossroad south to the battlefield itself. We were on the road the German center had taken as it pushed across the Marne. The country we had come along all the way from Châlons was level farming land, except for a sharp ridge running south from Epernay which we crossed through a hollow at Bergères. When we turned south, however, we soon found ourselves in a very hilly country with frequent woods and orchards so that there were no places for long-distance sighting. There were no signs of war here at all and we were rather surprised to see the Colonel pull up by the roadside and get out. We had just come through a rather steep little ravine where the Petit Morin empties out of the western end of the marshes of St. Gond. We had climbed the southern slopes and were on the rounding fields on the hilltop. This was the main line of battle for the Forty-second Division. There were no trenches in sight. The Division held the road from the fifth of September to the eighth. Temporary earthworks had been thrown up but these had disappeared, and the country was left for the farmers, who were busy then plowing the fields alongside. There were about half a dozen soldiers' graves in the middle of one field, but Réquin said that in the thickest of the fighting the ground before us and the light woods a hundred yards or so to our left were strewn with the dead, both the French infantry who had been mowed down by machine gun fire and the Germans who had suffered from the French 75's in the wood.

We were the only people in sight who were interested in history that morning; and the whole day through we found no other people interested in this first battle of the Marne although there were crowds of sightseers at Château Thierry.

A little farther south we turned down a back country road along the south edge of the wood, and Réquin pointed out the house where he had his telephone and general headquarters. A quarter of a mile farther up the road was the farmhouse of Chapton, a large barn-yard surrounded by the house and barn in a hollow square. We went across to the barn in the southeast corner, behind the manure piles; and Réquin pointed out the spot here where he found General Grossetti, the general of the Forty-second Division on the night of September 8, and awakened him with the orders from General Foch to take his Division out of the battle line and march at top speed across country to attack the Germans farther east. Grossetti's troops were in motion by dawn and at four o'clock in the afternoon had reached the heights along the French center, fourteen kilometers away. This was after three days of continuous battle.

Then we turned east along the upland to the hill at the village of Mondement which looks out over the battlefield of the Marshes of St. Gond and the low country beyond. The château at Mondement was the farthest point the Germans got, just on the edge of the hill, and was still in ruins. We had our lunch on the terrace overlooking the whole plain.

After lunch we ran down to Broyes and again from the hilltop looked out to the northeast, this time with the whole battlefield in view. It was down the roadway next to the east and in plain sight across the fields that Grossetti's troops came marching on the afternoon of the ninth. An old peasant who had watched the battle that afternoon joined us here, and he gave a very vivid description of the marching columns and the distant bursting of shrapnel on the battle-line. We went down the very steep hill and lost our way in the muddy farmers' roads below but finally pulled up in an open plain beside some airdromes in perfectly open country with a very slightly rolling wheat field in front of us. There is nothing by which anyone could recognize the spot as being different from any other, but Réquin said that this was where he saw the Forty-second go into action at six o'clock on the evening of the ninth, and that was perhaps the most important single action in the whole battle of the Marne. There was a strawstack standing there, and as Grossetti had followed his troops over the ridge, he had left word with Réquin to set fire to it half an hour afterwards as a signal or landmark as it was already growing dark. By the next day the Forty-second had pushed on into the German center and the great retreat had begun.

Of course, in following the fortunes of a single division this way one gives a false perspective of the whole, but the Forty-second was to the French army of the center what the Canadian troops were to the British, and in having the guidance of the man who actually gave them their orders on the field of battle we were as fortunate as we had been up on the Canadian front.

We came home through Montmirail and from there to Château Thierry were on the route the American troops took on their first attack, for Montmirail had been the American headquarters. There were few signs of war until we got up to the hilltops back of the Marne; but that long straight road that went up and down over the hills must have witnessed some strange scenes as those American camions raced along it into action that summer day, not a year ago now.

We came to the high edge of the hill south of the Marne rather suddenly and found ourselves looking down over Château Thierry and beyond it over to the hilltops that had been German for a short time. From Château Thierry to Paris is an old traveled road for me now, and the only change in our program this time was to stop long enough in Meaux to look at the outside of the cathedral, which was already closed.

When I came back to Paris I gave my clothes to the chambermaid to be cleaned, and remarked that the white mud was hard to get out, that it was the dust of Verdun. She took the clothes reverently and said with a tone that I shall never forget, "That is very precious dust, sir."

I found waiting me a bunch of official documents, showing that the Germans were calling for a new answer in the labor matter, and so got ready for a busy week to make up for the lost time.

The Terms Imposed, with Some Revisions

Monday, May 26, 1919

The second German reply to our labor proposals took a hard day's work. Our Committee met at eleven, the British as usual coming along with a proposal for our adoption, but it seemed to me very feeble and particularly poor as an appeal to the public. So, with Mr. Miller's help, I dictated an alternative reply after lunch. I wove in the two texts in the afternoon session, with the result that the document as given out answers the German objections at every point. It took the entire day. Had been writing part of an article for the *Round Table,* attempting to forecast the reaction of the United States to the Treaty; no easy task.

[The last days of the Peace Conference presented only one item of importance in connection with social legislation, that of securing protection for social insurance for German citizens in the territories taken from Germany. The chief problem discussed at this time by the heads of the Allied Governments was not the fate of Germany, for that matter was regarded as settled, but the fate of the Austro-Hungarian monarchy and the conflicting claims of the new Danubian and Balkan nations, and Italy. These questions were not settled prior to President Wilson's departure and were left for a second phase of the Peace Conference history, that which lasted on through the summer and autumn and finally produced the Treaties of St. Germain, Neuilly, and Trianon.]

Tuesday, May 27, 1919

Morning spent in a final session of the Committee verifying the text of our reply. I had lunch with di Palma-Castiglione, the Italian member of the Committee, at the Hôtel Edward VII, where the Italian Delegation lives. The dining room and the vestibule were filled with Italian statesmen, including the Prime Minister and Sonnino, and I was struck with the attractive quality of the gathering. The faces of the Italians are less hard than the French and the whole meeting had a genial tone.

The afternoon was spent in the Ministry of Labor with Fontaine and Butler, who hurried over from London to help at the labor negotiations but got here too late, so instead we worked out the rules of procedure for the October conference, taking as a basis the work of M. Pone of the French Ministry who had been studying the rules of the Chamber of Deputies and the Labor Conferences. It is interesting to find that the workingmen in their own conferences have developed stricter rules of procedure than parliaments, apparently out of self-defense, in order to curtail their own speech-making tendency.

I took Butler over to dinner at the Inter-Allied Club, which I had almost never gone to. It is the Rothschild mansion on the Faubourg Saint Honoré, and we dined out on the lawn at the back of the house looking into the good-sized park that runs over to the Champs Elysées. It was the most beautiful sight I have seen in Paris. At nine o'clock I called on Professor Cestre of the Sorbonne who lectures on American institutions and is about to take another trip to the United States. Some other Sorbonne people joined us and it was an evening much like one in my own apartment, with the genuine university atmosphere.

Wednesday, May 28, 1919

Began to prepare memoranda concerning labor legislation for Miller to take to America, pointing out what a work of constructive statesmanship we have accomplished!

Spent the afternoon in Fontaine's office finishing the work on the procedure for the Labor Conference. As a compromise between the purely parliamentary debate in public session, which would be the only way of getting popular support for the conference, and the method of commissions, which was the only way of making sure that the work of the conference would actually accomplish something, I proposed a study of the commissions of the French Chamber of Deputies. French parliamentary procedure had always seemed to me to have a better balance between public oratory and commission reports than either the British or the American system. A detailed study of the rules of procedure furnished the definite clue for organization for which I had been hunting.[1]

[1] Cf. *The Origins of the International Labor Organization*, I, 292 n.

[This application of history to politics had a further chapter added to it when the Washington Conference actually met. The League of Nations was already studying its own procedure, and members of its staff in London examined carefully the model we had worked out. When the Washington Conference met, Sir Eric Drummond sent Major Abraham of the Secretariat to see how it actually worked, with an eye to the adoption of similar procedure by the League at its first Assembly, which met shortly afterwards. These details are of little interest to any but those who have had to do with the long and tedious process of creating a wholly new organization; but the success or failure of the institutions themselves depended very largely on the careful planning of matters of this kind.]

I had invited Max Lazard and his wife to dinner, as I had been their guest many times. We had a quiet time with them and Beer and afterwards drove out through the Bois de Boulogne, through the long rows of scented acacias. It was a restful end to a long hard day. It also seems like the end of the long task of creating for Labor its international parliament. Butler left for England today.

Tuesday, May 29, 1919

Worked with Robinson and finished the Miller memoranda. At lunch I invited Dr. Mezes and Beer to the Inter-Allied Club, as Mezes is to leave tomorrow for America, and he much appreciated the courtesy. So far as I know it was the only one extended to him. I felt sorry for him in spite of the past, which now seems a long way off. I am to have his office. Just what this means I do not know, but it will relieve the pressure somewhat.

In the afternoon I went to say good-bye to Miller. We parted close friends. I have great admiration for him. Mrs. Miller is staying over a little longer and Warrin and I have promised to show her some more sections of the front. I shall take the occasion to see the sector between Soissons and Amiens and then shall have completed the whole front from Verdun to Ypres.

I had dinner with Fontaine and his family. He had invited as well a number of young French authors and it was quite a literary circle, including a young Chinese from the Delegation. We had a very pleasant evening and Madame Vandervelde drove me home.

Friday, May 30, 1919—Memorial Day

I was up early to say good-bye to Mezes, who left about seven. The morning spent in dictating routine work. In the afternoon I drove out, taking some soldiers along, to the cemetery of American soldiers at Suresnes, west of Paris. The cemetery is away up near the top of the hill known as Mont Valerian, the highest hill around Paris, and from the edge of the cemetery one looks over the whole of the Seine Valley. The cemetery is, of course, very new and the crosses at the soldiers' graves are all of wood, but on every one a wreath had been hung and there was a great profusion of flowers strewn on the graves and half-withered in the sunlight.

The President's speech was very impressive and I was close enough to hear most of it. There were thousands of American soldiers there and the band that played was the best I have heard, although the bugler who sounded taps seemed rather nervous.

I drove back hurriedly to the hotel to finish up the day's work and at eight in the evening was up at the Hôtel Majestic at a very interesting dinner. Lionel Curtis had got a group of Americans and British together to form institutes for international affairs, one British and one American, with a joint publication. Lord Robert Cecil presided and then turned the meeting over to General Bliss. Other speakers were Sir Eyre Crowe (with whom I had a very interesting conversation at dinner), Lord Eustace Percy, Headlam-Morley, Latham of Australia, Temperley, the historian, etc. They appointed a joint committee to draw up a scheme and report at a subsequent meeting. The three English members were Lord Robert Cecil, Sir Sidney Peel and Commander Latham, and the American members were James Brown Scott, Coolidge of Harvard and myself. The object of the institutes is to furnish a better fund of information on policy as well as on mere facts, and there will have to be a publication later. In any case, the committee will be an interesting one to work with. Beer, Hornbeck and I drove home with General Bliss, who was very genial.

[This was the origin of what later became the Royal Institute of International Affairs in London and the Council on Foreign Relations in New York. In the case of the American organization, a plan had already been started in New York, which, however, did not work out successfully until it was reorganized to meet substantially the plan drawn up in our meetings in Paris, Professor Archibald Coolidge of Harvard taking the initiative.]

Saturday, May 31, 1919

The day was spent mostly on the German negotiations: a hard day's work drafting the reply. I got the reparations committee to take up again the question of opening the Austrian archives and spent some of the rest of the day on the text of the reply to the Germans, which is to be discussed with Barnes at dinner this evening.

Sunday, June 1, 1919

When I arrived at the Majestic last night Mr. Barnes met me with a most apologetic but funny little smile and said, "You'll think I am a strange kind of man to invite you to dinner and not be able to stay, but there are some disadvantages in being a member of the Cabinet. The Prime Minister has just summoned us to dinner at his apartment, and has brought the rest of the Cabinet over from England." He wanted to take me over to the group of them who were standing ready to go to dinner but I knew it would be one of those casual meetings, and besides I had met some of them before and had nothing in particular to say, especially as I couldn't ask them what they were going to do. So I stayed for dinner with Mr. Hodgson, Mr. Barnes's private secretary, a very nice young man, and allowed the British Empire to go on.

As a matter of fact, that was intended to be one of the most momentous meetings in the history of the British Government. They meet again this morning at eleven and are considering major revisions in the Treaty. Things have got into a very bad condition here. This is no secret, although I have not referred to it before. A part of the British Cabinet is up in arms.

A remark was made to me last night that just as it was Lord Milner who came in at the critical point in the War and forced through the Single Command, it may be Milner who will save the situation again. In any case, whatever comes of it, this meeting of the British Cabinet is of great historical importance. Just how the Conference will develop now is hard to say. We may conceivably have an entirely new peace conference.

However, the Labor Section of the Treaty is not likely to be changed and so I feel free to go off on a trip to Toulouse to lecture to the American army, or a section of it, on the work of the Peace Commission.

[This grew out of a request from the American Expeditionary Force University for lectures by technical experts from the Peace Conference, a request which the Commissioners strongly endorsed and sent along to the various Heads of Divisions. One of the strongest posts was down in Toulouse, and by agreement with Dr. Bowman, I was chosen to lecture there, a choice which I always regretted because, although the Labor Section of the Treaty did not come under fire, the rest of the Treaty was subjected to a bombardment from all quarters during the few days of my absence from Paris. The account of the journey which follows was dictated from my notes upon my return from Paris.]

The station was filled with American soldiers. On the platform I had hard work crowding through a mass of American soldiers and officers intermingled with a few French travelers, and when the train came in we had a big rush for seats. I was lucky enough to get one, but there were many who had to stand for hours. In my compartment were four young American officers and one middle-aged Frenchwoman in black. The American army was at first a little suspicious of a civilian who talked American, which interested and pleased me, for those young fellows were certainly on their guard. They soon saw I was to be trusted, however, and the young captain beside me turned out to be a graduate student of the University of Wisconsin with some thought of going to Columbia or else going into politics. In fact, I found quite a number of the Expeditionary Force with political ambitions on their return. They say they are going to tell the folks back home something about world politics. I hope they do, for very few of them have any militaristic ambitions. The captain across the corridor had an interesting tale of the war. He asked me if I had been at Soissons and if I had seen those ruined tanks by the roadside between Soissons and Villers-Cotterets. I have described them before and have a very vivid memory of their battered hulks out in the fields not far from a little crossroads farm. The road runs straight across the fields, lined on both sides with tall trees, and with a little ditch with its slight embankment on each side. The captain described how his men advanced across the fields there and got as far as the road, where they lay all night, with the Germans just over the brow of the slightly rounding field in front. The tanks were French and I was glad to learn from this captain that they were abandoned by the French before the Germans actually blew them up. He said he saw the farthest one set on fire by the Germans and burned. In his advance he and a sergeant saw something that looked like a groundhog's hole in the field with a mound of new earth thrown out and walked over and found it to be a German dugout. The sergeant had his bayonet fixed and the captain his revolver drawn and they called in to the Germans to come out, and thirty of them came out holding up their hands and were herded back of the lines. He had one machine gun bullet through his helmet, one in his knapsack; one cut the lapel of his coat, another grazed the back of his neck and a fifth hit him in the arm. He said that he wouldn't have missed his experience over here for a million dollars, but he wouldn't take another million to go through it again. A bit of soldier psychology came out when we were approaching Vierzon, where they were to change cars. The French were crowding in the aisle with their valises, but when they asked the soldier by the window if this was Vierzon his reply was: "Either it is or it isn't."

The landscapes of France in June are wonderfully beautiful with their patches of clover in bloom and great fields of yellow blossoms that may be some kind of clover but in any case shine very gaily in the sunshine. The country just south of Paris is an undulating stretch of mixed garden and woodland. But about ten or fifteen miles farther on it flattens out to the same kind of great level plain that I have described in the country north of the Seine and Marne. This flat land continues right across the Loire, which we crossed at Orléans. The railway station at Orléans was a busy Franco-American spot with the women in the newspaper booths selling *Saturday Evening Posts*. One sees little of the city from the train and the main memory of Orléans is of railway yards. The river itself is a shallow stream with drifting sandbars, continually changing so that dredges are all the time employed to keep the channel clear. The low banks furnish no dominating point for cathedral or castle, and if there is any castle at all, I saw no sign of it. The cathedral, however, is impressive enough as it rises over the flat city, with its two square towers blocked out in receding stories and surrounded by galleries and its great rose window marked out on the southern face. I passed through Orléans on the day in which Jeanne d'Arc became a saint, but I saw no sign in the railway station of any memories of the delivery of Orléans from the English. A few British Tommies were in sight, but the boys who saved France this time, like the fellow in the seat opposite me, were no formal candidates for saint-ship.

The country from Orléans south for fifty miles or so runs through a poor, sandy, rather swampy country, a mere continuation of the flats of the Loire. At Vierzon most of the American soldiers left, for it is the junction for the central business offices of the American army, at St. Aignan. From here on the country starts to show a better type of farm, though still not so good as north of the Loire. At Issoudun there was a fine old feudal tower sticking up over the roofs of the town. Then out on a long, level stretch a huge army encampment came into sight, and as we swept past it I recognized the sign-post of America in a football and a baseball ground and on the baseball ground were sure-enough negroes in khaki. This big camp is at the junction of the railroad from Bordeaux with the American railroad that stretched over to the front northeast; so at least they told me. Anyway, there were freight trains in the yards with long lines of American artillery, and all in all it was about the most warlike exhibition I have seen America put up. We were now approaching Châteauroux and from here on the country is poorer. There are vineyards on the hillslopes for quite a while, the vineyards being closely cropped. The grapevines seem hardly big enough to bear grapes, being cut back to a mere stump each year. The road climbs up over the farming hills through a lovely rolling country—poppies and bluebells in bloom—past the valley of the Creuse, which winds in behind the back gardens of the long street of Argenton, past the two round towers of the made-over château at Célon, looking rather foolish in its modern dress, through steeper hills, past poorer farms with unkempt hedgerows, woodlots and meadowland; and then suddenly across the rounding hilltop we come upon the city of Limoges, with its single-towered cathedral and the slender spire of a more modern church standing out over the roofs. I had always thought of Limoges as a city in muddy flats, mainly I suppose, because I thought of brickyards where they got the clay for making pottery, but it is picturesquely situated on the rounding intersection of a group of hills with a nice little river running down along the southern side.

Southward from Limoges we run into still higher country, winding up along mountain streams, none of them grand but all rather restful and secluded. This is the western fringe of the Auvergne mountains and the run lasts for some fifty or a hundred miles. Suddenly the road strikes a broad transverse valley with vineyards on the slopes again and the slightest suggestion of a change in architecture with the white walls and red roofs of the Midi. Little villages are grouped on the hilltops instead of in the lee of the hills as they are farther north, and feudalism has left its mark in strongholds that increase in frequency as we go on.

South of the modern looking town of Brive in the valley of the Corrèze we pass over another divide and come out on the Dordogne at Souillac. From the windows of a twentieth century restaurant car, I suddenly caught a glimpse of caves on the cliffs facing south. There was a footpath up to them and they were apparently inhabited. We were right in the midst of the cave country where primitive man passed the long stretch of centuries through the ice age. I suppose cave dwellers from the Dordogne fought in this war along the valley of the Somme, where the earliest fist hatchets mark the site of the Krupp factories of the nth millennium before the ice sheet came down over northern Europe. It is hard to keep one's mental poise in such a mixture of time and space.

From the Dordogne valley we crossed another hilly country and came out suddenly again upon the broad stretches of the valley of the Lot, passing under a high, battlemented, feudal castle along the river cliff to the city of Cahors, which lies just in the circle of the river with a fourteenth century bridge surmounted by three great towers, one in the middle of the stream. A thunderstorm was bursting over the hills with strong evening sunlight flecking the northern slopes. We settled down into twilight quickly and the train wound on across the next upland to the valley of the Tarn, which we crossed at Montauban. From here the road runs through the broad, flat valley system of the Garonne to Toulouse, where we arrived at ten-thirty in the evening. I asked an American lieutenant about hotels and he recommended the Grand Hôtel de la Poste, so I took him along in the one-horse cab, as he was going my way. The grand café at the main corner of the town was crowded with hundreds of Toulousans, sitting out taking their late coffee and looking at each other and the people passing, with that animal-like satisfaction of gazing at nothing which seems to make a satisfactory chemical compound in the Latin peoples. Anyway, there they were by the hundred and there were plenty of soldiers and casual pedestrians in the streets.

The city was rather gaily decked with little tricolors and here and there an American flag, only a very few. Next day I learned that the decorations were in honor of Jeanne d'Arc, but I learned as well that the troops in barracks had mutinied that day and had torn down some tricolors and hoisted red flags, protesting against being sent to Russia and also against their food and treatment. Other troops had been rushed in from Montauban and the little insurrection seems to have ended without serious consequences, although some of the American boys told me that the mob threw paving stones and anything else they could get at the police. There was no sign of that when I arrived, but in the night I heard the sound of marching troops through the streets below.

Monday, June 2, 1919

The city of Toulouse is a much more modern city than I had expected to find. It is the finest provincial city I have seen in France. The buildings in the business part are uniformly five stories high and the shops have large plate glass windows. In the center of the town it is much more impressive than Lille, although the streets are not so wide. I went out after breakfast to find my way to the university, and wandered over to the cathedral. It is a red brick building, dating from the Romanesque period, and has remained practically untouched from the early Middle Ages. Its long, barrelled vaulting did not permit of any large-sized windows, and as the day was cloudy the effect inside would have been quite gloomy but for the fact that the tapestries which had been brought out for the festival of Sainte Jeanne were still hanging on the pillars with long rows of silken banners above them. The tapestries were mostly rich red in color and gave a note of true magnificence to the massive but somber nave.

Back to the main square, where a market was being held. There I saw an American major standing on the street corner waiting for a car. He was as usual very surprised to be spoken to by an American civilian and we soon chummed up and he turned out to be in charge of the science section of the American army university. There are about twelve hundred soldiers left. He was in civil life chief chemist to the Federal Sugar Refining Company at Yonkers and has taken courses at Columbia. He told me that the student center was housed in a disused powder factory about a mile or so away and courteously escorted me to the proper street car. There are a number of these powder factories along the muddy Garonne (how anyone can be proud of that stream I can hardly understand), with enormous sheds and great tall chimneys reminding one of Bridgeport or Wilmington, and one of them had been turned over to the American soldiers for barracks and classrooms. They were very comfortable there, they said, but most of them availed themselves of the privilege of boarding with the French down in the city.

The commandant was not in his office, but soon a car drove up bringing a young lieutenant by the name of Wright, who got out with apologies, having missed me at the station. He took me back to the city and transferred my belongings to the Grand Hôtel, where I found that the largest room and drawing-room with bath attached —in fact, the suite de luxe of the finest hotel in Toulouse—had been placed at my disposal. On the way down he explained that in Toulouse I was the guest of an American student organization known as the International Trade Relations Society of the University of Toulouse, a group of students who had got together for the purpose of studying the foreign relations of the United States and who proposed to go into diplomacy, politics or business after the war. The commandant joined us shortly and we had lunch together informally at the hotel.

From half past two to five, I was quizzed on the work going on in Paris. After this examination was over, they took me out to a country home in the outskirts where a kind-hearted French matron had made the boys at home. Their respect for her was the nicest single incident connected with the American Expeditionary Force that I have seen. They said that there were other homes in Toulouse open to them in the same way, which is a vastly different story from what one hears in the north. Unfortunately, there was no one home, but I saw the rose gardens through the fence and I don't wonder that the boys liked to go there. I may add that there seemed to be two young daughters, besides roses and food, of whom the boys spoke in very appreciative terms.

I just got back in time for the six o'clock banquet of the International Trade Relations Society! There were about fifty at the table, and of course I had to talk on the Treaty, etc., which I did from seven to eight. Then at eight-thirty I was due at the hall, which apparently had once been a church but was now a student center. It was hot and stuffy and the ventilation was poor but those lads listened to me for two solid hours and called for more. They were extremely interested in the Treaty that was closing the war they had fought, and of all the audiences I ever talked to, this was by far the most attentive. In the first place, they were picked students, all of them university men; in the next place, they had all been through hard fighting, for only combat troops were chosen for this post; and finally, they had kept a keen interest in affairs. One of them told me afterwards that it was the first time in his experiences that a part of the American Expeditionary Force had listened for two hours to a lecture but that the subject was of compelling interest. I told them in the first place about the difficulties of making a treaty and then explained in detail the International Labor Organization. After the lecture I had still a group of men crowding around.

Tuesday, June 3, 1919

I was somewhat undecided whether to stay over to the night train and spend the day with one of the men who wanted to take me down to Carcassonne, which is only an hour away, or else run up to Bordeaux to see the docks the American army had built; but thinking it over in the night, I decided that I had been long enough away from Paris at this juncture and so six o'clock found me at the railway station.

I got to Paris at half-past seven in the evening in time to have dinner with Slosson at the Crillon. It seemed that the same luck had been against me as on the "George Washington" when I missed meeting the President, for on my desk was a very urgent call signed by the secretary of the American Delegation for all chiefs of divisions to meet in Secretary Lansing's office that morning at eleven o'clock; and, going with Beer to his room, I learned from him the whole story of what I had missed. The President had got them together for the one time at the whole Peace Conference to talk over the answer that we should make to Germany on its last protest. There had been a most interesting session, the details of which reside in more than one diary, I imagine. I should not have had anything to contribute to it, for we had already made the labor reply and the questions at issue were in other fields, but I missed the chance of seeing the President in action in the presence of all his advisers, with Lansing, House, White, Bliss, Hoover, etc.

In addition there had been a meeting of the Labor Committee at three in the afternoon, but I learned on calling up Barnes that nothing much had happened at it and that they would meet again at three the next day and I could ratify or not what had been done.

Wednesday, June 4, 1919

The Labor commission began work at three, mainly to deal with the question of employing German laborers in the reconstruction of the devastated regions. Two Belgian statesmen had come along especially to make sure that no Germans were to be allowed to go back to Belgium to do this work, as there were hundreds of thousands of Belgians out of work. Colliard, the French Minister of Labor, considered the question important enough to interrupt his negotiations with the strikers' committees (Paris is suffering a perfect epidemic of strikes just now, particularly in the subways which are almost entirely tied up, and the labor situation is very tense) to look after this question of German labor; but Fontaine had the situation much more in hand than Colliard and we passed a resolution that Allied labor was to be given first chance, that current rates of wages should be paid and that German labor should be kept in separate camps.

I brought up the question of additional safeguards to secure social insurance funds in territories ceded by Germany or Austria, but could not bring the matter to a vote and so another meeting is necessary. I spent the evening attempting to draft a satisfactory clause to be added to the Treaty and finally Slosson and I pounded one out on the typewriter, a clause which I think is likely to get into all the treaties drawn up in Paris.[1]

[1] See below, p. 357.

Thursday, June 5, 1919

The affairs of the world paused today while President Wilson himself decided that my wife and two daughters might have a special passport to come over here before I leave! What a commentary on bureaucracy that he should be bothered with trifles like this.

Still working part of the time at the social insurance clause. But most of the morning spent with Dr. Putnam, making arrangements by which he can secure for the Library of Congress records of the Peace Conference that otherwise might go astray or be locked up in the State Department's archives. I sent a memorandum in to the Commissioners pointing out the need of having many of the records of the Peace Conference kept in the Library of Congress in view of the fact that the Conference covered much more than the purely political material which would normally go to the State Department.[1] It took a good deal of urging to put this through, for the State Department has its own designs on this material. Finally, however, I got enough authority to start going, and so Miss Wilson, working under Dr. Putnam, is happily fixed once more, cataloguing the documents she so loves to handle.

More memorandum writing in the afternoon.

[The Spanish Government had submitted a memorandum through their ambassadors both in London and in Washington stating that Spain, "as one of the leading neutrals during the war," would be extremely gratified if invited by the Powers to take part in the Council of Organization of the Washington Labor Conference. This called for a great deal of personal consultation among those representatives of the Labor Commission still left in Paris, and my memorandum was a recommendation to the American Commissioners asking a ruling against Spain's being admitted, as it would involve difficulties with other Powers.]

In the evening a dinner at the Majestic with the British members of the committee, that had invited some half dozen of us to found an international institute, with branches in London and in New York, which we had planned last week. Lord Robert Cecil opened the meeting and General Bliss presided. I had a good time talking to Sir Eyre Crowe of the Foreign Office but failed to convince him of

---

[1] After President Wilson left, Dr. Slosson and Dr. Louis H. Gray were commissioned to go through the records of the Conference and prepare them for the State Department files.

the need of opening the British archives. His point is that the documents have been given to them in confidence and that it is a violation of that confidence to throw them open; that however much it might help at the present, it would make future negotiations difficult, and that documents would not find their way into files that were open to researchers, so that the real question of public diplomacy with deferred responsibilities would remain unsolved. I have been wanting to get a middle course accepted which would permit non-official individuals properly certified to examine the materials, but the old Foreign Office officials are against even this. The younger men, like Lord Percy, are for it, of course.

We decided to form the Institutes and they put me on with Coolidge, James Brown Scott and Shepardson as the American members of the organizing committee. I drove home again, as at the first meeting last week, with Beer and Hornbeck in General Bliss's car.

Friday, June 6, 1919

Spent the morning on arrangements with Dr. Putnam and further work on the suggested clause for social insurance.

The Labor Committee met at three o'clock, and I found that it was possible to get through the clause unanimously in the widest possible form, applying to all territorial cessions, even Alsace-Lorraine if the French did not otherwise meet the situation. It was quite nice to pull it off to the credit of our Government, for Barnes had had the same idea, only he let it slip and I put it through. He was very good about it. As a result there will now be a clause in all the treaties safeguarding the savings of workers and all others in these territories that pass from German, Austrian or Hungarian sovereignty, so that their old-age, accident and sickness insurance will not be taken from them under any pretext by the new government under which they will have to live.[1] As it is a very technical matter, the details, if not satisfactorily settled by the Governments themselves, will be handled by a committee appointed mainly by the International Labor Office. That alone is a pretty fair week's work, although after all, relatively simple.

Coming back to the Crillon, I sent a memorandum to the President telling him the news and then happened in on Colonel House,

---

[1] The article in question is number 312 in the Treaty of Versailles, 275 in the Treaty of St. Germain, and 258 in the Treaty of Trianon. It was also inserted in the Treaty of Neuilly, Article 203.

who was quite tickled with the item. He was very cordial and even enthusiastic.

[This was one of the incidents of my work in Paris which I am especially happy to recall. The social insurance and labor legislation of Germany prior to the War had to be taken care of in the territories ceded by Germany to its neighbors. It would have been a serious step backward, for instance, if the section given to Poland were to have no provision against Polish denial of the established safeguards of labor. Unless there were a guarantee clause in the Treaty, private individuals would have no redress in case of arbitrary action by the new government. The article in the draft treaty had recognized the situation but left the redress entirely in the hands of the state receiving the territory. I insisted that there should be provision for international arbitration and that the former German subjects should have the chance to appeal the case to such a tribunal. There had been no opposition to this on the part of my colleagues, Mr. Barnes or M. Fontaine. On the contrary they were heartily for it, but there seemed no way to get the question considered. The Labor Commission had dissolved by this time; but as Barnes was Vice-President, I prevailed upon him to call a special session and brought my draft of the clause along. I had, however, not been able to reach my own Commissioners or get the attention of Colonel House. When the meeting took place and we were asked to present our credentials, I took the risk of assuring my colleagues that I was accredited to the meeting, although as a matter of fact I had no authority to act in this improvised meeting, nor any backing for the text which I presented. Fortunately the case was so clear that it took only a short session to have the clause accepted by all. Then I hurried back to the Crillon to get my action ratified. Secretary Lansing, to whom I explained the situation, reported it to the President, who heartily approved what I had done.

The clause of the Treaty which I inserted stated that if, within three months after the signature of the Treaty, the countries receiving territory from the Central Powers had not made treaty agreements adequately safeguarding social insurance in the ceded territory, then the conditions of the transfer of territory should be referred to a commission of five members, one appointed by the German (or the Austrian, Hungarian, or Bulgarian) Government, one by the other interested Government, and three by the Governing

Body of the International Labor Office from the nationals of other States. This commission should then by majority vote, within three months, adopt recommendation for the Council of the League whose decision would be final. The important point was that a majority in these arbitration commissions would be from disinterested nations, so that the adjustment of social insurance would be made solely on the basis of the justice of the case. This arbitration procedure has been effective in more than one instance in maintaining the higher standard of social legislation against the natural tendency of the newly established governments to break it down. In addition to the cases in which the procedure of the Treaty was actually invoked, the threat of its possible action has also operated to secure agreement between employers and employed, as for instance in Upper Silesia.]

Saturday, June 7, 1919

Had lunch with Macleay of the Far Eastern Department of the British Foreign Office, discussing with him, Beer and Hornbeck the arrangements between China and Japan. I learn that Japan has given written assurances that make the cession of German rights in China much less objectionable.

Called on Colonel House at five o'clock to see if it is going to be possible to follow up in the League of Nations the question of the opening of archives to research. Found him very responsive to the idea of taking it up at the first meeting of the League of Nations. The Committee on the League of Nations met today and submitted something for the reply to Germany which will please liberals, if accepted.[1]

A quiet dinner with Beer and Shepardson with discussion of the formation of the government of the League of Nations. My guess is that Beer will be one of the cabinet. Tomorrow I shall be once more in the country, this time as Warrin's guest, with a French officer, to see the extreme western end of the battlefields of 1914, which will complete my survey of that page of history.

[1] I have not the slightest idea now to what this refers, but the entry shows that some of us were concerned about securing more liberal terms.

The Battlefield of the Ourcq

Sunday, June 8, 1919

For the motor trip, Warrin brought a French officer named Jirodaux who had fought through the first battle of the Marne on the extreme northwestern end of the French line. He could therefore give us a first-hand account of how they drove in on von Kluck's extreme flank and forced him to turn around to meet them.

We left Paris by the gate of St. Denis, turning north. St. Denis itself presented a busy scene, for the working people were out getting their morning supplies at the market; but it is a poor and squalid town. We were soon running through the open fields, however, and just north of Pierrefitte branched slightly toward the west on a road that cut straight through the undulating country now approaching hay-harvest time, till we came to the little village of Moisselles. It is about fifteen miles out from Paris and was as far as the retreating French troops withdrew before the Germans on the road to Paris, in September 1914. The end of the retreat was a gentle valley running across the fields with a little brook in it, while at the east the high, forested hill of Ecouen furnished a pivot with its concealed fortress protecting Paris across the broad, northeastern plains. Across the road to the west was the forest of Montmorency. The Germans had not come down this far; it was the turning point of the retreat. We took the little country road to the right to follow the line of march to the field of battle. For the next three hours we were most of the time on these little country lanes going across from one hamlet to another in a general easterly direction. First there was the little village of Attainville, then Villiers, where we stopped to see the old church, a twelfth century Romanesque, as most of these village churches are, but with a Renaissance adaptation on the façade. Battlefields apart, this section of France is a perfect mine of medieval art treasures in the old village churches and châteaux. There was hardly a town we went to that had not a church dating from before the thirteenth century, and the quaint old streets were jumbled down on gently sloping hillsides if the town were on a brook, or, here and there, clustered on the hilltops with the spires visible for long distances. Somehow the impression grew upon us all, so that we spoke of it, that they were strangely silent. There were very few people along the track of the whole cross-country run, and one felt almost as though in the presence of the silence of the battlefield after the fighting was over. Even at the little town where we took lunch, Mareuil-sur-Ourcq, where they were having the first fête day in five years, the celebration was a very quiet affair, except for the children at the merry-go-round.

We turned across fields to follow a cow track which our Cadillac had difficulty in navigating until it came out on the fine national way leading into Luzarches. This is a most lovely spot, with a beautiful château overlooking a gentle valley with avenues of trees along the roadside. The Germans had got this far; Jirodaux's friend and comrade was shot by Uhlans at the crossroads where we turned. He was on scouting duty at the head of the French army and was cared for while dying by an old servant in a well-to-do house to which we turned, for Jirodaux wanted to find the old woman and see what had become of her during the rest of the war. She had refused to let the Uhlans touch her soldier and dared them at the point of his revolver. We found the house, but weeds were growing in the lawn and on paths. It had been deserted for four years, and the family had gone no one knew where. That is but one story of the universal dislocation of northern France.

From Luzarches we turned east following the 1914 route taken by the Germans, whom one could still imagine skirting the fields to the northeast, on the way to Dammartin. Dammartin is on a main trunk road leading north from Paris. Just a word about these roads. They spread out from Paris like the spokes in a wheel and therefore furnished the army of defense with a quick way of reaching out to the circumference. We had gone out on one of these running pretty straight to the north. At Luzarches we crossed another. At Survilliers we crossed a third. At Dammartin a fourth. But this last one is of more historic interest, as along it the "taxicab army" drove out from Paris on the eighth of September unloading some twelve thousand men near Nanteuil, a village still farther on beyond Dammartin, which gave the French enough weight at the extreme end of their line to alarm the Germans and force them back across the Marne.

Dammartin itself is on one of those dominating ridges, or rather hills, like Ecouen, and its church spire is visible for long reaches. The town itself is stretched along the main road, a clean little place, which is one advantage of living on a hill. I may say that there were some places we went through that were not on hilltops. From Dammartin on across toward Meaux on the long straight road with its marvelously complete line of elms stretching across the country as far as one could see until we struck a little country road turning off from it just west of St. Soupplets. Here we were almost in sight of the villages which I had seen from the road to Meaux on the south, for the next town beyond St. Soupplets was Monthyon, where the first cannon of the Marne battle was fired at noon on September fifth. All that day the troops of Jirodaux had been hurrying along the road we were now following, to strike in on the battle-line to the north. They had reached Dammartin from Luzarches by night but at eleven o'clock were roused again and told that they must continue the march, and so all night they marched as well. Just as dawn was approaching they were entering these fields we were now in and received the first German shell fire as they advanced over the brow of a long slope toward the little village of Oissery. Here they pushed the Germans out, but their losses began to tell; and the graves still dot the little meadow down by the brook that runs through Oissery. It was nine o'clock on the sixth of September when they pushed through here, but still they kept on fighting, pushing across the fields where our little winding country road led us, through Brégy to the hamlet of Fosse-Martin. This is hardly more than a farmyard with great barns and an enormous courtyard surrounded by farm buildings. We drove right into the farmyard itself and out the gate into the lane behind, and there suddenly came upon a little cemetery of French graves which the peasant women had cared for with carnations and sweet williams. The inscriptions on the crosses were already obliterated except for one or two where one could read that it was the grave of an unknown soldier or officer. It was one of the most lonely and pathetic spots I have seen on the whole war front; but Jirodaux was looking over to the slight ridge on the east about a mile or a mile and a half away where another long row of trees indicated a cross-country road and the red roofs and stone walls of a single farm house were in plain sight. The field between us sloped very gently and was almost entirely open and under cultivation. There was a single spot in the middle of it where two or three trees stood out above a little sand-bank. This was the scene of hardest fighting on the flank of von Kluck's army. For five days they fought back and forth across these fields, and of the 2700 men who went in with Jirodaux only 610 and 7 officers were left at the close of the fighting. We found the little hollow in the roadside where he had slept during the battle, coming back each night to crawl into it, and though the farms have all been repaired and have new roofs and freshly plastered walls, it was not difficult to imagine the scene of battle with the ambulance pulled up under the cow-shed and the tired troops moving back and forth across that ghastly road to the next farmhouse. It was at the group of trees that he and his men captured a German regimental flag.

The battle at this part of the line never lessened in intensity until the whole German army was extricated from the Marne, for if the French could have pierced von Kluck's flank here, it would have meant more of a rout than actually took place. So when the Fifty-Sixth in which Jirodaux fought was reinforced by the "taxicab army" to its left, von Kluck brought back across the Marne heavy reserves and threw them against this little band of French, until on the ninth they almost gave way. The Germans continued the pressure; but by that critical time Foch had driven in the German center and the whole battle-line withdrew to the heights along the Aisne.

We followed the line of the retreat on through Acy-en-Multien, a little village where the Americans went in later when the Germans came down this country again a year ago now on their way to Paris, then through Betz and over a road to the east till we struck the Ourcq at Mareuil, a quaint little village still living in the four-teenth century. It was two o'clock now, so we engaged the dining room of the hotel of the Golden Sun, which was a little back room opening in from a thirteenth century front room with a smoky old fireplace and a few shiny pieces of brass. It was saint's day in Mareuil and the hotel room was filled with country people having their lunch and their glass of wine; for every town in France, I suppose, has its patron saint and has a sort of civic holiday in his honor once a year. In Mareuil it was St. Médard, which shows that the festivities go back to Merovingian times. A group of soldiers were singing around a rather rickety piano, and we sat down to eat to the music of ballads of the war. Outside the hurdy-gurdy was starting up with children gathering around it, for Sunday really ends at noon in Catholic countries; but as I said before, the festivities were rather sober on the whole.

From Mareuil we ran along the valley of the Ourcq to La Ferté Milon, a town in the narrow valley of the stream dominated by a magnificent old feudal castle whose great walls were visible for some distance across the country. Of a sudden we found ourselves in the midst of the new devastation of 1918, for here is where the Germans tried to smash through towards Paris on the southern flank of the great forest of Villers-Cotterets. The town is close under the side of a very steep hill which terminates in cliffs just beyond, and on the sloping hillside just above the road there was a new soldiers' cemetery, and side by side with the French graves a half-dozen American, distinguished by their slightly larger crosses. The names were Magie, Johnson, Feldmann, Kowilski, Donovan and an English name which I forget. It was strangely typical of the make-up of the American army.

We crossed the stream and mounted the hill on the north and were soon running into the forest of Villers-Cotterets, a wonderful stretch of woodland in which Foch hid his preparations for the attack on the German flank last July. We didn't see much of it in detail, however, for the road was long, straight and perfect and I counted sixty miles an hour on the speedometer. In a few minutes we were in the town of Villers-Cotterets, where there is a large assembling plant for salvage of the war. It is uninteresting, level country and the town has been sufficiently shot up to have that unkempt, despondent air of the towns behind the lines. From Villers-Cotterets we took the road to Soissons which I had taken once before. The north end of the wood through which we still ran for five miles or more was badly shot into and at the crossroads where the woods suddenly terminated the little group of farm buildings was badly smashed. The road from here on ran right over the battlefields where the Germans pushed through Soissons a year ago, and we soon came to the crossroads with the deserted tanks still standing along the fields at the spot where the captain I met on the road to Toulouse had such vivid memories of the fighting. There is an American cemetery a little beyond which must have several thousand graves. The American flag was flying from a high flagpole in the center and a great wreath furnished the only ornamentation. Just the long rows of wooden crosses inside a low railing.

In a minute or so more we were fringing the deep valleys that concentrate on the Aisne at Soissons and running down the long hill into the desolation of the main front. The sight of Soissons cathedral struck me this time, as it did before, as much more affecting than that of Rheims. All that part of the city around the cathedral is smashed, as at Rheims, but the Germans showed that this was done on purpose by the fact that whole blocks to the north and to the east were relatively little touched. One point should be noted very definitely. The old hospital (Hôtel Dieu) just a little east of the cathedral seemed hardly injured.

It was now five o'clock and we left for Compiègne, running for miles along the valley of the Aisne on a road that was once along the front line trenches. Out at Fontenoy, about five miles west of Soissons, we turned to the river itself, for at this point Jirodaux had crossed with his men to drive the Germans from the heights above. There was only a narrow lock across the stream and they crossed at midnight in the midst of a blinding rainstorm and under a heavy fire. The passageway across was so narrow that when a man fell they simply threw him into the stream, for otherwise the bridgeway would have been blocked and those already across cut off; but what a ghastly story! The bridge was down, however, so we could not cross the Aisne. Beside it was a little cemetery, and Jirodaux explained that these were the graves of the engineers who kept the bridge open during the succeeding months. From Fontenoy we ran rapidly along to the great forests of Compiègne and through them into the town itself. The palace here, one of Napoleon's favorite residences, is one of the famous royal palaces of the old régime but we were too late to stop and see it, and so, with only a little pause to look around, we left for Paris, going at a terrific rate through the long forest road, faster, indeed, than I care to remember. At Verberie we left the lowlands of the Oise valley and went up a long, winding hill to the high plain which stretches from here away across to the Marne. A pleasant farming world with broad open fields.

We reached Senlis at about seven o'clock, having been delayed with a blow-out on the road, and ran up in the quiet square beside the cathedral. This is to me the most like a country cathedral in England of any in France, not in style, but in setting. All the styles of the different centuries have been built into it. The front recalls the severity of the Romanesque St. Etienne in Caen. The spire is a glorious suggestion of Coutances or Chartres. The southern portal of the transept shows the fifteenth century mastery of ornamentation, its delicate and not too elaborate tracings hiding the firmer walls of the older church while not concealing their massive proportions. It is not a large cathedral but perfectly proportioned to the little, quiet city where it stands.

There are many signs of the Middle Ages in Senlis. Old ramparts as well to wander around. Luckily we had another blow-out here which gave us an excuse to loiter. The streets were almost deserted and the town showed the effect of the German occupation when in their march to Paris they burned systematically a quarter of the city because they claimed they had been shot at by civilians. The Mayor was shot as a hostage. It was from Senlis they swung toward the east on that flank movement which gave a chance for the troops from Paris to attack them at the side.

Through the forest of Chantilly, which skirts Senlis on the south, our road ran over gently rolling stretches back to Paris, the same road I had taken on the previous trip from Soissons, and we came in through the great airport of Le Bourget, reaching home about nine o'clock.

Paris, saved by that sacrifice on the fields behind the barn of Fosse-Martin, and again by the tanks that hid in the glades of the forest of Villers-Cotterets, was peacefully enjoying the Sunday evening twilight, the streets being unusually quiet, owing to a strike on the tramway. Somehow the town seemed unusually French as one approached it through the memories of the old historic Ile de France, and unusually magnificent in contrast with the squalor and ruin of the towns along the battle-front.

June 9, 1919

Spent the day working on memoranda for Colonel House and getting my files in shape for permanent cataloguing. Learned, to my great satisfaction, that Beer has been appointed on the staff of the League of Nations in control of mandates, which will mean that he will be looking after all colonial problems and dependent peoples like those in the Near East. It is a big, responsible job, and they have the right man for it.

In the evening I ran over the plans for the new international institute with Shepardson, after a walk through the Champs Elysées with Beer in the twilight.

Tuesday, June 10, 1919

Worked on memoranda and then at eleven went over to the Committee of the Sir William Ramsay Fund on which I had got, by mistake, an appointment among a group of scientists. I tried to resign but they insisted on my staying in on some mistaken idea that I could be of help. I am now out gunning for some distinguished American chemist to take my place. The idea of the foundation is to send American students to Europe and French to England, etc., so as to have a real chemical union of the inter-Allied sciences.

At noon saw Curtis for a moment on the American Institute plan. In the afternoon Dr. Putnam and I planned with Mr. Harrison, of the State Department archives here, for a proper handling of the documents of the Peace Conference.

Wednesday, June 11, 1919

Spent the day closely at the Crillon inventorying papers which Slosson found in the cubbyholes and clothes closets of Room 444 where they had been left by the Central Territorial Committee. Also dictated memoranda at the suggestion of Colonel House on the difficulties of making a world treaty.

Summer has come. I forgot to mention the fact earlier, but last week all of a sudden a hot wave struck Paris and we blossomed out in our summer clothes. In the evening Beer, Hornbeck and Millet were the guests of Chadbourne, an American liquidator of army affairs, at the Inter-Allied Club, where we ate picnic fashion, on the lawn. Then I got a car and drove Millet home out near the Bois de Boulogne.

[The memoranda for Colonel House were in response to a request for a survey by the Division of Diplomatic History of the work of the Peace Conference itself, its scope, organization, and the nature of its negotiations. With Colonel House's consent the substance of some of this was subsequently recast for an article on difficulties in treaty making, which appeared in *The Independent*.[1]]

[1] It is quoted in Appendix IV.

Thursday, June 12, 1919

Wrote to President Butler and to Professor John Bates Clark suggesting that the Carnegie Endowment take over the publishing of the semi-official monographic material which the Conference has produced, such as the Inquiry reports.[1]

In the evening, Beer, Hornbeck and I dined at the Majestic with Curtis, Headlam-Morley, Hurst (who has drafted the Treaty clauses for the British) and a few others. We met a larger group later in the evening and worked away on the constitution of the proposed International Institute for Foreign Affairs. The editor of the *Register* is to be Lord Eustace Percy. I do not think much of the plan for the first table of contents, which Beer and I examined along towards midnight after we got back.

In the afternoon Professor Anderson dropped in from Beaune looking like a bronzed veteran of the war. He is on his way for a fourteen day leave in the devastated regions. He has got much more out of his experience in the Army University than if he had stayed with me to write memoranda on diplomatic history.

[1] This was finally undertaken by the Carnegie Endowment, though in somewhat different form, in the series, "The Paris Peace Conference, History and Documents," of which the first two volumes, *The Origins of the International Labor Organization,* were published by the Columbia University Press in 1934. The volumes on Reparations are to appear in 1937.

If Germany Should Not Sign. The Troops
on the Rhine

Friday, June 13, 1919

Routine work dictating memoranda and letters. In the evening I dined at the Majestic at Barnes's guest. He has planned to take me to the British front on the Rhine at Cologne and I have been trying to adjust my arrangements so as to accept his invitation and see the British army as the guest of a member of the British War Cabinet. Then I want to take him on up to Coblentz as my guest to see the American army. Some arrangements made in order to square obligations with Mr. Miller stand in the way, for I promised to take Mrs. Miller over part of the Canadian battlefields along with Mr. Warrin, Miller's assistant. It can be done, perhaps, but involves a strenuous week ahead.

Mr. Barnes and I had a very interesting evening together, just the two of us. He had lunched with Lloyd George who sent him along with Bonar Law to see Clemenceau. They were trying to secure a modification of the terms of armed occupation of Germany and got Clemenceau to agree to a formula which will give Germany a chance to get rid of the burden by good behavior.

Saturday, June 14, 1919

Trip to Soissons and beyond, with Warrin and Mrs. Miller. We took the train to Soissons, arriving there about nine-thirty. There Mrs. Miller's private French car met us, and after a view of Soissons we went up the road towards Laon across the intervening hill just at the west end of the Chemin des Dames, where the battered mound that once commanded the fort of Malmaison commands the pass through the valley of the Ailette. The long, barren ridge told the same story as it did at its eastern end by Craonne towards Rheims where I had been before, but now the whole hilltop was ablaze with masses of poppies. I never saw anything like this great wilderness of a battlefield covered with this cloak of blood-red flowers. It was inconceivably beautiful. How it has happened I can hardly understand. Weeds and grass cover most of the desolation of the front, but nowhere else have the poppies made a battlefield so entirely their own. Here and there blue cornflowers mingled, especially in the gun-tracks, but they only accentuated the harmony of color. Not a soul was in sight for miles across this waste, and the rude and neglected character of the graves showed that the final work of tracing the dead had not yet been undertaken.

We wound down a road that was still rough from shell holes, over the sickly looking marshes of the Ailette canal and then through the German front, on into the relatively untouched country behind the German lines where the isolated hill on which Laon stands loomed up through the long avenues of poplars.

A long climb up the hillside that reminds one of the Tuscan hills, crowned with the medieval walls and terraces of Laon and then a picnic lunch on the northern terrace beside the cathedral looking out over the vast prairie country of northern France. It stretches below one here as from an airplane view, with the straight white roads, the little villages and groves dotting it all the way to the distant horizon. If the French could only have held this fortress and the whole rough hill country behind and kept the Germans in the plain—as was planned in their textbooks on the defense of France—there would not have been four years of war.

Laon is almost untouched by the war, for although it was the headquarters of the German staff in the western area, the French did not bomb it as one might expect. The railway station down in the plain below, however, is a mass of ruins.

From Laon we struck the northern outskirts of the woods of St. Gobain, where a little spur runs in from the main railroad line to the emplacement of the great gun that fired on Paris from seventy-five miles away. We had a local guide who said that the Germans never fired it singly but always fired two or three others at the same time so that the Allies could not locate it by the sound. They never allowed civilians, either, to get a sight of it, and once when there was a forest fire and they called out the civilians to help fight it, they placed special guards around that corner of the wood where the gun was stationed. It took the Germans about eight months to mount it, and the soldiers told the villagers that the first time it was fired the breech blew off and killed all the engineers. In any case, they never saw those engineers again. Only the cement foundation and the section of the iron track on which the gun revolved is left, so that there is less to see than in the one north of Château Thierry which I described before. There were in the same wood two other emplacements for other Berthas, but the wood was infested with a savage big fly which struck me as having disease possibilities of a kind not to be trifled with, so we didn't hunt up the other emplacements. From there we went on to La Fère, the railroad junction on the Oise, which is as far as the Allies got. It is an ugly town, although with some quaint old buildings, and is only half destroyed; but what is left is foul and desolate. From here west one can see the long reaches of the plains of Picardy, while along the eastern horizon the wooded slopes of St. Gobain, two or three miles away, mark the main key position to the whole German line.

We took the road along the Oise through Tergnier to Chauny and then instead of running over to see Coucy, as we had planned, Mrs. Miller, who is quite delicate, felt that she had gone as far as her strength would stand and we took the train for Paris from the improvised railway station of that ruined village.

The railroad runs along the valley of the Oise and we soon came in sight of Noyon, which has been only partly destroyed. The cathedral walls seemed to be standing, viewed from the railroad a quarter of a mile away, but a flattened new roof recalls the fact that it was burned in the last German drive. Our train came through Compiègne and Chantilly back to Paris where we arrived about half past eight.

Sunday, June 15, 1919 [1]

I had hoped for a day of rest but found that there had been a hurry call for me the afternoon before to insure a proper statement about the Labor Clauses in the reply to the Germans. At nine-thirty Slosson and I set to work on the problem of getting the proper text, working over at the Quai d'Orsay in the rooms where the Peace Conference committees are at work. It was lucky I was back in Paris, for I changed their draft entirely. That was not all, however, for the committee was running into all kinds of other difficulties. I recast a

[1] From the trip to Amiens and the Rhine to the end of the diary there were full but rough notes taken at the time from which this last section of the narrative was reconstructed.

number of other paragraphs in the reply and also saw to it that the drafting committee of the treaty itself put in the addition which we worked out on social legislation on ceded territories.

I go tonight to Amiens where I arrive about midnight, and in the morning take Mrs. Miller, who, with Warrin, has already gone there, over the battlefields to Lille. There Mr. Barnes is to meet us for a trip to Ypres and from there he and I go on to the Rhine, while Warrin brings Mrs. Miller back to Paris. I shall be three or four days at least away from the Crillon.

I was busy up to the last minute before rushing off to the train; for after the day's work at the French Foreign Office, Mr. Barnes and his secretary came to dine with me at the Crillon, so as to get our plans worked out for the trip. I flung a few things across the room at my valise, jammed them in it, left my guests to finish their dinner with Beer, and rushed off with just time to catch the train for Amiens, leaving the crowded Gare du Nord at eight o'clock. I missed the fast express, but had a comfortable compartment with two English officers in a train which arrived at Amiens at half-past twelve.

Twilight across the plains of northern France! Little hamlets set in the folds of the long slopes, pegging them down like quilting pins; the gray walls of farmhouses of the old Romanesque churches of the Ile de France clustered so tightly as hardly to be noticeable between the patchwork of the fields. It was dark from Chantilly, where the road leaves the high plains of the Ile de France, and, cutting through the forest, descends to the valley of the Oise. From there on, however, the moon, which was at the full, lent enough elusive interest to the landscape; so that I was rather sorry when, after stopping at every imaginable place, we pulled into Amiens, where Warrin was waiting to take me to the hotel. The station was crowded with refugees and soldiers, some asleep on the floor or on piles of baggage, and in the smoky light the grimy figures of those tired people gave me as much of the suggestion of the presence still of war as anything I have seen.

Monday, June 16, 1919

Amiens: Visited the cathedral in the early morning. They were taking down the sandbags that had protected the high altar. The colored glass has not been put back into the windows yet. As we left the town for Albert the huge mass of masonry rose higher and higher above the roof tops. Although the town is really a busy little provincial capital, the cathedral dominates it even more than in most cathedral towns, and from the far-off hills where the German line was, the only thing one sees against the western horizon is the slender flèche that crowns the nave.

In the countryside around Amiens itself all sign of war has now disappeared except for broken tree trunks along the roadway. Farmers are going in carts to market and working the fields. Then a dramatic change, as the road enters a deep woods. In the shadows there are army huts and prisoners coming and going, guarded by poilus. It is the west bank of the Somme. Across on the other shore the lines of trenches are being filled in by the farmers. There are white chalk marks still from the thrown up stone but most of it will be covered with crop this year. Down in the valley, hidden from both sides, is a little village with British signs still standing in the streets, some of them comical enough. Up from it, the road climbs steadily and then tops a ridge and down below us lay Albert.

From here on we covered about the same ground that Currie showed us two months before, but this time going in the opposite direction, omitting only Vimy Ridge and the country around Longueau. While there were still hours of motoring over absolute deserts along the Somme, and the horror of places like Delville wood seemed even more terrible than when we had studied it with Currie for its strategic importance, yet here and there refugees had returned to live in the dugouts or in little corrugated iron sheds. There was still not a house with a roof on it from Albert to Bapaume; but the German prisoners were actually rolling up the barbed wire of the Hindenburg line. Explosions could be heard from time to time as the corps of workmen destroyed stray shells that were scattered over the farms.

Cambrai is still a spectral city. From the distance its church towers and the walls of houses look untouched, but within it we found not a single house that was not gutted by either high explosives or fire, and there was no hotel except the little café at the railway station.

Back to Arras to the railway station, where we took the train for Lille, connecting up with Mr. Barnes, with whom I am to travel up the Rhine.

Tuesday, June 17, 1919

From Lille we motored west along the low-lying swampy country, strewn with "pill-boxes" and barbed wire, out to Armentières which lay just behind the German lines. Another hollow shell of a place, but restaurants are again starting in sheds and one hardware store had tools displayed. From here we followed the country roads over to Mt. Kemmel and on to Ypres. There are four chief centers of devastation, Verdun, the Chemin des Dames, the Somme front and Ypres. The rest can be farmed again in at least a year or two, but these great battlefields seem utterly beyond recovery. Swamps and the debris of war and the ground churned up as though there had been an earthquake; no sign of habitation as far as the eye can see, not for miles on end.[1]

Ypres has already become the prey of vandals carrying off souvenirs, and a huge sign stands in front of the ruins of the Cloth Hall:

> "This is Holy Ground
> No stone of this fabric may be taken away
> It is a heritage for all civilized peoples.
> By order,
> TOWN MAYOR, YPRES."

There are hawkers in the hot empty streets selling souvenirs and postcards. Temporary sheds mark the beginning of the return of the population.

Back to Lille along the Menin road through Passchendaele, where a flower garden is already planted beside the heap of brick that marks where the village church once stood.

Wednesday, June 18, 1919

Mr. Barnes and I were up at four-thirty to catch the train for Brussels, a local train which stops at every crossroads and invents stations. Signs of the devastation disappear. After we leave Tournai

---

[1] Yet when I revisited Ypres in August of this same year, they were already plowing the fields along the road from Ypres to Passchendaele and planting gardens not far from Sanctuary Wood, the very center of this appalling desolation. First, companies of workmen explored the fields with sounding rods for what lay just beneath; then other bands of workmen gathered whatever could be found where the little stakes had been placed up and down the fields; then came the plowmen in the fields behind; and so, steadily and rapidly, they brought the battlefields back to the gardens they had been before.

the country is slightly rolling with white farmhouses of one story, and I note that the only visible change in this part of Belgium is that the railway bridges have been blown up by the Germans on their retreat. We stayed in Brussels from eleven to two. Busy city; no sign of hardship in the main street at least. Walk over to the central squares. They are getting ready for Wilson, who is to arrive this evening, having followed us to Ypres. From Brussels to Louvain along the great plain that slopes up to the divide with Germany. Cannot see any sign of damage at the railway station at Louvain. Liége—suddenly down the long hill to the picturesque valley of the Meuse—no sign of war. Up the eastern slope to the defile by a winding stream to the German frontier at the watershed at Herbestal.

Germany. At once one sees larger and better houses, even in the rough meadow country that slopes down to Aix-la-Chapelle (Aachen). There is no more sign of war on the landscape than in Aachen itself. There are herds of cattle in the fields. We have seen none in Northern France. Aix in its broad valley, the old capital of Charlemagne, where he lies buried, is today a fine large modern city with railway and electric cars running from the station to the heart of the town. The railway line is distinctly better than anything in France; the roadbed is excellent, although the German armies have passed over it for the last four years. There is smoke from the high chimneys of mining towns, for the furnaces are going and the iron works running. The fields around the factories are well cultivated. British Tommies are on guard at the bridges. At the industrial city of Düren there are new houses and up-to-date looking factories.

Cologne, Headquarters of the British Army of Occupation, just at twilight. No one at the station to meet us, to Mr. Barnes' chagrin. We went to the office of the British Military Headquarters and were assigned rooms in the Kaiser Friedrich Hotel. The street car which we take is partly filled with Tommies, who talk of the Treaty among themselves, saying it's undoubtedly hard on the Germans; but they want it all settled and over so that they can go home. The night in the hotel showed that behind the façade Cologne was very much down at the heels. The rooms were horribly dirty and the only safety for a night's sleep was to throw the mattress and bedclothes away and sleep in our overcoats.

Breakfast at the Kaiser Friedrich corresponded with the bed-room. We strolled through the main streets of Cologne, a fine, big, American looking city. We reached the cathedral square just as a detachment of the British Army was passing Headquarters, which are established in a massive building on the north side of the street that leads to the Rhine bridge. A huge British flag from the balcony lent a note of color to the otherwise drab city buildings. It was a detail of engineers with all accoutrements, including boats on wheels. Everything had been polished up and was shining. The horses were well groomed and in excellent condition and there was all the snap and go of an army on parade. Perhaps one noticed this all the more by contrast with the civilian population, which looked apathetic and dull. Sir William Robertson, the commanding general, arrived; bugle calls sounded out across the square.

We made our call and Robertson had a long conversation with Barnes. There were many apologies for the failure to look after us properly on our arrival. It seems the notification had miscarried. Robertson hopes he will be out by Christmas. He is not satisfied with what we have been doing in Paris and is afraid that he may be kept in the occupied area holding down an unfriendly population. There are no serious troubles but it is disagreeable. When we left, Barnes told me how Robertson had broken down in the War Cabinet when he opposed the unified command, was reduced in rank for his insubordination, but still offered his services.

We wandered over to the cathedral where the Cardinal (Archbishop) was conducting services, having his procession of Corpus Christi around the aisles of the cathedral instead of in the town.

After lunch we left for Bonn, a long good run. There were Corpus Christi flags in little villages and a large procession in Bonn itself, with enormous crowds watching in the public squares. We went through under the arch of the University and out to Princess Helena's home on the Rhine. She is the Emperor's sister. We had tea with General Morland on the terrace, and then went through the rooms—the princess herself was in a little tea room at the foot of the stairs. The pictures on the walls were mostly those of English royalty—Victoria and Albert had the places of honor on the stairs; a strange family mix-up.

Then back to Bonn, where there were thousands in front of an open-air altar at which the clergy were officiating. Unable to proceed we turned aside and crossed the bridge over to Solingen, where the great knife factories are. Once, shortly after we arrived in Paris, I bought a small souvenir jackknife on the Rue de Rivoli. On one side was stamped "Foch," and on the other "La Victoire" but at the hilt of the blade was stamped "Solingen." And still wars are fought and barriers erected to stop the movement of trade. Some day the laws of economics will assert themselves, but not fully or openly in our lifetime.

Beyond Solingen, on the way to Burg, we ran into British Tommies marching out to the fifteen mile radius from the bridge head, to be ready for the dash to Berlin if that should be necessary. There were long lines of troops, dirty and hot in the late afternoon sun. Soldiers dropped out, overcome by the heat in their heavy uniforms and the heavy packs they were carrying. Heavy howitzers were on the move, dragged by tractors; there were light horse batteries as well. We reached the hill country after the long run up and down hill into Burg, where General Henniker, in command, came over to the car. We watched the Tommies unload into new quarters. We climbed a very steep hill to the castle and then skirted along country roads with troops marching everywhere. One company had a goat as a mascot. Kitchens were dragged along the roads cooking as they came. Lorries picked their way through the troops, with about thirty-five men crowded into each. How an army staff can keep track of all these different companies, moving and milling on the march, is beyond the civilian mind. On our road back we passed big airdromes. General Salmond of the Air Corps, who was with us, said they had more than they needed. If there were opposition the defiles were narrow and they would use the air.

Back across the great Rhine bridge, to dinner at the Château and quarters in a private house of a wealthy chocolate manufacturer. It was embarrassing for us, because while the owner's family was most correct, it was quite clear that we were uninvited guests.

Friday, June 20, 1919

Today we left for Coblentz, motoring up the Rhine through Bonn and Andernach to the highlands, where the cliffs of Siebengebirge and the Drachenfels appeared. There American sentries replaced the British. The Americans have the most picturesque section of the

Rhine. There were not many in sight, mostly Military Police. But here and there we saw parks of caterpillar tractors and artillery.

At Coblentz we were given quarters in the official residence of the provincial governor, opposite the palace, with rooms on the Rhine. We called on General Liggett, whose office looks out over the Rhine across the gardens of our house to the fort of Ehrenbreitstein, which is surmounted by the largest American flag in Europe or perhaps anywhere else. General Liggett wants no more war and does not want to see more French negro troops on the Rhine. Barnes asked him if the American negro troops fought well and he said, "Yes, when under white command." Then he told the story of the negro who was stopped behind the front. When his officer asked him why he was running away he explained that he wasn't running away but he had passed some others who were.

We have a colonel to conduct us to each divisional commander on the American section of the front. Our troops had only moved up yesterday from the Rhine to the extreme edge of the occupied area, fifteen miles east of the bridge heads, at the same time as the British. We found them encamped in little "pup" tents under the trees along the wayside, all tucked away as unobtrusively as can be, but waiting for the command to march to Berlin if the Germans do not sign the Treaty. Again there were parks of autos and lorries and airplanes. We returned, crossing the Rhine at Bendorf on a bridge said to have been built by Russian prisoners during the war. We met a detachment about 7500 strong marching along the Rhine bank with their flags shining in the sunlight.

Back for dinner at the Officers' Club, where we dined in the open, with the band playing beside a fountain sparkling under the electric light.

Home through quiet streets to sleep in the private rooms of the Vice-President of the Rhineland.

Saturday, June 21, 1919

Car back to Cologne—9 A.M. General Robertson has been to Paris and back. Barnes wrote a memorandum to Lloyd George commenting on some of the things we have seen. Back again by train to Liége. Then instead of going to Brussels we followed the Meuse south through the narrow gorge past miles of foundries all destroyed, with their great doors open or off the hinges. From Namur the country flattens out. We went up the Sambre through broad meadows with mowers at hay-making. There are lines of poplars by the road and here and there mine heaps with smokeless chimneys.

There is a tank on a siding, "Erobert, 5 armée" (Conquered by the fifth army), which the Germans hadn't managed to get away. From here on mines and steel works, like one long Pittsburgh, solid to Charleroi. All the bridges were down (six or more) to Erquelinnes, on the French frontier, which is destroyed. No wonder the French have fought so hard to have their reparation claims put through. In all the motoring and travel from Amiens to Brussels and back again from Liége, there were only two tall chimneys with smoke coming out of them, and they were close by Brussels. On the other hand the moment we crossed the frontier into Germany the whole industrial life seemed untouched so far as one could judge by externals. The contrast was simply overpowering.

Night over the battlefields as we slept on our way to Paris. We were awake by Chantilly.

Paris. We rode from the railway station with a British Army observer just in from Germany who had sympathy for the Germans as to the Treaty but says they will surely sign. This finishes my impressions of Germany.

Sunday, June 22, 1919

All morning at correspondence. Lunch with Barnes to listen to his memorandum which summarized some joint impressions.

Saw Colonel House at half-past six to discuss Gompers' difficulties in accepting the Labor Charter in its changed form. Shepardson, in my absence, had answered him by a long cable which the President signed. The Colonel agreed with me that there was no need for any further explanation.

Dinner with Beer. Exchanged news and impressions, for he had been at Metz.

Monday, June 23, 1919

Decide to sail for home. See Colonel House. Packing books and papers.

7 p.m. Peace! The news has just come that Germany will sign. The guns are firing from the batteries around Paris. They announce the end of our work.

Tuesday, June 24, 1919

Packing and correspondence. Continue to work at the problem of the record for the future.

Wednesday, June 25, 1919

I am to go over to Washington for a week or so to help straighten out the labor legislation program. Colonel House and I agreed that this was necessary, so I sail on the "George Washington" with President Wilson; to come back to England the following week.

Thursday, June 26, 1919

The Library is being packed and Captain Gilchrist sends me in his report, which will not be without interest to librarians. In view of all the demands made on us and the improvised conditions of housing, it shows what the American trained librarian can do. Of the 4612 volumes in our keeping, many of them borrowed from the Library of Congress and universities, all but a half dozen or so were accounted for at the end.

Friday, June 27, 1919

Lunch and afternoon at the Hotel Majestic working on Labor problems and the Washington Conference.

The Signing of the Treaty and the End
of the Story

Saturday, June 28, 1919

In the morning we had a special meeting of the Organizing Committee of the International Labor Conference.

Saturday afternoon—the signing of the Treaty of Versailles.

Although the morning was spent in routine work there was an air of excitement in the Crillon as the final hour approached. The soldiers on guard were all spruced up, the officers were in parade uniforms with much gold lace, and diplomats could be distinguished at last from their professorial colleagues by silk hats and full diplomatic regalia.

The Secretariat had taken immense pains to make sure that the signing of the Treaty would be witnessed only by those who in some way or other had had a share in its making as plenipotentiaries or commissioners. There were several kinds of tickets admitting the bearer to different parts of the Palace of Versailles, and the bearer himself had no idea of the exact meaning of them. When the hour came to leave the hotel there was a whole company of American army cars waiting in line in front of the Crillon, each with a huge colored label on its windshield and hood and a special list of its passengers. Beer, Haskins and I had a car together, and just as we were getting into it a well dressed civilian American stepped up to us and pointed to the empty seat and asked if he might go along. We explained how impossible this was, but he told us how equally impossible it was to find a taxi and that all he wished was a ride to the gate of the city of Versailles. He was a business man and was merely sight-seeing for the day. There was no reason under the circumstances why he should not ride with us that far, and when we reached the city gate and showed our credentials to the guard posted there he quietly left the car and disappeared. When the ceremony was over I found him on the terrace at the doorway to the grand staircase of the Palace. I asked him how he had managed to get in

381

and he pulled out of his pocket a Pall Mall cigarette case, bright red with a coat of arms in gold at the corner and said that had been his "laissez-passer." It was the only touch of comedy in the high drama of the day.

Our road lay through the forest of St. Cloud and perhaps it was the contrast with its shadowy avenues and restful glades which lent an added magnificence to the military pageant that stretched out before us in the sunlight from the city gate to the Palace. On each side of the broad avenue, as far as the eye could see, regiment after regiment of cavalry stood motionless in line with lances upright, their spearheads glittering in the sun and little blue pennants fluttering from the shafts. Horizon blue is as fitting for parade as for battle; it forms an indistinguishable mass, and while it lacks the gay rich note of the old red uniforms of French soldiers it gives a tone to the picture that is entirely lacking in the business-like drabness of the khaki. It must be over a mile to the Palace gate and on either side the troops stood in exact alignment.

Inside the grille of the Palace there were other regiments more gaily caparisoned, until finally the climax came at the main doorway. Here we found the Garde Républicaine, who are in France what the Life Guards are in England. Dismounted but in full regalia they reached in long lines from the doorway up the grand staircase to the Hall of Mirrors, where the Treaty was to be signed. There was something that reminded one of the days of the Grand Condé, who had been greeted by Louis XIV on this same stairway in that other victory over the Germans three centuries before. For these troops still wear the shining cuirass and the great crested helmet with its long black and red horsehair *crinière* and huge black riding boots with spurs. Step after step up the grand staircase they stood in double line with their swords at rest in front of them ready for salute. Draped on the walls behind were the flags of all the Allies, with the Tricolor to the fore, giving a richer glow than tapestry to the great gilded hall itself.

It was, as everyone knew, the moment for the *revanche* of France, to force Germany to sign its treaty of defeat at the very spot where Bismarck had had its triumph proclaimed in 1871. But Bismarck had chosen the spot for Germany's *revanche* for what it had suffered under Louis XIV. With these reminders of war and of a civilization so largely based on war, the one thing that seemed incongruous in the event ahead of us was not the humiliation of a conquered Power, for that was a commonplace in the past of Europe, but the fact that this Treaty proposed at last a way of escape from such a vicious circle.

The seats in the hall were all low, red-upholstered benches without backs, giving as clear a view as possible of the proceedings. The seat assigned to me was close to the front and over by the wall, so I stood during the ceremony itself against the embrasure of a window and saw everything close at hand. The Allied leaders came up the grand staircase through the central aisle of the hall escorted by military attendants to their seats behind the table where the signing was to take place. Then there was a pause and the hall grew absolutely still as the two German delegates were ushered in and given their places at the side of the table, more like men facing sentence at a trial than the representatives of a great Power at an act of sovereignty. They were both deathly pale and nervous, and the nervous tension grew while the Treaty received the signature of the Allied Powers. When finally came the turn for Dr. Bell and Herr Müller to sign, one of them found that the pen wouldn't work, and one of Colonel House's secretaries stepped over and pulled his fountain pen from his pocket and handed it to him, and I suppose has the pen as a souvenir still. No sooner had the Germans completed their signatures than immediately, as from some electric signal in the hall, the guns of St. Cyr on the southern slopes of Versailles began to boom the announcement to the world outside. Then, fort after fort on the hills around Paris, the heavy guns broke into a salute in a vast reverberating chorus. With a stiff bow, but not exchanging a word of greeting with anyone, the two Germans left the room by the same side door which had admitted them. It seemed to me an added and unnecessary humiliation, but perhaps it saved them from embarrassment.

The crowd then broke up into little groups, talking in a subdued way about the drama we had just witnessed. Everyone with whom I spoke was sorry for the Germans. The effect intended had miscarried.

Out on the terrace below, the crowd now came to life like a lawn party in the gay afternoon sunshine. The great fountains had started playing at the same moment that the guns had begun to boom. There were hundreds out there who had not been admitted to the ceremony but who could nevertheless tell their friends—and record for their descendants—that they had been invited to the Palace of Versailles for the signing of the Treaty that closed the World War.

I had no time to stay and look around, for I had to finish packing, have an early dinner, and catch the presidential train.

I never expect to leave any city again in such state. Red carpet reached down the stairway from the street and all the ugliness of the station was hidden by a forest of high palms. There were troops at salute and a band playing the national airs of France and America as President Wilson left Paris at the Gare du Luxembourg.

Sunday, June 29, 1919

The train was filled with dignitaries of all kinds, ambassadors and ministers and their attachés. At Brest the whole line of the railway for seven or eight miles was picketed with American troops. The ships in the harbor were all decked with flags, and as the "George Washington" left we were given the parting presidential salute from the guns of both forts and battleships. A French battleship and destroyer accompanied us until we left the shores of France behind. Then we put out to sea with two American destroyers on each side and the big battleship "Oklahoma" in front of us.

Thursday, July 4, 1919

For the first time in the history of the United States the President is spending the Fourth of July on the high seas. The navy had great plans for a unique celebration but failed to carry the President along with it. For days the wireless engineers on board have been planning and experimenting to see if they could have the President's address on board ship wirelessed from over a thousand miles at sea to the Navy Department at Washington for broadcasting or for listeners at telephone receivers. While they were testing the apparatus I listened in for the return signal from Washington; for the naval engineer in charge, an electrical specialist from Schenectady, was an old Columbia man and had looked me up to talk things over. As we heard the faint reply there was a sudden loud interference by a Morse code call. My friend was much annoyed, for he explained that the navy had the full use of the air during the hours of experiment and no one had a right to break in. A little later he hunted me up to tell me that the message was from R-34, the British airship,

President Wilson's Fourth of July address to the returning soldiers and sailors
on the "George Washington"

making its first trip across the Atlantic and at that moment putting out its first call for America from beyond Newfoundland.

They had rigged up a microphone in the middle of the rear gangway of the upper deck, which was to be the platform from which the President would speak to the several hundred doughboys swarming the covered hatches on the deck below and clambering up into the rigging. When the President saw the apparatus and discovered that he would be talking to the American people and not merely to the ship's company, he stepped over to the side, completely avoiding the microphone. I have never seen navy engineers nearer a state of mutiny than at that particular moment. While I had every sympathy with them over the failure of their long planned demonstration of the capacity of wireless, still I think the President was right, for if his voice had reached the land in anything like the broken and distorted whispers I heard on the trial message, the effect would have been anything but favorable.

Monday, July 8, 1919

I have not kept a diary on board ship for there is little to record. The President has kept more to his cabin than when going over, and from time to time calls in his advisers, especially those of the financial group. Apparently reparations continues to be the chief problem. I had a very strong letter to him from Colonel House about the job ahead of me in Washington, and yet it was not until today that the President sent for me. I had a good long talk with him alone in his study and we went over the whole Labor program together. I explained the points of difference and the final settlement and found him keen and interested, but I could see that he had never given the problems any serious consideration before, at least not on a par with the other parts of the Peace Treaty. He agreed with my plans and suggestions for getting things under way in Washington and told me to come and see him again about them there.

The voyage has been uneventful. We have been pounding away steadily on a tranquil summer sea, a quiet but dignified procession with the little destroyers on each side and the battleship leading about half a mile ahead. About eleven o'clock last night there was a slight fog and the battleship threw its powerful searchlights back across our path, lighting us up so that any approaching ship could easily see us. I never felt so fully the protecting arm of our convoy. It was a beautiful sight to see the powerful lights playing on the water in front. Nightly there were movies in the salon which the President and Mrs. Wilson generally attended. Most of them have been stupid films, but tonight, the last night at sea, we are to have war scenes on the American front.

Tuesday, July 9, 1919

Morning. We are coming in! We are still out of sight of land, but at breakfast time we heard the whir of airplanes and rushed up on deck to see half a dozen navy planes playing around us. It is very impressive to see these daring flyers out on the ocean this way; they look like enormous sea birds, dipping and rising, one of them even settling on the sea and then taking off from it with great clatter and splash. I can hear them as I write now, for I have come down to pack my things so as to be free to watch the rest of the display. The flags are out gaily at top-mast and our destroyers have released long ribbon-like streamers of bunting that fly out behind in the wind. We are now in a long file, two destroyers in front, then the battleship, then the "George Washington," then our other two destroyers. The sea is calm; sunlight shines on the white uniforms of the sailors; everyone has an expectant, happy look. Home again!

The navy has just come out in force to meet us—four big battleships in two lines and thirty destroyers. They have fired a salute and now have turned out in a long lane. There is an airship above us floating slowly along; a dozen airplanes are darting over the sea, all sparkling in the sunlight. The sailors are lining the decks, all of them in white. Flags are flying from every masthead; it is a royal scene. More airplanes, squadrons of them, the roar of their engines is constant. Land is in plain sight now on both sides. New York is ahead!

The Statue of Liberty; I shall never look at it again without recalling that magnificent phrase of Samuel Gompers: "Men do not know how safe a thing freedom is." To which I should add: "Nor the price that must be paid for permanent peace."

APPENDICES

THE HATCHET

The Largest Circulation On The Atlantic Ocean

Published On The High Seas

You Can Mail The Hatchet To The Folks Back Home

Vol. 9   Saturday, December 7, 1918   No. 3

MANY NOTABLES BESIDES PRESIDENT ON GEO. WASHINGTON

Cabinet Members - Diplomatists - Ambassadors - Army and Navy Officials

It is probable that not for five years has any group of such important personages entrusted their lives in any single vessel to the dangers of the deep as the representative assemblage who are undertaking this voyage.

Besides the leading figure in the eye of the present world and his staff are ambassadors to England and from France and Italy. Distinguished officials of the army and navy, well known publicists and specialists are also among those to be found on the decks of this ship.

That the larger reading public of The Hatchet may know of their identity, a much abbreviated list of the more distinguished passengers follows:

The President.

Mrs. Wilson.

The Honorable Robert Lansing, Secretary Of State.

Mrs Lansing.

The Honorable Henry White, Ex-Ambassador to France,

The Honorable John W. Davis, The American Ambassador to Great Britain.

The French Ambassador

and Mme. Jusserand.

The Italian Ambassador.

and Countess Macchi di Cellere.

Admiral Harry S. Knapp, U. S. N.

Rear Admiral Cary T. Grayson.

Captain Pratt, U. S. N.

Brigadier General Churchill.

Col. L. P. Ayers.

Mrs. W. S. Benson.

R. B. Fosdick.

Mr. George Creel.

PRESIDENT AT MOVIES ON THE HIGH SEAS

President and Mrs. Wilson headed the guests of honor attending last night's performance in the Martha Washington theatre. Both apparently enjoyed the entertainment very much. The stars of the occasion were Douglas Fairbanks and Charlie Chaplin.

Incidentally the work of the Mount Vernon Symphony Orchestra is a real feature of all the entertainments in this theatre. There are many professional organizations who could learn a good deal about music from them.

AIX-LA-CHAPELLE OCCUPIED

LONDON, Dec. 7.—Victorious troops have entered Aix-la-Chapelle and have compelled the Prussians to doff their hats and pay respect to the uniforms of the Belgians. They have laid down a martial law in a proclamation in almost identical language to that which the Germans used in Belgium. The inhabitants are ordered to remain indoors at night.

CHILE - PERU APPROACH WAR

LIMA, PERU, Dec. 7, — The situation growing out of the dispute between Chile and Peru is gradually becoming more tense. The Bolivian Consuls have taken over all Pervian interests in Chile and the entire Peruvian cabinet has resigned. M. Barreto has been commissioned to form a new cabinet. Meanwhile the preparations for war in both nations continue.

FRENCH PLAN DEMOBILIZATION

PARIS, Dec. 7. — Prem. Clemanceau will probably make an official announcement to the Chamber of Deputies on De emb.r 17th regarding the necessities of a prolonged armistice. He believes the demobilization of all soldiers in active service should be complete by April, the remainder to be mustered out as soon as peace is signed.

BUENOS AYRES, Dec. 7, — An earthquake has destroyed the town of Vallenar and partially destroyed Capiapo in Chile killing one hundred persons. In the devastated districts bodies of men women and children are still buried in the ruins. The shocks continued four minutes and the disturbance was unusually severe.

LLOYD GEORGE EXPLAINS CABINET POLICY ON PEACE

Punishment for Murders on Sea and Land - Indemnification - Land for Troops

By Radio to The Hatchet

LONDON, Dec. 7—Premier Lloyd George, in a political address today, lifted a part of the veil of secrecy that has surrounded the attitude of the British coalition government toward the coming peace conference. However the Premier continues significantly quiet regarding the proposed League of Nations with its accompanying general disarmament.

Summed up the British attitude on foreign matters as outlined in his address is as follows:

First—The Kaiser must be subjected to the doctrine of personal punishment for personal guilt.

Second—All responsible for the murders at sea and for the maltreatment of prisoners of war must be held answerable for their crimes.

Third—The Central Empires must pay the cost of the war and a joint commission will decide amounts and methods of payment.

Fourth—Government land must be given to soldiers and sailors and national resources must be developed to the utmost in conformity with a program of intensified industrial development.

The failure of the Premier to make Great Britain's position on what admittedly is the greatest problem that the peace conference must settle, establishment of the League of Nations to provide absolute and impartial international justice, has displeased the London newspapers. The Times, owned by Lord Northcliffe, in endorsing the League says it is the most important matter to be decided and declares that it should be so organized to insure justice, repress wrong doing and guarantee the sense of international security which alone can obviate the need of competing armaments. The British people are greatly in earnest regarding the League of Nations.

APPENDIX II

MEMORANDUM ON INTERNATIONAL LABOR LEGISLATION

(Prepared for the Press Saturday, January 18, 1919)

NOTE:—The following matter is issued for the confidential information of correspondents on the same terms as matter given out verbally at the Conferences and with the express understanding that they will not provide copies to unauthorized persons or attribute the facts included to any official of the Commission or government, who assume no responsibility therefor:—

INTERNATIONAL LABOR DEVELOPMENTS

The placing of "Legislation in regard to International Labor" among the questions on the Order of the Day for the first session of the Peace Conference throws this question into a position of prime importance in the world settlement now being framed. The great end in view is to prevent the destruction, in the difficult economic situation which is certain to follow the war, of the safeguards which have been painfully secured in recent years amongst the nations, and to incorporate in the peace treaty and as an essential purpose of the League of Nations the principle of regulation by international agreement of certain labor conditions which properly lend themselves thereto, including the protection of women and children in industry, the regulation of certain sanitary conditions, and in that relation the hours of labor.

It is felt that there can be no real political peace under the threat of an economic competition which might destroy the safeguards of labor. It is recognized, of course, that the demands for labor in the debt-crushed nations of Europe may very likely force a slackening of various national laws for the protection of workers and that once this process begins in one country it is apt to spread throughout all competing nations. Not only are the claims of labor as such distinctly recognized but it is felt that such recognition is one of the most practical and solid foundation-stones for the League of Nations.

This point of view finds support in the recent development of international labor protection, in the tremendous increase in power and unity of purpose of labor during the war, and in the traditions and machinery already existing to this end. Not only is there a realization such as has never before existed of the economic interdependence of the various nations and their responsibility one to the other for satisfactory labor conditions throughout, but there is at hand in the various national labor organizations and in the International Association for Labor Protection, a semi-official body composed of delegates from similar national bodies, the elements of a good working machinery which might be taken over by the League of Nations as the basis of its labor bureau.

The conception of international protection for labor is not new. It first entered European diplomacy in Switzerland in 1876, obtained support in the Congress for the Protection of Labor at Zurich in 1897, the Conference of Berlin in 1890, and the Congress of Paris during the Exposition of 1900, and took concrete and permanent form with the foundation of the International Union for the Legal Protection of Labor in 1901. Out of this came the first international stipulation for the protection of labor, the Fontaine-Luzzatti agreement of April 15, 1904, by which France agreed to protect the Italian laborer who moved to France against any abridgement of his title to accident compensation and to interfere to prevent abuses of child labor, while Italy agreed to meet the complaints of French industry as to the alleged faulty enforcement of Italian labor laws by introducing an effective system of inspection, and both agreed to future conferences to consider questions of standardization of labor legislation.

This agreement, followed shortly by the British elections of 1906 which brought the labor party strongly to the fore, created a strong moral pressure for international labor protection which formed a good background for the Berne international labor Conventions of September 26, 1906. These conventions condemned the employment of yellow phosphorus in the match industry, which as a result has since been prohibited in all considerable producing nations except one, and urged a nightly rest of 11 hours for women in industry, which also has since been generally obtained.

At the Berne conference of September 1913, attended by all the large European nations, two main projects for international agreement were recommended to the governments, the prohibition of all industrial night labor for persons under 16 and the establishment of a minimum ten-hour day for women without distinction of age and for males under 16. The attempt to set the age limit at 18 failed because of the great increase which would have been created in the difficulty of securing a supply of labor which already in several states had led to an undesirable influx of foreigners.

The war broke off this form of international co-operation but gave birth to the new form which is culminating in the present situation at the Peace Conference. Whereas the conference which was to have been held in September 1914 to prepare the third and fourth Berne meetings had to be called off, the demand grew in many quarters for a Labor Congress to be held at the same time and place as the Peace Conference. This was formally suggested by the American Federation of Labor and accepted by the British, French, Italian, and Belgian labor organizations on May 1, 1916, when M. Jouhaux, Secretary of the Confédération Générale du Travail was commissioned to prepare the agenda for a Congress to be held in Leeds in July.

The Leeds Conference, at the suggestion of the British delegates, came to the decision that if the labor Congress were to be held simultaneously with the Peace Conference, its conclusions would be framed too late to be of assistance. Consequently the calling of the Congress before the Peace Conference was agreed upon and the report of M. Jouhaux concerning the minimum demands of labor accepted.

This Leeds program, distributed broadcast through the labor press, declared "that the peace treaty which brings to an end the present war and secures the political and economic liberty and independence of the peoples should likewise assure to the working classes of every country, free from international capitalistic competition, a minimum of moral and material guarantees relative to the right of employment, the right of labor organization, change of residence, social insurance, and the duration, hygienic conditions and security of labor." It urged freedom to work in any country where employment was available and under equal conditions with its nationals, the institution in all countries of sickness, accident, unemployment, and old-age insurance, prohibition of child labor under 14 years, prohibition of night work to women and to adolescents under 18, broadening of legislation to assure the health and safety of workers, especially in unhealthy or dangerous industries, and the creation of both national and international bodies to study, codify and interpret labor statistics, laws, and tendencies.

This program was communicated to the International Gewerkschaftsbund by the Scandinavian Trades Union Organizations in November 1916 and in the following February the latter invited the former to meet with it to consider the problems involved. As a result the labor organizations of Germany, Austria, Hungary, Bohemia, Bulgaria, Denmark, Norway, Sweden, the Netherlands, and Switzerland met at Berne on October 1, 1917, and approved the Leeds program, thus assuring agreement by Allied, Central Empire and neutral labor organizations on the labor policies to be pressed before the Peace Conference.

Shortly after, on November 12–24, the American Federation of Labor at Buffalo, at its 37th annual convention, where President Wilson said: "While we are fighting for freedom, we must see among other things that labor is free," voted the following proposals for incorporation in the world peace treaty: that no article of commerce shall be transported or delivered in international trade in the manufacture of which children less than sixteen years of age were employed; the basic eight-hour day shall not be exceeded in commerce and industry; compulsory labor shall be imposed only as punishment for crime; and general introduction of trial by jury.

Within the past few weeks the French Chamber of Deputies has drawn up and adopted a plan for international labor protection at the Peace Conference. The report of its commission, prepared by Deputy Justin Godart, was based upon the interrupted, pre-war Berne conferences amplified by the Leeds Conference. The Chamber, in accepting it with little modification, went on record as the supreme French legislative body in favor of international protection of labor, a subject of especial importance to France in view of the eventualities in Germany.

Meanwhile the British were also taking action. The British Labor Party, in its long and detailed analysis of War Aims, urged "the need for an international agreement for the enforcement in all countries of the legislation on factory conditions, hours of labor, and the prevention of sweating and unhealthy trades necessary to protect the workers against exploitation and oppression." Similarly British plans for the League of Nations seem to contemplate establishing an international labor council as a broad humanitarian measure of prime importance in the League of Nations plan.

Some confusion has arisen as to the connection between these labor programs and the various socialist congresses, especially the International Socialist Conference scheduled for Berne. It should be pointed out that the labor plans discussed above contemplate only specific labor problems and are confined to remedial humanitarian legislation without regard to the existing social and economic order. The Socialist conferences, however, include not only these specific labor problems, but look forward also to the socializing of the state.

APPENDIX III

THE CONSTITUTION OF THE INTERNATIONAL LABOR ORGANIZATION

PART XIII OF THE TREATY OF VERSAILLES

LABOUR

SECTION I

ORGANISATION OF LABOUR

Preamble

Whereas the League of Nations has for its object the establishment of universal peace, and such a peace can be established only if it is based upon social justice;

And whereas conditions of labour exist involving such injustice, hardship, and privation to large numbers of people as to produce unrest so great that the peace and harmony of the world are imperilled; and an improvement of those conditions is urgently required: as, for example, by the regulation of the hours of work, including the establishment of a maximum working day and week, the regulation of the labour supply, the prevention of unemployment, the provision of an adequate living wage, the protection of the worker against sickness, disease and injury arising out of his employment, the protection of children, young persons and women, provision for old age and injury, protection of the interests of workers when employed in countries other than their own, recognition of the principle of freedom of association, the organisation of vocational and technical education and other measures;

Whereas also the failure of any nation to adopt humane conditions of labour is an obstacle in the way of other nations which desire to improve the conditions of their own countries;

The HIGH CONTRACTING PARTIES, moved by sentiments of justice and humanity as well as by the desire to secure the permanent peace of the world, agree to the following:

393

Chapter I

ORGANISATION

Article 387

A permanent organisation is hereby established for the promotion of the objects set forth in the Preamble.

The original Members of the League of Nations shall be the original Members of this organisation, and hereafter membership of the League of Nations shall carry with it membership of the said organisation.

Article 388

The permanent organisation shall consist of:

(1) a General Conference of Representatives of the Members and,

(2) an International Labour Office controlled by the Governing Body described in Article 393.

Article 389

The meetings of the General Conference of Representatives of the Members shall be held from time to time as occasion may require, and at least once in every year. It shall be composed of four Representatives of each of the Members, of whom two shall be Government Delegates and the two others shall be Delegates representing respectively the employers and the workpeople of each of the Members.

Each Delegate may be accompanied by advisers, who shall not exceed two in number for each item on the agenda of the meeting. When questions specially affecting women are to be considered by the Conference, one at least of the advisers should be a woman.

The members undertake to nominate non-Government Delegates and advisers chosen in agreement with the industrial organisations, if such organisations exist, which are most representative of employers or workpeople, as the case may be, in their respective countries.

Advisers shall not speak except on a request made by the Delegate whom they accompany and by the special authorisation of the President of the Conference, and may not vote.

A Delegate may by notice in writing addressed to the President appoint one of his advisers to act as his deputy, and the adviser, while so acting, shall be allowed to speak and vote.

The names of the Delegates and their advisers will be communicated to the International Labour Office by the Government of each of the Members.

The credentials of Delegates and their advisers shall be subject to scrutiny by the Conference, which may, by two-thirds of the votes cast by the Delegates present, refuse to admit any Delegate or adviser whom it deems not to have been nominated in accordance with this Article.

Article 390

Every Delegate shall be entitled to vote individually on all matters which are taken into consideration by the Conference.

If one of the Members fails to nominate one of the non-Government Delegates whom it is entitled to nominate, the other non-Government Delegate shall be allowed to sit and speak at the Conference, but not to vote.

If in accordance with Article 389 the Conference refuses admission to a Delegate of one of the Members, the provisions of the present Article shall apply as if that Delegate had not been nominated.

Article 391

The meetings of the Conference shall be held at the seat of the League of Nations, or at such other place as may be decided by the Conference at a previous meeting by two-thirds of the votes cast by the Delegates present.

Article 392

The International Labour Office shall be established at the seat of the League of Nations as part of the organisation of the League.

Article 393

The International Labour Office shall be under the control of a Governing Body consisting of twenty-four persons, appointed in accordance with the following provisions:

The Governing Body of the International Labour Office shall be constituted as follows:

Twelve persons representing the Governments;

Six persons elected by the Delegates to the Conference representing the employers;

Six persons elected by the Delegates to the Conference representing the workers.

Of the twelve persons representing the Governments eight shall be nominated by the Members which are of the chief industrial importance, and four shall be nominated by the Members selected for the purpose by the Government Delegates to the Conference, excluding the Delegates of the eight Members mentioned above.

Any question as to which are the Members of the chief industrial importance shall be decided by the Council of the League of Nations.

The period of office of the members of the Governing Body will be three years. The method of filling vacancies and other similar questions may be determined by the Governing Body subject to the approval of the Conference.

The Governing Body shall, from time to time, elect one of its members to act as its Chairman, shall regulate its own procedure and shall fix its own times of meeting. A special meeting shall be held if a written request to that effect is made by at least ten members of the Governing Body.

Article 394

There shall be a Director of the International Labour Office, who shall be appointed by the Governing Body, and, subject to the instructions of the Governing Body, shall be responsible for the efficient conduct of the International Labour Office and for such other duties as may be assigned to him.

The Director or his deputy shall attend all meetings of the Governing Body.

Article 395

The staff of the International Labour Office shall be appointed by the Director who shall, so far as is possible with due regard to the efficiency of the work of the Office, select persons of different nationalities. A certain number of these persons shall be women.

Article 396

The functions of the International Labour Office shall include the collection and distribution of information on all subjects relating to the international adjustment of conditions of industrial life and labour, and particularly the examination of subjects which it is proposed to bring before the Conference with a view to the conclusion of international conventions, and the conduct of such special investigations as may be ordered by the Conference.

It will prepare the agenda for the meetings of the Conference.

It will carry out the duties required of it by the provisions of this Part of the present Treaty in connection with international disputes.

It will edit and publish in French and English, and in such other languages as the Governing Body may think desirable, a periodical paper dealing with problems of industry and employment of international interest.

Generally, in addition to the functions set out in this Article, it shall have such other powers and duties as may be assigned to it by the Conference.

Article 397

The Government Departments of any of the Members which deal with questions of industry and employment may communicate directly with the Director through the Representative of their Government on the Governing Body of the International Labour Office, or failing any such Representative, through such other qualified official as the Government may nominate for the purpose.

Article 398

The International Labour Office shall be entitled to the assistance of the Secretary-General of the League of Nations in any matter in which it can be given.

Article 399

Each of the Members will pay the travelling and subsistence expenses of its Delegates and their advisers and of its Representatives attending the meetings of the Conference or Governing Body, as the case may be.

All the other expenses of the International Labour Office and of the meetings of the Conference or Governing Body shall be paid to the Director by the Secretary-General of the League of Nations out of the general funds of the League.

The Director shall be responsible to the Secretary-General of the League for the proper expenditure of all moneys paid to him in pursuance of this Article.

CHAPTER II

PROCEDURE

Article 400

The agenda for all meetings of the Conference will be settled by the Governing Body, who shall consider any suggestion as to the agenda that may be made by the Government of any of the Members or by any representative organisation recognised for the purpose of Article 389.

Article 401

The Director shall act as the Secretary of the Conference, and shall transmit the agenda so as to reach the Members four months before the meeting of the Conference, and, through them, the non-Government Delegates when appointed.

Article 402

Any of the Governments of the Members may formally object to the inclusion of any item or items in the agenda. The grounds for such objection shall be set forth in a reasoned statement addressed to the Director, who shall circulate it to all the Members of the Permanent Organisation.

Items to which such objection has been made shall not, however, be excluded from the agenda, if at the Conference a majority of two-thirds of the votes cast by the Delegates present is in favour of considering them.

If the Conference decides (otherwise than under the preceding paragraph) by two-thirds of the votes cast by the Delegates present that any subject shall be considered by the Conference, that subject shall be included in the agenda for the following meeting.

Article 403

The Conference shall regulate its own procedure, shall elect its own President, and may appoint committees to consider and report on any matter.

Except as otherwise expressly provided in this Part of the present Treaty, all matters shall be decided by a simple majority of the votes cast by the Delegates present.

The voting is void unless the total number of votes cast is equal to half the number of the Delegates attending the Conference.

Article 404

The Conference may add to any committees which it appoints technical experts, who shall be assessors without power to vote.

Article 405

When the Conference has decided on the adoption of proposals with regard to an item in the agenda, it will rest with the Conference to determine whether these proposals should take the form: (*a*) of a recommendation to be submitted to the Members for consideration with a view to effect being given to it by national legislation or otherwise, or (*b*) of a draft international convention for ratification by the Members.

In either case a majority of two-thirds of the votes cast by the Delegates present shall be necessary on the final vote for the adoption of the recommendation or draft convention, as the case may be, by the Conference.

In framing any recommendation or draft convention of general application the Conference shall have due regard to those countries in which climatic conditions, the imperfect development of industrial organisation or other special circumstances make the industrial conditions substantially different and shall suggest the modifications, if any, which it considers may be required to meet the case of such countries.

A copy of the recommendation or draft convention shall be authenticated by the signature of the President of the Conference and of the Director and shall be deposited with the Secretary-General of the League of Nations. The Secretary-General will communicate a certified copy of the recommendation or draft convention to each of the Members.

Each of the Members undertakes that it will, within the period of one year at most from the closing of the session of the Conference, or if it is impossible owing to exceptional circumstances to do so within the period of one year, then at the earliest practicable moment and in no case later than eighteen months from the closing of the session of the Conference, bring the recommendation or draft convention before the authority or authorities within whose competence the matter lies, for the enactment of legislation or other action.

In the case of a recommendation, the Members will inform the Secretary-General of the action taken.

In the case of a draft convention, the Member will, if it obtains the consent of the authority or authorities within whose competence the matter lies, communicate the formal ratification of the convention to the Secretary-General and will take such action as may be necessary to make effective the provisions of such convention.

If on a recommendation no legislative or other action is taken to make a recommendation effective, or if the draft convention fails to obtain the consent of the authority or authorities within whose competence the matter lies, no further obligation shall rest upon the Member.

In the case of a federal State, the power of which to enter into conventions on labour matters is subject to limitations, it shall be in the discretion of that Government to treat a draft convention to which such limitations apply as a recommendation only, and the provisions of this Article with respect to recommendations shall apply in such case.

The above Article shall be interpreted in accordance with the following principle:

In no case shall any Member be asked or required, as a result of the adoption of any recommendation or draft convention by the Conference, to lessen the protection afforded by its existing legislation to the workers concerned.

Article 406

Any convention so ratified shall be registered by the Secretary-General of the League of Nations, but shall only be binding upon the Members which ratify it.

Article 407

If any convention coming before the Conference for final consideration fails to secure the support of two-thirds of the votes cast by the Delegates present, it shall nevertheless be within the right of any of the Members of the Permanent Organisation to agree to such convention among themselves.

Any convention so agreed to shall be communicated by the Governments concerned to the Secretary-General of the League of Nations, who shall register it.

Article 408

Each of the Members agrees to make an annual report to the International Labour Office on the measures which it has taken to give effect to the provisions of conventions to which it is a party. These reports shall be made in such form and shall contain such particulars as the Governing Body may request. The Director shall lay a summary of these reports before the next meeting of the Conference.

Article 409

In the event of any representation being made to the International Labour Office by an industrial association of employers or of workers that any of the Members has failed to secure in any respect the effective observance within its jurisdiction of any convention to which it is a party, the Governing Body may communicate this representation to the Government against which it is made and may invite that Government to make such statement on the subject as it may think fit.

Article 410

If no statement is received within a reasonable time from the Government in question, or if the statement when received is not deemed to be satisfactory by the Governing Body, the latter shall have the right to publish the representation and the statement, if any, made in reply to it.

Article 411

Any of the Members shall have the right to file a complaint with the International Labour Office if it is not satisfied that any other Member is securing the effective observance of any convention which both have ratified in accordance with the foregoing Articles.

The Governing Body may, if it thinks fit, before referring such a complaint to a Commission of Enquiry, as hereinafter provided for, communicate with the Government in question in the manner described in Article 409.

If the Governing Body does not think it necessary to communicate the complaint to the Government in question, or if, when they have made such communication, no statement in reply has been received within a reasonable time which the Governing Body considers to be satisfactory, the Governing Body may apply for the appointment of a Commission of Enquiry to consider the complaint and to report thereon.

The Governing Body may adopt the same procedure either of its own motion or on receipt of a complaint from a Delegate to the Conference.

When any matter arising out of Articles 410 or 411 is being considered by the Governing Body, the Government in question shall, if not already represented thereon, be entitled to send a representative to take part in the proceedings of the Governing Body while the matter is under consideration. Adequate notice of the date on which the matter will be considered shall be given to the Government in question.

Article 412

The Commission of Enquiry shall be constituted in accordance with the following provisions:

Each of the Members agrees to nominate within six months of the date on which the present Treaty comes into force three persons of industrial experience, of whom one shall be a representative of employers, one a representative of workers, and one a person of independent standing, who shall together form a panel from which the members of the Commission of Enquiry shall be drawn.

The qualifications of the persons so nominated shall be subject to scrutiny by the Governing Body, which may by two-thirds of the votes cast by the representatives present refuse to accept the nomination of any person whose qualifications do not in its opinion comply with the requirements of the present Article.

Upon the application of the Governing Body, the Secretary-General of the League of Nations shall nominate three persons, one from each section of this panel, to constitute the Commission of Enquiry, and shall designate one of them as the President of the Commission. None of these three persons shall be a person nominated to the panel by any Member directly concerned in the complaint.

Article 413

The Members agree that, in the event of the reference of a complaint to a Commission of Enquiry under Article 411, they will each, whether directly concerned in the complaint or not, place at the disposal of the Commission all the information in their possession which bears upon the subject-matter of the complaint.

Article 414

When the Commission of Enquiry has fully considered the complaint, it shall prepare a report embodying its findings on all questions of fact relevant to determining the issue between the parties and containing such recommendations as it may think proper as to the steps which should be taken to meet the complaint and the time within which they should be taken.

It shall also indicate in this report the measures, if any, of an economic character against a defaulting Government which it considers to be appropriate, and which it considers other Governments would be justified in adopting.

Article 415

The Secretary-General of the League of Nations shall communicate the report of the Commission of Enquiry to each of the Governments concerned in the complaint, and shall cause it to be published.

Each of these Governments shall within one month inform the Secretary-General of the League of Nations whether or not it accepts the recommendations contained in the report of the Commission; and if not, whether it proposes to refer the complaint to the Permanent Court of International Justice of the League of Nations.

Article 416

In the event of any Member failing to take the action required by Article 405, with regard to a recommendation or draft convention, any other Member shall be entitled to refer the matter to the Permanent Court of International Justice.

Article 417

The decision of the Permanent Court of International Justice in regard to a complaint or matter which has been referred to it in pursuance of Article 415 or Article 416 shall be final.

Article 418

The Permanent Court of International Justice may affirm, vary or reverse any of the findings or recommendations of the Commission of Enquiry, if any, and shall in its decision indicate the measures, if any, of an economic character which it considers to be appropriate, and which other Governments would be justified in adopting against a defaulting Government.

Article 419

In the event of any Member failing to carry out within the time specified the recommendations, if any, contained in the report of the Commission of Enquiry, or in the decision of the Permanent Court of International Justice, as the case may be, any other Member may take against that Member the measures of an economic character indicated in the report of the Commission or in the decision of the Court as appropriate to the case.

Article 420

The defaulting Government may at any time inform the Governing Body that it has taken the steps necessary to comply with the recommendations of the Commission of Enquiry or with those in the decision of the Permanent Court of International Justice, as the case may be, and may request it to apply to the Secretary-General of the League to constitute a Commission of Enquiry to verify its contention. In this case the provisions of Articles 412, 413, 414, 415, 417 and 418 shall apply, and if the report of the Commission of Enquiry or the decision of the Permanent Court of International Justice is in favour of the defaulting Government, the other Governments shall forthwith discontinue the measures of an economic character that they have taken against the defaulting Government.

CHAPTER III

GENERAL PRESCRIPTIONS

Article 421

The Members engage to apply conventions which they have ratified in accordance with the provisions of this Part of the present Treaty to their colonies, protectorates and possessions which are not fully self-governing:

(1) Except where owing to the local conditions the convention is inapplicable, or

(2) Subject to such modifications as may be necessary to adapt the convention to local conditions.

And each of the Members shall notify to the International Labour Office the action taken in respect of each of its colonies, protectorates and possessions which are not fully self-governing.

Article 422

Amendments to this Part of the present Treaty which are adopted by the Conference by a majority of two-thirds of the votes cast by the Delegates present shall take effect when ratified by the States whose representatives compose the Council of the League of Nations and by three-fourths of the Members.

Article 423

Any question or dispute relating to the interpretation of this Part of the present Treaty or of any subsequent convention concluded by the Members in pursuance of the provisions of this Part of the present Treaty shall be referred for decision to the Permanent Court of International Justice.

CHAPTER IV

TRANSITORY PROVISIONS

Article 424

The first meeting of the Conference shall take place in October, 1919. The place and agenda for this meeting shall be as specified in the Annex hereto.

Arrangements for the convening and the organisation of the first meeting of the Conference will be made by the Government designated for the purpose in the said Annex. That Government shall be assisted in the preparation of the documents for submission to the Conference by an International Committee constituted as provided in the said Annex.

The expenses of the first meeting and of all subsequent meetings held before the League of Nations has been able to establish a general fund, other than the expenses of Delegates and their advisers, will be borne by the Members in accordance with the apportionment of the expenses of the International Bureau of the Universal Postal Union.

Article 425

Until the League of Nations has been constituted all communications which under the provisions of the foregoing Articles should be addressed to the Secretary-General of the League will be preserved by the Director of the International Labour Office, who will transmit them to the Secretary-General of the League.

Article 426

Pending the creation of a Permanent Court of International Justice, disputes which in accordance with this Part of the present Treaty would be submitted to it for decision will be referred to a tribunal of three persons appointed by the Council of the League of Nations.

ANNEX

FIRST MEETING OF ANNUAL LABOUR CONFERENCE, 1919

The place of meeting will be Washington.

The Government of the United States of America is requested to convene the Conference.

The International Organising Committee will consist of seven members, appointed by the United States of America, Great Britain, France, Italy, Japan, Belgium and Switzerland. The Committee may, if it thinks necessary, invite other Members to appoint representatives.

Agenda:

(1) Application of principle of the 8-hours day or of the 48-hours week.

(2) Question of preventing or providing against unemployment.

(3) Women's employment:

    (*a*) Before and after child-birth, including the question of maternity benefit;

    (*b*) During the night;

    (*c*) In unhealthy processes.

(4) Employment of children:

    (*a*) Minimum age of employment;

    (*b*) During the night;

    (*c*) In unhealthy processes.

(5) Extension and application of the International Conventions adopted at Berne in 1906 on the prohibition of night work for women employed in industry and the prohibition of the use of white phosphorus in the manufacture of matches.

Section II

GENERAL PRINCIPLES

Article 427

The High Contracting Parties, recognising that the well-being, physical, moral and intellectual, of industrial wage-earners is of supreme international importance, have framed, in order to further this great end, the permanent machinery provided for in Section I and associated with that of the League of Nations.

They recognise that differences of climate, habits, and customs, of economic opportunity and industrial tradition, make strict uniformity in the conditions of labour difficult of immediate attainment. But, holding as they do, that labour should not be regarded merely as an article of commerce, they think that there are methods and principles for regulating labour conditions which all industrial communities should endeavour to apply, so far as their special circumstances will permit.

Among these methods and principles, the following seem to the High Contracting Parties to be of special and urgent importance:

First.—The guiding principle above enunciated that labour should not be regarded merely as a commodity or article of commerce.

Second.—The right of association for all lawful purposes by the employed as well as by the employers.

Third.—The payment to the employed of a wage adequate to maintain a reasonable standard of life as this is understood in their time and country.

Fourth.—The adoption of an eight hours day or a forty-eight hours week as the standard to be aimed at where it has not already been attained.

Fifth.—The adoption of a weekly rest of at least twenty-four hours, which should include Sunday wherever practicable.

Sixth.—The abolition of child labour and the imposition of such limitations on the labour of young persons as shall permit the continuation of their education and assure their proper physical development.

Seventh.—The principle that men and women should receive equal remuneration for work of equal value.

Eighth.—The standard set by law in each country with respect to the conditions of labour should have due regard to the equitable economic treatment of all workers lawfully resident therein.

Ninth.—Each State should make provision for a system of inspection in which women should take part, in order to ensure the enforcement of the laws and regulations for the protection of the employed.

Without claiming that these methods and principles are either complete or final, the High Contracting Parties are of opinion that they are well fitted to guide the policy of the League of Nations; and that, if adopted by the industrial communities who are members of the League, and safeguarded in practice by an adequate system of such inspection, they will confer lasting benefits upon the wage-earners of the world.

APPENDIX IV

DIFFICULTIES IN TREATY–MAKING [1]

The Treaty of Paris may be either worse or better than what people think about it now. It is hardly ever possible to anticipate the judgments of history, but one thing is certain—that just as the War which it brings to a close was the most difficult of all the wars that have ever been fought, so the Treaty of Paris is the most difficult of Treaties that has ever been made.

The Treaty has about 80,000 words and over 400 Articles. It deals with almost every kind of problem in international affairs. About a thousand specialists drawn from all parts of the world worked at it, and they were not all there to help—some were there to block it, most were there to change it from whatever else it might have been. There is hardly a clause in the whole long document that has not been the object of controversy and debate. It is difficult now when looking at the clauses as a whole to realize how many other alternatives were examined and discarded before the final wording was agreed upon.

It is especially the difficulties of detail which are likely to escape attention; yet the Treaty is a mass of details. Principles may be agreed upon but they can seldom be applied without conflicting with other principles which in themselves have perhaps an equal claim to consideration. And yet, a single decision must be reached and a single formula must be found which will embody that decision.

In this finding of formula a single instance may furnish an indication of the final difficulties even after general plans have been agreed upon. Article 409 deals with the problem of erecting an International Labor Office with a right of supervision over the carrying out of International Labor Legislation. It states that a Governing Body *"may* communicate" the criticisms concerning Labor Legislation to the government involved, "and *may* invite that government to make such statement on the subject as it thinks fit." The question arose whether the verb "may" was strong enough, and "shall" was suggested as a substitute. Between the two verbs "may" and "shall" lie whole worlds of discussion, and back of them the

[1] See June 11. This article appeared in *The Independent* on August 2, 1919, under the journalistic caption, " 'Shall' or 'May': How We Handled Verbal Dynamite in Making the Peace Treaty."

accumulated forces of national histories, institutions and interests of the industrial nations of the world. Representatives of some of the nations at the Conference felt that the Governing Body of the International Labor Office should not be a mere agency for registering pious resolutions. On the other hand, representatives of other governments felt that if "shall" were used it might be interpreted as giving power to send impertinent notes to the governments of the world, or else, on the other hand, would lessen the discretion of the Governing Body by forcing it to subscribe to complaints with which it would be unwise to be identified.

There is many a point in the Treaty in which a single word contains the explosive power of these divergent principles of "shall" and "may." It is hardly too much to say that there are hundreds of instances where the choice of words opens up as many possibilities as this. Indeed, the art of drafting is only second in importance to the determination of the principles themselves.

Take another instance from the same general section of the Treaty: In Article 405, which was formerly Article 19 of the International Labor Proposals, a paragraph is inserted stating that in the framing of International Labor Legislation "the Conference shall have due regard to those countries in which climatic conditions, the imperfect development of industrial organization, or other special circumstances make the industrial conditions substantially different." It was, to say the least, somewhat difficult to suggest to the State which particularly profited by this clause (Japan) that its industrial organization was below the standards of the great European powers—yet the admission had to be secured in order to include the exception in a way satisfactory to the more advanced nations.

Still another instance: That same important Article has another clause which refers almost by name to the United States—"In the case of a federal State, the power of which to enter into conventions on labor matters is subject to limitations, it shall be in the discretion of that government to treat a draft convention . . . as a recommendation only." This sentence proved to be a formula to which the other nations could not take exception, for in noting the privileged position of the United States it did so by simply describing its government. In the earlier stages of the drafting the exception was stated in an adverbial rather than an adjectival form and other nations objected to its inclusion.

These are simple instances of the difficulties of finding a satisfactory expression to items upon which there could in the last instance be little disagreement, and they illustrate the difficulties of reaching a statement even where the points at issue were relatively beyond dispute.

When one turns from this set of difficulties to the subject-matter itself we reach at once a set of most interesting and difficult problems. In the first place there is the question of boundary making. Under the spell of the map most people think of boundaries as something almost as real as the rivers, mountains or seas along which they may run, with some one definite principle determining them, almost like a law of nature. This is true, perhaps, of districts like Alsace-Lorraine; but from the Rhine east there is hardly a single boundary which can be drawn that does not do violation to some important principle to which from one angle or another the Conference was pledged.

The new nations in the east of Europe unfortunately do not live on different sides of any clearly defined line. They fringe out into each other over a wide borderland through which it is possible to draw several lines each one of which would have a distinct justification. Still harder is the problem of dealing with islands of people set in the midst of other races.

The City of Lemberg is solid Polish, but is surrounded by Ruthenians who form the majority of the country population of that part of Galicia. Add to this fact the further complication that many of the Poles are Jewish, while on the other hand much of the land in the country of the Ruthenians is owned by Polish nobles. The people themselves cannot decide the question and are at war. What is to be done?

Take again the case of Greece. The real center of Greek civilization is the Aegean Sea with a fringe of Greek settlements all around it. Shall one consider that here we have a new form of state essentially maritime with its frontiers fringing the land rather than the sea? Most states run their frontiers from the land to the sea. This would reverse the process. The Greeks, as traders, may claim the ports along the Aegean as definitely as the American may claim the outlets for his railroads and compare the water rights of the Aegean to the overland rights of a continental country. It is a new point of view in political theory, but not without a good deal of weight. Shall one, therefore, consider the Aegean civilization as a unit and turn over to it the ports which are claimed as essential to its trade? Or shall one regard the hinterland as of more importance since they may claim that the Greeks shut them off from their own natural outlets to the sea? One thing is clear—whichever way one decides, one is both right and wrong.

Boundary making on the basis of statistics of population is difficult enough in itself, but is doubly difficult when measured up against the claims of culture and of history. It is possible for a small section of the population to give the tone culturally to the whole and to dominate the country politically. The Italians, for instance, claim that they have the cultural domination in the Adriatic, and visitors to the Dalmatian Coast are struck with the outer marks, at least, of this old Venetian quality of the maritime towns—while the Czechoslovaks claim that the steady pressure of racial movement offers a dynamic counterclaim less visible but more powerful. Magyars admit the statistical claims of Rumanians in Transylvania and of Slovaks in Slovakia, but cherish the proud memory of centuries of domination among these people since the Turks were driven out. Should one count heads and decide upon the basis of population, the result might lead to a distinct decline in the standards of civilization.

Again, the sentimental claims of history are often just as real as the demands of nationality. The fact that Upper Silesia had never belonged to Poland since the rise of modern states is as real a fact in its way as the national history of Bohemia. The century-long submission of the Slovenes to the Hapsburgs makes difficult a correct reading of plebiscites in that section of the new kingdom of the Serbs, Croats and Slovenes. In planning for the future one cannot ignore the bearing of these historic factors in the erection of new states.

From more than one point of view there could be no settlement of these problems that was not wrong, and when one adds to racial claims the legitimate demands of economics, the need for provisions for transit and for markets, the rival claims for territories with supplies of raw material, the geographical and strategical elements in boundaries that would overrun cross-country railroad lines, and a dozen other considerations varying with each new boundary, one realizes that the decisions of the Paris Peace Conference, no matter what they were, would leave the door open to further controversy.

It is quite possible, of course, that the actual boundaries drawn in the Treaty are open to objection, but it should be remembered that no boundaries can be drawn which will meet the approval of all parties concerned. This being the case, it would surely be well for liberal minded people the world over to concentrate a little less upon the map itself and more upon the international policies of the new States which have been erected.

The question of policies is of course even more difficult than that of boundary making. The one fact which stands out from history and geography as well as from a study of the present situation is, that the whole Danube Valley is intrinsically one and that the erection of new states with intensified national feelings along that great international waterway may result in retrogression rather than in progress, unless some means is found to unite them to some degree in common policies. Their boundaries must not be rigid barriers to trade or they will mutually suffer, and yet the one great solvent for their difficulties is impossible— namely, Free Trade. Even a Zollverein or Customs Union is perhaps beyond the limits of immediate possibility. How can they be brought together, suffering still, as they do, from the antagonisms of the War, to face the future constructively and in a co-operative spirit? Obviously, the

League of Nations cannot go too far in assuming the supervision of this relatively incoherent mass of peoples. It is in no position to succeed at a single step to an enlarged Hapsburg Monarchy. And yet, the constructive scheme proposed must be elastic enough to include these possibilities, or at least suggest ways for meeting them in the future.

It is this question of elasticity which is the most difficult to appraise. If the international agreements of the Conference of Paris were to be made rigid it would seem as though much more were accomplished than to leave them frankly incomplete, but carried along as far as is possible now and fixed so they can be adjusted to changing conditions.

The only institutions which last are living institutions; and the very condition of living is change. It was the problem of constructive statesmanship at the Peace Conference to set going rather than to set up understandings, so that they would keep pace with changing events and secure the future as well as the present. Two parts of the Treaty dealt specially with this constructive planning, the one dealing with the League of Nations and the other with International Labor. In both these sections two schools of thought soon showed themselves even among the most ardent supporters of the general plan. On the one hand there were those who wanted to see something like a Super-State erected to which governments would abdicate some portion of their sovereignty. On the other hand, there were those who felt that true international action lay as much with the governments of the different States as through the congresses which they should set up, and that it was a grave mistake to lessen the authority and prestige of governments even in co-operative enterprises. Upon the whole, the latter view prevailed. The international arrangements in the Treaty are not of a kind to weaken governmental control, but continue to use governments as national organs in the international community. The national line-up on these questions was of great interest. The Continental European Powers feel that in spite of the War which has so divided them, there remains a need for a Continental community of nations. Stimulated by the radical thought, and particularly by certain sections of the syndicalists and socialists, they are prepared to enter into a closer league with closer international guarantees and sanctions than the non-Continental Powers could entertain. In questions, for instance, of International Labor Legislation it must not be forgotten that an almost imaginary line ran through the great industrial regions at the north of France setting over some communities into Belgium and some into France, and that different Labor laws will affect the output of these two communities so that they feel obliged to come to an international agreement. The case is far different with the British or the American employers and workmen.

One of the most difficult problems to solve, however, in the League of

Nations was the setting in the League of what amounted to a League of Nations in itself—the British Empire. The Dominions demanded to be regarded as nations. They remained at the same time parts of the great imperial League. From almost every standpoint excepting that of allegiance to a common sovereign they were acting as independent nations— much too independent in fact, for the comfort at times of the home government. There was every reason, therefore, from that angle for giving Canada, Australia and South Africa at least as much recognition as Jugoslavia, not to speak of a dozen or more smaller States. The Dominions make their own tariff treaties, and they fought in the War with distinct armies which they raised by their own free will according to their own laws. But if each Dominion were to receive a single vote, that would mean that the British Empire would have five votes in the League of Nations and the United States one, which obviously does not seem fair. If the British were to have only one vote, however, the Dominions would hardly care to enter into the League for they do not wish to give up the independence which they have already acquired, by surrendering to a purely British statesman their participation in international affairs. The League of Nations was, therefore, obliged to choose between the one and the other alternative. It chose to recognize the different Dominions as States members of the League, and America agreed to this, although with some misgivings on the part of some Americans in Paris. That the decision to do so was wise is becoming every day more and more apparent, for as far as the United States is concerned the different Dominions, young democracies so similar in spirit to the American and so analogous in institutions and traditions of liberty, are bound to support in the main lines those policies which America will be supporting. It is, therefore, in this group of young Anglo-Saxon States that America will be likely to find its strongest allies in the councils of the League in the future. If backward countries are to be admitted to the League, as must be done, it is surely essential to have a fairly large proportion of those peoples with the political experience and training which comes from Anglo-Saxon history as a makeweight against the inexperience and theoretic tendencies of the newer states.

It is only by looking far ahead and considering the probable attitudes of the different States when actual questions arise that one can judge the wisdom of such decisions as these.

The more the objections that are raised to the Treaty, the greater the importance grows of the League of Nations as the one means of readjusting solutions and rectifying blunders. Otherwise there is chaos ahead; and chaos means the end of civilization.

APPENDIX V

THE "BRITISH EMPIRE" IN THE LEAGUE COVENANT [1]

The arrangement which I suggested for listing the British Dominions and India under "British Empire" in the signatures of the original Members of the League of Nations turned out to be one of the revolutionary acts of the Paris Peace Conference. Accepted by the various British governments there represented and by all the other States as well, it was an official recognition by all the world that the "British Empire" was a sovereignty among the other sovereign States, a fact neither claimed nor granted in diplomatic dealings before. Strictly speaking, the symbol of that sovereignty has been a royal, not an imperial, Crown, although popular usage and even ceremonial references at coronation employ the more exalted title.

The confusion is not of recent date. Anson has noted that "from Athelstan to Canute imperial styles were used and 'emperor' is applied to Edward I, Richard II, and Henry V." [2] Firth has traced the use of the term "British Empire" through the early modern period, when the new national sovereignties were rising to supplant the traditional claims of the Holy Roman Empire.[3] But, as Keith has pointed out, there never had been a formal legislative definition of it.[4] The King is also Emperor of India but not "British Emperor." The congeries of dependencies and autonomous governments over which he rules are, except India, united under a Kingship. The Covenant was the first treaty with other States in which the designation of Empire was used to cover the whole vast fabric. As a matter of fact, it embraces more than British territory. "In addition to the Indian States, it includes large areas of territory designated as 'Protectorates,' over which the Crown exercises full control, while attached to it in various degrees of relationship are 'Protected States' and 'Mandated Territories.' " [5]

The way in which all this came about has been described in the Diary.

---

[1] See above, February 12.
[2] Sir William R. Anson, *The Law and Custom of the Constitution* (4th ed., Oxford, 1935), II, Part II, 255 n. "Empire" in such cases was limited to England.
[3] C. H. Firth, " 'The British Empire,' " *Scottish Historical Review*, XV, pp. 185–189.
[4] A. Berriedale Keith, *Constitution, Administration, and Laws of the Empire* (New York, 1924), pp. xvii–xviii.
[5] Keith, *op. cit.*, p. xvii. See also his *Governments of the British Empire* (1935), pp. 118-119.

The draft of the Covenant was being put together in printed form. It had to be ready for the Commission in the morning. The night was already far spent when the question of signatures came up. The American printing establishment was in a somewhat remote part of Paris. There was no time for consultation, and there was no precedent to follow. The British Members of the League of Nations obviously had to be grouped together. It would not have done to have listed them so that Australia would follow the United States of America, and South Africa come between Salvador and Spain. Moreover there was need of indicating the slightly different status of "States Members of the League" from "Members of the League." Hence the indention in the printed list, marking out this group of Members from the rest.

The term "British Empire" as the name for this group was especially suggested by the presence at the Peace Conference of the "British Empire Delegation." Indeed, this was the deciding factor. The way in which that Delegation functioned has been described in some detail in the Diary. But it, too, had its history. It was largely due to a direct migration from London to Paris of the members of the Imperial War Cabinet, the one organ of an imperial government that had been functioning. The antecedents of this carry us back to Queen Victoria's Golden Jubilee in 1887, when the Colonial statesmen inaugurated the periodically recurring Conference, which in 1907 changed its style to Imperial Conference. This slight and infrequent mechanism had given the semblance of political and even of legal reality to the concept of a British Empire, but the term remained somewhat indeterminate, being confined to domestic use within the territories under the Crown. This process of imperial development, slow and hesitant in peace time, had reached its climax in the World War, in the Imperial War Conferences of 1917 and 1918 and the creation of the Imperial War Cabinet. At the close of the War in which they had played so notable a part, Canada, Australia, New Zealand and South Africa could not be denied status at the Peace Conference, and their Prime Ministers made known in no uncertain terms their demand to participate in the settlement. The result was that the Foreign Office was almost snowed under in Paris and at times forced to yield to the vigorous leaders of the Dominions. The descriptions of the scenes in the Hotel Majestic given in the Diary show clearly enough the corporate existence at Paris of a British Empire—puzzling, self-contradictory, but effective. The fact that India was a part of the British Empire Delegation accounted for the inclusion of India, an empire in itself, in the list of States within the British Empire. The reason that this was left untouched was probably the uncertain significance of the indented margin which grouped these states together.

But there could hardly be both a British Empire on the list of States

Members of the League and a United Kingdom as well, without giving the appearance of double representation. There was opposition enough already, especially in the United States, to the number of votes that the various British governments could mobilize in the League. That, in a word, was the chief reason for leaving the United Kingdom off the list when inserting in it the new, as yet undefined "British Empire." There was also the additional fact, however, that the non-self-governing colonies were popularly referred to as parts of the Empire, while their relation to the United Kingdom was not always clear. Although governed from Whitehall, they differed in the degree of achievement of autonomy on local rights and privileges.

But does the absence of the United Kingdom from the list of League Members mean that the Mother State is not herself a Member of the League? Strangely enough—or, perhaps, naturally enough—this question was not asked at the time, so far as I know. Years later, however, Sir Cecil J. B. Hurst, who was Legal Adviser to the British Delegation and who shared with Mr. David Hunter Miller the editorship of the very draft of the Covenant in question, commented upon the signatures as follows:

If you look at the Covenant, which is the charter or constitution of the League, you will see that a list of the original members of the League is given in an annex. The form in which British membership is provided for satisfies both the two outstanding characteristics of the British Empire: the unity of the whole and the autonomy of the parts.

The names of the states come in alphabetical order. When you reach the words "British Empire," you will see immediately after them, but set back a little so as to show that they constitute part of the British group, the names Canada, Australia, South Africa, New Zealand, and India. The Irish Free State was only admitted as a member of the League at a later date.

Satisfactory though the form is in one respect, in that it recognizes the distinct international personality of the dominions, it is unsatisfactory in another respect, in that it entirely omits Great Britain, and Great Britain is not a wholly negligible part of the Empire. Great Britain only finds herself within the League as an unmentioned element in the British Empire.

How this came about it is a little difficult now to tell. It probably originated in the fact that the plenipotentiaries representing Great Britain at the Peace Conference were furnished with full powers from the King which contained no words of territorial limitation and enabled them to act on his behalf generally. Their signature to the Peace Treaty was not limited in its operation to Great Britain. Technically it applied to all the King's dominions.

Whatever the purpose of this arrangement in the Annex to the Covenant, it has not worked well in practice. If the object was to lay stress on the unity of the Empire as a political entity, the effect has been the opposite, because in the ordinary work of the League it has tended to render the words "British Empire" synonymous with Great Britain and to create the impression that the dominions were something outside the Empire. If at a meeting of the Assembly the representatives are called upon to come up to the tribune to cast their votes in, let us say, the election of the president, and the South African delegate is seen to vote in the name of South Africa while the delegate of His Majesty's Government in Great Britain is seen to vote in the name of the British Empire, it necessarily suggests that South Africa is no part of the Empire.

Until the terms of the Covenant are amended and account is taken of the existence of Great Britain it is bound to happen that for some purposes the words "British Empire" are taken as meaning Great Britain— for instance, the share of the expenses of the League which falls to the lot of the Empire must be paid by Great Britain.[1]

One utterly unforeseen effect of this use of the term "British Empire" in the list of League signatures has been a modification in the form of treaties generally. At the Imperial Conference of 1926 Lord Balfour's Report raised the issue in these terms:

Some treaties begin with a list of the contracting countries and not with a list of Heads of States. In the case of treaties negotiated under the auspices of the League of Nations, adherence to the wording of the Annex to the Covenant for the purpose of describing the contracting party has led to the use in the preamble of the term "British Empire" with an enumeration of the Dominions and India if parties to the Convention but without any mention of Great Britain and Northern Ireland and the Colonies and Protectorates. These are only included by virtue of their being covered by the term "British Empire." This practice, while suggesting that the Dominions and India are not on a footing of equality with Great Britain as participants in the treaties in question, tends to obscurity and misunderstanding and is generally unsatisfactory.

As a means of overcoming this difficulty it is recommended that all treaties (other than agreements between Governments) whether negotiated under the auspices of the League or not should be made in the name of Heads of States, and, if the treaty is signed on behalf of any or all of the Governments of the Empire, the treaty should be made in the name of the King as the symbol of the special relationship between the different parts of the Empire.[2]

"In the name of the King." This was the only solution for the Imperial Conference which laid the basis for the Statute of Westminster of 1931, by which the "British Commonwealth of Nations" was at last accepted as the proper term for the traditional "British Empire." But the formula also had a counterpart in the practice of the American Government, using the title "The President of the United States of America" instead of the name of the country.

[1] Sir Cecil J. B. Hurst, *Great Britain and the Dominions, Harris Foundation Lectures, 1927* (Chicago, The University of Chicago Press, 1928), pp. 91–93.
[2] *Imperial Conference, 1926. Summary of Proceedings,* Cmd. 2768, pp. 22-23.

APPENDIX VI

CHRONOLOGY OF THE PEACE CONFERENCE [1]

1919

Jan. 12. The Supreme War Council, with President Wilson and Secretary Lansing and the Premiers and Foreign Ministers of Great Britain, France, and Italy, lays out the procedure of the Peace Conference at the Quai d'Orsay, Paris.

Jan. 18. Conference convenes; President Poincaré welcomes it and President Wilson nominates Premier Clemenceau of France as permanent Chairman; he is unanimously elected by the delegates.

Jan. 19. Council of Five—United States, Great Britain, France, Italy, and Japan—instituted, which is to take part in all meetings, hear all commissions, and execute all decisions. Other Powers are to take part in questions which concern them, the neutrals appearing only on invitation.

Jan. 22. Council approves of President Wilson's proposal inviting representatives of all belligerent Russian groups to meet representatives of the Council at Princes' Island (Prinkipo), Sea of Marmora.

Jan. 24. Council warns belligerent nationals in Southeastern Europe that acquisition of territory by force would prejudice their case at Conference.

Jan. 25. Conference votes for a League of Nations.

Jan. 26. Clemenceau appoints various committees: On Responsibility, Reparation, Labor Legislation, and Regulation of Ports, Waterways, and Railways, etc.

Feb. 3. League of Nations Commission meets at the apartment of Colonel House, President Wilson presiding.

Feb. 11. French member of the League Commission, Léon Bourgeois, proposes that the League enforce its decision by an international army. On the ground that the United States had recognized the political cohesion of Serbia, Croatia, and Slavonia, on Feb. 7, the Jugoslav delegates ask President Wilson to judge

[1] Taken from "Chronological Review of the World's Remaking," *New York Times,* January 4, 1920.

between them and the Italian delegates on the Adriatic question.

Feb. 14. President Wilson expounds the League of Nations Covenant before the Conference.

Feb. 18. Italian delegates decline to accept President Wilson as arbiter in the Adriatic question on two grounds: The question is not a matter for arbitration and the Croats and Slovenes, included in Jugoslavia, are still enemy peoples.

Mar. 10. Supreme War Council formulates terms for German disarmament—100,000 effectives and a twelve-year enlistment.

Mar. 18. Navigation of the Rhine to be controlled by an international commission and Heligoland forts dismantled.

Mar. 21. Italian delegation threatens to withdraw from Conference unless Fiume be rendered to Italy. (In the Treaty of London, Fiume is given to Croatia, but on Oct. 30, 1918, the people had declared their union with Italy.)

April 6. Report that owing to the military demands of France and Italy President Wilson contemplated an immediate return to the United States.

April 8. Commission of Responsibility for War, presided over by the American Secretary of State, Lansing, excludes the death penalty from contemplated legal procedure against William of Hohenzollern, the former German Emperor.

April 10. The League Commission incorporates in the covenant a passage intended to leave the Monroe Doctrine inviolate.

April 12. Claim of France to the Saar Valley accepted by the conference.

April 14. President Wilson privately addresses Italian delegates on Fiume.

April 16. Conference agrees to provision Russia under the Nansen Commission, provided the Whites and Reds cease fighting.

April 23. President Wilson, emphasizing his statement of the 14th, tells the Italian people that Fiume must go to Jugoslavia as the only available port for the nations of South Central Europe.

April 24. Premier Orlando, the head of the Italian peace delegation, in a reply to the foregoing, demonstrates Italy's claim to Fiume.

April 25. The council settles Poland's access to the Baltic—a traffic highway is to be opened through East Prussia to Danzig, which will be made a free city under the League.

April 26. As a protest against President Wilson's attitude on the Fiume question Premier Orlando and his colleagues, Sonnino and Salandra, return to Rome to lay the matter before Parliament.

April 27. The text of the labor article in the covenant is made public.

April 28. President Wilson, as Chairman of the League Commission, expounds the revised text of the covenant before the conference.

April 30. In answer to Japan's note verbale promising military and political surrender of Shantung, the Council agrees to the Chinese-Japanese arrangement in regard to the former German lease of Kiao-Chau.

May 5. Sir Eric Drummond takes office as Secretary General of the League, which organizes its first committee.

May 6. The council designates the mandatories for the former German colonies.

May 7. The Italian delegates accept an invitation to return to the Conference, their conduct having, meanwhile, been indorsed by the Italian Parliament and public demonstrations in Italy.

May 29. The German delegates formally protest against the terms of the treaty presented to them at Versailles, May 7.

June 12. Council to give qualified material aid to Admiral Kolchak, head of the All-Russian Government at Omsk.

June 15. Council finishes changes in the Versailles Treaty.

June 26. Council declares it can promise nothing in regard to Turkey.

July 18. Council places General Allenby (British) in charge of the British, French, Italian, and Greek armies of occupation in Asia Minor, the principal fields of operation being the British in Palestine and Mesopotamia, the French in Syria, the Italians south of Smyrna, and the Greeks in Smyrna.

Aug. 4. Tokio Government in a statement to the Council ratifies the note verbale given it by its delegates on April 30.

Aug. 15. Conference informs Rumania that it will make readjustments in Hungary and not Rumania.

Aug. 22. The Council orders the Magyar Archduke Joseph to retire from the head of the new Hungarian Government.

Sept. 5. The Council completes the text of the Bulgarian peace treaty.

Sept. 27. Conference issues a note to Germany demanding evacuation of former Russian Baltic provinces.

Oct. 16. Council invites Germany and Baltic nations to join in a blockade against Soviet Russia.

Nov. 7. Council issues ultimatum to Rumania to withdraw from Hungary.

Nov. 21. Council gives Poland mandate over Galicia for twenty-five years.

Dec. 22. Supreme Council sends Germans ultimatum in regard to acceptance of protocol.

APPENDIX VII

THE ORGANIZATION OF THE AMERICAN DELEGATION AT THE PARIS PEACE CONFERENCE

Looking back upon the preparations of the Inquiry for the Peace Conference, it seems now that the problem of the organization of the American Delegation and its relation to the Peace Conference as a whole was fundamental, because it affected in a major way not only the procedure of the Peace Conference but even the terms of the Treaty. Yet no adequate study of these problems of organization has yet been made. Something of their nature may be gathered from the short description given in the Retrospect of the way in which they were dealt with by the Inquiry, and in the discussion attached to the entry for January 29, at the time when the organization of the technical experts began to be integrated with that of other similar bodies.

In this connection the following two charts will be found of interest. The first one was prepared for the Research Committee of the Inquiry and was discussed at its meeting on September 20, 1918. It is a modification of one submitted to the Committee on September 10. These two plans did not differ with reference to the place of the American Delegation in the Peace Conference, but only with reference to the organization of the technical bodies serving the American Delegation, especially the Inquiry and the Washington "Central," that is, the Central Bureau of Planning and Statistics, under the chairmanship of Dr. Edwin F. Gay. It is important to note that the Inquiry at that date fully expected that the Peace Conference would include representatives of the Central Powers, and that the American Delegation would be composed of representatives of the Executive and the Senate, a representative at large, and the Secretary of State. An additional blank space indicated some uncertainty as to the size of the Delegation.

The second chart reproduced here was drawn at Paris to indicate the actual structure of the American Delegation. As is evident from the narrative in these pages, the relative places occupied by General Churchill's staff and by the Division of "Intelligence" under Dr. Mezes and Dr. Bowman should be reversed.

INDEX